READING & WRITING
TOGETHER

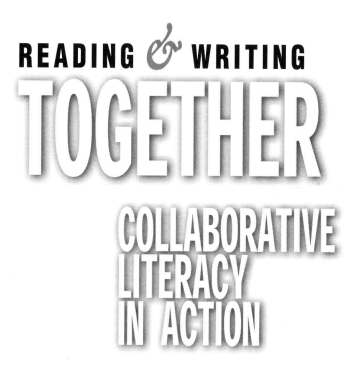

READING & WRITING
TOGETHER
COLLABORATIVE LITERACY IN ACTION

NANCY STEINEKE

Foreword by Harvey Daniels

HEINEMANN
Portsmouth, NH

Heinemann
A division of Reed Elsevier Inc.
361 Hanover Street
Portsmouth, NH 03801–3912
www.heinemann.com

Offices and agents throughout the world

The author and publisher wish to thank those who have generously given permission to reprint borrowed material:

Figure 4.1: "Rude, disrespectful doctors" is reprinted from the *Chicago Tribune*, November 25, 1994, by permission of The Associated Press.

Figures 8.13 and 8.14: "Observation Sheet" is adapted by permission from *Cooperation in the Classroom* by David Johnson, Roger Johnson, and Edythe Johnson Holubec. Copyright © 1991, 1998. Published by Interaction Book Company.

Figures 9.8 and 9.9: "Same-Different: Outer Space" is reprinted by permission from *Cooperative Learning Structures for Teambuilding* by Laurie, Miguel, and Spencer Kagan. Copyright © 1997 by Kagan Cooperative Learning. Published by Kagan Publishing. *Same-Different* books are available from Kagan Publishing at <www.KaganOnline.com> or 1-800-933-2667.

Figure 9.26: "Examples of RAFT Assignments" is reprinted from *Classroom Strategies for Interactive Learning, Second Edition* by Doug Buehl. Copyright © 2001. Published by the International Reading Association. Reprinted by permission of Doug Buehl and the IRA.

Appendix B: "Social Skill Lesson Plan" is adapted by permission from *Cooperation in the Classroom* by David Johnson, Roger Johnson, and Edythe Johnson Holubec. Copyright © 1991, 1998. Published by Interaction Book Company.

Appendix G: "Night Club" by Katharine Brush is reprinted by permission of Harold Ober Associates. Copyright © 1927 by Katharine Brush. Renewed.

Library of Congress Cataloging-in-Publication Data
Steineke, Nancy.
    Reading and writing together : collaborative literacy in action / Nancy Steineke.
      p.   cm.
    Includes bibliographical references.
    ISBN 0-325-00443-9 (pbk. : alk. paper)
    1. Language arts (Secondary)—United States.   2. Group work in education—
United States.   I. Title.
    LB1631 .S733   2002
    428'.0071'2—dc21

                                     2002005928

Editor: Leigh Peake
Production: Lynne Reed
Cover design: Lisa Fowler
Cover photograph (front): David Carroll
Cover photograph (back): William Steineke
Typesetter: Publishers' Design and Production Services, Inc.
Manufacturing: Steve Bernier

Printed in the United States of America on acid-free paper
06 05 04 03 02 RRD 1 2 3 4 5

For George H. Hurst:
father, teacher, school principal,
the most influential educator in my life.

CONTENTS

FOREWORD

BY HARVEY DANIELS

The popular "teacher books" in our field are a peculiar genre indeed. Most of them are professional autobiographies told by a fabulous, magical, master teacher. The author recounts stunning successes with students, usually over daunting odds. Whole classrooms of teenagers are held at a steady state of intellectual arousal, a fever pitch of academic engagement; elaborate lessons unfold according to flawless plans; and the students churn out staggeringly precocious products, work of Nobel Prize quality. And at the center of these miracles is one huge, amazing personality—a maestro, a superhuman life-force.

By and large, every one of these magical-master-teacher books could have the same subtitle: "Be Like Me!" The trouble is, most of us can't be anyone else, whether we emulate, imitate, or channel them. So these miracle books sometimes have the opposite of their intended effect. They make us regular, everyday, journeymen teachers feel, well, a little inferior. We know very well that we can't be like the gurus. Their tomes of triumph just confirm that we don't have the gift, the grace, the right stuff. They make us believe that great teaching needs to be inborn, wired into the genes—and that our own DNA is definitely deficient.

Or worse, maybe it is our lack of commitment that's the problem. Maybe we don't read enough books, publish enough articles, appear at enough professional conferences. Maybe we succumb to the distractions of friends and family more than the truly great ones do, the ones who sacrifice all, because they **really** care. Maybe the paragon is showing us the shining path: maybe we need to be more driven, more obsessed, more perfect, like him.

"Nah," says Nancy Steineke.

This is a different kind of teacher book, and Nancy Steineke is a different kind of teacher. Don't get me wrong, she's a wonderful educator, one we can all learn a lot from. If you read this book ten times (which I recommend), you still won't dig out all the practical and generous teaching ideas here. But Nancy did not write this book to show off, to brag how great she is, or to dazzle you with how much better her students' work looks than yours. Instead of showcasing only her triumphs, she honestly shares her struggles and problems, too. Instead of making you feel inferior, she makes you feel capable. Instead of spurring you on toward perfection, she offers you a license to fail. When a new strategy flops in your classroom, Nancy says, treat yourself to a massage or buy a new outfit. Celebrate your own risk-taking.

Nancy takes risks in her own classroom every day. Even though most of her routines and procedures already work well, she changes them anyway, experimenting with things that might work even better. The pace is incredibly fast; kids group and regroup, write, talk, report, quote, debrief, reflect, regroup, and start again. Nancy is not shy. She moves around the room announcing instructions, enforcing time limits, coaching individual kids, bursting into laughter, nudging and cajoling, or donating ideas to groups.

This is high school teaching at its best—full of life, friendship, people you can trust, and ideas that matter—and features lots and lots of books. It's exciting to let all this activity swirl around you; the engagement of students, and the level of responsibility they take for themselves and classmates is something to see. Being in Nancy's classroom reminds us that high school doesn't have to be hell; in fact, it can be pretty much fun, for both teachers and kids, when the work is fresh, real, and challenging.

Do Nancy's kids behave in these exemplary ways for every minute of every class, every day, all year long? Of course not. Nothing always works. Two minutes ago, I opened an email from Nancy, telling about a student who was conspicuously not contributing to his group today. When Nancy inquired, the student explained that he was busy drafting a letter to the school board, complaining about all the pressure Ms. Steineke was putting on him, as well as her outrageously unfair grading practices.

The most distinctive thing about Nancy's classes, on the many good days and good moments, is the way the kids work together. They collaborate on a wide range of projects, in ever-shifting cooperative groupings—pairs, teams, discussion circles, and writing response groups. They pay attention, respect, and listen to each other. They move crisply in and out of different groupings and tasks, sharing jobs, keeping records, reporting results, reflecting thoughtfully upon their own social process as well as upon the ideas they have developed.

If you have ever taught high school, you know that this is an exceedingly rare occurrence. We would love to see this happening in our own classrooms! After all, if you can get kids working productively and reliably in small, student-led groups, then you can diversify readings and assignments, do more coaching and less yakking, and better meet the wide range of needs we encounter in today's increasingly heterogeneous classrooms. So how did Nancy and her kids get to this point?

We all studied cooperative learning at some point in our careers. We took a half-day workshop back in '73, attended the district-wide inservice session in '84, or sat through that summer workshop in '92. After this brief exposure, we went back into our classrooms, threw kids into small groups, then watched them crash and burn. Our fledgling groups didn't look the way the presenter described them at all. They were ragged, noisy, off-task, and chaotic; they lowered the intellectual level and raised our blood pressure. So we put the kids back in six rows of five desks, defaulting to the instructional baseline: the whip-and-a-chair model of whole class instruction. If anyone in the faculty lounge ever mentioned cooperative learning, we'd roll our world-weary eyes and opine: "Yeah, I tried that back in '95, and it didn't work."

What didn't work, of course, was us. Nobody has "a gift" running a collaborative classroom. It's about studying, practicing, reflecting, and revising. Nancy has done that work, over many years. The cooperative literacy strategies in this book do not stem from Nancy's personality, adorable as it is, or her grace. This is about what she has learned to do with real kids. Nancy's is not a cult of personality—it is a cult of patient, steady, thoughtful work. This book explains clearly and completely what that work is, if you want to undertake it.

This doesn't mean you are supposed to ape Nancy; indeed, she'd be mad if you did. There is no one true path to a literate classroom community, but a thousand alternative trails, each practical and scenic. Nancy offers you scores of strategies to choose from, to adapt, refine, and personalize for yourself and your particular students. Indeed, the book may overwhelm you with its generous detail and concrete specificity. Among other curious things, you will learn:

How to give your students "home court advantage" in your classroom

Why kids should not always work with their friends

How to make term papers fun

How to handle Mr. Angry

Why not to give "group grades"

How to make a family newspaper

Why steel wool is an important survival tool

Why kids and teachers should leave their "personal baggage" at the classroom door

How to quiet domineering group members with "talking chips"

How a neighborhood map can help spur narrative writing

Why large group sharing time can be both risky and unimportant

What you will not find in this book is magic; there's no smoke, no mirrors. You don't need to be a "gifted" teacher to put these ideas to work. But there's also no downside. If you take a patient, stepwise approach such as Nancy's, collaborative literacy will work, with your kids, in your school. Guaranteed.

The last time I visited Nancy's classroom, I sat down with a Literature Circle that was discussing *There Are No Children Here* by Alex Kotlowitz. The kids paid little attention to my arrival except for Joey. In an entirely typical spasm of sophomore attention-getting, with a brand new audience (me) at hand, Joey smirkily directed my attention to the floor. One girl in the discussion group had casually kicked off her shoes. Joey decided it might be amusing to try on the platform sandals and take a little walk around. He slipped the shoes on, stood up wobbly, and pranced a few steps around his book discussion group. Renee, the owner of the shoes, looked over her shoulder, groaned disgustedly, and turned back to the discussion. She utterly ignored him, and so did everyone else in the room. Joey teetered there for a moment, looking puzzled, then sat back down, gently slipped off the shoes, and shouldered his way back into the conversation.

So-called clowning or goofing off like Joey's, and the enthusiastic reception it usually gets from peers, is a routine manifestation of some teenage psychological imperatives. But we can also see it as an attempt by kids to interject some life, some laughter, some fun, into the too-dreary daily life of high school. We can also see it as a control-seeking gesture, a brief and symbolic attempt to seize the agenda from the teacher, to grab some airtime, to have a voice. In genuinely cooperative classrooms, such gestures are beside the point.

Joey has no audience in Nancy's class, because students are engaged, respected, and in charge. They don't have to fight for the spotlight; they're in it. No, Nancy hasn't transformed these teens into the alien super-beings encountered in some other professional books, as Joey has just demonstrated. What she *has* done is make normal, regular kids truly believe that what they have to say really matters, that books and ideas are really cool, that they can be part of a lively and caring community, reading and writing together. And that's a real gift.

ACKNOWLEDGMENTS

Danielle Taylor, my fabulous student teacher. Without Danielle at the helm, I never would have found the time to write this book.

Smokey Daniels, friend and mentor. As I took those first tentative steps down the authorial path, Smokey's advice cut away the brush and smoothed the trail.

Kimberly Campbell, revision expert. Before her input, my manuscript was like a messy closet. After taking Kimberly's comments to heart, I found "outfits" I didn't even know I had!

Bill Steineke, loving husband and willing proofreader. After my third manuscript overhaul, I knew I had it right when Bill said, "Now this is making sense to me, and I don't even teach English!"

David Carroll, photographer and historian. Thanks for aiding me in my photo emergency!

Jim Vopat, friend and enthusiast. Thank you for repeatedly saying, "Your book is going to be great!"

Edye Johnson Holubec, cooperative learning expert. Though she and her brothers developed the model described in this book, it was Edye who worked with me over several years, imparting her knowledge, wisdom, and warmth.

The students of Victor J. Andrew High School. If they weren't willing to take some risks with me, I'd never learn anything new!

Leigh Peake, editor and red zinfandel fan. Always attentive to my desperate emails, Leigh's expertise and encouragement have been invaluable.

READING & WRITING
TOGETHER

CHAPTER 1

Magic Versus Methodology
Or, Good Teachers Are Made, Not Born!

About ten years ago I had a student by the name of Lance who wanted to be a magician. He was a sophomore and could perform a few magic tricks that were pretty rough around the edges. During impromptu classroom performances, Lance's card tricks worked about half the time. His best trick was changing an ordinary dinner napkin into a brassiere; leave it to a sophomore boy to get that one right! Due to his lack of skill and his white "John Travolta" suit, Lance took a lot of ribbing; kids and teachers rolled their eyes and wondered when he'd figure out what he really wanted to do with his life.

But Lance wanted to be a magician, so he practiced and sought the help of other magicians. He went to performances and trade shows and introduced himself. He found mentors. About five years later, I saw him perform tableside magic at a local restaurant. And you know what? He was good, he was funny, and he made it all look real. Was he gifted? He sure didn't seem like it his sophomore year. Did he practice, refine, and hone his originally modest skill? Absolutely!

Remember Michael (Air) Jordan? Did you know that he was cut from his high school's varsity team his sophomore year and bounced down to junior varsity? Years later he led the Chicago Bulls to six NBA championships and earned a reputation as the best player in the world. Was he gifted? He sure didn't seem like it his sophomore year! Did he practice, refine, and hone his skill? Absolutely! Fred Lynch, then assistant coach at Laney High School said, "He didn't sulk, he worked."

When you look at top people in any field, we assume that a lot of training and practice brought the top doctor, lawyer, or athlete to where they are today. Why isn't teaching viewed in the same way? Fueled by unrealistic media portrayals, the definition of a great teacher has taken on a mythological flavor. Great teachers are characterized as talented, creative, gifted, spontaneous, intuitive, sensitive, and selfless; they live for their students and can reach them all. They are "naturals." When they die, these teachers are automatically elevated to sainthood. The underlying message is—unlike other professions that one can learn to do well—good teaching can come only from the heart. Either you're born a teacher or you're not.

Many professional books about teaching seem to unconsciously support this premise. Have you ever read a "teacher book" and left the experience feeling totally inadequate, that no matter how hard you try you'll never match that teacher who wrote the book? For me, that book was Nancie Atwell's *In the Middle*. Before *In the Middle*, I hadn't even heard of reading/writing workshop. The first time I read that book, I was awed and astounded that Atwell had the courage and conviction to engage in a model that turned almost every conceivable English teacher convention on its head. What amazed me even more was that it worked, it *really* worked! Her students were writing and reading up a storm! After attending a few workshops on reading and writing across the curriculum, I read *In the Middle* a second time. Boy, were her ideas great, and now I was ready to implement a workshop in my basic writing class. I was gonna be like Nancie!

The following fall I acted on my plan. Writing workshop went okay, maybe a little better than the old way, but my classes just weren't as good as Nancie's. Though the kids seemed happier about writing, I'm not sure their writing was really that much better. I confided in our district workshop expert, and she consoled me saying, "If the kids like writing more, then you're still making progress." But jeez, Atwell's kids were on their way to winning Pulitzers while some of mine were still struggling with remembering to put their names on the papers. Looking for answers, I returned for a third time to *In the Middle*. This time I felt truly deficient, defeated, and shamed. And that same sad feeling followed me again and again as I searched other professional books for the answers that would reward me in my quest for Atwellian perfection. After much reading and much self-flagellation, I had an epiphany: these teachers must not be telling us the whole story! They're leaving something out! Don't these teachers ever struggle? Where are the stories about the kids who refuse to lift a pen despite these incredibly rich environments? If I have these kids in my class, then they must be in other classes too, right? These were stories of classroom perfection minus the warts, stumbles, problems, and potholes that are so much a part of the reality of teaching.

My quest eventually taught me that I would never be one of those perfect teachers. I am not Nancie Atwell or Don Graves or Jaime Escalante. I doubt anyone will ever make a feature film focusing on my greatness. As much as I would love to be an instructional goddess, preferably one with the wisdom of Athena and the body of Aphrodite, I've had to let go of the dream. I'm learning how to be happy with being a good teacher who's trying to get better. I've made a ton of mistakes, learning from some while trying to forget others because the nightmares were disturbing my sleep!

See, we're all in the same boat. While we're all trying our best, we're also trying to learn from our mistakes. I want this book to reflect this reality. To begin with, let me promise you that the strategies and techniques I describe in this book will never work for every kid in every class. But, hey, get real—what does? I can distinctly remember a couple of kids I've had who could be poster children for the National Passive–Aggressive Society. Sabotaging my instructional agenda gave them power, while passing classes or developing positive relationships held no interest for them. In the end, I did not succeed in teaching them but I did succeed in doggedly writing enough detailed deans' office referrals to eventually get them removed from the room. Let's face facts: if a kid has been practicing schoolwork avoidance for ten years, it's going to be a big challenge to turn him into a believer in one or two semesters. I've won some tough games, but I've lost some as well. Anybody who promises across-the-board-student-achievement-miracles either hasn't been in the classroom in eons, or is not telling you the whole truth. I will tell you, though, when creating a collaborative classroom became my focus, it definitely raised my student engagement batting average and team morale.

Why Collaborate?

Humans are innately social creatures and naturally want to interact with others. If the students in my high school were polled on the number one reason for going to school, I'd bet that a majority would list "seeing their friends." Of course, I have faith that "learning" would rank within the top ten, but I still think that the social aspect of school would rank higher. Therefore, one reason to collaborate is to capitalize on the already overwhelming desire that teenagers have to talk to each other rather than listen to a teacher talk. The greatest thing about tapping into this natural desire is that the result of good collaboration is increased learning and a positive classroom climate. It's well established that people who talk about what they're learning will remember far more than those who only listen to a lecture. Also, the positive exchange of ideas results in the development of new friendships and working relationships. When students begin to respect and appreciate each other's similarities, differences, and talents, a strong community emerges. I typically find that if students are offered the opportunity to collaborate, 90 to 95 percent of the class is highly engaged in learning; even the kids who don't generally do schoolwork still try to pitch in because they feel like part of the community. An added benefit of collaboration is that kids who are happier and prepared to work create fewer discipline problems, a huge time waster.

The importance of collaboration must also be addressed in the entire school community. Have you noticed how much attention has been given lately to the topic of bullying? When you boil it down, the recipe for a bully includes a desperate need for recognition, a lack of empathy, and an objectification of others. Equally disturbing is the unwillingness of bystanders to stand up to bullies. Students who are not "bully prey" breath a sigh of relief and often assuage their discomfort by concluding that the victim "had it coming." The end result is a school community in which fear and "looking out for number one" rule while higher-order thinking takes a back seat to survival. Everyone suffers when students are not taught how to positively interact and support one another. Socially inept students grow into socially inept adults. Even scarier is that the victims of bullies sometimes seek revenge in violent and tragic ways.

Teaching students how to collaborate will help them long after they leave the confines of your classroom. In 1991 the Secretary's Commission on Achieving Necessary Skills (SCANS) released the federal government report "What Work Requires of Schools." While the SCANS report focused on reading, writing, and mathematical skills, an equal portion focused on speaking, listening, creative thinking, and interpersonal skills. The report named specific workplace skills such as contributing to a group effort, justifying a position, attending to body language, taking an interest in what others say, and showing empathy. Sounds like a short list of desirable classroom behaviors contributed by a bunch of teachers! In fact, employers generated this list in an effort to get schools to teach skills that would enhance the employability of high school graduates. Though teaching students to collaborate successfully takes more time and effort than relying on lecture and individual assignments, the sophistication of their collaborative skills will ultimately enhance their employability.

Finally, collaboration requires that students take others into consideration. It requires them to use empathy. It requires them to consider other opinions and viewpoints. It requires them to listen. It requires them to help each other. It requires them to look beyond themselves and try to create a community where everyone can feel safe and supported, a community where students and teachers can thrive and do their best work. In light of the events that transpired on September 11, 2001, I truly believe that our nation and our world can only grow stronger when empathy, caring, and compassion are valued in our schools in the same way as reading, writing, and arithmetic.

Trial and Error

Though now I work mostly with freshmen and sophomores, I used to teach a lot of upper-level classes, one of which was Grammar. Before I learned how to use cooperative learning, Grammar class was deadly in its mind-numbing sameness. Day after day after day, the class repeated the same format: check the homework, learn something new, work on that night's homework. The number of worksheets we went through in a semester was at least two inches thick. The students quickly fell into one of two categories: those who got it and those who didn't. The ones who understood the subtle differences between a noun clause and a relative clause liked me and the class; they clearly saw visions of higher scores on the English Usage part of the ACT test. The ones who hit the brick wall of Grammar sometimes caused disruption, but more often quietly fell into a well of apathy and depression. The ones who got it and the ones who didn't seldom talked to each other about grammar; both subgroups kept their successes and failures private.

The worst case was a girl who gave up quite early in the semester. Sometimes she was absent but never asked about make-up work. Most of the time she was there but seldom seemed mesmerized by my fantastic grammar lessons delineating the differences between sentence patterns six and seven. She never spoke, never raised her hand, never asked a question; her goal was to become invisible. Quite predictably, when the time arrived for her to take the final exam, she didn't come close to passing. Since she was a senior and needed the class to graduate, her guidance counselor begged me to let her take the exam a second time. She did, and her score on the second attempt was even worse. It was sad; she had fallen through one of those gaping high school cracks. She was just one of my class load of 150 students who didn't cut it.

> **Moral:** *Even the most deadly and dull tasks improve when a social element is added. Luckily for later students, I learned how to incorporate collaboration. Partners became helpful friends, and a feeling of probable success replaced that feeling of impending doom.*

Learning How to Teach Collaboration

When I started teaching English, I taught others in the manner I had been taught: five-paragraph essays, whole class novels, large group discussion, and machine-graded unit tests. These strategies had a very low engagement rate. I can remember teaching a short story class early in my career. On any given day, half the class failed to read the assigned story, and, much to my chagrin, they didn't seem to regret the decision in the least. Most of the kids seemed to have a good sense of how to do just enough to skate by with a C or D. Of course, there were those six or so kids who actually enjoyed reading the short stories and volunteering in discussion while the rest of the class feigned interest or watched the clock. However, the devotion of those six just didn't leave me feeling gratified. I knew something had to change, but I was clueless as to what.

That summer I had the good luck to participate in our district's staff development program. Two of the topics on the agenda were *Cooperative Learning* and *Reading and Writing Across the Curriculum.* While the reading/writing training gave me some fresh and interesting replacements for that tired five-paragraph essay and stifling whole-class novel, cooperative learning gave me the strategies for structuring student learning teams that worked. Before that summer, I avoided putting students in groups because they didn't get along, they wasted time, and the final products often reflected the conscientiousness of one overworked and under-appreciated member. That fall I started using pairs in a semester-long class called Grammar. I began structuring assignments so that the students worked with a regular partner versus on their own, and I tried to teach them to use some specific skill when working together: asking for help, giving help, explaining one's answer aloud, and praising someone for a positive contribution. While the kids worked with their partners, I walked around the room, answering questions but also trying to model the skills the kids were supposed to use. What I didn't change at all was the class curriculum; we were still doing endless and pointless worksheets on the parts of speech, sentence patterns, and *who* versus *whom*. Even so, adding the element of structured pairs with specific skills to practice changed that class from dreary to fun.

Smug from my Grammar class success, I tried to transfer what I learned to my Short Story class the following semester. I saw some success, but I also saw quite a few disasters. That's when I decided I still had more to learn. I took two more courses from David and Roger Johnson and continued to go to the trainings our district offered. As I practiced using student discussion groups, my craft in structuring interactions grew. After awhile, I developed a reputation as the teacher who could get kids to work together. Sometimes interested teachers would drop by to observe student groups in action, but afterwards they often concluded that my finesse with structuring collaboration was directly connected with my personality, my "giftedness" related to teaching. That's part of the problem when it comes to observing skillful teachers; they make it look *too* easy. I found these comments frustrating because my skill with groups was the result of study, hard work, and continual learning. I mastered these strategies because of my willingness to learn and implement a new strategy and my determination to keep trying in spite of many failures!

This book is based on the premise that unless kids are carefully taught how to function in highly interactive ways, collaborative "best practice" strategies are just not going to work very well. Though many professional book authors hit briefly upon the topic of classroom climate, usually describing their favorite beginning of the year "get to know you" activities, where do they go from there? Can those few starter activities really sustain the supportive environments described in these books? I think the answer is "no." When I start working with a class, I have a vision for them. I want them to appreciate each other's ideas, help create a positive environment, and learn successfully as individuals, as a class, and as small group members. Probably few teachers would argue with these goals. My guess is that many master teachers/authors are doing a lot of other things to shape the group dynamics of their classrooms but are taking those strategies for granted rather than literally sharing everything they do with the reader. After all, how can peer conferencing work if the kids are not interested in what their classmates have written or how can literature circles work if kids aren't good at listening? Putting kids together in groups doesn't guarantee any kind of collaboration; without guidance and training, students can just as easily obstruct each other's learning instead of facilitate it. Just as children need to be taught good manners, group members need to be taught the behaviors necessary for successful collaboration.

Believe it or not a wealth of information on the topic of group dynamics is out there for us to use. In their book, *Group Processes in the Classroom*, Richard and Patricia Schmuck clearly define the phases a teacher must move through when training students to work in groups. At the beginning of the year, there is a very real need for those icebreaking activities that some of your colleagues view with suspicion. Those activities begin the bonding and trusting process. Until they know each other and feel comfortable together, students cannot move to the next stage when they sincerely begin to value each other as important resources and group members. Moving students from stage one to stage two takes careful planning. It doesn't happen by accident. Once students value each other, a class can move into high gear in collaboratively pursuing academic goals. In any setting, be it family, school, or work, real cooperation will never occur until all members of a group can trust one another. Explicitly training students in how to work in groups creates a new set of classroom norms. If students expect each other to be friendly and helpful, a lot more learning will take place.

Speaking of learning, David and Roger Johnson along with their sister Edye Johnson Holubec have devoted most of their lives to researching the effectiveness of cooperation as a learning tool. Their meta-analysis of over 375 studies conducted over the past ninety years clearly indicates that cooperative learning results in significantly higher achievement and retention than individual or competitive learning. Another researcher and author, Alfie Kohn, fully confirms the Johnsons' findings in his book *No Contest: The Case Against Competition*. Ironically, many aspects of the standard school system promote competition within the classroom, pitting student against student. Kohn's review of research found that competition only motivates those who have a significant chance of winning. Those who perceive themselves as potential losers avoid the pain of defeat by giving up. Furthermore, Kohn found that competition in learning tends to inhibit creativity for all those involved. Highlighting the learning power that cooperation can offer students, the Johnsons have been refining their cooperative learning model for the past thirty years. Using that model, student collaboration for any learning goal can be teacher designed and implemented. It is the Johnson model that I rely upon in my own teaching and will refer to often in this text.

In addition to those just mentioned, Elizabeth Cohen and Spencer Kagan have also broadened and strengthened the field of cooperative learning. All of these authors/researchers would agree that positive group dynamics is a result of careful consideration and structuring of such components as building friendships, sharing tasks, maintaining positive working relationships, and examining group functioning. I think one reason professional books often glide over the intricate details of collaboration is that dissecting group interaction is rather unromantic; it flies in the face of the belief that great teaching and learning depends upon charisma and spontaneity. The reality is that when successful small group work becomes the norm of a classroom, it is because of the teacher's careful and continual planning and strategizing, not because that teacher always has "good" kids. As the Johnsons repeatedly pronounce, "Good group members are made, not born."

However, I must warn you. Designing effective group work is hard; it takes quite a bit of training and practice. I've seen many school districts offer the disservice of a one-day cooperative learning inservice. Teachers leave with enthusiastic visions of collaboration, thinking they know a lot when, in actuality, that workshop only gave them a little bit. Back in the classroom, teachers soon give up on groups when they aren't working right. Rather than celebrating their courageousness while searching for better training, instead, these teachers fall victim to those nagging internal voices, those nasty voices that taunt all teachers in their quest for unattainable perfection! What I've found in my own teaching is that a truly collaborative environment is the result of a thousand experiences that can be steered very reliably and predictably. A classroom climate conducive to engaged learning is the result of craft, not magic. The key is being willing to invest in group development. It takes time, and you've got to have a plan because each encounter should reinforce the last group experience and dovetail with the next one. *Planning carefully for group development is the ingredient so often missing from otherwise great learning strategies.*

My goal for this book is to save you time by not having to reinvent the wheel. You'll find lots of collaborative strategies that build upon each other. I've included many of the forms I use along with some student samples, though I've tried my best to refrain from excessive show and tell. As I worked on this book, I often returned to my own favorite teacher books and examined what I had highlighted. Without exception, the only student samples I ever bothered to read or highlight were those that directly illustrated a new strategy I was trying to use. Therefore, I'm not going to bore you with my kids' poetry or personal narratives. On the other hand, if I have a good sample of something that might clarify a strategy, I've included it. I've looked for the best examples so that you can have a clear idea of what you might want to see in your own students' assignments. However, in my desire to unmask the magician, I want you to know that the samples you see are not representative of the complete range of my students' work. Most of my students are competent, but all are not stars. I'm not perfect, and neither are my students, so please don't look at these examples and imagine that Nancy Steineke waves her magic wand and everyone lives happily ever after.

This book will be most useful to you if you read the chapters in order. Each chapter represents a progression in teaching kids how to work together and how to refine their interactions with text, that dovetailing I mentioned earlier. Chapter 2 begins with the foundation strategies I use at the very beginning of the year. Once a positive learning climate is established, you're ready to move on to refining a class's skills as you simultaneously use strategies that build and strengthen a community of readers and writers. Please notice that literature circles and peer conferencing are purposely found in later chapters. By the time I challenge students with these models, I want them to have a solid skill foundation on which to rely. Also, somewhere in each chapter, you'll find a special section called "Trial and Error." Rome was not built in a day, nor is it ever finished. In my teaching life, I have made mistakes galore, so I figured I might as well share some of my most humbling and humiliating experiences so that you can rest assured that I didn't lie when I told you I wasn't perfect.

Learning how to orchestrate true student collaboration is never an easy task, but it will be much easier and enjoyable if you find a colleague who's willing to work with you on this project. Working with a colleague made a huge difference for me when I was starting out. Read together, commit to trying new strategies, and then afterwards talk about what happened. Don't forget to celebrate your successes and use your failures as springboards for revision. You'll know you've mastered collaboration strategies when at the end of the year or semester the kids will remember you, but also remember all of their peers. And remember, we're all unique. While you'll never be Nancie, you will be _____ (fill in your name here). Now get out there and start teaching those kids how to collaborate!

CHAPTER 2

Getting Kids to Like Each Other and Work Together
Building a Positive Class Climate

Trial and Error

The start of my 2001–2002 school year was particularly rough. School started later than planned due to construction delays. A classroom shortage resulted in the loss of the room that had been "mine" for the last twelve years. The new dry erase boards refused to erase. Capping it all, the new "student friendly" desks and chairs turned out to be far too large for our rooms. No longer could I circulate effortlessly throughout the classroom during the course of my teaching. I now had to slowly edge my way up and down narrow aisles, trying to keep my rear end out of anyone's face. Our first day of school was September 10, 2001. Our second day of school was September 11, 2001. The catastrophe of the World Trade Center and the Pentagon seemed to intensify my students' misbehavior; the kids were wild! They didn't listen, talking to whomever they pleased whenever they pleased. Some of them wouldn't even stay in their seats, impulsively jumping up for a stroll at any time. The stress of horrific world events combined with much higher than normal school stress just about pushed me over the edge. Aside from lesson planning, I split my afterschool time pretty evenly between sobbing at my kitchen table and sending "woe is me" emails to all of my friends. Had I gotten five bucks for every utterance of, "If I could retire right now, I would," I probably could have retired! Teaching seemed pretty grim those first few weeks.

Now it's the day after Thanksgiving and, thankfully, our nation seems to be moving forward. First quarter ended a few weeks ago. The desks still don't fit in the room and the boards are still refusing to erase, but I'm no longer praying for a really early retirement option to miraculously appear in my contract. As a matter of fact, I'm feeling rather enthusiastic about the remainder of the school year. When we need to form groups, the kids have learned how to cooperatively move all that stupid furniture out of the way in under two minutes. Those "wild days" are coming to a close as my students move down the road towards becoming consistently positive contributors. The major difference between September and November is that now the processes of community building and collaboration are in full swing.

Every year I make the same mistake: I always want to "take-off running" while my students are often "learning to walk." I trip myself up every time by expecting the latest crop of students to enter my room with the same interpersonal skills with which the old class left the previous June. Talk about unrealistic expectations! I always forget that it takes time for students to get to know and care about one another, to learn how to listen, and to consistently contribute to the success of others. If I could jump into Sherman and Peabody's "Wayback Machine" to revisit the start of the previous year, I'm certain that those "wonderful kids" I remembered so fondly exhibited the same wildness as the current kids did during those first few weeks. What's the solution? You need a plan for developing the norms that will carry you and your students through the school year. And, you need to remember, "Rome was not built in a day."

> *Moral: A class will almost always be better behaved and more skillful in their interactions at the end of fourth quarter than at the beginning of first quarter. My problem with summer vacation is that I only remember that happy fourth quarter, so I set myself up for a rather rude awakening every fall. Since I've proven so adept at repressing my demoralizing first quarters, I'm going to start videotaping my students at the beginning of the year so that I don't forget that all classes rise from humble beginnings.*

The Importance of Community Building

- What is the best class you've ever had? *Best*, however, means that both students and teachers were learning from each other and enjoying each other's company.
- Describe a time you enjoyed learning something; this event could be in or out of school.

I always use the preceding writing prompts in the first days of the semester. Thinking about enjoyable learning experiences gives students a chance to reflect on the nature of what a learning community is and how learners and teachers need to be supportive of one another. However, even though students will acknowledge the importance of such behaviors, the vision of a powerful learning community will not transform them overnight. Hard to believe, isn't it? This is why you need to *explicitly* teach students how to successfully interact with one another and also how to reflect on those interactions. Building a foundation for positive climate means doing three things early on: helping kids get to know one another, establishing basic behavior expectations and negotiating class norms, and teaching students procedures for organizing their work and their reflections. Unfortunately, taking time for what some consider "non-academic" activities seems to fly in the face of our standards-driven curriculums. However, a positive classroom climate will enable your students to work at levels of engagement, collaboration, and self-direction that otherwise would not be possible. Here is a comment from a former student that emphasizes the rewards reaped when the classroom climate is positive.

> Working with others is something I should not be afraid of. I have learned, while working in groups, that the uniqueness and variety of people who I haven't known before is tremendous. I have also learned that people share many similarities.

Still not convinced? Give the following list some thought.

1. Students who are part of creating class rules are more likely to invest in the behavior code. This means less time is wasted on discipline problems.
2. Students who are given time to plan and reflect are more likely to take responsibility and control over their own actions.
3. High-quality task collaboration cannot take place unless positive relationships are developed first.
4. Learning cannot take place without risk. Risk cannot occur unless students feel they can make errors without threat of put-downs.

One other thing to keep in mind is that most of your class period will still be spent on content activities. Except for negotiating the class rules, the activities described in this chapter take only ten to fifteen minutes per day. Even when I am focusing a bit more intently on community building, the other items on my teaching agenda might include reading or writing minilessons, sustained silent reading, teacher read-alouds, journal writing with prompts, responding to a partner's writing, or learning how to write questions that really create conversation.

Breaking the Ice: The Art of Getting to Know Others

Recently, our school toyed with the concept of putting freshmen into heterogeneous integrated teams. The proposal was defeated for a variety of reasons, but one of the most frequent criticisms of the concept was that students would have fewer friend-making opportunities since they would spend three or four periods with the same group of one hundred team members. This concern got me thinking about my own high school classes, and I quickly concluded that these multiple friend-making opportunities described by the critics were largely a myth, a romanticized high school memory. As I mentally reviewed my freshman through senior schedules, I could only remember a friend here and a couple of acquaintances there. All of my real friends were connected with my extracurricular activities: band, choir, and theatre. Though part of the problem in my classes was that they were all pretty traditional and didn't provide many opportunities for interaction, the other problem was that meeting new people and introducing oneself was not a part of the classroom norm. No teacher ever stopped me from introducing myself to a classmate and engaging in some conversation before the bell rang, but no teacher ever encouraged this behavior either. Likewise, I don't recall any of my classmates engaging in the outgoing friendliness necessary for getting to know someone new. Being a "good student" who wanted to fit in, I devoted my energies to paying attention, being quiet, and doing my seatwork.

Reflecting on my high school experiences, I concluded that no matter how many different people students have the potential for meeting throughout the day, they will actually meet very few of them unless a class is structured for interaction. Early in the school year, students need to learn the names of their classmates and practice the art of "ice-breaking" conversation.

Names

If we expect students to work together collaboratively and be interested in each other, then learning everyone else's name becomes pretty important. There are probably lots of different name games out there, but this one has worked well for me. The day before, I tell the students to think of an animal or food that has the same sound as their first name (Dolphin Deanne, Bagel Brad, etc.). The following day, I first have the students check in with their pre-assigned partners in case they need help with their alliteration, sending the kids to the dictionary if necessary. Then I have everyone sit or stand in a circle so that we can all see each other. A volunteer begins by saying his name along with the alliteration. Then the person to his right speaks, saying, "That's (fill in the name) and I'm (fill in the name)." Each person in turn must repeat the previous names before introducing himself. As the game progresses, it becomes more difficult. When a person forgets a name, it is the responsibility of the name owner to coach that person. There is no shouting or laughing by other class members since that is counterproductive to concentration. After getting completely through the circle one way, then the game starts over with a new "starter" and moves around to the left rather than the right.

Once students have mastered the game at this level, they are required to think of a descriptive word that extends the alliteration (Diving Dolphin Deanne, Big Bagel Brad). The game repeats

PARTNER GRID

TOPICS		

Figure 2.2   *Blank Partner Grid*

- Favorite vacation
- Pets
- Best place to live
- Favorite sports/sports team
- Favorite music/songs/groups/radio stations
- Hobbies
- Scary experience
- Best gift you ever received
- Best gift you ever gave
- Favorite food/ice cream flavor/restaurant
- Favorite movie/television show
- Favorite holiday
- Most overrated holiday
- Dream car
- Favorite store/mall
- Best/worst hair cut
- Most valuable possession that isn't worth money
- Best thing you can cook
- Best field trip ever taken
- Famous person you'd like to meet/date
- Future careers

Figure 2.3 *Partner Grid topic ideas*

listening carefully and taking notes on what one has heard, a tangible indicator that someone is respectfully paying attention. Also, recording the questions asked enables students to re-examine their interviewing skills later.

At the beginning of the semester, I try to use the Partner Grid activity daily so that students begin to hone their questioning and listening skills but also because it is an excellent icebreaking activity that helps the class get more comfortable with each other. Once a side of the Partner Grid is filled in, I have students evaluate them. They highlight their best questions in one color and the yes/no questions in another. Then they set an improvement goal for their next round of interviews. While they work, I walk around, look at what they've marked, and stamp that side of the sheet. (The stamp system will be thoroughly explained in the "Getting Organized" part of this chapter.) This technique gives me the chance to look at their papers without actually having to collect them. When both sides are filled and stamped, the kids save them in the Leadership section of the binder (also explained in "Getting Organized").

Appointment Clock

When students have a handle on most of the names and the Partner Grid procedures, the next step is to have them work with a greater variety of partners. One of the best ways to facilitate this

APPOINTMENT CLOCK

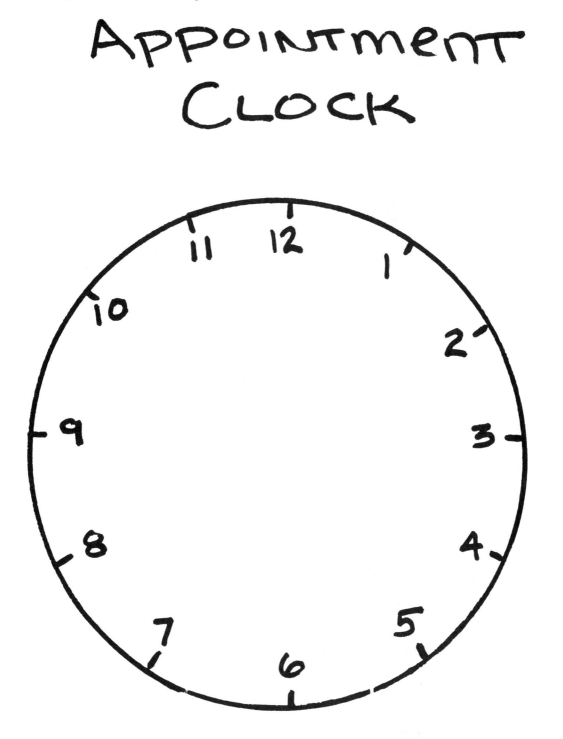

Figure 2.4   *Appointment Clock*

activity is the Appointment Clock. Before starting, push all of the desks out of the way; everyone needs to stand and move around. Each student starts with a blank clock face handout; their goal is to find twelve different partners.

To get the process going, I start by giving some criteria for the first few appointments.

1. Same hair color
2. Same eye color
3. Wearing the same color
4. Total stranger
5. Owns the same pet you do/Owns no pets
6. Plays the same sport/Doesn't play any sport
7. Someone you have/had in another class
8. Has the same teacher (another class), counselor, coach as you
9. Went to same junior high or grade school as you
10. Same birthday month or day number
11. Opposite sex
12. Different height than you
13. Has moved in the past ten years
14. Speaks a second language
15. Has relatives or friends in another country
16. Different year in high school than you

When students pair up, they write each other's name down by the designated number. After about six criteria partners, I let them look for six more new names on their own.

Once all twelve appointments are made (this takes about twenty minutes), it's important on subsequent days for the students to begin using the clock by meeting with all their partners for quick, fun activities. One example is playing the game "Would You Rather." The following are guidelines for this game:

1. Students find their first appointment and greet each other by name. When finished, they are to stop talking, turn towards the teacher, and practice Silent Patient Waiting.
2. Once everyone has stopped talking, a forced, and hopefully silly, choice is read aloud. For example, "Would you rather have eyebrows that crawl around your face whenever you start to daydream or would you rather have ears that grow larger or smaller depending on the change in barometric pressure?" Students confer with their partners and get each other's opinions; they do not have to agree on a choice.
3. Then they thank each other and move on to their next appointment. Each appointment has a different set of choices to discuss. You can continue the game for all twelve appointments or stop at six and save the other half for a different day.

Between Appointment Clock days, have students work in pairs to write new "Would You Rather" choices. If you're tired of "Would You Rather," try riddles. Type up enough riddles so that each person can have one. Be sure to leave enough space on the page between the riddles so that you can easily cut them apart. Give each student a riddle. After greeting the first appointment, each partner takes a turn reading her riddle aloud and seeing if the partner can guess the answer.

After both have taken turns, they trade riddles, thank each other, and move on to the next appointment.

In the subsequent Appointment Clock activity, I use a stopwatch to time the class. I give students their time and ask them to list three ways they could move through the activity more quickly. As a large group we talk about this and then set a time goal for the next time. When the goal is met (it almost always is if students review their plans before starting the next Appointment Clock game), students reflect afterwards on what people were doing differently this time compared with last time.

At this point, you're probably wondering why I spend so much time on these Appointment Clock activities. Believe it or not, a lot of skill-building is going on in an activity that might be labeled "fluffy" by the uninitiated. These include:

1. Getting to know who the appointments are for each hour
2. Becoming familiar and comfortable with each appointment
3. Learning how to meet new people
4. Staying on task
5. Careful listening (choices are only repeated once)
6. Practicing names
7. Practicing quiet, patient waiting
8. Fun, movement, positive and low-risk interaction
9. The clock becomes a source of partners for more serious assignments later on
10. Getting used to working efficiently under time restraints

Rather than me listing these preceding reasons, I have students brainstorm what skills they are practicing when they go though this exercise. Actually, this is a great way to approach many class activities. When students can identify the skills they are practicing, they tend to value it more.

Finally, the Appointment Clock is a great way to expand the use of the Partner Grid. Rather than having students always work with the same shoulder partner (that's the partner you get when two rows are pushed together), the kids can meet with a different appointment on each Partner Grid day. The only problem with this idea is that if you do the grid the first five minutes of class, the kids won't be in their seating chart assigned seats, so you may need the class's help to figure out who is absent. In addition, the Appointment Clock comes in handy anytime the kids need to do something with a partner. It saves time pairing up, and it gives the class some variety, because after awhile most kids do get sick of working with the same partner. When students want to work with a variety of classmates, that's evidence that a solid community is beginning to form.

Trial and Error

Trying to follow my own good advice, I had my new freshmen fill out their Appointment Clocks. On a subsequent day I scheduled "Would You Rather" so that they could visit all of their partners. For my 4th and 6th hours it was working okay, but the kids were noisy and not listening very well when I read the choices. They seemed more focused on trying to talk to nearby friends than their own partners. Though annoyed, my stubborn streak told me to persevere rather than reverse course and try something simpler.

Then 7th hour came. Wired from the previous six periods along with the Ho-Ho's, cheese fries, and soft drinks they consumed at lunch, I should have paid attention to the cues. But hey,

I did this the other two hours; I wasn't gonna budge now! Never mind that the previous success rate was questionable. As the activity progressed, this class was worse than the two others combined, but did I stop? No! We hadn't gotten to appointment number twelve yet! In an attempt to regain order and reiterate the instructions once again, I gathered the students around me. In the middle of my "pep talk," a boy blurted out something incredibly outrageous and definitely unrepeatable. To top it off, it was directed towards a girl. I was stunned. Nothing like seeing your class go down in flames within the first week of the new school year. Luckily, it was close to the end of the period, and the kids had sense enough to recognize the value of putting the desks back in rows and sitting down until the bell released them.

> **Moral:** *"Would You Rather" won't work until the kids have mastered the skills of Silent Patient Waiting and Quiet Attentive Listening. Assessing maturity level is not a bad idea either!*

Establishing Classroom Behavior Norms

As students get to know one another, they also need to begin practicing some basic classroom behaviors. First of all, students need to master the art of listening and following directions. Almost any collaborative activity requires students to listen to the directions and then interact with their team members. All interaction, whether social or academic, requires attentive listening. Attentive listening is an essential skill that must be taught early in the year and then consistently reinforced from the first day on. Also, since the daily agenda in any language arts class almost always includes the individual activities of reading and writing, students must learn how to keep from disturbing classmates when they are finished before others. Another very important skill that cannot be overlooked is teaching students how to avoid putting each other down. Hurtful words can shut down learning in a second. Finally, students and teachers *together* need to negotiate the rules or norms under which everyone can work productively.

Silent Patient Waiting

Are your kids wild in the afternoon or is it just my 5th, 6th, and 7th hours that are overloading on sugary snacks and soft drinks? Years ago when I taught early morning classes to apathetic seniors, it seemed like I didn't have to spend much time teaching them how to be quiet and listen; who knows maybe by senior year some other teacher had already done this task or maybe they figured it out for themselves. In any event, I just don't see that automatic quiet behavior exhibiting itself amongst most of my students. They want to blurt things out and visit with their friends (nearby or seated on the opposite side of the room) whenever the urge strikes. After several years of "hallway talks" and some nasty referrals to the deans' office, it finally dawned on me that the best way to get the kids to stop disturbing others and to start listening to each other during large group was to explicitly teach them. After all, if the kids can't do these two things, they probably aren't going to learn much during the course of the year. Before the year goes any farther, this is the lesson I have to teach. I explain to the kids that not much learning can go on unless they can be quiet during solo work and listen during large group. With their "shoulder partner," I have them introduce themselves and then brainstorm what someone should do when he finishes his work but doesn't want to disturb anyone else. Then we make a master list, which usually includes suggestions such as these:

- Reads a book
- Writes a note

- Daydreams
- Puts head down
- Reviews homework
- Listens to the soothing classical music

I add this last item and explain that often during solo time I'll play music that's soothing and supposed to help them think. Until Silent Patient Waiting has become a norm, I throw the overhead of suggestions up every time the skill needs to be used.

Quiet Attentive Listening

The following day I start by teaching that second basic and so necessary skill: Quiet Attentive Listening. Working with their shoulder partners again, each pair needs a sheet of paper; I usually just hand out scratch paper, which they fold in half (hotdog style) to make two columns. The left-hand column is labeled "Looks Like" and the right-hand column is labeled "Sounds Like." Then I ask the class what students and teachers would be doing if they were listening carefully to someone speaking during a large class discussion. Students brainstorm with their partners and then we combine the lists. The chart ends up looking something like this:

Looks Like	Sounds Like
Looking at who is talking	One person talks at a time
Sitting up straight	Giving new information
Raising hands	Asking a new question
Sitting quietly	Adding to what has been previously said
Taking notes	

With both of these initial charts, you might have noticed that there are no negatives. This is not accidental. When social skills are defined, it's more effective to focus on what students should be doing rather than listing what they shouldn't do. That way, the behavior expectations are very clear. Our "Quiet Attentive Listening" list becomes another frequently viewed overhead. It's also not a bad idea to run off a lot of copies of that chart and, at first, have the kids check off which behaviors they are using and which ones are giving them trouble. Then, with your guidance, they can work on their own behavior modification plans! Once these two skills are somewhat intact, I can now begin the process of negotiating classroom policy.

Home Court

I bet you've noticed that many of your students actively engage in the art of the "put-down." Thanks to some very popular sitcoms (*Seinfeld*, *Friends*, *The Simpsons*) the comic use of the put-down among fictional characters has been confused with the way real people should be interacting. The problem with put-downs is that they quickly create an atmosphere of mistrust. If classmates cannot trust one another, they are highly unlikely to share opinions or even listen to each other. Furthermore, one sarcastic comment can completely shut down a person's ability to concentrate and learn. How logically and rationally can you think when you are angry or upset? It's almost impossible to do any higher-order thinking when your negative emotions have taken center stage. Students need to understand this and avoid put-downs.

I begin by telling students that statistically teams win more games at home than when they are away (LaMeres 1990). This fact is consistent across sports and also between amateur and professional players. With their partners, I ask students to make a list of all the reasons this might be true, and I emphasize that brainstorming means quantity over quality. They should put every reason down. After a couple of minutes, students then prioritize the list according to how much they believe each reason actually affects a team; number one makes the most difference, and so on. Then, after pointing to the Quiet Attentive Listening chart and reminding the students to practice the skill, pairs take turns reading an idea to the class following these instructions. *When it is your turn, read your number one idea. If that has already been mentioned, read your number two, etc. If all of yours have been taken, go back to your number one and read that. As you listen, check off the ones that are mentioned and add the new ones to your own list.*

The results are very consistent. Students almost always believe that the top reasons that home court advantage exists is because of fan support and because teams are comfortable with their playing field. Now the composition books (these will be explained more thoroughly in the next section) come out along with the "Silent Patient Waiting" chart. I put out the following question to the class:

- *How do fan support and a comfortable playing field relate to the academic success of the people in this room? How can we create a home court advantage here?*

Students write for a couple of minutes and then share their pieces with a partner. I ask for a few volunteers to read their responses aloud. I end by telling students that this is home court for us. One of the most important ways to keep that advantage is to avoid using put-downs. From now on, if anyone hears a put-down, just gently say "Home Court" to remind that person to stop. Ever since I've started the year with this activity, the number of negative comments has plummeted. "Home Court" becomes a friendly joke, but when one student says it to another student who is "being mean," the message gets across. It's not unusual to hear the phrase "Home Court!" shouted in the hallways. Though kids insist that put-downs are just jokes and that others don't mind the ribbing, deep down they all know that it hurts when the teasing is directed at them. That's why "Home Court" is something that sticks.

A helpful follow-up activity, particularly if your students are expecting a very traditional learning environment (the teacher lectures and asks the questions while the students take notes and hope they won't be called on to answer) is to have students examine the roles of coach and team player. Working with a partner, have the students fold a paper lengthwise, making two vertical columns. Label one Coach and one Players. Under each column, the partners should list things that coaches say and do that help a team succeed. Students should do the same thing for players. Like the Home Court list, students should brainstorm first and then prioritize according to importance. A quick, large group share should get some of the most important ideas up in front of the room.

Now have the students return to their partners and give them these instructions. *In this class I'll be working more like a coach than a traditional teacher, and you'll be working more like team players than traditional students. If that is the case, what winning behaviors would you expect from the teacher and students in this room? Make two new columns on the back of your sheet and jot down your ideas.* Follow the routine: brainstorm, prioritize, and then share in large group. Conclude this activity by tying together "Home Court" and coach/team behaviors in a journal response. You could ask students to respond to the following question:

- *As a team member, what's something specific I can offer my teammates so that they can learn and enjoy this class? What's something I can do to help the teacher/coach create a great class? How do the ideas of team and Home Court go together?*

Negotiating the Rules

Negotiating classroom policy is something that is commonly done in grade school but seldom touched again once students get to high school. I wrestled with this when I considered all the "yeah, buts." Yeah, but our high school already has a very detailed discipline code. Yeah, but it's required that I write a dean's referral after four tardies. Yeah, but I teach five different classes; how am I going to have a different set of rules for each class? Yeah, but . . . (fill in your own argument here). Okay, here's the good news. All of your classes can negotiate their own rules. Though the words may be different, the spirit and sentiment behind the words will be pretty consistent. As a matter of fact, the rules will probably look pretty similar to the ones that you would have come up with on your own. Check out the rules that emerged from three of my classes:

First Hour

- Don't disrupt people when they are working or talking.
- Don't hurt anyone physically or mentally.
- Be a good friend and help those in need.
- Care about other people's feelings.
- Treat everyone equally and with respect.

Second Hour

- Help when others need help.
- Treat other people kindly.
- Be friendly.
- Care about other people's feelings.
- Don't exclude others.

Third Hour

- Treat everyone fairly and equally.
- Don't make fun of others.
- Make everyone part of the group.
- Treat others the way you would like to be treated.

These are three different classes. Though they had no opportunity to collaborate, their rules were very similar. I think the problem with our narrow thinking on many occasions, my own included, is that we forget that our humanity gives us a lot in common. When it comes down to how we want to be treated, most people want the same things. These class rules do not contradict school policy; instead they create some important and more personal ground rules that define how students want to interact with each other.

Remember those "best class" prompts from the beginning of the chapter? Though I usually wait until the second week to begin rule negotiation, I have students write on those prompts the very first day. If your students are like mine, on the first day of class they've brought a pen but for some reason forgotten their paper (I guess in an attempt to stave off work for at least one more day). That's why I have a stack of 4" × 6" index cards ready. While the students are writing, I play soothing music. You've probably heard all about the "Mozart Effect," and I have absolutely no idea if playing the right classical music improves learning, but I do know one thing: soothing instrumental music is a great cue for quiet, reflective thinking. Even if you give students a short time to write, it is a guarantee that they will finish at different rates. Rather than immediately looking for a friend with whom to converse, they can now sit quietly, listen to the music, and reread the Silent Patient Waiting suggestions featured on the overhead.

I collect the cards from everybody before they leave that day. Besides giving me a little glimpse into each student's experiences, this activity also offers an initial writing sample. As I read through the cards, I try to give some quick responses in the style of a short personal note. Since much of the writing in my class requires responses from other readers, I want to start modeling this immediately.

The following week, I pass the pieces back. Working in pairs, one student reads his story (based on the prompts from p. 9) to his partner while the other listens carefully. Of course, that Quiet Attentive Listening overhead is glowing up front! Afterward, the listener asks three detail questions and a bit of conversation is pursued. Then the roles are reversed. This whole process takes about five minutes. Before I ask for some stories to be shared, I get three volunteers to help me: board writer, spelling lifeline, and note taker. The board writer puts the class's ideas up on the board, the spelling lifeline advises the board writer if he gets stuck on a word, and the note taker copies down the board writer's notes on a piece of paper. After each story, I mention what basic characteristics of positive learning the experience possessed so that the board writer has an easier time. Since students are taking care of the note taking, I am free to lead the discussion and walk around the room, moving in on those who need to clarify their focus (i.e., forgotten the meaning of Quiet Attentive Listening!). A summary of what comes out of these stories looks something like this.

Positive Learning Experience Characteristics

- Wanted to learn, choice in learning
- Collaborative, friendly relationships
- Coaching, willingness to help
- Mutual respect
- Learning by watching others
- Risk-taking, making mistakes is okay
- Practice
- One-on-one guidance
- Useful for real life
- Learn something new
- Had fun
- Time goes by quickly

The following day I display a transparency listing the Positive Learning Experience Characteristics that we created together the day before. Then I pose the question: If we were to do our best to recreate a positive environment for learning, what rules would we all have to follow? Working in pairs, the students brainstorm a list. After about five minutes, I call time and tell them to go back and star the three most important rules. Next, I pass out strips of paper (recycle old handouts by cutting them in half lengthwise) and one marker to each pair, instructing them to write in big letters each of their top three rules on a separate strip. As a rule is written, one of the students takes it up to the board and tapes it under one of the following headings: Respect/ Courtesy, Responsibility, Kindness/Helpfulness, and Miscellaneous. If the rule doesn't seem to fit under any of the other categories, it goes under Miscellaneous (*Ways We Want* 1996).

After about five minutes, there are quite a few rules up on the board. Students are invited to walk up and read them, think about which ones repeat the same idea or move ones that seem to belong in a different category. Once again seated, I combine nearby pairs into groups of four. Now that everyone has had a chance to look at the board, together in their new group, they create the five most important rules, being sure to discuss why those rules would be important to everyone in the class. I give each group a transparency and marker to record their decisions. Once each foursome has its rules, a reporter from each group goes to the overhead, reads them aloud, and explains why they are important to the class. After all are heard, someone needs to collect the transparencies and distill them into four or five class rules. This person can be the teacher, but if you can get a kid to do it instead, you'll have better student investment from the very start.

The next day the final draft of the rules is displayed. Rather than immediate class discussion, now is a good time to return those "Positive Learning Experience" cards from the first day. Play the soothing music and have them write on the reverse side of the cards using one of these prompts:

- *How might following these rules create a "best class" this year?*
- *Which rule do you think is going to help the class the most?*
- *Which rule might be hardest for the class to follow? If it's important to creating a "best class," how might we deal with the problem?*

After the writing, have the kids share with a partner and then invite some students to share their cards and open the discussion up. Have you noticed that almost everything gets shared with a partner first? The reason I do this is that it gives students the opportunity for low-risk rehearsal. Before being called on to explain their ideas to an entire class, everyone has practiced articulating and refining his thoughts before an audience of one.

The problem with rules, any rules, is that after awhile, people forget about them. The real trick with class rules isn't how to negotiate them, but how to revisit them frequently and thoughtfully enough so that they remain at the forefront of everyone's consciousness. One of the best ways to keep a class's focus on these rules is through the use of a composition book.

Getting Organized

One of the ongoing dilemmas of my teaching career has always been how to handle the paper load, not just on my end but on the student's end as well. On the one hand, I was trying to figure out how to collect fewer papers without eliminating useful assignments. On the other hand, I was trying to figure out how I could get the kids to hang on to everything so that early assignments could be retrieved later for portfolios and reflection. The good news is that after ten years of thinking, I finally figured it out!

The Composition Book

One of the handiest little products you can pick up at any office supply store is the composition notebook. Smaller than a spiral notebook, these have firm cardboard covers and a black cloth binding, a real plus if you've ever been snagged by one of the wayward wires from a spiral. Creating a community of responsible classroom citizens requires students and teachers to monitor and reflect on their own behaviors. As you read the rest of this book, keep in mind that most of the reflective writing prompts would be recorded in the composition book. Though the composition books are also used for learning log and literature response assignments, reflecting frequently on one's personal contributions to the class is of key importance. The earliest reflections need to get the kids focused on the characteristics of a leader. Leadership means striving to improve and meet one's own goals while setting a positive example and actively helping others towards their own successes. Leadership includes following the class rules. After negotiation is complete, the students copy their rules into the composition book. Then I ask them to reflect on each of the following two questions:

- *Which rule will be easiest for you to follow—why?*
- *Which rule will be most difficult to follow? Since the class has decided that this is important, what is your plan for dealing with that "difficult" rule?*

A few days later I might ask one of these questions:

- *How is your plan working?*
- *How have the rules benefited you this week?*
- *What was something you did these past few days to help someone else in this class?*

A little later on, I use prompts that branch out beyond the class rules yet still continue to focus on leadership.

- *How am I contributing to my own success?*
- *What successes have I experienced in the last week?*
- *How have I contributed to the success and well-being of others in this class?*
- *What are my personal improvement goals for reading, writing, speaking and listening, and leadership? What accomplishments so far this semester prove that I am working towards these goals?*

Though the entries are not always incredibly deep or elaborate, the composition book is particularly useful in keeping leadership and personal responsibility at the forefront of consciousness. Also, taking a few minutes every few days to examine personal work/behavior habits or the success of a collaborative activity helps students understand that they have much more control and responsibility regarding their own personal successes and the success of the whole class. Here is Todd's series of reflections.

The trick with the journal is not to let it fall by the wayside. Good intentions often flourish and then die. I'm guilty of this myself. I tend to do well with the journal for about the first four weeks of school and then the compulsion to cover the content blinds me. Reflective writing only takes three to five minutes two or three times a week. Also, always have the kids copy down the prompt they've chosen and make sure to date each entry. That way when they look back on these reflections one or two months later, their responses will make some sense to them. Also, I assign points based on dated entries, so if the kids don't have them dated it's hard for them to cash in on the points. Rather than collecting the comp books, I have kids count up their entries and then I do quick spot checks while they're doing sustained silent reading.

Binders

Another lifesaver for me has been the use of three-ring binders. I require my students to get a $1\frac{1}{2}$- or 2-inch D-ring binder along with a set of five binder dividers. I encourage the D-rings because they seem to endure adolescent abuse much better than O-rings, whose clasps never seem to match up after the first week. Also, a D-ring keeps the papers flatter and neater. All work is kept in the binder. Everything has it's place and good organization is very important because much of the class work and homework receives points via stamps, which are counted up only a few times a quarter.

8/31/99   Goals

Reading—Read faster and understand what I read better

Writing—Be able to write more sentences to help explain what I'm saying

Speaking—Give a good speech that keeps everyone interested

Listening—Pay better attention and get something out of what I hear

9/1/99   How would I like to be treated in class?

The way I would like to be treated is the way everyone else wants to be treated. I want to be treated with respect. I want to be talked to and treated as if I were an adult. Nobody should make fun of or laugh at someone else, and nobody should be excluded from anything or anybody.

9/2/99   Class Rules

Don't disrupt people when they are working or talking

Don't hurt anyone physically or mentally

Be a good friend and help those in need

Care about other people's feelings

Treat everyone with respect

- How will these rules affect learning?

By doing all these things, it will help make you able to succeed. You'll get help from your peers as well as your teacher, and there will be a better environment for learning.

- What do you personally have to do in order to follow these class rules?
    1. Try answering questions when people ask them.
    2. Ask others how they are doing.
    3. Talk to other people in class, not just my friends.

9/3/99   How did you contribute to your own success and the success of others today?

    1. I did not disturb people while they were working on their writing.
    2. I listened to everything everyone was saying while we were playing the name game, and by doing that I remembered their names.

9/7/99   Goal for the week—What would you like to accomplish? How will you do it?

I'd like to pay better attention in class and make sure I finish my homework. I can plan my time to make sure I have enough time to do my homework.

(continues)

Figure 2.5   *Todd's composition book reflections*

9/9/99   Homework—How am I doing? Where am I messing up? How can I do better?

I think I'm doing okay. I've got most of my homework in. I think I'm messing up sometimes because I forget to write in my planner. I forgot to turn one assignment in because I didn't write it in my planner, so I didn't know I had to do it.

9/10/99   "Loss of Pet" story quiz—How did I do? How could I change the way I read/study in order to do better next time?

I did well on this quiz because I read it before going to sleep in my quiet room, and I went over the important parts a couple of times to understand it better.

9/13/99   "Loss of Pet" story partner discussion—How is discussing with a partner new to you? What did you learn about the process? What will you remember and do differently the next time?

I've learned how to pay better attention and to ask myself as well as my partner good, interesting questions on the reading which helps me to understand and remember better. Next time I'll try to think of better questions.

9/17/99   Homework—In what order do you do your homework? How do you study?

1. Science
2. Honors World History
3. Spanish
4. Honors Algebra
5. English

I work in my room at my desk. I've got everything I need there. I listen to the radio doing some subjects, others I don't.

9/22/99   Tableau Practice—What process did you use to plan and rehearse it?

First, we read the paper with the directions of what we had to do and which characters were in the script. Next, we chose who was going to be what characters. Usually the taller people were the older people in the script. Last, we began to act the play out and see where the characters should be standing.

9/28/99   Pick a Card—What were three successes you experienced doing this activity?

1. We worked as a group.
2. We had interesting follow-up questions.
3. We answered the questions well.

Figure 2.5   *(Continued)*

9/30/99   Silent Patient Waiting during the announcements—How can you listen better?

I think I'm doing pretty good with the announcements. Sometimes I'll talk if I hear something interesting, but otherwise I listen pretty well.

10/1/99   Illustration Discussion—What was interesting/fun? What would help make the discussion better?

It was fun looking at the drawings and asking them why they drew certain things the way they did. I don't know what we'd do differently the next time. It seemed good enough.

10/4/99   Improving tableau performance—List the steps for a successful rehearsal.

Assign characters and organize where everyone stands.
Make sure everyone knows what they are doing. Practice holding the positions.
Practice facial expressions.

11/17/99   How did following the class rules help you and the sub yesterday? Why did the sub enjoy working with this class?

1. Except for a few, we paid attention.
2. We were very kind, generous, and respectful.
3. We talked to the sub about ourselves.
4. We were quiet during the movie.
5. We participated a lot when the sub asked us about the movie.
6. We listened to the sub's instructions.

Figure 2.5   *(Continued)*

As you look at the following divider categories, you'll notice that all sections also have one or two subsections. I create these by photocopying the titles of the subsections onto heavy stock paper; each subsection divider is a different color. New assignments go in the front of each section while old papers reside in the archive sections. *Writing* has a subsection called *Writing Reference*, the place where I tell students to put all of those grammar handouts, and *Reading* has a subsection called *Reading Sheets*; this is where all of the weekly reading logs go after they're recorded. If any of the example Binder assignments have you puzzled, I assure you that all will be explained in one of the subsequent chapters.

1a. Miscellaneous

This is the place for work that is in process, ongoing partner activities, class rules, and other papers that need to be right in the front for quick retrieval.

1b. Miscellaneous Archive

2a. Reading

> Reading Log Sheets, Book Talk Sheets, notes from Literature Circles or other reading, written reading responses.

2b. Reading Archive

2c. Reading Sheets

3a. Writing

> All drafts, reference materials, prewriting activities.

3b. Writing Archive

3c. Writing Reference

4a. Speaking and Listening

> Notes, speech evaluations, readers theater scripts, tableaux rubrics.

4b. Speaking and Listening Archive

5a. Leadership

> Completed Partner Grids, group processing, accomplishment reflections, and completed teambuilding activities.

5b. Leadership Archive

Say It with a Stamp

The binders work for me on several levels. First, the stamp and binder system is a great way to cut down on the number of grades in your grade book. My class grade is divided up into thirds: a third is for reading log sheets, a third is for homework/class work, and a third is for final products. Final products include unit tests, projects, and final drafts. Every day there are always one or two assignments completed in class or for homework. In the old days, I was always assigning points, recording them, and then adding them up. I can remember quarters where I'd have up to thirty different grades in the homework/classwork category. Why did I even bother to give grades for this stuff? Because the school experience taught the kids that if something doesn't get a grade, it's not worth doing. This value system is well established by the time kids reach high school. Of course, I'd love to work at a school where students did the assignments for the intrinsic reward of greater knowledge and skill. However, since that school hasn't called and offered me a job yet, I had to figure out how I could give credit for all these mini-assignments without driving myself crazy. That was when I realized how I could make the binders do the work for me.

Now, instead of homework/classwork assignments getting individual grades, they get a quick scan and stamp if they met the quality criteria. When I pass back the papers, it's the kid's responsibility to put them in the right section. I tell them which section to put the papers in, but I also list the returned items along with the corresponding sections on the board; that way, instead of repeating the directions, I can just smile and point towards the board. Recently stamped items always go in the front of each section. I tell the kids that these assignments are like money. Since the points haven't been recorded in the grade book yet, they need to take good care of those papers and not lose any. Two or three times a quarter, the students read a little longer during SSR, and I do the binder check. I've even made out little forms so that the students count up and record their points. I ask the students to count up and record their points first. During my verification check, we recount the stamps together. The stamp count is very visual and makes it really clear to a student whether she's been pulling her weight. Also, since I started using the stamp system, the students keep their binders much more organized. If the binder is a mess, I won't check it; the student has to get everything in order before the stamps get counted. I record the total number of stamps in my grade book. After a check, I change the stamp or the ink color so that it's always clear what is currently being counted. After a binder check, the kids take the archive section out and place it back in the binder on top of the papers just counted. That way each section is now ready to accept papers with the new stamp without mixing them up with the papers just counted.

Good binder organization facilitates any process-driven activity; knowing where to find all of the old drafts of the paper under construction comes in handy. The binder also acts as a working portfolio. Unless the kids keep their old stuff, they have no way to document their growth and change. Keeping everything and keeping it organized also gives students a much wider selection to choose from when developing their end-of-semester presentation portfolios.

How Do I Assess This?

Since it's still early in the year, lighten up and relax. Participation in community building can be assessed. For example, when a class has filled up one side of their Partner Grids, I have them highlight their two best interviews, the ones where they really asked good follow-up questions and took detailed notes. While they're working on something else, I walk around, stamp, and have quick conferences with the students that don't seem to be writing much down.

At this time of the year, most of the assessment takes the form of reflection and self-evaluation. Exit slips work well for this. I pass out 4" × 6" cards towards the end of the period and ask students to give three examples of how they've been practicing an important leadership behavior such as quiet patient listening. Before writing, I remind students to look back in their composition book to review their other reflections. I collect the cards, write short responses, and pass them back in a week or so for another skills update. If you notice certain students having skill trouble but not confronting it, ask them to make a plan. You might write, *"I noticed that you tend to talk when I'm trying to give directions, and then have lots of questions on things I've already explained. What are three things you can do to listen better?"* In cases like these, be sure to have the class reflect on the cards more frequently so that a dialogue begins. That way you can note improvements in your short response. Better to catch them being good than waiting until you must nag again. After the cards have several entries, stamp them and have the kids store them in the Leadership section of the binder.

Finally, remember that community-building activities only take between five to fifteen minutes per day. That means you'll still have time for most of your usual first-quarter assignments. Whatever grades you normally count on for academic assessment should still be in place.

Parting Words

I can't emphasize enough how building the foundation for a strong classroom community needs to start the moment students walk through that door on the first day. Though it takes time for norms to take root, the seeds need to be planted immediately. Creating a community goes far beyond just negotiating some rules. A real community is created when its citizens are prepared to work, ready to help each other, and skillful in their interactions with others. A positive classroom climate supports each student's desire for academic success but also fosters social success. In a strong classroom community, students are recognized and appreciated by their peers, and everyone enjoys each other's company. Rachelle's letter attests to this.

5-29-91

Mrs. Steineke,

I was waiting for another processing letter to tell you this, but I don't think that I can wait anymore. I want to thank-you for clearing up some confusion I had my freshman year. My boyfriend was in your Grammar class and so was this one girl with red hair. Well, I had gym the same hour that he had your class. Sometimes I would get out of gym early, and I would come by your class and look in the window. I always saw my boyfriend and that redheaded girl laughing and hanging out together. Naturally, I thought that they were flirting with each other. We had a lot of fights about it. He tried to make me understand that his class was very close and nobody ever thought anything about it. It took me until this year (my junior year) when I am finally in your class to understand how close you get your classes to be. I think it's great. Being close to everyone cuts out all the fighting and chaos that goes on in classes where there are people who hate each other.

Rachelle

Figure 2.6   *Student Letter*

Resources

Negotiating the Rules

Kohn, Alfie. 1996. *Beyond Discipline: From Compliance to Community.* Alexandria, VA: ASCD.
Well-supported reasons on why developing a classroom community aids students in both cognitive and affective development.

Ways We Want Our Class to Be: Class Meetings that Build Commitment to Kindness and Learning. Oakland, CA: Developmental Studies Center, 1996.
This book offers detailed instructions for running a variety of class meetings. Unfortunately, no examples go beyond grade six.

Building Classroom Community

Kagan, Miguel, Laurie Robertson, and Spencer Kagan. 1995. *Cooperative Learning Structures for Classbuilding.* San Clemente, CA: Kagan Cooperative Learning.
Kagan defines class-building as those activities that require the entire class to get up out of their seats to talk and mingle with each other. This book has enough ideas to last for several lifetimes.

LaMeres, Clare. 1990. *The Winners Circle: Yes, I Can! Self-Esteem Lessons for the Secondary Classroom.* Newport Beach, CA: LaMeres Lifestyles Unlimited.
Though the "self-esteem" part of the title might be off-putting, this is a great collection of community-building activities. The "Home Court" idea is adapted from this book.

Riddles, Would You Rather?

Heimberg, Justin and David Gomberg. 1997. *Would You Rather . . .? Over 200 Absolutely Absurd Dilemmas to Ponder.* New York: Penguin Putnam.

_____. *Would You Rather . . .?* 1999. *Over 300 Absolutely Absurd Dilemmas to Ponder.* New York: Penguin Putnam.

These books are fun, but they are written for an adult audience. Be sure to preview and choose carefully since many do have rather racy references to sex.

Rosenbloom, Joseph. 1976. *Biggest Riddle Book in the World.* New York: Sterling Publishing Co., Inc.

_____. *Zaniest Riddle Book in the World.* 1984. New York: Sterling Publishing Co., Inc.

More riddles than you'll ever be able to use!

Classical Music CDs for Quiet Solo Work

Beethoven at Bedtime, Philips, #446 485-2

Mozart Adagios, Decca, #289 460 191-2

Mozart at Midnight, Philips, #442 493-2

Mozart for Meditation, Philips, #446 378-2

Mozart for Your Mind, Philips, #446377-2

CHAPTER 3

Sustained Silent Reading
Creating a Community of Readers

Seeing value in reading is one of the most critical norms that must be developed in a language arts classroom community. If reading isn't viewed as an enjoyable experience, students aren't going to talk about their reading in any depth, nor will they be very excited about choosing books for literature circles. During the first week when I start shaping a classroom community, I set aside a period for a class trip to the library. The sooner my students can get into the daily habits of reading, choosing books, and recommending good titles to others, the sooner their attitudes about books will change. Yes, I know this book is supposed to be all about collaboration, but here's the news flash: successful collaboration is the culmination of many individual efforts. To see collaborative literacy in action, the collaborators have to *value* literacy. Sustained Silent Reading opens the doors to the enjoyment of reading. And, as you know so well, whenever a person has just finished a good book, collaboration often happens spontaneously. Readers want to talk with those who have read the same book, and they want to encourage others to read that title. Unfortunately, even after I began to experiment with cooperative groups, I endured some pretty painful moments before I figured out that a strong Sustained Silent Reading program is an integral component of creating a classroom community of readers.

I'll never forget when I first began teaching English. As any new teacher will, I started out with the handouts that other more experienced teachers had generously given me. One of my favorite handouts was a first day "Getting to Know You" questionnaire. One of the questions asked, "What is your favorite book?" Some students did list titles (many from early childhood reading experiences) while the vast majority answered with the words "None" or "I don't like to read." As a beginning English teacher, this was pretty disturbing information. My impression of teaching English was that reading and discussing literature was a standard component! How was I going to teach English if students didn't read? As I soon learned, it *was* pretty difficult. Of course, there were always those five or six students who did do their homework and were willing to engage in what is erroneously called large group discussion, but the vast majority remained unengaged and uninterested. Once I started using small group discussions on a regular basis, more students started doing the reading since it was far more uncomfortable to sit unprepared with a small group of one's peers than it was to sit unprepared in a large group. I even had one student compliment me on avoiding large group discussions (i.e., teacher lectures!). He said, "You don't talk much, do you? That's good."

Though more engagement was occurring, an underlying current still unnerved me: my students were doing the reading, but they still thought reading was boring. My first impulse was to find more interesting books for them. After attending a reading conference where I heard Robert Cormier speak, my wheels started to turn and I thought of the brilliant idea of having my sophomore Basic English students read *The Chocolate War* and *Beyond the Chocolate War*. My head filled with wonderful project ideas, and I envisioned exciting group discussions. I expected that the kids would be thrilled to death to be able to carry around an eight-ounce paperback rather than an eight-pound anthology. If anyone could identify with Jerry and his outsider status, it had to be those alienated kids in my sophomore Basic English class. WRONG! The kids hated that book. The one class who liked me, did humor me and agree to read both books, but it wasn't a self-actualizing experience for anyone in that room. In the other class, the one that didn't like me, I'm not even sure we finished the first book. All I can remember is rebellion, class disruption, and unhappiness. Boy, who says reading can't influence behavior! My argument that we were reading a real book versus a contrived anthology fell on deaf ears. What I later gathered from that horrendous experience were a few hard-earned kernels of wisdom that I will always remember.

1. Just because a teacher likes a book, even one that is supposedly geared to young adults, doesn't mean that young adults are going to like it, too. The one part of Cormier's speech that I had forgotten was that he had originally written *The Chocolate War* with an adult audience in mind. It was not a young adult book until the publisher decided it was a young adult book.

2. Even in tracked classes, students come to you with widely varying reading experiences and abilities.

3. Most readers hate to be told what to read. As an adult, I don't really like it either. The difference is that I am a confident reader. Even if my graduate course readings were excruciatingly boring, I also knew that I was still going to like reading because the pathetic choices of my professors didn't define the entire world of literature. I have read lots of good books and, given the time, I will read a whole lot more of them. Non-readers or poor readers do not draw the same conclusions. Because most of their assigned readings of the past have been classified as "boring," these readers assume that all reading is boring.

4. Few books fit an entire class. It is extremely difficult to find one book that most students in a class will like because of individual interests, experiences, and reading abilities. I once had a "discussion" with a supervisor about the wisdom of forcing poor readers to slog through *To Kill a Mockingbird* when I knew they didn't have the prior knowledge, vocabulary, or skill to read and enjoy the book. The response was the traditional, "Students don't have to like what they read; we're here to teach the classics." For the life of me, I couldn't figure out how we were servicing the classics if the end result was that students swore to never pick up another book once they graduated from high school.

5. Even if a text falls into a certain readability level, students must be ready developmentally. Though the readability level of *The Chocolate War* was age appropriate, my students weren't ready developmentally to tackle a story that focused on a kid who bucks the system and loses big time. Talk about a feeling of hopelessness. That is not a message most fifteen-year-olds want to contemplate because it forces a person to acknowledge his own weaknesses and vulnerabilities. In a similar vein, most classics were not written with fifteen-year-olds in mind. These are books about adult situations, and the authors were counting on their readers to have enough adult experiences to identify with the characters and their struggles.

Once I took these five kernels to heart, I realized that one of my main goals as an English teacher was to create positive reading experiences. If students become confident and skilled readers who enjoy reading, I fully expect that those same readers will eventually pick up those classics and enjoy them as adults. The key is getting kids to change their attitudes about reading.

When a lot of us who are now middle-aged adults were growing up, reading didn't have the stiff competition for a student's time that it does now. My family did not have a color television until I was in eighth grade. Even when we did, there were still only about six local stations to watch. If I wanted to listen to a record or 8-track tape (ha, ha), the stereo was in the family room with the color television. The use of my family's minimal multimedia had to be negotiated. I read that a typical teen in 2001 spends less than one percent of his time reading and about thirty-three percent of his time in media-related activities. Nowadays it's not uncommon for students to have complete home entertainment systems (CD, DVD, VHS, cable television, video game systems, and computers with Internet access) in their bedrooms, so this statistic really isn't that surprising. During my childhood, reading was a cheap and accessible entertainment that had very little competition. However, if I had all of the entertainment choices that are available to students now, I wonder, would I be such an avid reader? Now more than ever before, I think whether a student becomes a reader is highly dependent on the number of positive reading experiences she encounters at home and at school. Since teachers have little control over those home experiences, attention needs to be focused on what we can do when the students come to us.

Typically, most students enjoy reading until about the third grade and then interest in outside reading tends to wane until middle school, when outside reading takes a complete nosedive. Blame hormones, extracurricular activities, peer pressure, or lack of societal modeling, but the average student is a nonreader by the time she gets to high school. Ironically, high school teachers bemoan the fact that students can't read or won't read, but few teachers value reading enough to provide time for it in their classes. Jim Trelease summed it up succinctly in his book *The Read Aloud Handbook,* "We make time for what we value most." What follows are some ideas for making that time for reading.

Finding the Time to Read

Starting to read for many students is like starting an exercise program. Most students would like to be better readers and know that they should read, but they just don't like to do it so they don't read. Providing 10–15 minutes daily for in-class reading is the start of that exercise program. Some teachers like to reserve Fridays for free reading. Though that easy Friday lesson plan is attractive, I don't think it is nearly as beneficial as the daily short spurts. Going back to the exercise analogy, when a person starts a walking or running program, she accomplishes fitness goals at a more rapid pace by doing a little every day than by trying to exercise for an hour once a week. Why? Because when you're out of shape, you cannot keep up the same level of endurance for a full hour. You'll walk or run fast for the first fifteen minutes, but by the end, if you even make it for the full hour, you'll be moving slowly and gasping for breath. Reading is the same way. Out of shape readers have trouble sitting still for an entire period. They lose their focus and start daydreaming. They don't have a repertoire of skills to get them through the difficult or boring parts of a book. Let's face it, very few books are perfect.

One way to put books front and center is through the use of Sustained Silent Reading. Though I know we've all got curriculums to cover, many benefits can be achieved when just fifteen minutes a day is devoted to individual reading. SSR time needs to be structured and predictable; it's not something you just throw in when there are a few minutes to spare. In my classroom, I aim for fifteen minutes on a daily basis. Typically I try to schedule SSR in the beginning of the period just after the students have done their Partner Grids. This way students get into the habit of having their books ready to go. Now, that doesn't mean that I still don't have to say, "Get your books out!" It just means that they're not surprised by it; it also means that they know they must have their books in class every day. The other thing I like about starting the period with SSR is that it seems to have a calming affect on the students, something that will come in handy later in the hour when you want the kids to listen to your minilesson on the Globe Theatre! When we read, I use a kitchen timer so that students can start getting a feel for their reading speed. Every day they log their reading on the official form.

Since we sometimes get shorted by a few minutes (think impromptu fire drill or extra long morning announcements), I also have the kids star the days when we have read exactly fifteen minutes. Being able to pinpoint those days lets them begin to compare reading speeds between books and also between school reading versus home reading. Furthermore, these starred dates give students the documentation they need to see their reading speeds increase.

Out-of-Class Reading

In addition to in-class reading, I also require that students read two-and-one-half hours per week outside of class. This reading is recorded on the bottom half of the log sheet. I strongly encourage students to limit their reading to half-hour intervals. Unless a book is absolute dynamite (think *Go Ask Alice*), out-of-shape readers often lose focus when they read for longer intervals. When the in-class reading time is usually fifteen minutes, it's easy to compare reading consistency by looking back at what's recorded on the top half of the sheet. I talk with the reader when I notice a glaring inconsistency. When a student can read ten pages in fifteen minutes but can cover only twelve in thirty minutes, I ask why that is. Sometimes it's because they're fudging their time. More commonly, I find out that the reading is taking place right before going to bed. I guess it's nice that the kids like to end the day with a good book, but on the other hand, I know that our football team practices a lot earlier in the day even though it's the team members' favorite sport. The bottom line is that you can't give your all to anything when you're half asleep. In those cases, I try to get them to put that half hour of reading earlier in their homework schedule. A reading slow down also often signals inefficient multi-tasking. More than one student has confessed that he reads while watching television or wearing headphones. If those habits slow down the reading and lower the comprehension, I try to get the student to rethink his reading environment.

Weekly Time Goals

I've chosen to set a weekly time goal rather than a weekly total pages goal for a couple of reasons. While a time goal allows a student to choose just about any book, a total page goal often narrows student choice. Students might be tempted to look for easy books that can be read quickly rather than more challenging titles that would require a greater time investment for the same total page requirement. Also, a total page goal puts an unfair burden on a slower reader who might take much longer to finish the same number of pages than a faster reader.

Cheating

What about cheating? Well, kids cheat, and this approach is not foolproof. I originally asked for a parent's signature to verify the out-of-class reading, but after a couple of years I realized that many parents will blindly sign any school form that their child thrusts in front of them. Then, when I did catch a blatant cheater and phoned the parents, they were usually "honked off" at me rather than their kid. I soon concluded that the "signature plan" wasn't meeting my accountability needs, but still I wanted some sort of parental involvement.

Due Date_____   Name_____

Book Title_____   Date_____Hour_____

Author_____ Pages_____

In-Class Reading

Date	Pages Read	Total Pages	Points
Ex: 12/1	36–43	7	1

Out-of-Class Reading

Break reading into 15–30 minute intervals

Date	Place	Pages Read	Total Pgs	Time In/Time Out	Total Time
Ex: 12/1	Homeroom	43–50	7	11:20–11:35	15

_____pages = _____hours

**Late sheets are only given half-credit!
Only novels or previously approved books count.
Newspapers, magazines, or text books do not
count. Credit is given to only one title at a time.
That book needs to travel to and from school
on a daily basis.**

In-Class Points_____

Out-of-Class Points _____

Total Points_____

Parent/Guardian Signature _____

Yes, this week I have discussed my
student's reading with him/her.

Figure 3.1   *Reading log sheet*

The form I use now still asks for a signature, but that signature indicates that the student talked about the book with his parents. Readers who actively talk about what they read see skill increases faster than those who don't, so this is one of the ways I try to increase the frequency of those conversations. How do I catch cheaters? It depends on how much energy I have. First, I won't give outside reading credit for books that I have never seen. I'm pretty strict on the one book at a time rule. When a kid argues, I just tell her that she can read as many books at the same time as she wants, but she can only count one book at a time on the log sheet. That cuts down on the number of "mystery" books. From time to time I also eyeball pages covered in class versus out of class; huge discrepancies result in point deductions and some impromptu conferences, but now the conferences just involve the student and me. Usually I can squeeze a confession out, but sometimes allowances are negotiated as well. Sometimes a faked reading sheet is the result of some serious problems occurring outside of school.

One of the best ways to cut down on cheating is to know what the kids are reading. Once or twice a week at the beginning of SSR, I like to take a quick walk though the room to see who's reading what and where they are in the book. I stop here and there in a random fashion and ask a question. What's the best part of the book so far? Which other books have you read by this author? How did you get interested in this book? One question is enough. In general, the more you can talk to your students about what they are reading, the less they will cheat and the better they will become as readers. Also, the faster you can pinpoint a student who has made a bad selection, the faster you can get her to a more suitable book. In the vast majority of cases, the students who are off-task during SSR are the ones who have chosen books that are not holding their interest.

Attracting Kids to Books

When I first started using SSR, I brought the kids to the library and told them to browse. After all, that's what I did when I went to the library, and I had no trouble finding a good book. Au contraire! I quickly discovered that one of the primary skills nonreaders lack is the ability to pick out books they will enjoy. When you think about it, why would they be good at picking books for themselves? For the most part, their reading encounters have been whole class books or individual selections restricted by an Accelerated Reader list. Left to their own devices, nonreaders base their choices on title, cover design, and familiarity. Often I see slower, less-skilled readers choose a 700-page novel by Stephen King, usually a title that has already been made into a movie. When questioned, these students stubbornly hang on to their choices even though I know the book is not going to fit them as a reader. Stephen King is a brand name when it comes to the horror/suspense genre. All of those movies have been commercials for his books! Though some students will stubbornly cling to an inappropriate choice, I try hard to get them to consider some alternatives. While I've found that the right book can truly change an attitude, the wrong book choice only confirms and strengthens the belief that reading is boring.

Helping Them Choose

How do I get kids to choose the right books? I read a lot of young adult fiction myself. That's the beauty of SSR: while the kids read, the teacher reads as well. If I graded papers or spent all of my time monitoring their reading, the message would be reading is important for you but not for me. I want kids to see me reading, too. I've often thought it would be wonderful to schedule "guest readers" to drop in at the appropriate time and say something like, "I've heard this is a good place to read; mind if I join you?" Ideally, I'd work on recruiting adult male readers since this group is sadly under-represented when it comes to modeling. From what kids report to me, it is far more typical that mothers read aloud to their children than fathers. Even in high school, I notice that it is overwhelmingly the mothers who deal with school concerns. In the world of media, Oprah energetically touts her favorite authors, but I can't think of any prominent males promoting reading with equal enthusiasm.

The advantage of you reading during SSR is that while the kids only clock fifteen minutes, you'll have put in close to an hour by the end of the day. I use that time to read books that I think my students might enjoy. Thanks to that time over the years, I've been able to read hundreds of young adult literature titles. I've made a real commitment to find books for my students during SSR. Consequently, my reading of adult literature is not as extensive as I wish, but part of the fun of being a reader is having those impromptu discussions with others about books we've read. While my students offer me those conversations, I have few counterparts in the adult arena. Never forget that conversation is indeed a motivator when it comes to reading.

As a teacher, knowing what books to recommend is the key to a successful SSR program, but the other part of the puzzle is having the books to recommend. Through the years, I have developed a fairly respectable classroom library. I started the collection by combing the used book sales of local libraries. I also offered some bonus points to students who could donate useful titles. Eventually some administrative support developed, and I now have some brand new books specifically chosen by me for the classroom library. I view the classroom library as a stop gap between our visits to the school media center. Classroom libraries are a very important tool, but I've got to warn you right now: the books just don't last. Students do fill out an index card with name, title, and date checked out, and file them in a little box, but some books still disappear. That's the nature of a classroom library, so you've always got to be working on ways to replenish your book supply.

The Media Center

That's why I take my students to the school media center every three to four weeks. The MC has an even bigger selection of novels, probably due to their bigger budget and their computerized check-out system; they're much better at getting their books back than I am! Prior to any library visit, I request the media specialist to set up a cart of books that I think my students will find interesting. I do this by keeping track of popular books from previous classes and then giving the MC a list. Before I set students free to browse, I give a quick talk, featuring some of the books I've read and those that other students have enjoyed. I was surprised by a recent *English Journal* article written by Donald Gallo. A survey conducted by a former graduate student of his revealed that few teachers ever recommended books to their students and when they did, those books were usually classics rather than books teenagers might enjoy. Now, I have nothing against the classics, and I am always willing to point out a few good but more difficult books if I have readers who are ready for them. Sometimes it is truly surprising what kids will tackle on their own when it isn't assigned. However, my primary objective here is to help kids find books that they will truly like. Often, after my book talk, students still insist on browsing the stacks. Adolescents, for the most part, are a stubborn bunch and hate it when it looks like their decisions might be influenced by an adult, but those titles I talked about often turn up in their hands later on in the semester.

Other Sources

If you haven't read any young adult titles besides *The Outsiders*, don't berate yourself; get started! The American Library Association and the International Reading Association as well as *The ALAN Review* and *Voice of Youth Advocates* journal all offer great reviews and bibliographies. ALAN even has a great website to check out. Consult with your school and public librarians. The local bookstore is also a great resource; you'll always find at least one person who is an expert in young adult literature. Given these resources, you'll have no problem deciding on which books to read and recommend to your students.

Your increasing knowledge of good books for adolescents can help you in another way. Oftentimes teachers need to take an active role in book acquisition. Most school media centers encourage teachers to make book order requests. Take advantage of this; do not leave ordering good books strictly in the hands of the media specialist. After all, you probably have a better feel for what your kids will read because you know them best. Every year I fill out book orders worth thousands of dollars, knowing full well that all of those books won't be ordered. However, over the years, I've found my school's media center often has monies that turn up mid-year via grants or budget transfers, so I want to have my orders in just in case. Taking my students to the library on a regular basis is also another way to encourage media center specialists to take choice reading seriously. Most media center specialists want students to find the books for which they are looking; if they see that a particular resource (in my case, novels) has a high usage, more money will be budgeted for that part of the collection in subsequent years. Whenever we go to the library, I tell my students that they are obligated to check out at least one library book. Circulation rates provide hard data that proves to the media specialists that the money spent on books has been worth it.

Encouraging Good Book Choices

As I mentioned earlier, many students are clueless when it comes to their personal selection of books. Since they harbor the opinion that "all books are equally boring," it doesn't really matter what book they choose. Of course, this attitude creates a self-fulfilling prophecy. Reading will always be boring as long as selection is careless. Therefore, on our first trip to the library, which takes place about the third day of the new semester, I already have my first minilesson in mind: how do you pick books you know you'll enjoy? When I ask this question, most students immediately suggest cover design and title. They are surprised when I tell them that book covers are designed by a publisher's advertising/marketing department and editors often make the final decision on a book's title, based on what they think will sell the most copies. Realizing that title and cover design are ploys of the marketing department, the kids then suggest that getting recommendations from other readers is a good way to find enjoyable books. This idea segues nicely into my Book Talk.

Book Talks

While I give the kids a couple of minutes to practice their 12-inch voices (quiet conversation), I look over the book cart and grab about twenty surefire winners. Now it's time for me to talk about books and for them to practice Silent Attentive Listening. I talk about each of the books very briefly, trying to tell just enough to give the kids an idea of what the story is about while also grabbing them with a hook. Here's an example.

The Killer's Cousin is about a guy named David who has to repeat his senior year of high school. He's repeating it because he spent most of the previous year in court on trial because he was accused of killing his girlfriend, a death he claims was accidental. Even though the verdict was "not guilty," his hometown still thinks he's a cold-blooded killer, so his parents send him to live with relatives in another town where people will not connect him with the trial. As soon as he gets to his aunt and uncle's house, David knows he is not really welcome because they barely speak to him. The only person who does say anything is his eleven-year-old cousin, Lily, who greets him with a question. "What did it feel like to kill her?" As you might guess, David's problems are not over.

Every time we go to the library, I always do a ten-minute Book Talk because I want the kids to have lots of possible choices. On any given visit, I'd say about half the kids will jump for the books I've talked about while another twenty-five percent peruse the stacks with their friends, relying on each other's recommendations. Sometimes, a lone student will march towards the stacks with great deliberation and find a book that I know no one else in class has read. Of course, I always ask, "How did you decide on that book?" There is nothing more encouraging to me than when a student says that a friend in another class recommended it. This means that conversations about books and reading are extending beyond the classroom. Then there is the other twenty-five percent that didn't like any of the books I talked about. These are hard nuts to crack because they're so averse to reading. Often I can match them to a book by asking the following two questions:

1. What are some books you've read in the past that you've liked?
2. What are some of your favorite movies? Television shows?

As students read, they begin to realize that they like certain genres or story structures. They also begin to create an informal network of people whose book recommendations they trust; sometimes it's me, oftentimes it's their friends or parents. They even begin to develop reading source preferences: classroom library, school library, public library, books brought from home. The trick is to bring all these subconscious realizations to the conscious state and then discuss how these preferences dictate their reading. When a student is consistently abandoning books, I ask some questions.

1. Why do you think you keep picking out books that you don't like?
2. What is it that is initially attracting you to these books?
3. How do you go about picking out books?
4. How might you change the way you select your next book?
5. What books have you read in the past that you liked?
6. What kind of story are you looking for?

Trial and Error

I'll never forget the student who came back to my class with a book titled *The Frankenstein Diaries*. Since he didn't have his I.D. with him to check out a book during our class visit to the library, the following day he fussed until I let him go on his own. Even though he had been present during the Book Talk, apparently none of those books appealed to him. Back in class, it soon became clear that *The Frankenstein Diaries* was not holding this kid's interest, so I took a look at the book. For most kids, even Mary Shelley's classic, *Frankenstein*, proves pretty slow moving. Well, this book was even more boring by teen standards. There were no monsters in this book at all, just the musings of Dr. Viktor Frankenstein as his entries traced his gradual descent into madness. Try as I might to dissuade him, this kid insisted on hanging on to that book for at least six weeks even though it couldn't hold his interest. During SSR, he would open it up and then promptly put his head down for a nap or look around for an equally unengaged reader with whom he could converse.

Another recent student seemed to have a similar agenda. It almost seemed as though he purposely chose books that he knew he wouldn't enjoy. He chose a Stephen King book that another kid had already totally panned. He chose a book that his father recommended and stubbornly continued reading it even though he freely admitted that he couldn't follow the plot. Most of SSR was spent like the other kid: looking for someone to talk to. It just seemed like he purposely chose books that would confirm his opinion that "reading is a waste of time." In the course of one year, I think he only finished two books. One was his Literature Circle book (peer pressure has its positive side). The other was *Skellig* by David Almond. *Skellig* came highly recommended from another male in my freshman English class, who described it as weird and freaky. It's the story of a boy who finds what he thinks might be an angel. The part I couldn't figure out was why "Mr. I Don't Finish Any Book I Start" waited until fourth quarter before finally paying attention to his classmates' recommendations.

Moral: Every student runs on his own internal compass. The best you can do is point your students in the direction of lots of good books and hope that most of your kids' compasses are pointing in that same direction.

Creating Conversation about Books

Besides the fact that daily reading helps students improve their reading skills, having a class read together opens the door for many conversations about books and reading. The point to remember is, that even though all the kids are reading, these conversations will not necessarily take place spontaneously. Just as the friend-making skills introduced in the previous chapter needed specific structure and guidance, so do book-sharing skills. As always, it is important for the teacher to model first and then provide regular opportunities for these conversations to take place. Once students get into the SSR habit and have a few good books "under their belts," you'll begin to see them talking about books more spontaneously. Finding interesting books to read and getting others to read books they've enjoyed is something that is becoming important to them. However, in the beginning, a community of readers needs to be nurtured.

Partner Grid and Appointment Clock

Having students frequently interview each other on what they're reading and how they picked that title is another avenue for helping students share their lives as readers. At least once a week, I have students meet with one of their Appointment Clock partners to interview each other on the books they're reading. As usual, the questions and answers are recorded on the Partner Grid. The following two questions work well for this.

1. How did you pick that book? How do you decide on a book to read?
2. What is your book about and how is it so far?

Let students visit with their different partners and talk about these topics. Learning how classmates choose books and think about their reading is akin to learning the different ways people solve the same algebra problem. Sharing ideas almost always results in a revision of one's own thinking. Plus, the more you can get students to talk about what they've read, the better their comprehension will be. Always remember that students don't need to finish a book before they can talk to others about it. Talking about one's reading should be an ongoing and regular feature of class conversations.

The Reader Space-Out

Another way to use the Partner Grid is to get kids to talk about when their reading derails, otherwise known as the "reader space-out." I have to give credit to Stephanie Harvey and Anne Goudvis for coining this phrase in their book *Strategies That Work*. Have you ever read some text without reading it at all? Your mind was somewhere else. You saw the text and turned the pages, but whatever you read never got to your brain; instead it flowed straight from your eyes out through your ears. As a skilled reader, you probably caught yourself within a page or two, decided whether or not to reread, and then proceeded with the goal of staying better focused. Kids experience reader space-out all of the time, except they react differently. Because they think reading is boring anyway, they think that the space-out is a normal part of reading just as breathing is a normal part of living. Students will read for an entire chapter and never consciously notice a space-out. Afterwards, when they can't remember a darn thing, the typical response is something like, "I can never remember what I read anyway." Space-outs affect all readers from time to time, but good readers catch them, regroup, and go on. Good readers also recognize that when space-outs occur frequently, their needs as a reader are not being met by that particular text. Students need to be on the look out for their space-outs and think about what triggers them. Here's another good Partner Grid topic:

When are you most likely to space-out when you're reading and how do you deal with it?

Ideally, if students discuss this topic a few times, they will start to recognize the parts of text that often trigger space-outs. For myself, I know that I have to increase my focus whenever I read long narrative passages. I need to set myself up with some internal conversation by asking myself the question, "What will I need to notice in this part that will give me insight or become important to the story later?" Once kids realize what triggers their own space-outs and recognize that a ten-page space-out is not a natural part of reading, they'll begin to catch them before they've wasted much time (Harvey 2000).

Finding Good Passages

One of the components of being well prepared for a Literature Circle or Book Talk, both of which will be discussed in subsequent chapters, is picking out good passages to read aloud and discuss. Typically, teachers do a lot of modeling when it comes to this skill; after all, in most large group discussions it is the teacher who picks out the important parts of the text to discuss. Also, since teachers usually pick the same parts of the text to read aloud from year to year, they usually do it in a polished and dramatic fashion, the inherent result of repeated practice combined with that pent up "ham acting" talent most teachers possess.

Unfortunately, this modeling doesn't automatically rub off on students. Typically, when reluctant readers read, they view all parts of a story as equal and equally boring! Helping students learn how to find enjoyable books does begin to change their general outlook on reading, but it doesn't automatically translate into the skill of picking out the great parts of a story; this takes practice and guidance. Before SSR, tell the students to get out their sticky notes; as they read, have them mark a passage or paragraph that's important, exciting, interesting, or written with good description. After SSR, students can check their Appointment Clocks, move together with one of their partners, and take turns reading their passages aloud and talking about why they picked that part. Or, just have the kids read the passage aloud to their partners. After the passage, the listener must first explain why he thinks his partner chose that passage and then ask some questions about the book. If the chosen passage is truly good, it may convince a partner to check out a title.

This works better as just a talking activity; the Partner Grid makes it cumbersome. I have found, though, that students read better standing rather than sitting, so you might have everyone in the room up on their feet for a change. Repeating this partner activity often is a good idea because it helps get the kids into the habit of actively looking for good story parts while also reading with their sticky notes in hand. Both of these skills come in handy later for Literature Circles.

After practicing with their partners, I found that most students became much more adept at finding good parts of their books to share with others. However, my joy quickly turned to despair when I listened to how the kids were reading these passages. Their readings were excruciating in their blandness and atonality. To top it off, the kids didn't know how to adjust the length for ultimate listener attention; either they'd read one sentence or two pages. They had no idea how to cut a long section or splice shorter sections together. Talk about picking a really good passage and then stabbing it through the heart! Just when I thought this passage stuff was conquered, I realized that if I wanted the kids to turn into "ham actors," I was going to have to teach them that, too. That's when I thought of turning their passages into short performance speeches.

Students are required to choose a passage that's one-half to one page in length; the criteria for choice is that the passage get potential readers interested in the book. Cutting or splicing is okay, and I model this for them a couple of times using whatever book I'm currently reading. I show the kids a transparency of the page and then using a marker, I cross out cuts or draw arrows to spliced sections. As long as they use pencil or sticky notes, they can do the same thing with a library book. Once they've chosen and cut their passages, I have students practice reading them aloud to three or four of their Appointment Clock partners. Next, I have them return to their seats for a little solo work. They need to write an introduction and a conclusion. Before reading the passage aloud, they must first give some basic information about the book and also set the audience up so that everyone understands the passage. After reading, the presenter must explain why he felt the passage was important. After the introductions and conclusions are written, students work with a few more partners, practicing the entire speech. This time I insist that the speech giver stand before her partner. All of this preliminary work takes three or four days, about twenty minutes per day.

When the formal speeches begin, I require that each student bring in a videotape so that their presentation can be recorded. Afterwards, students can take their tape home and do a self-evaluation. Videotaping speeches is also very handy if there is any sort of grade dispute. All you need to do is watch the tape with the student and discuss the rubric together. After sitting through a first round of bad to mediocre passage speeches, my students finally realized that the best passage will die a slow and torturous death if the reader hasn't given it a proper introduction or offers an unenthusiastic delivery. Afterwards, it's easy to quickly pinpoint the many ways the first round of speeches went wrong. Therefore, to get the best results and most improvement in passage reading, you really need to do two rounds of speeches. Once the kids have to sit through several days of boredom inflicted upon them by their peers, they won't want to repeat the experience. The second set of speeches will be significantly better. Here's something else to keep in mind. Though individual speeches can be time consuming, learning how to sit still and be a good audience member comes in handy at the movies or graduation, and this assignment offers you the chance to revisit Silent Patient Listening!

Making Personal Connections with Text

It's well established that connecting text with one's own life improves comprehension and also retention of what is read, yet few students seem to know that this is an important reading skill. Very often the problem is that students can't come up with a connection because they think they need to relate to the entire story. Here's a good example. A student had just finished the novel

Book Passage

Name _____

Date _____ Hour _____

Performance Evaluation

- **First impression:** prepared, confident   yes   no

- **Introduction:** title, author, short summary,   3   2   1   no
  tie in to passage

- **Passage:** holds audience's attention,   3   2   1   no
  ¾ to 1 page in length

- **Voice:** audible, clear enunciation, correct pace   3   2   1   no

- **Interpretation:** practiced, shows emotion   3   2   1   no

- **Conclusion:** explanation of why passage   3   2   1   no
  was important, personal connection

Figure 3.2   *Passage speech grade sheet*

Book Passage

Performance Self-Evaluation

   1. What did you do well in your performance? Be specific.

   2. If you could repeat the performance, what would you change to make it better? Be specific.

   3. What will you focus on specifically so that your next performance improves? What will you do differently? How will you practice differently? How could your group members, family members, or teacher help you?

Figure 3.3   *Passage speech self-evaluation*

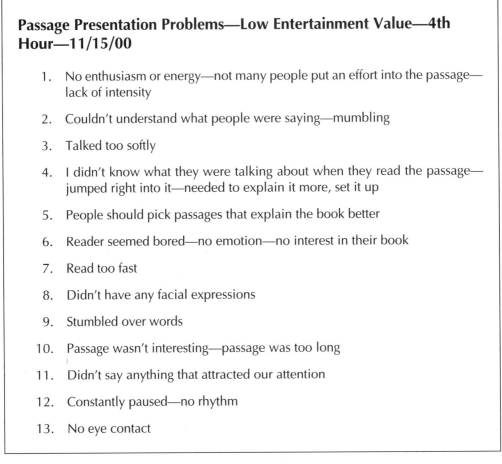

Passage Presentation Problems—Low Entertainment Value—4th Hour—11/15/00

1.   No enthusiasm or energy—not many people put an effort into the passage—lack of intensity

2.   Couldn't understand what people were saying—mumbling

3.   Talked too softly

4.   I didn't know what they were talking about when they read the passage—jumped right into it—needed to explain it more, set it up

5.   People should pick passages that explain the book better

6.   Reader seemed bored—no emotion—no interest in their book

7.   Read too fast

8.   Didn't have any facial expressions

9.   Stumbled over words

10. Passage wasn't interesting—passage was too long

11. Didn't say anything that attracted our attention

12. Constantly paused—no rhythm

13. No eye contact

Figure 3.4   *Passage speech weaknesses/improvements for next time*

Wrestling with Honor (Klass 1990), The story follows the star of the high school wrestling team who is wrongly accused of drug use when his urine sample tests positive. The reader, John, said to me, "I don't wrestle, I don't do drugs, and I have never taken a urine test. There's nothing I can connect this book with." Students need to know that a connection does not necessarily need to involve a direct personal experience; they also need to understand that you can make a personal connection with a solitary incident in the book. I asked him, "Have you ever been accused of something you didn't do? What have you heard about the Olympic medalists that were disqualified for drug use? How did you feel when a friend let you down?" The partner activity described earlier for passages can also be used for connections. Also, unlike passage modeling, teachers seldom explicitly model personal text connections, possibly because they are afraid of "getting off on a tangent." Ironically, those "off on a tangent" moments are when students get to see that teachers are real people with lives outside of school, rather than just teaching machines that the district warehouses in some boiler room during off hours.

    As students become more familiar with the idea of looking for personal connections, make use of that composition book I mentioned earlier. Remind students to have their sticky notes

Cassie 8th
September 29, 2000

Chicken Soup for the Teenage Soul III

Friendship

Me and my friends told ourselves that we would never let a guy come between us & if that did happen, to act mature enough to talk it over

Pg. 79

Friends are difficult to understand & have diffrent feelings & actions than you. Don't do something to hurt your friend just because you think its cool or its gonna make you popalar, b|c it won't

Pg 90

This reminds me of when my brother used to always get in trouble & his friends would be waiting until their parents came to get them & they wouldn't want to see them.

Pg 108

Figure 3.5   *Sticky note examples of connections*

ready and mark parts of the story where they've made a connection. By Friday, or whatever day you choose, they should have at least three connections. On the appointed day, each student writes about his favorite connection but also goes back to the text for details when comparing their connection with the story events. After spending five or ten minutes writing, students can meet with one of their appointments and trade composition books. Rather than having a talking conversation, students have a written one via a Dialogue Journal. After trading, students read their partner's entry and then write back to them in letter style. The goal is to share ideas, affirm opinions, and ask questions. After about five minutes, students trade back. Partners read the response and write back again. Depending on time, these written conversations can continue for several trades or just one response followed by a quick oral conversation.

Branching Out

A final part of making connections is to begin to differentiate them. More skillful readers usually begin with personal connections but then branch out by looking for connections that relate to another text, current or historical event, or something else they've studied. I try to guide this branching out by offering many short, supplemental readings that relate to what we're studying in class. For example, when reading *A Raisin in the Sun*, I brought in an article I found in the *Chicago Tribune* that detailed the story of a family whose house purchase was summarily cancelled once the current owners discovered that the purchasers' adopted child was African American. Students read the article, jotted some notes, and talked with a partner about how this article compared with the problems encountered by the African American family in *Raisin*. A quick large group share followed to emphasize the importance of looking for connections that go beyond personal experience.

A colleague of mine helps the connections process along in her sophomore team that combines English, Biology, and Geometry. While the students are studying genetics in Biology, they are reading the young adult novel *Star Split* by Kathryn Lasky in English. This short science fiction book takes place in 3028, a time when all embryos are screened for genetic defects and then genetically enhanced so that each person born can achieve his ultimate potential. The novel gives human faces and emotions to the abstract and complex topic of genetics, while the study of genetics offers the reader greater understanding of the dilemmas the main characters face when confronted with a government that controls and monitors the genetic history of all of its citizens.

Background Knowledge Inventory

In some respects, examining one's background knowledge is very similar to personal connections because it requires the reader to inventory his prior experiences and then connect relevant information to the text. Students need to consciously be aware that background knowledge, or the lack of it, is going to affect how well they comprehend and enjoy a text. A book I can think of off hand that makes this point is *Beyond the Reef* by Paul Zindel. The story focuses on a family who tries to make a living deep sea treasure hunting off the Florida Keys. Even though I've only visited Florida once and avidly avoid swimming and boating, I enjoyed the book, maybe because of my childhood devotion to the old television show *Sea Hunt* starring Lloyd Bridges. I never could get a student to read this book. Considering that I live and work in a Chicago suburb, my guess is that the lack of interest is because my students' experiences have so very little in common with the novel's topic. When a student actually did read the book this past fall, I had to ask him why he chose it. As it turned out, Dan had gone scuba diving off the coast of Florida while on vacation. Background knowledge or lack there of can make or break a reader's comprehension and enjoyment of a text. Some of the trouble students have when they pick books that they aren't enjoying is that they never stop to think about what they need to know.

Here is a quick partner activity for emphasizing the importance of background knowledge. Be on the look out for comic strips that require background knowledge in order to get the joke, and then make transparencies out of them. Throw a few up on the overhead each day. Tell the kids to turn to their shoulder partner and discuss why the comic is funny and what the reader needs to know in order to "get it." I can think of one comic I cut out during the height of the Firestone tire recall and another that made use of the word *chad*, a noun few people knew the meaning of before the Florida ballot recount in the 2000 presidential election. In both cases, without the correct prior knowledge, there's no way these comics would be funny.

Making Inferences

Being skilled at making accurate inferences is crucial when it comes to fully understanding fiction. While nonfiction tends to be less subtle, the reader of fiction always has to be alert to the significance of a tone of voice, a character's actions, or what might have happened during an unnarrated interval of time. Accurate inferences are derived from keeping track of the story's clues, the details that are revealed in the text. While students need to be keen observers of detail, they also need to think about how the details create the clues for "reading between the lines."

Comic strips are also very useful in teaching inferences. The best examples show characters who make incorrect inferences. For example, one "Blondie" strip depicts Dagwood demanding a raise from his unsympathetic boss. "You should pay me what I'm worth!" says Dagwood. What are the inferences? Dagwood thinks he should be paid more while his boss's expression clearly shows that he would love to pay Dagwood far less. Like the background knowledge activity, this also works well with shoulder partners. Display the transparency and have partners talk about the clues that make the comic funny. Once they have an answer, have pairs quickly share with another pair to see if others might have thought of something they didn't. Before calling the class back to order, make it clear that the talk time was a chance for clarification and rehearsal. Everyone should have an answer ready, so no one should raise his hand. Then call on students at random. This instruction makes it clear that partners need to talk together and everyone has to be ready to explain.

How Do I Assess This?

Even though students are largely making their own reading selections, there really are quite a few different ways to monitor progress and give grades.

1. **Weekly Reading Log Sheets:** I count these for one-third of each quarter's grade. At the end of each quarter, we put the sheets in order and graph the 15-minute average for each week. The graph gets stamped and goes into the Reading section of the binder.

2. **Reading List:** Students use this form to keep track of the books they've read. At the end of each quarter, we count the number of books read along with adding up the total number of pages. Each time the lists are updated they get stamped. Since these lists become a piece in their semester portfolios, it's super important that these updates become a specific assignment. Otherwise, the kids who aren't into keeping meticulous lists (about ninety percent of all teenagers) will have very incomplete lists at the end of the semester. The lists are stored in the binder with the reading log sheets. That way they are more likely to update the lists each time a graded log sheet is returned.

3. **Reading Self-Evaluations:** Students evaluate themselves at the beginning of the semester, in the middle of second quarter, and around the middle of third quarter.

Name_____

Date_____   Hour_____

Title, Author, Copyright	Total Pages	Date Finished	Genre

Figure 3.6 *Reading list*

Name _____

Date _____　　Hour _____

First Week Reading Survey

1. If you had to guess . . .

   How many books would you say you owned? _____

   How many books would you say you've read over the summer? _____

2. How often do you read at home for pleasure?

   _____

   _____

3. What kinds of books do you like to read? Do you have any favorite titles or authors? List them.

   _____

   _____

4. What magazines do you enjoy reading?

   _____

   _____

5. How does someone become a good reader?

   _____

   _____

6. How can being a good reader come in handy?

   _____

   _____

7. Computers

   Do you have Internet access at home? _____

   Do you have your own email address? _____ Address _____

   Which programs do you have on your home computer? MS Word MS Publisher

   (Circle the programs you have) _____ (other)

Figure 3.7　*First week reading survey*

Winter Reading Survey

Name _____

Date _____   Hour _____

1. On a scale of 1–5 (1 is the lowest rating while 5 is the highest), how would you rate yourself on the following reading skills? Explain why you rated yourself as you did. Give specific examples/reasons.

   _____ Choosing books you know you'll enjoy reading

   _____ Quickly catching yourself in a reader space-out

   _____ Making self connections to text

   _____ Recognizing and remembering/marking important passages

2. How many total pages have you read so far this semester? _____

3. Averaged between weeks, how many pages do you cover in 15 minutes? _____

4. Name the best book you've read so far this year. What made it enjoyable?

6. What are three specific reading goals you are going to work on this semester? How can you improve your speed, widen your reading repertoire, and change a habit so that you will be reading long after this class ends?

   _____

   _____

   _____

7. Name three books you'd like to read this semester. List title and author.

   _____

   _____

   _____

Figure 3.8   *Winter reading survey*

Spring Reading Survey

Name _____

Date _____   Hour _____

1. On a scale of 1–5, how would you rate yourself on the following reading skills? Explain why you rated yourself as you did. Give specific examples/reasons.

   _____ Setting time aside for reading

   _____ Using sticky notes to record what you notice and think as you read

   _____ Making inferences (drawing conclusions, filling in missing details)

   _____ Actively accessing prior knowledge while reading

2. How many total pages have you read so far this semester? _____

3. Averaged between weeks, how many pages do you cover in 15 minutes? _____

4. Name the best book you've read this semester. What made it enjoyable?

   _____

   _____

5. Name three books you'd like to read. List title and author.

   _____

   _____

   _____

6. How are you a better reader now than when school started last fall?

   _____

   _____

   _____

Figure 3.9   *Spring reading survey*

These evaluations encourage the kids to reflect on themselves as readers but also to set some personal goals in order to become better, more versatile readers. These goals play into the reading section of the semester portfolio.

4. **Book Talks:** About every four or five weeks, students must discuss their reading with their peers in an organized format. This will be discussed in detail in Chapter 5. I count these assignments as tests.

5. **Passage Speech:** Here's another grade that I count as a test. Also, this speech assignment is a nice way to meet your curricular goals of public speaking and oral interpretation while still focusing on honing skills that will be very useful when you get around to Literature Circles.

6. **Informal Skill Practice:** Students engage in regular conversations with their peers using the Partner Grid and composition book. I stamp a side of the Partner Grid when it consistently shows thoughtful questions and detailed notes. Completed Partner Grids are stored in the Leadership section of the binder. The composition book entries are counted during each binder check.

Parting Words

At the end of last year, I gave a book to Katelyn, a student in my freshman English class who also worked for me as an aide. Katelyn was an inconsistent reader, the kind of kid who reads a lot when she finds some good books but looses momentum quickly when her choices aren't right. She had mentioned that she enjoyed books written in a diary format, so as a parting gift, I gave her *The Perks of Being a Wallflower* by Stephen Chbosky. Written in the form of letters, it's the story of a boy trying to make friends and survive his freshman year despite some pretty serious personal problems. I didn't talk to Katelyn over the summer, but as luck would have it, she turned up in my sophomore English class. She loved *Perks* and had even loaned it to a couple of her friends. About a month into the school year, I noticed a girl in a different class reading *Perks*. Since this is one of my all-time favorite books, I couldn't help but start gushing. Laura endured my happy little rant, smiled, and said, "Yeah, this is good. Katelyn told me to read it." Talk about collaborative literacy in action! Once students become readers, their interest in connecting with other readers takes on a life fully independent of school and teachers.

Resources

Books

Atwell, Nancie. 1998. *In the Middle: New Understandings About Writing, Reading, and Learning.* Portsmouth, NH: Heinemann.
    Though Atwell's approach to reading focuses on reading workshop, many of her minilessons and strategies can be modified for use in an SSR program.

Harvey, Stephanie and Anne Goudvis. 2000. *Strategies That Work: Teaching Comprehension to Enhance Understanding.* York, ME: Stenhouse Publishing.
    These strategies demonstrate how to explicitly teach your students how to become more skilled readers.

Trelease, Jim. 1989. *The New Read Aloud Handbook*. New York: Penguin Books.

Jim serves up some great arguments about why reading is important, particularly in this multi-media age. He gives useful suggestions for parents and teachers on how to turn children into lifelong readers.

Periodicals

The ALAN Review (Assembly on Literature for Adolescents, NCTE)

Check payable to ALAN/NCTE and send to:

ALAN Membership
National Council of Teachers of English
1111 Kenyon Road
Urbana, IL 61801-1096
Yearly membership rate: $15

VOYA (Voice of Youth Advocates)

Scarecrow Press
4720A Boston Way
Lanham, MD 20706
(1-800-233-1687)
Subscription rate: $42.00 per year

Both of these periodicals offer reviews of the latest young adult literature titles, as well as genre retrospectives, "best of" bibliographies, teaching strategies, and interviews with authors.

CHAPTER 4

Teaching Students How to Collaborate Successfully

Once students are in the swing of using their Partner Grids with a variety of class members, you'll begin to notice a difference in the interpersonal skill levels of your students. There will be a few students who seem to work comfortably and successfully with most of the others, and there will be a few who can't seem to get along with anyone. Both of these examples are extremes. The majority of your students will fall somewhere in the middle: they'll show some strong social skills but also some very weak ones. Yet this shouldn't be surprising. Humans, though instinctively social, are not born with collaborative genes. These behaviors have to be learned, so if students are not using an important interpersonal skill, it needs to be taught directly.

Teachers often give up on collaborative strategies because of their students' inability to work together successfully. Students are mean to each other, ostracize group members, take over the group, scream at each other, or leave their seats in order to infiltrate and distract other groups. I could go on and on, but you get the picture. Actually, I remember a time in my own career when I avoided group activities for just those reasons. I wanted groups that shared the work, aimed for high quality, listened to each other, appreciated each other, and didn't disturb other groups. My groups didn't look like this, so I blamed the kids and stuck to individual assignments that were easily controlled by me. Luckily, I eventually learned that I could help students create positive interactions if I first examined a group task in regards to the specific skills it needed, and then explicitly taught those necessary skills.

What skills do I teach first? Skills can be roughly divided into two categories: maintenance and academic. Maintenance skills enable a group to function together in a positive and productive manner. Academic skills increase the level and depth of learning within a group.

Examples of Important Social Skills

Maintenance Skills	*Academic Skills*
Quiet voices	Asking questions
Forming groups quickly	Asking follow-up questions
On-task behavior	Summarizing
Praising	Asking for help
Taking turns	Giving help
Encouraging participation	Checking for understanding
Friendliness and support	Developing consensus

As I mentioned in the previous chapters, I get students to work together in pairs via the Partner Grid, Appointment Clock, and other short brainstorming assignments such as Home Court and Rules Negotiation. As students work, I observe and assess, looking for the skills that the students seem to lack. In the beginning I am most concerned with maintenance skills such as talking quietly, being friendly, using names, staying on task, focusing on your partner/group members, or encouraging participation. If you started your year with the activities discussed in earlier chapters, you've already begun teaching some basic group skills, so now the process is a matter of introducing a new skill or refining one that is already in use. Actually, introducing a new skill is the easy part. The hard part is getting the kids to actually use the skill on a regular basis. While talking quietly, sitting closely, and focusing on the group are skills easily learned, skills that require significant changes in behavioral functioning take longer. For example, it takes time, often an entire semester, to get students to listen carefully to a teammate's answer and then automatically ask him some thoughtful questions. Why does it take so long? Because this type of extended discussion rarely occurs in typical teen conversation. If you don't believe me, listen in on some lunchroom talk the next time you have the joy of being assigned cafeteria supervision. Typical lunch conversations are often purely expository. One student talks about how hard the geometry test was and then the next kid totally changes the subject and reports on who broke up with whom. No one stops and thoughtfully asks, "What went through your mind when the teacher said she thought the test was easy? How do you think you'll study differently the next time?"

Most of the academic skills and many of the maintenance skills listed above are really new skills, so it takes time for them to become truly integrated into a student's automatic behavior patterns. This means that only about four sophisticated skills can be focused on in any depth during a semester, so pick the ones that you most need for the academic goals at hand. But don't be tempted to just teach the academic skills! No higher-order thinking will ever take place unless a group is friendly, respectful, and trusting of one another. Another important key is that no matter what skill you teach, make sure that the students practice the skill within an academic context. Fun team-building exercises (i.e., puzzles, survival scenarios, etc.) that do not reflect your curriculum can serve as useful skill introductions. However, if students don't soon need the skill for an academic task, they will not value it. Last, but not least, keep reminding yourself that taking the time to explicitly teach a skill will save you time when the students are engaged together. Yes, time is always an issue, but stop to think about how much class time and productivity is wasted in the course of reigning in rowdiness and other counter-productive behaviors. Put in the time up front and reap the benefit later!

Teaching Group Skills

As I mentioned earlier, it's important to examine any group task in regards to the social skills the students will need in order to complete the assignment successfully.

Take a look at the directions for the collaborative study of a poem.

1. Each member takes a turn reading the poem out loud while the others follow along. After everyone has read, go around your group and get a response from each person for each of the following items:
   a. Which line stands out to you? Why?
   b. What's the best word the poet used? Why?
   c. Describe a connection, something the poem makes you think about.

    d. What's something about the poem that puzzles you? Ask the question and get every-one's input.

    e. What does the poem mean to you?

2. Afterwards, review the highlights of your group discussion and summarize your under-standing of the poem. Talk about it first and reach a consensus. Then each person should write down their group's summary in her composition book and be ready to present the summary to the rest of the class.

When I look at this lesson, I know that students are going to need the following skills: lis-tening, building on another's answers, asking interesting discussion questions, taking turns, sum-marizing, reaching consensus, and being friendly. Though all of these skills are important, I know that students already have some rudimentary training in listening, taking turns, and ask-ing questions because we've been using the Partner Grid regularly. Though summarizing and building on another's answers (piggybacking) are important, I'm going to choose to work on a maintenance skill instead. Since older students are often turned off to poetry because they have learned that they'll never figure out the correct (i.e., teacher's) interpretation anyway, I want the kids to be as positive as possible so that no one is afraid of contributing an idea. Therefore, I'm going to explicitly teach the skill of Friendliness and Support.

The first step in teaching any skill is to define it to students and explain why it's important. One of the best ways to introduce any skill is to show its real-life value. If you start reading Dear Abby, Ann Landers, or the employment section of any paper, it won't take long to find examples of how the inability to be friendly and supportive is not rewarded in real life. My favorite exam-ple came from a *Chicago Tribune* article. In 1994 I read a story titled "Rude, Disrespectful Doctors More Likely to Be Sued, Studies Suggest."

After reading this article aloud, I talk to the class about my own experiences working in groups. I've always gotten a lot more done in a group or committee when I felt like I was a val-ued and appreciated member. Work tends to be better and more fun when everyone gets along. Helpful as they are, the kids will now point out that if you just allow them to work with their friends, these skill problems will be solved. Good point! However, a true leader is someone who has the skills to work positively and productively with just about anyone. In the "real" world, how many people get to pick their co-workers, neighbors, children (once they're born, you've got to make the best of it), or in-laws? Actually, most of the people you work with in the course of a life-time are pretty random selections. Also, our closest friends tend to have very similar ideas and val-ues. An important academic strength of a group is the divergent thinking that can result. A group with different members often comes up with better ideas than one where everyone thinks pretty much the same way.

The T-Chart

Next comes the development of a T-Chart, a strategy originated by the Johnsons. This step is very important because it clearly defines both the non-verbal and verbal behaviors that would be observed if the skill were being used. Have students work in pairs for this brainstorming, using one sheet of paper between partners. Fold the paper in half lengthwise to create two columns. The kids should already be somewhat familiar with the T-Chart since they practiced this step once before when they discussed Quiet Attentive Listening. Head the paper "Friendliness and Sup-port." Label the left-hand column "Looks Like" and the right-hand column "Sounds Like." Pose this question: *If a group was talking about a poem together while being friendly and supportive of each*

26   Section 1   Chicago Tribune, Friday, November 25, 1994

Nation/World

Rude, disrespectful doctors more likely to be sued, studies suggest

ASSOCIATED PRESS

Doctors who want to avoid malpractice lawsuits should brush up on their bedside manner, two studies suggest.

Physicians are more likely to be sued if their patients feel the doctors are rude, rushing the visits or not answering their questions, according to the studies in Wednesday's Journal of the American Medical Association. The studies were done by doctors from Vanderbilt University in Nashville.

"A doctor can't get away with being a technical whiz and an interpersonal jerk," said Dr. Sidney Wolfe, a consumer advocate with the Public Citizen Health Research Group. He didn't participate in the studies.

"But the studies don't say that simply behaving well and having good interpersonal skills is a substitute for technical skills. People deserve and should get both."

One study analyzed 963 obstetric cases to find out what made patients unhappy with their medical care.

The patients were asked questions such as how long they had to wait before seeing the doctor, how much time they spent with the doctor, whether the doctor treated them with respect and whether the doctor listened to their concerns and questions.

The doctors who had been sued the most rated the worst on almost all the questions. Their patients even reported the doctors yelling at them twice as much as any other group.

But physicians who had never been sued were most likely to be seen by their patients as concerned, accessible and willing to communicate.

The other study examined the relationship between obstetricians with a history of malpractice claims and the quality of the clinical care they provided to patients five to 10 years after those claims.

The study used nurses and doctors to review patients' records and judge the quality of care. The study found no difference in the technical care provided by doctors who had been sued and those who hadn't.

"These studies show that a doctor might not have done anything technically wrong but generated enough misunderstanding and anger to provoke a malpractice claim," said Dr. Gerald Hickson, one of the studies' authors.

Dr. Wendy Levinson, in an editorial accompanying both studies, called on medical organizations to hold more classes in communication skills for doctors.

Figure 4.1   *Rude doctors article reprint*

other, what would you see as you walked around the room? This is "Looks Like." What would you hear people saying to each other? This is "Sounds Like." Then give an example for each column such as "smiling" for "Looks Like" and "Hi, how are you today?" for "Sounds Like." Notice that the Sounds Like column actually creates a script of phrases that students can say when using this skill. Have students brainstorm with their partners for a few minutes and then bring the class back around to complete a master list. Try to get a response from each pair (either column is fine) so that everyone gets an idea on the chart. Remember, though, that some pairs will have more ideas than others, and this activity will be harder for students who have not done much thinking about skills before. Be patient. When a student comes up with a negatively phrased suggestion such as "No one says shut up," ask the partners how they came up with that. Maybe they were thinking that everyone's ideas would be considered. Then ask how that statement could be turned into a positive one such as "Let's get everyone's opinions before we decide." The next page shows an example of what a T-Chart for this skill might look like.

T-Chart

Looks Like   **Sounds Like**

Figure 4.2   *T-Chart*

Friendliness and Support

Looks Like	*Sounds Like*
Smiling	"Hi, how are you today?"
Nodding in agreement	"What do you think?"
Group sitting close together	"That was a good idea."
Desks touching	"Thank you."
Eye contact	"Let's hear from everybody before we decide."
People taking turns speaking	"That's interesting; tell us more about your idea."
Taking notes on what others say	"Wow, I didn't think of that."

If I'm reading your mind correctly, you're probably looking at this chart and thinking, "Well, duh. This is so elementary; who doesn't know this stuff!" However, before skipping the skill of Friendliness and Support, think about the last few school committees of which you were recently a member. Now, go back and look at that T-Chart again. I've been on more than a few committees where the only way to get heard at all was to jump in when someone else finally had to stop talking in order to take a breath. To this day, I am still waiting for someone to say to me at a meeting, "Nancy, we haven't heard from you yet; give us your input," or "Nancy, that's an interesting idea; tell us more about it." You see, though these skills look simple on the surface, they are not. Many adults do not consistently use the skills of Friendliness and Support when engaged in group work, so why would our students be any better at it?

Reinforcing the Skill

Okay, enough of my soapbox chatter, back to the business at hand. Once the T-Chart is made and the kids understand the skill, the really hard part begins: getting the kids to actually use the skill. Believe me, the newer you are at this T-Chart stuff, the harder the kids will fight it. Have you ever tried to lose weight? Think about how hard it is to eat more healthfully on a *permanent* basis. Few people can do it. I think six weeks is about how long most people can stick with a diet and exercise program before they slip back into old habits. Learning to use a new skill requires new thinking and new behaviors; it is much easier to just act the same way and say the same things as you always have. Besides, if the kids' resistance is strong enough, caving in might mean you'll let them work with their friends! Be strong. You are older, wiser, and more experienced. You can *persist* longer than they can *resist*!

In order for students to practice the skill, the academic task must require it. Remember, that's why I chose this skill; I didn't want an unfeeling comment to shut down any member's ideas in regards to the poem. The use of Friendliness and Support is always important when students are discussing ideas, brainstorming, or problem solving. Also, discussion of a text should require significant input from everyone before a group begins to draw its conclusions. Even though a skill has been discussed, the kids still won't use it unless the teacher's expectations are clear. Before I set students loose on that poem, I'm going to put an "I'm Looking For . . ." list up on the board or overhead:

I'm Looking For . . .
- Following the directions
- Taking turns

- Getting ideas from everyone
- Staying focused on the group
- Looking friendly and supportive
- Saying friendly and supportive things

In the beginning, teacher monitoring is very important. Walk around a lot! Teach students how to set up their groups so that you can walk completely around them. Students like to bunch up together so they can goof off and you can't get close enough to really check out what they're doing. Don't let them fall into this bad habit. When kids whine about moving the furniture into a more "monitoring friendly arrangement," this is what I say, "Yeah, I know moving those desks is a lot of work. However, if you want to get any credit for today's assignment, I have to be able to observe you easily and so far I can't. I'll come back in a little while and see if I can observe then. I hope you decide to earn some points today." What group in their right mind wants a zero? I've never had a group that chose not to move the desks.

As you monitor, compliment and encourage groups who are using the required skills. Intervene in groups that are not and have them stop to say friendly, supportive statements to each other. Tell them that you want to hear them say nice things to each other; it's important to you! Yeah, of course their compliments will be phony and forced, but think about it: isn't every conscious behavior change uncomfortable and unnatural at first? Why would using a new skill be any different? The trick with nurturing the use of a new skill is not losing momentum. Just like that diet, we teachers will be gangbusters in reminding students to use a new skill in their collaborative work, yet several weeks later that skill is on the backburner while the class has moved on to something else.

Strategies that Keep Skill Usage in the Forefront

There are lots of different ways to help keep a new skill from falling by the wayside.

- Run off copies of the T-Chart or put it on an overhead. Before a discussion, have each student write down three Sounds Like statements he will use that day. Afterwards, have each student think of one new statement he could use. Add these to the chart.
- During monitoring, write down the skill statements you hear along with who said them. Report this back to the class later in the period.
- As you observe groups, keep a tally of each time you hear a specific skill being used. Give the class a total and make an improvement goal for next time. Graph ongoing results on a chart or overhead.
- Assign the role of Skills Coach in each group. It is that member's job to model and remind members to use the specified skill.
- Have students brainstorm assignments in other classes where the specified skill could be applied. Assign them to go out and use it and then report back to the class on what effect it had on the group interaction.
- As you observe, jot down good examples of skill usage on sticky notes and give them to the kids. I tell them to save the notes for their portfolio.
- Review the skill as a class. Talk about problems in usage and where refinement has taken place. Make up a new Sounds Like list.
- Teach students how to observe their own groups via a checklist or observation sheet. When a student must keep a tally of how his group is using some specific skills, it makes

that student and often the entire group more aware of when skills need to be used. (Observation Sheets are explained more thoroughly in Chapter 8, Literature Circles)

Trial and Error

No matter how hard you try to teach and reinforce interpersonal skills, Friendliness and Support will not stick to a kid determined to remain antisocial and untouchable. These are the students who feel most powerful when they are sabotaging a lesson plan and/or group. For these students, the guidance of a talented therapist may someday lead them to positive and productive lives; in the meantime, completing a T-Chart just won't be enough.

I distinctly remember one kid. School just didn't meet his needs. Period. Plus, this guy was angry, really angry. He obviously was angry about something that didn't involve me or anyone else in class, but he still chose to share it with all of us whenever he felt the need. Mostly, the anger expressed itself in passive–aggressive activities versus out-and-out explosions, though there were a few of those. During SSR, students kept a sticky note handy in order to add strong nouns and verbs to their own personal word lists, words that would later be used in writing. Of course, the kids were also instructed to look for new words, words that were not already a part of their vocabulary. Mr. Angry chose only to write down the words he could find that had drug connotations. Come to think of it, that was probably the main reason he chose to read *Go Ask Alice*. However, when he turned in his word list, I wouldn't give him credit because I felt all of the words he listed (*joint, doobie, uppers, acid*) were words he already knew. Of course, Mr. Angry, in traditional "bring the class to a screeching halt" fashion, became angrier and accused me of denying him credit for his hard work. I think there's a dent in the support post outside my old classroom from the doorknob hitting it as Mr. Angry slammed his way out on his way to the deans' office. Of course, thanks to my dogged persistence and also the fact that Mr. Angry refused to do any writing unless it pertained to illegal drug use, the deans got sick of the kid parked in their office and finally dropped him from my roster. Story over, right? Wrong!

The following year, Mr. Angry took to loitering by the lockers across from my room in order to offer his girlfriend some quality make-out time before making her late to her 4th hour class. Of course, being human, I still had it in for this kid. I took no small pleasure in telling him that lunch meant he needed to go to lunch; it was not carte blanche for roaming the building. Mr. Angry sent his girlfriend off to class, late again, and then proceeded to fire off a barrage of profanity towards me as he sauntered down the hallway towards the cafeteria. Repeatedly, and at the top of his lungs, he shouted, "You're a fat fucking whore Mrs. Steineke!" His pronouncement attracted attention. Students and teachers rushed to their doors, hoping to get a glimpse of the fat fucking whore. I could have used the incident to celebrate alliteration (gosh, maybe I did teach him something!) Instead, I stood stunned while my freshman resource homeroom boys attempted to rouse me from my stupor by offering to, bless their hearts, beat the guy up for me. They settled for hand delivering his referral for gross disrespect to the deans' office. Ironically, after the episode, Mr. Angry did not go to lunch but marched straight to the deans' office and turned himself in; he beat his own referral to the finish line! Later in the day during my prep period, I related the whole story to some of my office mates. One particularly sympathetic colleague said, "But Nancy, you're not fat!"

Moral: Sooner or later, you'll have a kid that drives you crazy. Teaching social skills or structuring engaging lessons won't make any difference because neither one of you is in the right place at the right time. Try your best to separate yourself from the infliction incurred and count your blessings that you aren't that kid's parents!

Refining Skills with Processing

The final step in teaching any skill is continual group processing. Unless the group frequently examines how they are interacting with each other and how their skill usage is progressing, it is unlikely that their functioning will evolve and their skills usage will become more refined. Here are some strategies to get your classes focused on examining their group interaction.

Ongoing Student Processing

Over the years, I have found the best format for processing is for each student to keep his own record on a sheet of notebook paper. Each meeting date is listed in the left-hand margin and to the right is the student's processing notes. Here's a typical question I might ask at the end of a group task:

> • *What were three things your group did today that helped with the discussion and enabled every-*
> *one to get along and enjoy each other's company?*

The group discusses the question, agrees on some answers, and every member writes them down on his Processing Sheet. A quick large group share is helpful so that you can get some ideas for skill refinement. For example, if the skill I just taught was Friendliness and Support but no group mentioned using this skill, I would have groups set a goal for next time related to that skill:

> • *List three specific ways your group will remember to use Friendliness and Support during the*
> *next discussion.*

Following is some ongoing processing from Gary. His class had been working together all year, so most of the goals set by his group focus on academic social skills; however, it is interesting to note that the group had to solve the "interrupting problem" before it could set the goal of "discussing passages in depth." In addition to processing the group's functioning, the heading "Discussion Highlights" encourages the group to recall the most interesting ideas from that day's group discussion.

Processing is always useful no matter how long a group works together. On average, I find that groups work together for about three to four weeks, the duration of a project or literature circle. On the other hand, once peer conferencing groups have bonded, I like to keep them together for the rest of the semester. Though students start a fresh Processing Sheet each time they switch groups, I make sure they keep the old sheets in the Leadership section of the binder. This makes it easy for newly formed groups to examine the problems and successes members encountered previously. These sheets provide data as students discuss the skills that really helped their old groups. Once skill usage becomes a conscious concern for students, there is little skill slippage when new groups are formed. As a matter of fact, when students own a skill, they'll even carry it to other classes. I've had a couple of teachers tell me about former students of mine instructing their new group members in how they must behave in order to be productive! Once a norm for successful group behavior is set, students expect others to adapt.

Compliment Card

Another processing activity that I like to use after a group has been together for awhile is the Compliment Card. Each student in the group receives an index card, writes her name and date on the red line, and passes her card to the right. On each card, each student writes a compliment

5/8/97   Group Goal: Not interrupt—wait until everyone's finished

5/9/97   Group Goal: Discuss passages in depth for better understanding

We met our goal because we did the following things:

1. We read aloud
2. We showed where the passage was in the book
3. We said why they were important so everyone had a full understanding

The two highlights of our discussion:

1. Scout's maturing
2. Scout's class's discussion of Hitler

5/12/97   Today will be our best discussion because we are going to . . .

1. Ask in-depth questions
2. Keep the discussion going
3. Stay focused

The two highlights of our discussion:

1. Boo Radley killed Bob Ewell
2. Will Boo Radley ever come out of his house again?

Our last discussion was memorable because . . .

1. We had a lot of fun
2. Pat told us his true feelings
3. Everyone shared their thoughts

Figure 4.3   *Student processing example*

to the card's owner stating a specific contribution that person made that helped with the group's learning or helped with everyone getting along and enjoying each other's company. The student signs her name to her compliment. After everyone is finished writing, the card is passed again. Be sure to tell students to practice Silent Patient Waiting and refrain from passing cards until all members have finished writing since it's rather disconcerting to be writing a compliment while another card is being shoved at you! The passing continues until the cards return to their original owners. After the writing, students read their compliments and thank each other. If students have taken the Home Court idea to heart, they'll refrain from writing inappropriate or hurtful comments on the cards because they know that this behavior will undermine rather than enhance their group. However, if you want to be on the safe side, be sure to emphasize that students must sign their compliments, but also tell them that you love reading the cards and will be collecting them from each group.

Art's personal goal: I would like to offer a better explanation of my book and ask follow-up questions. Also I would like to keep the group more motivated so they don't get bored so quickly.

Art—
I thought you did a very good book talk. I don't think anyone was bored while you were talking, and you made me want to read your book!

Molly

Art—
Well, I would have to say you did a good job of keeping us interested in your book. The passage just really made it.

Dana

Figure 4.4   *Processing that uses compliments*

Students can also use the Compliment Card procedure for their Processing Sheets. The example below shows how students can write compliments in response to a personal goal.

The Processing Letter

At the conclusion of a group's unit (whether it be Literature Circle, project, or paper), I like to have students look back on the experience and reflect upon their strengths and weaknesses. I have found that the best format for this is what I call the Processing Letter. While the ongoing group processing sheet focuses more on total group functioning, the letter focuses almost entirely on the individual. My instructions encourage students to take responsibility for their actions, explore their interpersonal strengths and weaknesses, and set goals for the future. The letter also gives me the *opportunity* to ask students about their lives *outside* of language arts. As I read the letters, I comment in the margins. Other than end-of-semester portfolio conferences, the high school schedule doesn't give me much opportunity for lengthy or reflective conversations with individual students. I like to think that the letter is a chance for that.

In his reflection, Rick noticed that he most enjoyed the group that seemed the friendliest. It sounded like the two girls were very skilled at encouraging participation. In comparison, the other groups got the academic work done but weren't as friendly, so the enjoyment/fun level was much lower. It's letters like these that remind me that group maintenance skills are just as critical as academic skills when trying to orchestrate groups that really function well.

Processing Tips

It's extremely important to set aside a few minutes for processing before the end of a group activity. Particularly when a skill is new, trying to incorporate it can be frustrating. Acknowledging even small successes via processing is extremely beneficial. Also, students will buy into using a skill faster when they become aware of the their own contribution towards practicing and refin-

---

1/17/96

Mrs. Steineke,

So the school's semester is at it's end. Well, here are a couple of comments about this year in class. I really didn't like my groups themselves to be honest. It is not how we worked together, but it's the people who were in them. I just don't get along with a lot of them. The groups I was in had a lot of strengths, though. We got along to do the job. We asked a lot of follow-ups, and we had good lead questions. The group I thought worked the best was with Lauren and the girl who sits next to her. They had interesting stories to tell. We could talk about anything. That's what I think made that group work. In the other groups we just didn't talk. We just did what we had to do; then we would sit and not talk. Most of the time this worked.

I, myself, asked more lead questions than ever. I did better I think at the beginning of second quarter than in the first quarter. My weakest skill was explaining my ideas to people. That's the one thing I have to improve besides my work habits.

Well, I looked in my binder, and I could see that I really liked the group work when I was with people I got along with. I think I've gotten a little better with the social skill of talking to people. Next time when you teach this class, you should find out from the students who they like to work with.

This year I read more books than ever. My favorite book was *Door to December* by Dean Koontz. I can read bigger and more mature books now.

In conclusion, you have helped me a lot with my work habits and my reading, and I thank you.

Rick

Figure 4.5 *Student example of Processing Letter*

ing a skill. Processing also offers closure and encourages ongoing reflection. Listed below are questions and statements that students might use to reflect on their skill usage and academic achievement. Be sure to have students reflect on both of these aspects at the conclusion of a group meeting.

Social Skills

1. List three actions that were helpful to the group.
2. What could we change or do better tomorrow?
3. How did using _____ (Friendliness and Support, Encouraging, Questioning, etc.) affect today's discussion?
4. We had fun when . . .

5. What is one thing that you could do better tomorrow? Set a personal goal and list three specific ways you will meet your goal.

6. What social skill could you use in another class? How?

7. List three statements your group used today that are good examples of _____ (Friendliness and Support, Encouraging, Questioning, etc.)

8. How did your group value differences today?

9. Make a plan for increasing your group's use of _____ (Friendliness and Support, Encouraging, Questioning, etc.) Come up with at least three ideas.

10. We noticed our group was using _____ (Friendliness and Support, Encouraging, Questioning, etc.) when . . .

11. I/we did _____ (skill) well today because . . .

12. I know I did my role well today because . . . (cite specific evidence)

13. List three new (skill) statements we could add to the T-Chart for _____ (Friendliness and Support, Encouraging, Questioning, etc.)

Academic Accomplishment

1. Who did you learn something from today? What was it?

2. What's one thing from the text that we understand better?

3. List three new ideas that came out of your discussion.

4. What were the most interesting topics your group discussed today?

5. Today I contributed to the discussion when I talked about . . .

6. The problem that was the hardest to solve was _____ because . . . Here's how we worked it out together.

7. One change I've/we've made in my/our thinking after today's discussion is . . .

8. After working together today on our _____ (academic task), we realized . . .

9. We discovered that . . .

10. We checked our facts and supported our opinions when we . . .

11. List two most useful suggestions the group came up with for each member's paper . . .

12. To summarize our group's discussion . . .

13. For our next meeting we are going to research _____ (topic choice) and bring the answers back to the following questions: _____

It Takes a While for a Skill to Stick

Depending on your students' previous experiences, their skill usage might be compared to an easy or difficult labor. Students who arrive with poor listening and friend-making skills are going to have a rougher time because these behaviors are really a stretch for them. Changing one's behavior is hard work. Consequently, the kids who need the skills the most are the ones who will fight you the most. I'll never forget the basic writing class I had several years ago: twenty-three boys and not a single girl, except for me. To top it off, the class met 7th hour! Boy, were these kids ready for action but not the kind involving reading and writing. There were many, many lessons on the skills of friendliness, listening, and staying in one's seat (not to mention about a dozen behavior contracts filed with the deans' office). We never moved beyond partners that semester. However, by second quarter, the skill lessons started to pay off. The kids knew what it took to stay focused on the academic work at hand, but they also found that functioning in a more productive social climate could still result in fun.

Another circumstance that sometimes conflicts with collaboration is the vision of school that students bring to the classroom. If you are surrounded by colleagues who are very teacher directed and rely on a combination of lecture, large group discussion, and individual seatwork, don't be surprised if this group stuff seems very foreign to the kids entering your classroom. As a matter of fact, some of the students might even question whether you're doing your job since the expectation is that students sit passively while teachers pour out knowledge. Stay firm in your commitment to teach students how to cooperate, and remember that the kids want that other class format because it's familiar and, in some respects, easier.

Even in the best of circumstances, getting kids to use new group skills consistently is a challenge that you must be prepared to meet. In their cooperative learning research, the Johnsons have established four distinct phases students go through as they learn a new skill (Johnson 5:16):

1. *Awkward:* Using the skill feels clumsy and uncomfortable. This is the stage in which you will encounter the most resistance from students. Kids will argue that this is stupid. Ignore them. They know it will be much easier for them if they can convince you to give up on teaching them any skills.

2. *Phony:* Students have given up resisting. They're using the skill, but it is still uncomfortable and unnatural. Often they'll complain that this isn't something they would normally do. Hey, neither is turning down that hot fudge banana split when you've finally decided to drop that extra twenty pounds!

3. *Mechanical:* Students are overusing the skill. They've finally grown comfortable with it, and now it is kind of fun to use the skill ALL OF THE TIME! If the skill you're working on is Friendly Encouragement, anything anybody says in the group will be rewarded with a friendly, supportive statement and a "high five." If the group counted forty skill usages last time, they'll be shooting for sixty today. It's no longer necessary for the teacher to remind students of the skill. Though this behavior seems silly and distracting, it is very encouraging because true skill integration cannot occur until overuse has occurred.

4. *Integrated:* The skill has truly become a part of the student's behavior. A student recognizes when the skill is needed and uses it appropriately and smoothly. While most students will reach the mechanical stage of any skill within a semester, not all students will use all skills in an integrated fashion. Different students will reach this stage at different rates depending on their prior collaborative experiences and the difficulty of the skill. For example, Giving Compliments is an easier skill to master than Asking Follow-up Questions.

How Do I Assess This?

The most important thing to remember when assessing students in groups is to try to keep the assessments individual versus giving everyone a group grade. One of the easiest ways I've found to assess students in regards to their skill usage is a checklist.

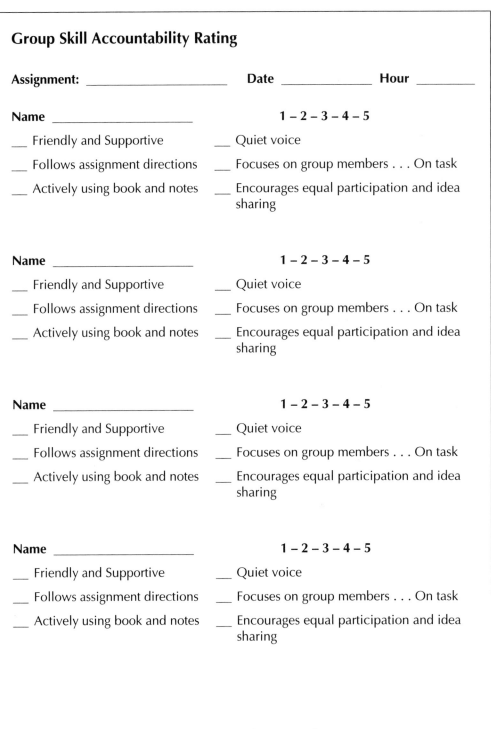

Group Skill Accountability Rating

Assignment: _____   **Date** _____   **Hour** _____

Name _____   **1 – 2 – 3 – 4 – 5**

___ Friendly and Supportive   ___ Quiet voice

___ Follows assignment directions   ___ Focuses on group members . . . On task

___ Actively using book and notes   ___ Encourages equal participation and idea sharing

Name _____   **1 – 2 – 3 – 4 – 5**

___ Friendly and Supportive   ___ Quiet voice

___ Follows assignment directions   ___ Focuses on group members . . . On task

___ Actively using book and notes   ___ Encourages equal participation and idea sharing

Name _____   **1 – 2 – 3 – 4 – 5**

___ Friendly and Supportive   ___ Quiet voice

___ Follows assignment directions   ___ Focuses on group members . . . On task

___ Actively using book and notes   ___ Encourages equal participation and idea sharing

Name _____   **1 – 2 – 3 – 4 – 5**

___ Friendly and Supportive   ___ Quiet voice

___ Follows assignment directions   ___ Focuses on group members . . . On task

___ Actively using book and notes   ___ Encourages equal participation and idea sharing

Figure 4.6   *Skill checklist*

Before a discussion, each group receives a form and each student writes in his name on one of the lines. As I monitor and observe the groups, this form makes it easy for me ascertain which students are using which skills. Rather than taking the sheet with me when I leave the group, I let the students stop discussion for a moment and look at it. My goal is for the checklist data to give them information for immediate skill improvement. Afterwards, students can use that data as they reflect on their Student Processing Sheet. I collect the processing sheets on a regular basis, stamp each processing entry, and then return them. This is an easy way to give points for productive group participation without taking up a lot of space in the grade book. The checklists main purpose is to spur immediate redirection and improvement, but they can be collected and photocopied if it's important for each member to have a copy. Students make use of the Student Processing Sheet and checklists as they reflect for their processing letter. Everything that is skills related is always stored in the Leadership section of the binder.

Parting Words

Teaching students the skills they need to successfully interact with one another is absolutely imperative. When groups aren't going well, don't blame the students and don't beat yourself up. Take a deep breath, step back from the chaos and disappointment, study the scene carefully, and ask the question: What skill do these kids need to learn so that they can get back on track? In the appendix, you'll find a skill lesson worksheet that I adapted from the Johnsons' 1991 edition of *Cooperation in the Classroom*. As you begin to teach the necessary group skills in an explicit fashion, this worksheet will help you to think through all of the steps. Expecting kids to work on an academic task together when they are socially unskilled is highly unproductive. Kids don't know which fork to use for the salad or when to say please and thank you unless someone teaches them. Neither manners nor group skills come naturally and automatically to most people; both need to be explicitly modeled and taught.

Remember that no skill is too small or too simple. Teaching students how to address each other by name is one of those simple skills that is frequently overlooked. I'll never forget the class who had trouble including all members in a discussion. About half the class seemed to belong to one loosely formed clique while the other half seemed to be outsiders looking in. Some of the outsiders had more problems to overcome than others. There was Mike, the boy who was sometimes a bully and an incredibly shy, reclusive girl, Joan, who came from an emotionally unsupportive home life. Since it was now November and the community was still somewhat shaky, I decided to teach and emphasize the skill of using names. From past experience, I found that using names could truly energize a group because it's hard to leave someone out of the discussion when the skill goal is to use everyone's name. Besides, kids always have fun using names; they often end up competing within a group to see who can use each other's names the most. When I introduced the skill, this is what the "Sounds Like" side of the T-Chart looked like.

- "Mary, how are you today?"
- "Chuck, read your passage to us."
- "Jim, what do you think of that?"
- "Susan, why don't you go next."
- "Anthony, we haven't heard from you. What do you think?"
- "Thank you for that great idea, John."

  • "Mike, how does your opinion compare with Ann's?" (That example was particularly
    popular because you could get two names in at once!)

First we practiced using names with a few Partner Grid discussions, but the moment of
truth came when the students counted off for their Book Talk groups. These groups were
purely random. As the students gathered with those of the same number, I gasped. That really
shy introverted girl, Joan, had ended up with a group of all guys. To top it off, Mike, the "on
again off again" bully, was in the same group. I crossed my fingers, held my breath, and
reminded the class that the skill of the day was "Using Names;" then I started monitoring the
groups. When I got around to Joan's group, I was pleasantly surprised, to say the least. Joan
was smiling and carrying the conversation. This was the happiest and most animated that I had
seen her all year. As Joan talked about her book, *Hang Time*, by Bob Greene, the three boys pep-
pered her with questions about Michael Jordan. "Joan, what do you think about Michael's
retirement from the Bulls?" "Joan, what other books have you read about Michael Jordan?"
"Joan, besides Michael, who's your next favorite Bulls player?" As it turned out, Joan was quite
an expert on Michael Jordan and the Chicago Bulls and absolutely thrilled to talk about the
team. Recognizing Joan's expertise, the boys listened carefully to what she had to say. Equally
fortuitous, it turned out that the other boys also had books about basketball, so the discussion
of Jordan threaded its way through all of the Book Talks. This student "dream team" was a
match made in heaven; no longer an outsider, Joan was definitely "one of the guys" that day!
It was lucky that Joan and the boys turned out to have so much in common, but I still honestly
believe that it was the skill of using names that unlocked the door to that wonderful discussion.
If the boys hadn't been compelled to see how many times they could use Joan's name, it would
have been very easy for them to have ignored her, particularly since Joan spent most of her time
in the shadows trying not to be noticed.

Resources

Avery, Christopher M. 2001. *Teamwork Is an Individual Skill: Getting Your Work Done When Shar-
    ing Responsibility*. San Francisco, CA: Berrett-Koehler Publishers, Inc.
    This book is written by a business consultant who coaches work teams. It affirms the need
    for learning interpersonal skills and shows how the skills learned in the classroom translate
    directly to being a successful employee.
Covey, Stephen R. 1989. *The Seven Habits of Highly Effective People*. New York: Simon & Schus-
    ter.
    Covey offers great examples of how getting along with others affects one's life positively. The
    chapters on "Empathic Communication" and "Creative Cooperation" are particularly useful.
Goleman, Daniel. 1995. *Emotional Intelligence*. New York: Bantam Books.
    When kids argue that learning should be an individual activity and that working in groups
    is a waste of time, shake this book at them and then read aloud some excerpts. Goleman's
    research shows evidence that people who have strong social skills show strong success in
    work situations while high-IQ workers with few social skills flounder.
Johnson, David W. and Roger T. Johnson. 1997. *Learning to Lead Teams: Developing Leadership
    Skills*. Edina, MN: Interaction Book Company.
    If you want more ideas on how to teach and reinforce specific social skills, this is the book
    for you! Many student activities for practicing social skills are included.

Packer, Alex J. 1997. *How Rude! The Teenagers Guide to Good Manners, Proper Behavior, and Not Grossing People Out*. Minneapolis, MN: Free Spirit Publishing, Inc.
As long as we're talking about social skills, might as well throw in manners as well. Along with a complete chapter on school civility, there is also a fine section titled "The Well-Mannered Conversation." Much of the book is in question-and-answer format, which makes it great for a quick read-aloud.

CHAPTER 5

Collaboration in Action
Student Led Book Talks

Creating Authentic Discussion about Books

In the beginning of the year, most of the talk about books is initiated by me, mainly because it's hard for most of the students to talk about books when they haven't read many. However, the sooner I can steer the kids to books that they finish and enjoy, the sooner they'll start talking about books on their own. It's part of human nature. Any time someone reads a book she loves, the almost automatic inclination is to encourage someone else to read it. Of course, as a teacher, I'm always trying to incorporate ways to facilitate this discussion both in and out of class. Thanks to the Reading Log Sheets, some students do have regular conversations with their parents about reading; some parents and children even recommend books to each other.

Another easy avenue of conversation is the Partner Grid. "Find out about your partner's book" is a topic that can be used repeatedly. After all, a reader doesn't have to be completely finished with a book in order to give his impressions. Informal chats about books also take place in the library when students ask me for help or when they start to value their peers' recommendations. However, I also use a more formal process for creating discussion about books, which I've come to refer to as Student Led Book Talks. These small group discussions take place about every four weeks and require all of the social skills mentioned in the previous chapter. Book Talks are a safe way to assess your class's skill level because the groups are only together for one period. If the kids don't get along, go off-task, or can't sustain the conversation, the disaster is minimal because the group disbands at the end of the period. The following day, you can start reviewing and practicing the skills that are still needed in order to ensure that all students in a class are capable of high-quality collaboration. Since one of my goals is to detect skill weaknesses, I like to form heterogeneous Book Talk groups by numbering off. These "let the chips fall where they may" random groupings are very useful because I get to see how my students interact with those they might not have worked with before. Having a handle on the "students who can work with anybody" and the "students who can sabotage any group" is useful information when trying to determine the best make up of more enduring alliances, such as Literature Circles and Peer Conferencing groups.

Trial and Error

I had a lot of really bad Book Talks before I ever had some good ones. I still remember an early Book Talk I had in a sophomore basic writing class. I don't think there was a single girl in the class. My first mistake was passing back their family newspapers, projects made from big sheets of newsprint. I had carefully rolled them up and rubber banded them ahead of time so that the kids could carry them easily, but I never considered how useful these rolled up newspapers would be for bopping each other over the head. Even though I admonished the boys to put those newspapers down, I caught quite a bit of sneaky style head bopping going on. Thank goodness the kids were content with that. I can just imagine all the lost eyes if the kids had realized they had the ammunition at hand for a rubber band war. I could have had an entire class of boys sporting a pirate look, each wearing a black eye patch.

Plunging into the Book Talks with the hope it would distract them from head bopping, each kid finished his talk in about thirty seconds, but they knew this wasn't good enough for Mrs. Steineke. They had to ask questions! The kids would pose the first lead question on the list that we had generated together. In response, the book talker would give a one-word answer that the rest of the group deemed fully sufficient, since they immediately plunged ahead to the next question. In under three minutes, a Book Talk that included thirty different questions was completed. On the one hand, I think the kids rushed through the talks because they had a lot more head bopping to do before the period was over. On the other hand, I think the kids rushed through the talks because they didn't know how not to.

Moral: Always break skills down and teach them before you need 'em, and never pass back projects with head bopping potential until after the Book Talks are finished.

Setting the Groundwork

From the beginning of the year, I start modeling the kinds of behavior that students need to exhibit when they talk about books to other people in the hopes of getting new readers. As I read books, I share what I think might hook other readers' interests. I read descriptive or exciting passages aloud and talk about why I like them. I describe plot points on our trips to the library or during informal passing period chats. I talk about incidents in books and how I've connected them with incidents in my own life. About a week before the first Book Talks, I model the steps, filling out the Book Talk Discussion Sheet on a transparency so that the students can see the notes I've written as I talk about the book. This sheet originated from the Jigsaw worksheet found in Harvey Daniels' *Literature Circles* (1994, 104) and then the instructions gradually evolved until students seemed to understand what I was asking for. I also show my classes several good examples from former students. The more I teach, the more I find that models are extremely important. When I give my Book Talk, I purposely avoid looking at my notes so that my speech is more conversational. I also emphasize the importance of having the book physically present so that the speaker can read aloud from it and the listeners can see the cover and look at the book if they desire.

Once my Book Talk is concluded, I open it up for questions. This gives me the chance to demonstrate how to pursue follow-up questions. Students take notes from the board, using a two-column format: Lead Questions in the left-hand column with the related Follow-up Questions listed across in the right-hand column. Sometimes after my Book Talk, the class sits dumbfounded; no one asks any questions. When this happens, I tell the kids to turn to their shoulder partners and brainstorm a question. Two heads are usually better than one, and the questions soon begin to flow. As I model, I always try to get students to ask at least three follow-up questions before moving on to a brand new lead question. When a question is asked in a yes/no format, I also ask the class how it could be rephrased. Here's an example of a class Lead/Follow-up Question discussion on the book *Midnight Express* by Billy Hayes.

Leads	Follow-ups
Why did Hayes think he wouldn't get caught smuggling drugs?	How come he didn't know about the laws in Turkey?
	What did his parents do when they found out?
	How did he feel about being in prison?

I continue the example discussion, trying out a few more lead questions, just until students get the idea. When students have difficulty coming up with lead questions, I have them work with their partners to generate a list of questions they'd ask someone if they were deciding whether or not to read a particular book. Here are the lead questions one class brainstormed.

Book Talk Lead Questions

1. Did you like the book? Why?
2. Would you recommend it to a friend?
3. Did you finish the book? How long did it take you to read?
4. Was it suspenseful? What parts were the best?
5. How did you rate your book on the scale? (1–10)
6. What is the book about?
7. What type of book is it?
8. What does the title have to do with the story?
9. Who was the main character? What was he/she like?
10. Did any of the characters remind you of yourself? How?
11. Were there any gory parts in the book? What happened?
12. Was the book interesting? Why?
13. Were any parts of the book funny? What parts?
14. Could you relate to the story? Why or why not?
15. When does the story take place? What was that time period like?
16. Where does the story take place? What is the setting like?
17. Was the book easy or hard to understand? Why?
18. Could this happen in real life? Why or why not?
19. Did the book have a good ending? Why or why not?
20. Why did you pick this book to read?
21. Have you read any other books by the same author? How did this one compare?
22. Is there a lot of action in the book? What kind of action?
23. Is there profanity in the book? What kind? Who says it?
24. Did you read the book outside of class?
25. What was the main problem in the book?
26. Did any of the characters change or learn anything?
27. What scene stands out the most? Why?
28. Would you read other books by this author? Why or why not?
29. Do you read many books? What kind are your favorite?
30. Do you think this book would make a good movie? Why?

I always get a laugh out of question #23: Is there profanity in the book? Though the question has multiple interpretations, that item came from a sophomore boy who viewed the author's use of profanity as a strong selling point! When that question was ventured, it gained enthusiastic confirmation from quite a few classmates who added that this kind of language lent reality to a book. Offering me the perfect teachable moment, I advised my students that though profanity has many fans, this fandom is not universal. When choosing a passage to read aloud, it needs to appeal to a wide audience; therefore, choose a part of the book that isn't loaded with swears. Instead, use those swears as a selling point with the phrase, "If want to hear that part, you'll just have to read it for yourself." Ideally, lead questions arise from what the reader has mentioned in his Book Talk, but a list such as this can often be helpful when students are first learning the procedure.

After my Book Talk example, I pass out the Book Talk Discussion Sheets and ask if the students have any questions about the assignment. Two questions frequently arise. "What if I've finished more than one book?" I always tell students to do their Book Talk on the book they liked the most, but also the one that they still have in their possession. "What if I'm not finished with the book?" As long as students have been reading regularly, I don't mind if they do a Book Talk on a book they haven't finished. If students were limited to only the books they knew they'd finish in time for the Book Talks, it would discourage them from reading longer or more challenging books. I just tell those students to base their talks on what they know so far about the book; after all, most readers have opinions within the first ten pages.

Book Talk Discussion Sheets

I usually make the Book Talk Discussion Sheets due the day before the actual Book Talk groups convene because it heads off some potential problems. First, the students who have forgotten to do it have a grace day before the actual Book Talks, but, yes, there is a late penalty. Second, and this is really the most important reason, having the sheets due the day before the talk allows the students to complete a self-evaluation of the sheet before I grade it. For assessment, I tell students that each section is worth a maximum of five points. Besides handing out a rubric, I also show them various student models that reflect different point values. Students score themselves against the rubric for each category and write those scores on a sticky note that they affix to their sheet. It's super important to have students write their names on the stickies because invariably one or two will come loose. Whenever possible, I always try to have students self-evaluate their work before I grade it. As long as you have some good models for comparison and some clear criteria, it's pretty hard for students to be dishonest. Finally, I can grade these sheets quickly enough so that returning them the next day is not a hardship. This way I have one less piece of paper to collect at the end of the period on Book Talk day.

Book Talk Day

I'll warn you now that your first set of Book Talks might be a little shaky; it really takes students awhile to get the gist of the entire procedure. Also, if you notice major group dysfunction, it probably means that the students haven't reached the group skills level necessary to conduct themselves at such a high task level. I'll never forget the nerve-wracking round of Book Talks I had with a freshman class when I miscalculated their skill and maturity levels. Instead of keeping the groups to a nice manageable three, I had the kids form groups of five, thinking that they'd be exposed to more books. Instead of joyously sharing their favorite titles, they loudly argued, ignored members, and hardly talked about books at all. By the time the Book Talks were over, the entire class was scowling and many complained of headaches, myself included. The next day we analyzed the

Book Title: _____   Name _____

Author: _____   Date & Hour _____

Book Talk Discussion Sheet

Do a good job. This counts as a test!

Plot Points

Main characters? Conflict? Rising action? Really good parts? Give some vivid details that will convince others to read your book.

    1.

    2.

    3.

    4.

Passage/Good Part

With a sticky note. mark a passage that will get others interested in your book. Be ready to read it aloud and explain why you chose this part. **Record the page number, location, and detailed notes on your opinion/thoughts/personal reaction.**

Connections

What does this book remind you of: another story, novel, personal experience, current event, television program, movie, play? **Jot down one specific connection with detailed notes that explain it.**

Illustration

On the other side of the sheet, **sketch a full page, detailed picture** related to your book. You can draw something that's specifically talked about in the reading, something from your own experience or feelings, or something the reading made you think about. **Color is always a plus!**

Figure 5.1   *Book Talk Discussion Sheet*

OCT 3 0 2001

Book Title: Blood and Chocolate

Name Gina

Author: Annette Curtis Klause

Date & Hour 10-30-01 5th

.35/30

Book Talk Discussion Sheet
Do a good job. This counts as a test!

Plot Points

Characters? Conflict? Rising action? Important details? Really good parts? What would readers need to know so that they want to read your book?

Characters (werewolf)   (human boyfriend)   (teenage werewolf clan)
1. Virian Gandillon, Aiden, Esmé (Virian's Mother), The Five-Willem, Finn, Rafe, Gregory, Ulf, Gabriel (leader, Vivians supposed Mate) Astrid (Mom), Kelly (Aidens friend), Quince (Aidens friend)

Conflict
2. Vivian and herself, She is confused of what she is human or werewolf, she struggles with her pack because she has finally been accepted as part of the human group but then struggles with the humans, for she has revealed herself to Aiden.

Rising Action
3. The Ordeal with the pack, Astrid jumps Vivians Mother and tries to kill her, Vivian attacks Astrid, and wins which makes her the leaders mate, she breaks up with her human boyfriend and struggles between making amends with pack and human

Details
4. Vivian changes in front of Aiden, Aiden throws things at her, he is scared, She jumps ou his window for fear of hurting him, couldn't change back into human until next morning, woke up with blood around her mouth and under her nails, she

Passage/Good Part *fears for him.*

Mark one good passage with post-it notes. Find a part that will get others interested in your book and give an idea of the author's style of writing. Be sure to be ready to read it aloud and **explain your opinion/thoughts in detail. Record the page number, location, and detailed notes on why you chose this part.** Pg. 148 end paragraph to the top of page 150 second paragr As I read this passage I thought of how neat it would be to be a werewolf or know someone who is. I thought of how much courage Vivian had to attack Astrid. She is so young and she has so much power and she never used it to kill humans, she used it to help protect her mother and take out anger on one who put All the pain in her life. I picture her fury and the violence one had held inside for so long, a massive picture of fur and blood flying everywhere.

Connections

What does this book remind you of: another story, novel, personal experience, current event, television program, movie, play? **Jot down one specific connection with detailed notes that explain it.** I connected with vivian and her struggles because whenever she had rage, she could change into a werewolf and run free, I would love to be able to change and run free in the wild whenever I had pain. Humans are somewhat forced to keep thier hate, anger, sadness, and fear inside of them, the werewolves were free to release thier burdens.

Revised 10/5/2000

I thought her boyfriend Aiden was A total jerk—
WHAT A POSER!   THAT ILLUS IS Gorgeous!

Figure 5.2   *Student example of Book Talk Sheet—front*

Illustration

On this side of the sheet, **sketch a full page, detailed picture** related to your book. You can draw something that's specifically talked about in the reading, something from your own experience or feelings, or something the reading made you think about. **Color is always a plus!**

Revised 10/5/2000

Figure 5.3   *Student example of Book Talk Sheet—back*

Book Talk Discussion Sheet Rubric

Plot Points

3	4	5
• Neat, easy to read • Points are delineated with some detail	• Character, conflict, rising action, good parts are addressed and clearly labeled	• Necessary points are accompanied by specific details

Passage

3	4	5
• Neat, easy to read • Page and location listed • Example is found beyond first 30 pages • Notes	• Notes focus on opinion/reader reaction instead of summary	• What I thought about/pictured during this part. Notes explain reader reaction with details versus general statements.

Connection

3	4	5
• Neat, easy to read • Chooses specific part of book to connect with rather than entire book • Comparison between text and connection	• Some specific details accompany comparison	• Lots of specific details accompany comparison

Illustration

3	4	5
• Neat • Fills the page • Some detail	• Foreground and background details	• Very detailed • Effort and thought apparent • Color used

© 2002 by Nancy Steineke from *Reading and Writing Together*. Portsmouth, NH: Heinemann.

Figure 5.4 *Book Talk Sheet rubric*

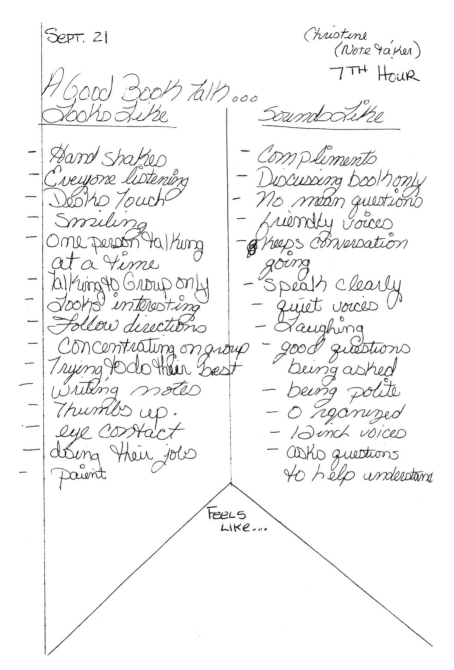

Sept. 21   Christine
                                       (Note taker)
                                      7TH Hour

A Good Book Talk...
Looks Like   Sounds Like

- Hand shakes   - Compliments
- Everyone listening   - Discussing book only
- Desks Touch   - No mean questions
- Smiling   - friendly voices
- One person talking   - keeps conversation
  at a time   going
- Talking to Group only   - Speak clearly
- Looks interesting   - quiet voices
- Follow directions   - Laughing
- Concentrating on group   - good questions
- Trying to do their best   being asked
- Writing notes   - being polite
- Thumbs up.   - O rganized
- eye contact   - 12 inch voices
- doing their jobs   - asks questions
  Patient   to help understand

                    Feels
                    Like....

Figure 5.5   *Book Talk disaster analysis*

experience. I asked them to imagine what good Book Talk groups would look like and sound like. Though it didn't get filled in, the class also mentioned that for "Feels Like," they would have left happy, interested in some books, and headache free. In the end, the class decided that they needed more work on how to be nice to each other and how to ask more follow-up questions. For my part, I decided to keep the groups to three instead of five for the next round of Book Talks.

I can't emphasize strongly enough that when students start working in groups, the results at first are sometimes unpredictable because the kids have lots more practice working alone than working in learning teams. When the situation turns sour, take it as an opportunity for analysis with the class. Believe me, the majority of students would much prefer productive group experiences than ones that make their heads hurt. Being able to reflect in this way is what helps teams grow stronger.

Book Talk day steps. Even though I clearly model how to give a Book Talk and how to ask Book Talk Follow-up Questions beforehand, that modeling doesn't really demonstrate the complexity of organizing and orchestrating the class groups, so here are the complete steps for Book Talk day.

1. At the beginning of class, students need to get out the following supplies: a sheet of loose-leaf paper, pen, and Book Talk book. While they're getting organized, I pass back the Book Talk Discussion Sheets from the day before.

2. Next, the students fill out the Book Review sheet. This short activity is actually a good writing assignment, since it requires a succinct summary followed by a well-supported reaction. Once again, showing students some good examples vastly improves the quality of their reviews.

3. After students have finished the reviews, they need to set up their Lead/Follow-up Question sheet. Be sure to have students put their names on and write the title of their Book Talk book top and center. Fold the paper in half lengthwise, labeling the left column Leads and the right column Follow-ups.

4. Before we count off, I review the roles. Though I don't normally use roles for Literature Circles, I always use roles for Book Talks and I encourage students to pick a different role each time since the different roles focus on different skills. Here are the roles.

Host
- Welcomes everyone and introduces members to each other
- Smiles, uses friendly body language
- Makes a point of using group members' names
- Keeps everyone included in the discussion and encourages good eye contact
- Makes sure the desks and chairs are arranged correctly and also put away after the Book Talk is concluded
- Asks lead and follow-up questions

Discussion Director
- Makes sure book talker discusses all parts of Book Talk Sheet
- Collects group papers that need to be turned in
- Asks lead and follow-up questions

Time Keeper
- Figures out how much time can be spent on each book

Name _____

                                    Date _____   Hour _____

Book Review

Category _____

Copyright _____   **Number of pages** _____

Book Title _____

Author _____

Rating (1 Lame — 10 Great) _____

Summary: In **one** sentence, tell what the book was about _____

_____

_____

Reaction: Tell why you would or would not recommend this book to another student. Explain the reasons behind your rating. Be specific and give some details!

_____

_____

_____

_____

_____

Figure 5.6   *Book Talk review sheet*

B)

Book Review

Name _Valerie_

Date _4/1/01_

Category _Fantasy_ Copyright _1995_ Number of pages _399_

Book Title ~~XXXXXXX~~ _The Golden Compass_

Author _Philip Pullman_

Rating (1 Lame → → → 10 Great) _10_

Summary: In **one** sentence, tell what the book was about _A little girl named Lyra has to grow up extremely fast and save the lives of many other children._

Reaction: Tell why you would or would not recommend this book to another student. Explain the reasons behind your rating. Be specific and give some details!

I liked how there were many characters in the book and none of them were what they appeared to be. This book is full of secrets, good and bad from the time Lord Asriel is almost poisoned to the time Lyra finds out who her real parents are.

Figure 5.7 *Book Talk review sheet student example*

- Helps the group stick to the schedule by saying, "We have two more minutes on this book; someone ask another question." OR "Time is up; let's move to the next book"
- Asks lead and follow-up questions

Questioner
- Works closely with time keeper when a book discussion needs to be continued
- Encourages members to ask another question
- Has a question ready if there is a lull in the discussion
- Asks lead and follow-up questions

5. Now I have students count off so that groups of four are formed. If the social skills are still tentative, form groups of three instead. After the groups have organized, each person signs his first and last name by his role on the Role Accountability Rating sheet. Once this is done, all sheets are turned in to the host. One other task must be completed before the talks begin. All members of a group pass their Lead/Follow-up Question sheet to the person to their right. When it is their turn to talk about their book, the person to their right records the leads and follow-ups the group asks about the book. Be sure to answer any questions after this step is completed, since this part is always very confusing for the first couple of Book Talks.

Book Talk Role Accountability Rating

Date _____ Hour _____

Host: _____   **1 – 2 – 3 – 4 – 5**

___ Correct set up and take down   disappointing   great job!

___ Actively uses support and liking skills

___ Monitors and enforces 12-inch voices

___ Asks follow-up questions

Discussion Director: _____   **1 – 2 – 3 – 4 – 5**

___ Makes sure Talker explains points, passage,   disappointing   great job!
connection, and illustration before group
starts asking questions

___ Asks follow-up questions

Questioner: _____   **1 – 2 – 3 – 4 – 5**

___ Asks lead questions that continue discussion   disappointing   great job!
if there is a lull

___ Asks **lots** of specific follow-up questions

Time Keeper: _____   **1 – 2 – 3 – 4 – 5**

___ Sets clear time limits   disappointing   great job!

___ Cues group to continue or conclude

___ Asks follow-up questions

Figure 5.8 *Book Talk Role Accountability Rating*

6. The Book Talks are finally ready to begin! I generally give groups about twenty minutes for Book Talks; this breaks down to about five minutes per talk. As students become more skilled, you might eventually want to lengthen the time by a few minutes. I usually work by the rule that it's better to give less time than more time. I let the students decide who will start, but if arguing ensues, I settle it by announcing that the member with the darkest colored shirt goes first. If a group still can't figure it out, I judge the shirt colors. By the next Book Talk there will be a volunteer!

7. As students engage in their Book Talks, I observe each group for a few minutes, checking off skills that I see being used and taking quick anecdotal notes on the accountability sheet. I try to write down specific words said or actions taken that demonstrate a skill. As I observe, I'm not concerned about evaluating the actual Book Talk each student gives. I'm concerned about observing how different members are contributing to the success of the group and its academic task. I also mark on the Book Review sheets whether or not the student has his book. B means "book"; NB means "no book." While I leave the Accountability Sheet with the group, I take the Review Sheets with me, attaching them to my clipboard, because it's one less item to collect later. A final tip: as you observe, make sure that your back is never turned away from the other groups. From a distance, you can still observe quite a bit in regards to group functioning. Besides, facing out makes it easier to catch the kid who's throwing the spitballs at another group.

8. In addition to my own observations, the students are taking turns keeping track of the leads and follow-ups asked for each specific book.

9. When the time is up, students retrieve their Lead/Follow-up Question sheet and turn to the reverse side. First, I always have them write down what role they had this time so that they'll remember to choose a different one next time. Next, I give students a few processing questions to discuss so that they can determine what their strengths and weaknesses were as a group. Generally, I'll give three questions: one that focuses on group successes and one that focuses on individual functioning. The third part of any processing is always setting an improvement goal for next time. Though students will be working in a different group for the next Book Talk, they can still set skill goals to carry with them. Here are some examples of questions that focus on group functioning as a whole and each individual's contributions to the group.

Group Processing Questions

1. List three things that your group did well (things that helped you get along, work together successfully, and get the task done with a high degree of quality).

2. What's one thing your group could do even better next time?

3. How well did your group do on asking genuine follow-up questions? Put stars by your best Lead and Follow-up Questions. (This forces the kids to look back on the front side and discuss their questioning.)

4. Write down your role. If you had the same role again, what's one thing you could do better next time? List the goal and number 1, 2, 3 below it. As a group, now brainstorm three specific actions/phrases each member could use to meet his goal. List them on your sheet.

5. What time did you actually begin talking about the first book? How many minutes did you talk about each book? Did any of the books get left out? How could your group use the time more efficiently next time?

Book Title: *This Place Has No Atmosphere*

What was the best part of the book?

___ Was the ending good?

___ How old was the character?

___ Why did they have to move to the moon?

___ How did the daughter adjust to living on the moon?

Book Title: *Please Don't Die*

What was the problem in the story?

___ Did they find a cure for her disease?

___ How did the mother react to her problem?

___ Was it a sad ending?

___ What does the daughter do after her mom dies?

___ Would you recommend this book?

Book Title: *Jack*

What is this book about?

___ How did he find out that his father was gay?

___ Does the boy meet his dad's boyfriend?

___ How does the kid react to this?

___ Did everyone else find out about his dad?

___ Does he get into a lot of fights?

___ What was his mom like?

Book Title: *All Around Town*

How does the title connect with the book?

___ What is the town?

___ How did she find the identity of her molester?

___ What effects did it have on her?

___ Were you really into the book?

Figure 5.9   *Student-generated questions asked during Book Talks*

2/1/01   Role: Questioner

Plan: Ways we can ask more/better follow-up questions

1. Listen to the person presenting the book
2. Figure out why it would be an interesting book to read

Plan: Three specific ways to get people interested in my book

1. Try to explain with more detail
2. Tell members that I recommend it and it's really good
3. Use more emotions when describing the book

Two good follow-up questions we asked today

1. Ashley asked Andy about the description of the devil
2. Katherine asked Ashley what the connection was with the ring

3/13/01   Plan: How to make the passage reading more interesting

1. Read with lots of enthusiasm and emotion
2. Introduce it: tell what, when, and where it's about
3. Read loudly and clearly so that people understand you

Role: Timekeeper
Plan: Making the book talk better for next time

1. Try to make it humorous at times
2. Monitor 12-inch voices
3. Speak loudly and clearly

4/11/01   Something I learned in my Literature Circle that I could use to improve this Book Talk:

- Using names and encouraging words a lot to get the speaker talking

We had a good time today because:

1. Everyone participated
2. We listened to everyone's opinions.

Figure 5.10   *Christine's Book Talk processing for semester 2*

Individual Processing Questions

1. List your role. Now study the job description and list specific things that you said or did that showed you were doing your role. Which parts of your role did you do best? Which parts do you need to do better next time?

2. How did you do selling your book? Describe how you convinced others to read it. What did you tell them about? How did you make the book look attractive?

3. How did you help the other members of your group do their best and enjoy working with the group? What did you do to help them feel welcome and comfortable?

4. How well did you participate in and contribute to the discussion? Which Lead and Follow-up Questions did you ask? Did you take other members' questions seriously and try to give them good answers that would help them decide whether or not to read your book?

5. What problems did your group encounter that prevented all of you from doing your best? What strategies and skills did you personally employ to try to get the group back on track? If you run into this problem again, what else could you try next time?

10. If time permits, it's nice to have some large group closure. First, having each group share a key observation from their processing can be very useful. It gives you the chance to ask some follow-up questions and elicit more specific documentation of successful skill behaviors, while giving the rest of the class ideas about how to positively examine functioning. Another nice closure activity is to have someone from each group share something about the Book Talks that took place in the group. The person with the best passage might read it aloud to the class or each group might vote on whose book sounded the best and then have that talker give a short synopsis to everyone. Before the groups break up, have the Discussion Director turn in the Role Accountability sheet and the Lead/Follow-up notes for the group. A reminder: remember that constant refinement of the skill Quiet Patient Listening is the only way these large group discussions will be able to take place.

11. On the following day, allow some time for students to meet with their different partners from their Appointment Clocks. Composition book in hand, the goal is to share recommendations and come up with a list of at least five books that they would be interested in reading.

Refining Student Led Book Talks

The best way for students to get better on the next Book Talk is for them to look back on their previous Processing and Book Talk Discussion Sheets. Early on I mentioned the use of binders. All processing goes into the Leadership section and all Book Talk Discussion Sheets go into the Reading section. Having old work at hand really facilitates reflection and goal setting for the future. However, sometimes Book Talks do go terribly wrong. As I mentioned early on, the first ones are usually the worst ones!

Tips for Starting Out

- Assess your students' social skill level *before* deciding on the group size. If your students are immature, have difficulty getting along, are loud, or fall off-task easily, stick with pairs or at most triads until the Book Talk routine is familiar.

- Even with pairs, students can still hear about two or three other books. After five minutes, every other row moves up one desk so that partners are changed.
- Keep the time short. Until your students' discussion skills become more sophisticated, three minutes per book is plenty of time.
- Be sure groups can successfully work in triads before moving to groups of four.
- Avoid groups larger than five. Going beyond five exponentially increases the likelihood of off-task behavior.
- Give clear, concise, and uncomplicated instructions. Before your first Book Talks, do a roleplay with student volunteers, modeling what a good Book Talk looks like.
- Discuss and give examples of encouraging, questioning, and support and friendliness before the first Book Talk. During the Book Talks, monitor and reinforce those behaviors.
- Determine ahead of time how students will be held accountable for their roles.
- Remember to process immediately afterwards or the following day if you run out of time. Improvement is much more likely to occur if the Book Talk is examined for what was done well and what changes need to take place.
- Expect your first couple of Book Talks to be less than perfect. It takes everyone a while to understand the roles and become skilled in discussion.

Other Book Talk Tips

As students become more adept at talking about books, do not let them look at their Discussion Sheets; tell them to put them face down so that only the illustration shows. Since these sheets can be a crutch with students reading off of them verbatim, the quicker they can work from memory, the better the Book Talk since they will be speaking in a much more spontaneous, conversational tone. However, even when students are not directly using the notes for the Book Talk, I still require that they fill out the sheets because it demonstrates going back to the text for support and it forces them to organize their thoughts.

Once students get into the habit of automatically asking follow-up questions, try doing a round of Book Talks *without* recording the Leads and Follow-ups. Though a useful tool for emphasizing the skill, this note-taking format is artificial and slows down the natural conversation process. I've also noticed that students can get so focused on asking the questions, particularly if some bonus points are involved, that they forget to listen to the Book Talker's answers! Remind students that the purpose of Follow-ups is to demonstrate good listening and to discuss a topic in greater depth. Once the Follow-up questioning becomes an automatically used skill, the Lead/Follow-up sheets can be abandoned.

How Do I Assess This?

My main individual assessment for the Book Talk is the Discussion Sheet. As I mentioned earlier in the chapter, students first evaluate the sheet against the rubric before turning it in to me. The Book Talk Discussion Sheet counts as a twenty-point test. Returned Book Talk Sheets are immediately stored in the Reading Archive section of the binder, since these grades have already been recorded.

In addition, students also get a stamp for each of the following items:

1. Having the Book Talk book
2. Filling out the Review Sheet with thought and detail

3. Participating positively in the Book Talk group

4. Recording the group's processing conclusions

You'll notice that the maximum for participation in the Book Talk is four points. Stamping each individual piece of paper would be a problem since the Accountability Rating Sheet is shared by three or four people and the Review Sheet isn't returned but placed on file in the classroom for others to read. After collecting the Rating Sheets, Review Sheets, and Processing Sheets, I run through a quick sorting/grading process. I start by setting up a temporary grade column in my gradebook. Next, I go through the Role Accountability Sheets and record a zero for anyone who was a real nuisance in their group; everyone else gets a one. Be sure to use a pencil when recording these scores because you'll be erasing the column later! After that, I look at the Review Sheets and record one or two points in the gradebook, depending on the quality of the review and whether the student had the right book with him. Finally, I look at the Processing Sheets while referring back to the gradebook scores. So far, each student has up to three points recorded; a good processing entry will make the fourth point. By the processing entry I mark a *X2, X3, X4*. This is my abbreviation for "multiply this stamp by this number of points." This part of the grading will move even faster if you can have a student alphabetize the Processing Sheets before you look at them; then you can just move straight down the gradebook column. When the Processing Sheets are returned, each has the current stamp and the number of points the student has earned. The Processing Sheet is placed in the front of the Leadership section of the binder and the points are counted during the next binder check. I recommend hanging on to that temporary gradebook column until after the next binder check. That way you have a back up if a student loses his Processing Sheet or has questions about the Book Talk score. Also, it's a reminder of who owes you make-up work.

Of course, it's a guarantee that someone will be absent on a Book Talk day. When that occurs, the student still needs to turn in the Book Talk Discussion Sheet, but to get the Book Talk participation points I require a poster rather than an oral report. I view the poster as an advertisement for the book. At the beginning of the year, I hang up some samples I've saved. They serve as models for future absentee students but also give me some immediate decoration for an otherwise bare September classroom.

Parting Words

With the help of processing and reflection, most students independently work to refine their own performance in future Book Talks, particularly when they notice that no one else has read the book they previously presented. Getting someone to read a book you enjoyed is very satisfying, particularly when the other person finishes and you have the chance to compare ideas. When no one picks their book to read, students often begin thinking on their own about how they can do a better job selling their next favorite. Also, I never worry about students hearing about books they aren't interested in during a Book Talk due to the random grouping. Usually there is something for everyone, but even if there isn't, I like the fact that students are finding out what other classmates are reading. Sometimes a Book Talk opens up a new genre for a student. The better the class knows each other as readers, the more each can serve as recommendation sources for the others. Students get credit for their expertise in certain genres and the word spreads.

I always enjoy listening in on the Book Talk conversations. I remember getting to one group fairly late in the hour, and I immediately noticed that no one was talking about the books they had in front of them. Always the taskmaster, my first question was "Why aren't you talking about

---

Book Talk Make-up Assignment

If you are absent on the day of a Book Talk, you need to make a <u>BIG</u> poster that advertises your book.

Size:	22″ × 28″ (standard size poster board)
Information:	Title
	Author
	Short Summary
	Big, attention-getting graphic (you may draw, cut out magazine pictures, or use computer clip art)

Grading will be based on your poster's ability to sell your book!

Figure 5.11 *Book Talk discussion make-up poster directions*

the books that you brought?" I discovered that the kids had finished their official Book Talks a few minutes before my arrival and the conversation had turned to other books the members had read. As it turned out, they all had quite a reading history connected with the books by horror/suspense author Dean Koontz. The kids were animatedly trading title highlights and comparing reactions to scenes from the different novels. When I got there, they were comparing Koontz's use of cockroaches as a horror/gross-out device that, as it turned out, he employed in several of his books. No wonder the conversation sounded strange when I arrived! Had the period not been drawing to a close, I'm certain that group could have continued to talk about their favorite books for quite some time. Once students see themselves as readers and know how to talk about what they've read, sharing favorite books starts to occur spontaneously. After all, readers are always looking for good books to add to their personal "must read" lists.

CHAPTER 6

The Elements of Group Design

When the Book Talks start to take off and flourish, it's not by accident. This collaborative experience is carefully designed and follows the cooperative learning model developed by David and Roger Johnson. There's no magic or special knack to creating a classroom that fosters successful group experiences. Groups that work are the result of the decisions a teacher makes when planning for collaboration. Any time you have students work together, you need to design the assignment so that all five of the necessary elements that follow are represented. Below I've briefly defined these elements and also pointed out how each was represented in the Book Talk discussion described in the previous chapter.

1. **Positive Interdependence** occurs when task completion requires the input and skills of all group members. Positive interdependence can be broken down into several categories: academic, role, skill, and environmental. Academic interdependence occurs because more than one person is needed in a Book Talk in order for a discussion to take place. Next is role interdependence. In the case of the Book Talk, each member contributes to the group by completing specific tasks connected with a role. Skill interdependence occurs because students need each other in order to practice asking Follow-up Questions. Finally, groups experience environmental interdependence since each group must be far enough apart so that I can walk around them and so that they are not distracted by another group.

2. **Individual Accountability** is the part of the task that each member must complete on his own. In the case of Book Talks, each member has to complete the Discussion Sheet on her own in order to participate in the discussion. During discussion, teacher monitoring via the Accountability Checklist further emphasizes the responsibility each student must accept with her role.

3. **Group Skills** refer to the specific collaborative skills needed so that the group can successfully complete the task. Book Talks require that students listen carefully, ask questions, and treat each other with friendliness and support.

4. **Group Processing** occurs when members assess the strengths and weaknesses of their group's functioning. After a Book Talk, students examine their group's successes but also consider how to improve their individual performances to make the next Book Talks more interesting.

5. **Face-to-Face Interaction** controls the size of the group, the composition of the group, and the arrangement of the groups within the room so that meaningful learning can

occur. One of the jobs of the Host is to make sure that the group is formed correctly. The teacher decides how large the groups will be based on her students' skill level.

Yeah, there is a lot to think about, but don't be overwhelmed. What follows is a thorough explanation of these components. However, before you continue reading, take a moment and make a two-column list. In column A, list a couple of different collaborative assignments that floundered. In column B, list the problems the groups ran into. Then, as you read the explanation of each of the five components, go back to your list and tweak the assignment. Based on the design elements of successful collaboration, what will you change, remove, or add for next time? Going back to these elements and comparing your lesson design against them is the best way to solve the problems that arise when students are expected to work together.

Positive Interdependence

Whenever you put students together in groups, you always need to ask yourself, "Why am I having students complete this task together rather than individually? How can the quality of the work be enhanced by the collaborative experience?" Now, if you honestly can't come up with any compelling reasons why an academic task needs a group to complete it, maybe that assignment should be an individual one. Kids don't need to do everything in groups, but they do need to work together if it enhances the learning. The tie that binds a group together is called positive interdependence; positive interdependence is the perception that each member's contributions directly benefit the other members.

A good way to illustrate the reality of interdependence is to use your students' actual career aspirations. First, have them list two or three specific jobs that they might like to pursue after high school or college graduation. Next, have them make a list of those with whom they might have to work. For example, a sales representative has his/her customers, an office assistant, a boss, a supplier, and a shipping clerk. Finally, have the students brainstorm how the different jobs are interdependent. In the case of sales, the representative could be the best salesperson in the world, but if the shipping clerk cannot fill the orders accurately there will be few repeat customers. People in the real world of work definitely depend on each other; the success or failure of one person ripples out to others. Frequent opportunities to work in cooperative groups give students skills that will come in very handy later on.

Now, how does this all translate into your classroom activities? When planning any lesson, try to aim for at least three different kinds of positive interdependence. If students still don't see the point in working together, increase the different types of positive interdependence to five and re-examine the other components to see what else is weak or missing. Thanks to the work of the Johnsons, the various types of positive interdependence are clearly defined.

Academic Goal Interdependence

This is the reason why the learning activity is shared rather than assigned individually. Whatever the academic goal, it has to be something that can't be accomplished individually. Here are a few examples of when groups are needed.

- The material is difficult and needs discussion and clarification.
- A problem needs to be solved and discussion can offer a variety of solutions.
- A complex project requires several different talents.
- A piece of literature requires the insight and perspective of a group discussion.

Have you ever seen group members say something like, "You take the even numbers and I'll do the odds"? This is a sign that the academic task has not been restructured in a way that requires group interaction. Almost any individual assignment can be redesigned so that it is cooperative, but it doesn't automatically happen just by putting kids together. When kids work together, be sure there is a clear need for collaboration; weak lesson design will devalue the group work experience. The strength of any group is its ability to think in a diverse manner and come up with ideas that no single person would think of on his own. Peer conferencing and Literature Circles are great ways to use groups. On the other hand, unless you really structure a grammar exercise so that it forces members to talk about it, the activity will break down quickly into individuals trading answers rather than working cooperatively.

One of the reasons why the better students traditionally hate working in groups is that they've always ended up shouldering the bulk of the work because they were the only ones invested, usually in the grade but not in the other group members. These students are accustomed to doing all of the work because they don't trust their group mates to get the job done or to do it right. Thinking that groups will work just because academic goal interdependence is present is a faulty assumption. While a group grade will not motivate slackers, a group grade is guaranteed to drive your high-achieving students into grade anxiety overdrive since they are the ones worrying about their class rank. No wonder they want to do everyone's job! For now, just remember to *never* assess the academic goal based on a group grade, and to always reinforce a group task with at least three different types of positive interdependence. And yes, before this chapter is over, I promise to give you some useful group grade alternatives.

Skill Goal Interdependence

While students are working together on an academic task, they should also be practicing the necessary social skills. Many times it is the skill usage that turns the academic goal into something that needs to be a cooperative venture. For example, let's say the academic goal is to complete a grammar exercise on punctuation. (Yes, yes, yes, we all know that grammar should be taught in context, but sometimes those exercises make a nice bridge to that context.) This is just the kind of exercise where the kids will divide and conquer. However, if the assignment instructions change slightly, this is far less likely to happen.

1. With your partner, decide who will do the evens and who will do the odds. You'll be taking turns.
2. When it's your turn, read the sentence aloud first. Then add the punctuation while explaining out loud to your partner the reasons for your decisions.
3. After you're done, your partner should challenge you on one piece of punctuation and then together you need to determine if any correction is needed.
4. While working with your partner, you need to use the skills of explaining, thinking out loud, praising, and questioning.

In the case of a literature discussion group, students might be practicing the skills of encouraging, praising, questioning, using the text for support, etc. The point here is that part of the expectation in the assignment is that the skills are used to complete the academic task. In order to reinforce the importance of skill usage, I often use an Accountability Checklist so that the students or I can quickly verify which skills are being used. Comparing checklists over the course of several meetings enables a group to monitor its growth in skillfulness.

Role Interdependence

Those of you who have dabbled in cooperative groups or training before are probably overly familiar with roles. Who hasn't had a reporter, recorder, and a discussion director at one time or another? Here's the news: roles are way overused. Roles need to have purpose, and whenever you choose to introduce roles into a group task, you've first got to think about whether these roles will really enhance group productivity. Often they are just something superficially tacked on because the teacher thought each person in the group needed to have a role. Don't mistake me. Roles do have their place; just make sure they're really needed before you assign them. My favorite roles are usually connected to skills or necessary jobs. The Host makes sure that the group is formed correctly and models using names and friendliness. The Discussion Director makes sure the assignment steps are followed and helps the group return to the task when lost on a tangent (fancy term for off-task!). The Questioner focuses on continuing the discussion through questioning and also reminds the others to ask questions as well. The Researcher looks up information in the text for support or to settle a dispute. The Materials Handler is the student who retrieves supplies, directions, and turns in papers. The Observer may or may not participate in discussion; her job is to keep track of who uses what skills, either by checking them off or making anecdotal notes. The Ambassador takes a question to the teacher and then returns with an answer that he must explain to the rest of the group. Roles are only limited by what the assignment requires and your imagination.

One good reason to use roles is that they increase the positive interdependence necessary to get the group to depend on each other and share the work. Roles work best when the responsibilities for each role enhance the academic task, the group's functioning, or the members' perceptions of fairness. As a teacher, the trick is for both you and the kids to easily remember and recognize who has what role and what tasks each is responsible for. If the work is tangible (is the Recorder taking notes?), it's pretty easy to keep track. However, a lot of roles are more discussion oriented and harder to recognize at a glance.

The best way to monitor roles easily is via a checklist. Notice that each role lists a mixture of task skills and social skills. What I like about the checklist is that if you want to give grades for group performance, you can grade each student's performance individually. Now, your honors student has a tangible reason for interacting with his peers; he can get an A for it! The example shown actually combines roles from several different assignments. Though several roles are listed, I generally try to make groups no larger than three to four members, so you need to create roles that best fit the nature of the task.

Another way to achieve role accountability is to have the groups make table tents out of 5" × 8" index cards, which are folded in half lengthwise. On one side, the student writes her role; on the other side, she writes the role again along with responsibilities. The label side faces out so that the other members and teacher can easily remember who has which role. The list on the reverse side faces the individual student as a reminder. I often use the table tents when I want each student to take the responsibility of modeling a different skill. On the front of the card is the skill and on the back are six phrases the student could say in order to model it. Here is an example one student came up with.

Staying Focused on the Task

"Hey guys, let's get back on task."

"Rich, it's your turn to do a question"

"Megan, you can talk to her about that after class."

Role Accountability Rating

Assignment: _____ Date _____ Hour _____

Host: _____   1 – 2 – 3 – 4 – 5
___ Correct set up and take down   disappointing   great job!
___ Actively uses support & liking skills
___ Monitors and enforces 12″ voices

Time Keeper: _____   1 – 2 – 3 – 4 – 5
___ Sets clear time limits   disappointing   great job!
___ Cues group to continue or conclude
___ Asks leads and follow-up questions

Questioner: _____   1 – 2 – 3 – 4 – 5
___ Asks questions that continue discussion disappointing   great job!
___ Asks specific follow-up questions
___ Encourages other members to ask questions

Observer: _____   1 – 2 – 3 – 4 – 5
___ Writes down lead and follow-up questions disappointing   great job!
___ Leads and records processing
___ Eliminates non-follow-ups and tallies

Dictionary Guy/Girl: _____   1 – 2 – 3 – 4 – 5
___ Looks up difficult/unfamiliar words and   disappointing   great job!
     explains the words' connection with the story
___ Points out context and importanceof
     vocabulary words

Historian: _____   1 – 2 – 3 – 4 – 5
___ Calls attention to footnotes and reads them disappointing   great job!
     aloud to the group
___ Points out historical and background connec-
     tions of posters and video

Figure 6.1   *Role checklists*

Note Taker: _____   1 – 2 – 3 – 4 – 5

___   Listens carefully and asks clarification questions disappointing   great job!

___   Orally summarizes group's ideas before writing
     them down

___   Quizzes members on group's conclusions so that
     all group members can explain when called on

Figure 6.1   *(Continued)*

Staying Focused on the Task *(Continued)*

"My vocabulary word is on page 111; everyone turn there."

"Amy, why don't you tell your connection now."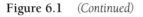

"Alright, quiet down and let Christine talk."

Depending on the task, sometimes I use roles; oftentimes I don't. As I mentioned earlier, roles are strongest when each role is required to produce something that is tangible. If a group has only two or three members and the task is discussion oriented, I don't use roles and rely on other forms of positive interdependence. However, when a project is complex and involves many steps, roles can be very useful.

Environmental Interdependence

Basically, this is when a group stays in one place and ignores the other groups. Nothing academic is ever going to happen if the kids in a group are sitting too far away from each other for quiet conversation or their desks are arranged so that everyone in the group cannot easily see all members. As the Johnsons say, "Knee to knee and eye to eye." However, as simple as this sounds, kids will resist you because their past experiences have shown them that group work can provide some major "goofing off" time. Sitting close together is going to impede their chances of talking with their friends in other groups. *Be explicit.* Draw a diagram of the way you want the desks arranged. Explain why this makes a difference. Ask a few students to drag some desks into correct formation and then sit down with them to model positive eye contact and body language. Once the kids have moved into groups, be stubborn. Rather than nagging a group that is poorly formed, I just say, "I noticed you haven't put the desks together correctly. Do you have any questions about how to do this? Okay, well, I hope you do it soon because I won't come back and observe until this is taken care of. And if I don't come back and observe, it's going to be hard for you to get any credit for this discussion." Once everyone knows what they're supposed to be doing, get the stopwatch out and see how fast the whole class can form the groups. For some reason I'm obsessed with time; if you can be more laid back, I congratulate you!

Resource Interdependence

An easy way to get a group more dependent on each other is to limit the materials. Instead of giving each kid a worksheet, give one to the group and pass it around from member to member; add to the fun by only letting the group use one pen. The only way the group can get credit for the assignment is if the handwriting keeps alternating. Want everyone to have a copy in the end? Photocopy the originals after the class has completed the assignment. Short on textbooks? Give one to each group and structure the assignment so that everyone has to look in it for information.

Instead of putting the markers in a big box, hit the "Back to School" sales and buy a bunch of cheap plastic pencil cases. I found mine for sixty-seven cents apiece; how can you go wrong? Divvy up the markers between the cases. Each group gets one case, and they've got to share and make the best of whatever colors are in there. Added benefit: this will cut down on those kids who are wandering the room in search of supplies, using the errand as an excuse to chat with their friends in other groups.

Celebration Interdependence

The Johnsons used to call this *reward interdependence* and often recommended using group grades, but revised their thinking after Alfie Kohn authored the book *Punished by Rewards* (1993). Kohn's review of research convincingly showed that people work harder and produce better quality material when they are working for intrinsic reasons, rather than extrinsic rewards. Tangible rewards often have no effect on motivation or even devalue the experience, making it less attractive. In light of Kohn's findings, giving group grades for collaborative work has come under some serious reconsideration.

The most common reason kids hate to work together is the group grade. Think about it. If your grade depended on your team members, wouldn't you want to choose exactly whom you knew you could depend upon? I know I would. I wouldn't want to take the chance of working with some new people; who knows what kind of workers they'd turn out to be? On the other hand, if I'm marginally invested in school, I'm going to group with some people who think like I do: one more failure or missing assignment isn't really going to change our lives much. What if the teacher assigns the groups? Now it's the teacher's fault when Johnny didn't get his "A" because Sally dropped the ball and didn't do the reading that had been assigned for homework. Believe me, Johnny's parents are going to blame you for his low group grade, and they aren't going to buy your argument that someday in business Johnny's salary may be based on how well his team performs. Gosh, group grades are actually the opposite of a reward; no one's happy, and the kids and their parents are dreading the next time you put them in groups. Luckily there's a better way.

Did you notice that this section is called *celebration*, not *reward*, interdependence? Well, that's what you've got to focus on, *celebrating group success either individually or as a class*. Want some ideas? Here you go.

1. Buy some silly stickers and give them to the kids as you roam the room and monitor for the skill of the day. Verbally compliment them on the skill you see the group using as you slap the stickers on their notes.

2. Count the number of times the kids use a certain skill as you monitor. Post a graph. Have the class set new numbers to shoot for. Don't forget that obsessive overuse of a skill is the key to it eventually becoming integrated.

3. Use the same count in number two and assign that number some bonus points, but *be careful*. The point is celebrating the successful skill usage or academic accomplishment; it's easy for kids to develop a maniacal preoccupation with bonus points. As teachers, we want to instill the belief that working together and contributing to the success of others is a reward in its own right. If kids start asking you, "How many bonus points is this worth?" it's time to back off the points. Also, remember that lots of bonus points might change a grade significantly, so I recommend using points as a class reward, not group reward. A group will quickly turn on a member who has lost them their bonus points. Though this is peer pressure to perform, the end results are pretty ugly.

4. Compliment individual students, groups, and classes. As teachers, we see tons of positive things occurring in groups, yet we often fixate on the one dysfunctional group. Put ten pennies in your pocket. Now start modeling the skills of praising and support and liking. Each time you make a positive comment, transfer a penny from one pocket to another. Play a game with yourself and see how many times you can move the ten pennies. As long as your comments are specific, this modeling contributes to the positive community and also gets the kids to start observing their own contributions in more specific terms.

5. Talk to the class about the great things you are seeing. Set up a roleplay that shows effective behavior. You never know, that one dysfunctional group might just get the message.

6. Have groups set goals and monitor their own successes. Take time in class to share these.

Identity Interdependence

Setting up a task that makes the group come up with an identity based on something they all have in common is an excellent way for getting new groups to work together. Coming up with a group name, motto, flag, or shield are all excellent icebreakers. Groups can share what they've come up with, but just be sure to keep this activity fun rather than competitive.

I'll never forget the time I handed the Group Shield exercise to a class of seniors. As I looked over the artwork, a part of one group's shield immediately raised my teacher red flag. The drawing depicted stick figures lying in hammocks while drinking beer and smoking cigarettes. Of course, I confronted the group. They laughed and reminded me that one of the shield questions asked what they would be doing in retirement. Well, I guess I couldn't fault them. I had forgotten that the last time I had used the shield handout was with a group of veteran teachers for whom retirement was soon becoming a reality. I thought about changing the question, but then kept it because it was so unusual for students to have to consider. The answers were too amusing.

A Little More on Group Grades

Now, I know that there are times when group grades are necessary, mainly when projects are on the menu. I must warn you, however, please do not attempt any large-scale group projects until the students know each other and are somewhat skilled at working together. If I assign the group, I set up the grading so that no more than twenty percent of the grade is actually a group grade; the rest is based on the individual evidence that a student presents in regards to his contribution. For example, if students were working together on writing a short story, each member would have to turn in drafts he wrote individually. If a group was working together to create a performance, all members would be required to write part of the script. In addition, each person would hold an individual role such as script coordinator, prop and costume collector, etc. Upon a project's conclusion, all individually produced artifacts are turned in with a letter explaining that person's individual contributions to the group. Also, when designing big projects of this nature, you need to build in checkpoints so that assessment is ongoing rather than one big lump in the end. The best way to build checkpoints is to have the students do it after they've finished a project. Here is what one class came up with after they finished memorizing, blocking, and performing Act V of *Othello*.

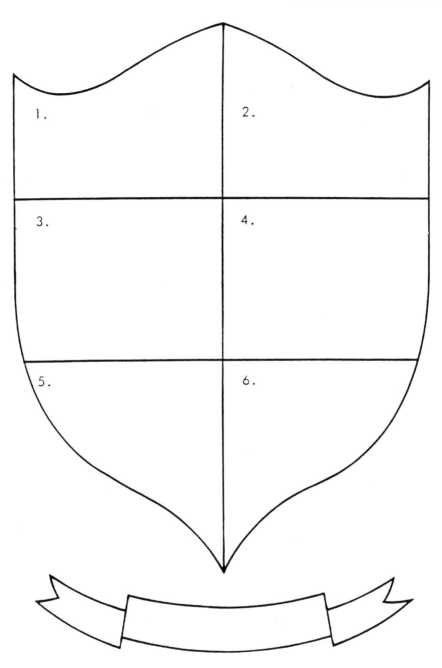

Figure 6.3   *Group Shield graphic*

Part I

- Have one person read the directions to the group.

- Read one shield topic at a time and discuss how it relates to each member's feelings and interests. Try to find commonalties in your answers.

- After the discussion of each topic, decide how the group's feelings and interests can be best represented visually. Record those pictures in the corresponding number on the shield. You may pass the shield around or assign an artist.

- Continue this process for each topic until your shield is complete.

Shield Topics

1. A significant event in your life

2. An important achievement or accomplishment

3. Favorite pastime activity

4. Something you are good at

5. The best place you've ever visited

6. A job that you would truly enjoy doing

Part II

Review your shield and think of a name for your group that best seems to reflect your members' feelings, values, and interests.

Figure 6.2 *Group shield directions*

Group Rehearsal Checklist

Day 1

- ❑ Assign a director who will follow the checklist and an assistant director who will take notes on blocking/staging and will also act as a line prompter.
- ❑ Quick read-through of scene.
- ❑ Divide up lines so that all actors have a part. If people double up on parts, consider smooth transitions between actors. Be sure to consider an actor's abilities such as portraying different emotions or being good at memorization.
- ❑ Second read-through with actors reading assigned parts.
- ❑ Cut lengthy speeches.
- ❑ Third read-through: stop and discuss how lines should be said and how other characters will react to those lines.

HOMEWORK: Practice lines. Think about blocking, gestures, and emotions. Find out how to pronounce the words correctly and what the character means in his lines. Read the footnotes. Use a dictionary. Reread packet on staging and blocking. Examine the character's internal thoughts and their relationship to the spoken lines.

Day 2

- ❑ Create a phone tree and assign rehearsal buddies who will practice lines together.
- ❑ Stand up and run through the scene slowly with movement.
  - Work out blocking and staging.
  - Make sure the actors know where to enter and exit from.
  - Be aware of who your character is speaking to.
  - Start practicing interaction with other characters on stage.
- ❑ Run through scene two more times so that actors begin to remember the blocking.
- ❑ Discuss props and costumes.

HOMEWORK: Each actor should start to memorize his lines. Start adding emotion to lines so that the character comes alive. It is helpful to read your lines with a family member or rehearsal buddy so that you will learn your cues. Start looking for props and costumes.

Memorization Tips

- Read the lines over several times until you understand what the characters are saying to each other. Then start memorizing.

Figure 6.4 *Group rehearsal checklist*

- Use common sense to think about how the lines are put together; the better you understand the conversation, the more sense the lines will make.
- Divide the lines into sections and set little goals for yourself.
- Repeat a line over and over and then test yourself.
- Find a partner to practice with; have the other person read the character lines that lead into your own.

Day 3

❑ Run through scene again:
  - Determine how transitions (when two actors play the same character) are to be made. Try to aim for smooth transitions that will attract the least amount of attention.
❑ Run through scene a second time. Make any needed changes in blocking and staging.
  - All characters should know their scene positions at this point.
❑ Run through scene slowly a third time and work on facial and vocal expressions for every character. Everyone must give ideas. Remember to overexaggerate expressions.
❑ Run through scene a fourth time; focus on remembering blocking and expressions. Director stops scene when necessary for acting/blocking notes.
❑ Discuss props and costumes; decide on what each person will bring in for tomorrow's practice. Remember that props should enhance the performance; do not bring props that might upstage the actors or distract the audience.

HOMEWORK: Have all your lines memorized for next day's rehearsal. Practice with your rehearsal buddy over the phone. Gather props for Day 4 rehearsal.

Day 4

❑ Run through scene without scripts and with props; assistant director acts as line prompter.
❑ Stop and discuss changes/additions to blocking, gestures, and facial expression.
❑ Run through scene a second time—no scripts! Practice improvements. Director stops scene when necessary for acting/blocking notes.
❑ Stop and discuss last-minute changes such as cutting lines that seem awkward or unnecessary or adjusting the use of a prop.
❑ Run through scene a third time so that blocking, gesture, emotion, and lines come together.
❑ Run through scene a fourth time; try to use the prompter as little as possible.

(continues)

Figure 6.4   *(Continued)*

HOMEWORK: All lines must be memorized. If someone is hazy, other actors can meet after school to help that person sharpen his memorization. Find and bring in any costumes and props. Call your rehearsal buddy to remind him of props/costumes to bring in. Practice over the phone; see if emotion and feeling come through in lines. Talk about what the character is saying.

Day 5

❑ Get into your costume and get into character by focusing on the role the character played in Acts 1–4.

❑ Full dress rehearsal. Do not stop until scene is complete; no stopping for mistakes. Director gives notes when scene has concluded.

❑ Director focuses on specific actors, watching and taking notes on cue mistakes, missing emotion/expression, or blocking errors.

❑ Keep practicing until rehearsal is flawless; director continues to give improvement notes upon the conclusion of each scene practice.

HOMEWORK: Be ready for the big performance. Make sure that your lines are confidently memorized so that you are saying them in your sleep! Do a walkthrough at home using family members as the other characters. Also, practice in front of a mirror or videotape yourself to get the facial expressions exact. Offer to help cast members who are struggling. This is a team effort. Make time to meet in the morning or after school if needed.

Figure 6.4 *Group rehearsal checklist (Continued)*

When projects offer students the opportunity to choose their own partners, I also give them the choice of working solo because I never want to put someone in the awkward position of feeling unwanted. It's always better to save "choose your own group" projects for later in the year when the classroom community is strong. A positive climate lessens the chance of ostracism. As a matter of fact, later on in the year you'll probably see more than a few students choosing to work with people who are not their "friends" but people with whom they have developed good working relationships. Even when a group project results in one final, communal project, I still try to build in as many pieces of individual accountability as I can. Each member has parts that they alone are responsible for and are graded individually. I also require that students keep a daily process journal that keeps track of the group's accomplishments, functioning, to do lists, etc. The journal and subsequent Process Letter are explained more fully in regards to the group writing projects in Chapter 9. A well-defined rubric is your strongest asset when it comes to assigning group grades. Always have the group self-evaluate their project against the rubric before turning it in to you. Don't just have them circle numbers; make them point out specific examples of quality related to each of the rubric categories. No matter how much a group wants to circle fives for everything and then loudly grumble when the mean teacher marks them down, they just can't give themselves a five for imagery when no one can find a single simile in the final draft! When my rubric is strong and I've been able to show students some high-quality projects from previous years, the group self-evaluations are seldom inaccurate.

Individual Accountability

The next component that you seriously need to think about when structuring groups is individual accountability. This is the work for which students are individually responsible for before, during, and after a group meeting (Johnsons 1998, 4:17). Between any group meetings, students need to be working on individual assignments that they will bring back to the group. When all of the work takes place in the group, it is easy for hitchhiking to take place. If completed homework serves as an admission ticket to a group and an individually graded performance is the post-group activity, students will work harder together. In the case of Literature Circles, individual accountability occurs at every stage. It is the reading and notes preparation needed for the discussion, the contributions and skill usage during discussion, and the test, writing assignment, or large group sharing afterwards. As group activities take place, all students should be well aware of what is expected of them as individuals later.

Group Skills and Group Processing

Though these elements were discussed at length in the previous chapter, it never hurts to be reminded that they are deeply important. Teaching, monitoring, and reinforcing the social skills necessary for a collaborative academic task strengthens the group's chances of success. Even if the collaborative task is clear, the kids have roles, they're sitting close together, and they know that eventually they will all be taking tests on their own, this is no guarantee that the students know how to talk and work with each other in a productive way. You've got to define those skills explicitly and make it important to the students that they use those skills. Likewise, once students start working together, they've got to frequently assess their growth as individual members and their growth as a group. It is the processing part of collaboration that ensures refinement in the various skills needed to work together.

Trial and Error

The very first class I began practicing cooperative learning on was my rowdy 7th-hour junior/senior Grammar class. As I recall, they spent a lot of time with their partners working on the skills of 12-inch voices and taking turns talking. By the end of the semester, they were a pretty happy bunch that enjoyed working together. Several had me the following semester for Short Story, and most were looking forward to another opportunity to work in small groups.

At the beginning of Short Story that semester, I made several tactical errors. First, I immediately increased the group size to three. Second, I only used icebreaking activities in the very beginning of the semester. Third, I gave them group grades. It only took about two weeks before one of my most positive students, a girl who had spent first semester in my Grammar class, was ready to drop the class. She blamed her group mates, two low-achieving, immature, socially unskilled males, for the bad grades she was receiving. This student knew what cooperative behavior was supposed to look like and these guys just weren't cutting it. She was angry with me and with them. What went wrong? Besides using group grades, I forgot to assess the skill level of this new class before deciding on the group size and tasks. I remembered how well the previous class had worked together in the end, but I'd forgotten what they looked like when I first put them in groups six months earlier.

Moral: Assume nothing when a class is new to you. At first, keep the kids in pairs and the tasks short and simple. Observe carefully, figure out what social skills need to be taught/reviewed, and go from there. Unless you want to guarantee mutiny, avoid group grades at all cost.

Face-to-Face Interaction

The size and structure of a group can make a *huge* difference between a group that fails and one that functions. One of the biggest mistakes teachers make when trying to teach students how to work collaboratively is making the group too big. Before I learned how to structure collaboration successfully, my groups were way too big, somewhere between four to six members. I hear the voices already. "Hey, wait a minute, how can you have a group smaller than four?" The answer: very easily. Stop and think about the task at hand. How many people do you really need to get the job done? Most academic tasks can be completed with greater efficiency and quality when the group is no larger than four. Actually, two or three often is the ideal size. Why is that? The larger the group, the greater the number of interactions. A group of two can only have two interactions: one person speaks while the other one listens. A group of five, on the other hand, has a potential for twenty different interactions. A group of fifteen, the typical size of a committee in my district, has a potential for 210 interactions; no wonder it takes so long to make a decision! However, you know what actually happens: a handful of people monopolize the conversation while the rest of the members feel frustrated because they cannot be heard. In any event, the situation is neither as productive nor as intellectually fulfilling as it could be.

Group Size

How do you decide the group size? If students are new to each other and/or to collaboration, design assignments around pairs. Pairs rate high for on-task behavior because at any moment fifty percent of the class is talking. Pairs are less easily distracted by other groups and require less sophisticated social skills in order to function well. Pairs can work faster at a task than a group of three or four; always consider how much time you have for an activity. Finally, pairs can be formed instantaneously. Maybe your school is different, but mine is tremendously overcrowded; everyone shares classrooms. Luckily, the desks are not bolted to the floor, but there is the unspoken courtesy of leaving the desks in rows just in case your colleague has a different approach. Push those rows together and you've got pairs! Be sure to keep the pairs shoulder to shoulder; don't let the kids convince you that the desks should be facing each other. The only certain feature this arrangement offers is that it's much easier for the pairs to ignore each other and lean over to talk to their friends on either side. Now, if you can't stand restricting collaboration to pairs, here's the compromise. Have pairs complete the task first and then move with another pair to share.

When students are accustomed to working in pairs and have developed some skill at encouraging, questioning, and supporting, that's the time to move them into larger groups. However, I must warn you, I'm never happy with the functioning of a group larger than four. When there are five or more people in a group, someone always gets left out because, typically, the others are not doggedly attentive enough to continually bring the reticent person back into the discussion. Usually the most outgoing member will give it a couple of shots, but then not have the patience to keep the encouraging up. In the end, that fifth member ends up being a silent observer, which I guess is not a terribly bad thing. On the other hand, the person who talks the most is the person who learns and remembers the most. Why do you think teachers are so smart!

The other half of the group equation is deciding how to form the groups. At the beginning of the year, I use pure random selection, making sure to keep the tasks easy, stress-free, and pretty short. I never want to throw harder tasks at groups until they've got some skills in hand, and I know who the difficult people are. During the first six to nine weeks, I usually stick with pairs. After that, the kids are ready for groups of three or four that stay together for a unit, project, or literature circle, all of which last about three or four weeks. The easiest way I've found to form new groups is to photocopy enough class lists from my attendance book so that every student gets a copy. At the top they write their first and last name. Underneath on successive lines they write their birthday numerically (3/31/89, for example), phone number, and student ID number. Next, they add up the digits in each and get a total. Finally, they add up the three totals for a fourth total. Here's an example.

Susie Que

Birthday	3/31/89	=	24 (look at each digit separately)
Phone Number	532-7300	=	10
Student ID Number	777001	=	22
Sum		=	56

Before the lists are turned in the first time, I also give them the option of crossing off one name. I don't guarantee that they'll never have to work with the individual, but at least I'm giving them a good faith effort. Most kids don't cross off anyone, so take special note of the ones that do, because those crossed out names often indicate a serious and yet unresolved conflict. From years of experience, I've found that sometimes it's better off not to group some kids together.

Each time new groups need to be formed, I give the lists back to the students and have them cross off the names of the people they've just worked with. I recollect the lists and put them in order based on one of the numbers listed at the top; lowest number is first, highest number is last. Then I use what I call "adjusted random order." Depending on what group size I want, I grab the first three or four lists, compare the cross outs, and then look at the names to see if the group will function productively. I make the kids think the groups are based on the random order of the numbers, but I try to form groups so that everyone in class gets to work with everyone else, including the room's most difficult people. Painful as this can be, everyone needs some practice for dealing with difficult co-workers later in life! I also consciously try to balance groups in regards to gender, group skills, and academic skills. If I know a kid is great at praising but a weak questioner, I'm going to try to form a group whose skills compliment each other.

Of course, if you love adventure, by all means give purely random grouping a try! There are all sorts of fun ways to go about this. If you are looking for groups of two or four, line-ups are great. Have the kids line up according to birthday, height, shirt color, number of siblings, you name it. Then have the end of the line walk around to face the beginning so that there are two lines with people facing each other. At that point, split them off into pairs or fours. If you want three in a group, the easiest way is to use a deck of playing cards. Figure out how many groups of three you need and then pull out sets of numbers from the different suits so that you have three ones, three twos, etc. Shuffle the deck, pass 'em out, and watch the fun as the kids search for their new group or surreptitiously try to trade cards so that they can be with their friends.

Speaking of friends, have you noticed that I'm not real big on the kids choosing their own groups? Having suffered through many team selections in grade school and high school physical education, I am still psychologically scarred from the repeated experience of being picked close to last because I was grossly untalented at team sports. My only comfort was that there was another person, the social pariah, who was consistently dead last because she picked her nose in public. Some comfort! At my ten-year high school reunion, I found that some of the least popular people in 1974 had become some of the most successful, talented, and best looking of 1984. Thank goodness those classmates had enough inner strength to put their team selection experiences behind them. Now that I am a teacher, I try to purposely avoid those approaches that will guarantee a painful memory for some. Left to their own devices, teens choose to work with their friends; and, usually, adults behave the same way. However, one of the goals of a collaborative activity is that it creates the potential for diverse ideas and viewpoints. Typically, people are attracted to their friends because they have a lot in common; they are more similar than they are different. While this comes in handy when trying to figure out what movie to rent at the video store, similar viewpoints generally weaken a group. What's there to challenge or explore if everyone pretty much agrees with each other? People also choose their friends because of the fear of the unknown. Obviously, it is always more comfortable to hang with one's friends rather than purposely choose the discomfort of being in a group of strangers. However, start thinking about all of the times you haven't been able to choose your group: your boss, college roommate, colleagues, committee members, students in your class; the list could go on and on. Actually, other than choosing whom I married, the majority of times I've worked in a group with others it has been based on random selection or someone else's selection. That's called being an employed adult. Being able to work successfully with new people in new situations is an important life skill. Assigned groups force students to learn how to break the ice and positively shape new working relationships.

Rest assured, I'm not a complete meanie. I might let students choose groups for a quick activity when I feel confident that no one is going to be left out. I also let students choose groups in project situations when a group grade is assigned; however, when the outcome is a group grade, I also give students the option of working independently.

How Do I Assess This?

When groups miss their mark, it's because one of the five elements is weak or missing. When it comes to structuring successful collaboration, I think the teacher needs to begin by modeling her own assessment. I've found it very helpful to make a chart of the five elements and post it right in the room. I use the chart to check my planning and also educate the kids.

1. Positive Interdependence
2. Individual Accountability
3. Group Processing
4. Social Skills
5. Face-to-Face Interaction

When I give directions for a group assignment, I point to the corresponding component on the chart. The kids will value your directions more if you explain the reasons behind your lesson-design decisions.

Another reason why groups sometimes fail is because the task is more complex than the skill level of the students. In the beginning of the year, you need to monitor and informally assess how well students work together. Who seems friendly? Who can carry on a conversation with just about any partner? Who ignores everyone but her friends? How long can pairs work on an activity before falling off-task? As the teacher, you need to observe these interactions closely since this determines the social skills you teach, the size of the groups, and the complexity of the academic tasks. I can't emphasize enough that in the beginning of the year, it's best to start with short assignments of no more than five minutes and to stick with pairs. As students become accustomed to working together, refine skills, gradually increase the time, and then make the groups a bit larger. Do not start grading kids on their skill usage until they've got a handle on what it takes to be a good group member.

Once students are somewhat skilled, this is your chance to branch out into Literature Circles, peer conferencing groups, project groups, etc. The key to assessment is a combination of teacher assessment and self-assessment. Use the checklists, but have the students record their ongoing processing as well. Whenever possible, let groups individualize their goals to fit their needs. Let them choose to work on the skills that they think will most improve their performance.

Maintain strong individual accountability. Most of your grades should come from the homework students bring to the group and the individual assignments students complete after a group has met. Avoid group grades whenever possible. Even group tasks can be graded individually. For example, in a conferencing group, let's say the task is for each member to read his paper aloud and get five revision questions from the listeners. Though each paper will be stamped individually, no one gets any stamps until everyone has his questions written on his draft. This second requirement ensures that the group takes a look at everyone's paper. In the case of group projects, if you can't make most of the grade an individual one, remember to make the grading criteria clear and let the group self-evaluate their product against the rubric before turning it in.

As far as the binders go, I have the kids put their project process letters, process journals, group processing sheets, and checklists in the Leadership section. The placement of other assignments depends on the academic skill they emphasize.

Parting Words

Successful groups come from careful planning. Though some classes will work better together than others, careful lesson planning, assessment, and revision should enable almost all students to collaborate successfully. While more than enough studies show that well-structured collaborative experiences produce better learning, it is the small victories that I remember best. In Short Story class I had a boy who continually and bluntly told his members that they were wrong. By the end of the semester, he had learned to disagree in a more socially palatable manner so that his partners wouldn't feel attacked. Furthermore, he also learned that literature can often have more than one correct interpretation, that it was indeed possible for two people to have differing opinions yet still both be right. In Grammar I had a girl who was not a worksheet whiz but did have the ability to get along with just about anyone. She didn't just endure a less socially skilled partner. Her patience and positive attitude helped others become better partners. In return, her partners wanted her to be successful and found the patience to explain and re-explain the intricacies of recognizing noun clauses versus relative clauses. By herself, she might have failed the class but when teamed with others she succeeded. Finally, I'll never forget the boy, a transfer student, who wrote in a final Processing Letter that at the beginning of the semester he had no friends, but by the end of the semester he felt he had many. That student, now twenty-four, reappeared to me just the other day. I hadn't seen him since his junior year. He greeted me with, "Hey, Mrs. Steineke, are you still teaching that Short Story class?" Years later, the memories of the fun and the friendships remained sharp. Strong collaborative experiences reap rewards that last well beyond the last day of class.

Resources

Johnson, David W., Roger T. Johnson, and Edythe Johnson Holubec. 1998. *Cooperation in the Classroom*. Edina, MN: Interaction Book Company.
   This is my bible when it comes to cooperative learning. Absolutely everything you need to know is there, somewhere. However, in order to decipher the book's organizational structure, you really need to take a course from the Johnsons. See the Workshops/Courses section.

———. 1994. *The Nuts & Bolts of Cooperative Learning*. Edina, MN: Interaction Book Company.
   This book is a great review of cooperative learning elements. Short chapters with clear titles make it easy to find the information that you want.

Kagan, Spencer. 1995. "Group Grades Miss the Mark." *Educational Leadership* (May): 68–71.
   Still thinking about group grades? This article presents all the arguments why group grades don't work but also offers some solutions.

Kohn, Alfie. 1986. *No Contest: The Case Against Competition*. New York: Houghton Mifflin Company.
   If you need any ammunition for a parent or administrator on why kids should be working together, this is the book for you. Kohn summarizes the research in an interesting manner.

Schmuck, Richard A. and Patricia A. Schmuck. 2000. *Group Processes in the Classroom*. New York: McGraw-Hill Higher Education.
   This book really offers a fantastic overview of the way groups evolve in their functioning. Each chapter focuses on a specific facet of group development accompanied by practical classroom strategies.

Workshops/Courses

The Cooperative Learning Center at the University of Minnesota: (612) 624–7031,<www.clcrc.com/index.html>, or <www.co-operations.org>.
   This is the headquarters of David and Roger Johnson. Every summer they offer a variety of very useful cooperative learning courses in a variety of locations.

Kagan Professional Development (800) 266–7576 or <www.kaganonline.com>.
   Like the Johnsons, Kagan offers a variety of workshops during the summer. Spencer Kagan's structure system makes an excellent introduction and bridge to the trainings done by the Johnsons.

CHAPTER 7

Questioning
A Key Collaborative Skill

One of the main things I notice early in the year as I observe the first round of Book Talks or other small group discussion activities is that most of the kids lack the ability to extend conversation. Typically, student A voices a rather vague, inarticulate opinion. Then, since getting everyone's opinion is one of the targeted social skills, student B robotically asks if anyone else has something to add. Rather than voicing a variety of ideas, all members agree with student A's opinion and that's the end of that, time for a new topic! Why are kids so uninterested in each other's viewpoints? My gosh, any teacher would be thrilled to have someone ask us for our opinion, and then we'd bend the person's ear in half while we explained our ideas in great detail. What gives? Well, think about it. Who does all the talking and questioning in a traditional classroom? Yes, you guessed it, the teacher! Now, even if your classroom is student centered, there is a strong likelihood that your kids' classroom experiences still weigh in heavily on the teacher-centered side. We've all spent time in those classrooms. Frankly, in my entire career as a student, kindergarten through post-graduate school, I only had two or three classes that were not teacher centered; therefore, I consider myself somewhat of an expert on traditional pedagogy.

What goes on in those traditional classrooms? The teacher stands in front of the room giving information in the form of a lecture or under the guise of a large group discussion. During the latter, the teacher asks questions, calls on volunteers, and tries to keep everyone involved. Though the questioning effort might be valiant, in the end most of the discussion still only involves a relatively small group: those six students who actually enjoy this format and, of course, the teacher. Some of the rest of the class might be passive participants, but most focus on turning invisible or volunteering an answer early in the hour so that they can relax. The kids that really don't want to be a part of the discussion stubbornly answer with "I don't know." No matter how hard a teacher tries to involve everyone in a large group discussion, the bulk of the conversation will always gravitate back to those five or six students who want to answer the questions because they are good at giving the teacher the right answers. For the teacher and these kids, it's a win-win situation: the teacher gets the content coverage she wants and the kids get the attention they want. Maybe, in a sense, it's a win for the rest of the class as well. If those six can keep the teacher busy, the rest are free to pursue their own agendas: write notes, daydream, sleep, watch the clock, or talk without getting caught. Now that I think about it, a lot really does go on during large group discussion; however, I'm not sure these are the activities teachers are striving for. Even if you look more closely at the kids who are involved, they still aren't talking all that much. The pattern of answering during a large group discussion begins with a short student response followed by a much longer piece of teacher elaboration. This all boils down to the fact that in a large group discussion, students seldom have to explain their ideas in depth or listen carefully enough to question someone else about his ideas.

Now, after years of training students in the protocol of large group discussion, we suddenly want our pedagogy to be student centered. Unfortunately, the kids just haven't seen or developed a lot of skills that automatically help them in this kind of environment. If the teacher asks all of the questions, does most of the talking, and ultimately decides what's important to remember, why would these kids be very good at directing their own discussions? Few people can excel at a skill until they see it modeled, get some lessons, practice, and then refine the skill via coaching or mentoring. Unless you're lucky enough to inherit students that have been doing reading/writing workshop, Literature Circles, and negotiated projects regularly, you're going to have to decide on how to train the kids so that they have the discussion skills necessary for these structures. Here's a big tip: work to refine the skill of questioning first in the social arena and then move it to the academic. Use of the Partner Grid, which was introduced in Chapter 2, is one way to reinforce careful listening and questioning. What follows are a few other social activities that get the kids into the mode of extending conversation through questioning.

Index Card Trade

Once you are confident that students are listening and questioning in a more skillful manner, they don't have to write everything down as they do with the Partner Grid. After all, most social conversation does not involve elaborate notetaking. The day before you plan to use this activity, pass out a 3 × 5 card to each student, telling them to write their name, date, and class period on the top line. If possible, use a different color of card for each period; the color-coding will come in handy later. Next, each student should write an interesting interview question to ask others in the class. Remind them that the questions should be open-ended versus yes/no. Emphasize that the question should not embarrass anyone and should be school appropriate. After they're done, collect the cards and take a look at them. There is almost always one joker in the group who comes up with a question about underwear. Catch that kid at the door before the bell rings, ask her what's wrong with it (she'll know), and hand her a fresh card so that a new question can be written on the spot.

On the day after you've screened the questions, pass the cards back and clear the desks out of the way. Students are going to mix and mingle using the same format as they did with the riddles.

1. Find a partner and greet them by name.
2. Darkest shirt starts by reading his question to his partner. After his partner responds, the interviewer needs to ask two or three follow-up questions.
3. Partners trade roles and repeat the process.
4. After both partners have been interviewed, they thank each other and trade cards.
5. Students look for a new partner by waving their cards in the air.

As kids get better with questions, have them think of new ones. If they're stumped, pick out some thought-provoking examples from any one of the myriad of question books available at any bookstore.

Card Pick

Don't throw those index cards away; save them for another day. This more complicated activity requires a group of four to five and at least two questions for every member. Use cards from other classes; the kids love to see what questions their friends wrote. If you've used a different color for each class, it's easy to mix them up and then sort them later if necessary. This activity is an adaptation of a Spencer Kagan structure called "Fan and Pick." I learned it at a Kagan workshop but was unable to find the instructions in any of his books.

1. Count off to form groups of four to five.
2. Within the group count off so that each person has a number.
3. #1 picks up the deck, shuffles, and fans them like playing cards.
4. #2 picks a card, turns to #3, and reads it aloud.
5. #3 answers the question. Then #4 and #5 each ask a follow-up question.
6. #1 finishes by offering a Support and Friendliness statement.
7. #2 takes the deck, reshuffles the cards, and the process begins again. Each group can decide on its own whether to reinsert the used card or remove it from the deck.

As you can see, this activity is more complex, so save it for later in the school year. However, once the kids have learned the steps, this is a strategy that can easily be adapted to many academic activities.

Neighborhood Map and Life Graph

A strategy often suggested in teacher books is the "Life Map," a supposedly wonderful prewriting device that gets a person to review the events of his entire life. Whenever I tried this activity, it never worked. The kids would just draw a blank, probably because I couldn't figure out how to draw my own life map either. Then I attended the Walloon Institute and had the good fortune to attend a workshop given by the poet Terry Wooten. Instead of drawing a "Life Map," he suggested drawing a map of your neighborhood first and then jotting down all the memories associated with the landmarks. Since I was able to complete this map, I knew it would work for my students.

When I do this activity, I tell the kids that they can draw their current neighborhood, their old neighborhood, the resort where their family rents a summer cabin year after year, Girl Scout camp, anyplace that represents a neighborhood to them. Of course, I show them my sad, messy, and inartistic map of my childhood neighborhood, and the kids are duly unimpressed until they notice the memory of "hippies in the park." Now they're intrigued. The assignment is to draw a map with twenty-five memories, not places/landmarks, but memories. It's important the kids understand that distinction because the next step just won't work unless the maps have lots of memories. I also tell them that since these are memory maps, they don't need to worry about scale or accuracy. The purpose of these maps has nothing to do with geographic directions.

The next day everyone gets their maps and Appointment Clocks out. With a student volunteer, I model the steps they'll follow for sharing.

1. Greet your Appointment Clock partner by name.
2. Trade maps.
3. The person with the lightest color shirt picks a memory that interests him from his partner's map.
4. The partner talks about the memory for one minute while his partner listens and keeps an eye on the clock. One of those overhead transparency timers works great for this.

Figure 7.1 *Neighborhood map student example*

5. If time is left, the listener asks two follow-up questions based on what he heard and the speaking partner answers.

6. After a minute is up, the roles are reversed. Now it's the other person's turn to talk about something from his map.

7. When both are done, partners thank each other and move on to their next appointment.

When using the Appointment Clock, you can have a class meet with appointments one through six one day, and seven through twelve on another. It is important for the teacher to signal when partners should trade roles and when the time is up so that everyone is moving to his next appointment at the same time. I like this activity because if students have done the map for homework, it plays directly into the day's activities. Early on, I try to emphasize that homework is almost always directly tied to a subsequent group activity. This is individual accountability, an important element of group design. Once the kids understand how personal responsibility ties into social interaction, homework completion rises substantially. The map trade is also a great activity because it is kinesthetic; the kids get to walk around and burn off some energy.

Another assignment that fits the above sharing procedure and also successfully gets at the same type of information is the Life Graph. I got this idea from Linda Rief's book *Seeking Diversity* (1992), which is chock full of great reading/writing ideas. Here are the steps.

Part 1: Gathering and Ranking Memories

1. Fold a piece of notebook paper in half lengthwise (hotdog style!) and then open it back up so that there are two columns.

2. Label the left-hand column with a minus sign and the right-hand column with a plus.

3. Under the left-hand column number one to seventeen and then start making a list of life's disappointments, life's "downs." These can be big events and little events, anything that's important to you. Brainstorm. Do not censor; you won't be required to share anything on the list that you don't want to.

4. Under the right-hand column number one to twenty-one and then start making a list of life's happy moments, life's "ups." These can be big events and little events, anything that's important to you. Brainstorm. Do not censor; again, you don't have to share.

5. After completing your lists, review them and check off the ten events in each column that meet these two criteria: the event is important to you, and the event is something that you are willing to share with others.

6. Go back to the items in each column that you've checked off and determine how old you were at the time and what year it was. Mark this information next to each checked event.

7. Get out a second sheet of paper and once again create minus and plus columns. In each column re-list the checked off items in chronological order, starting with the earliest memory. Before listing a memory, write down your age at the time and the year it took place.

8. Take a look at each memory listed on the paper and rank it between 1 and 10, with 10 being the happiest or saddest you can go.

Part 2: Creating a Graph that Illustrates Your Memories

1. Fold a piece of blank paper lengthwise, open it back up, and draw a vertical line on the center fold. Now turn the paper so that the line is horizontal. Draw a second vertical line about an inch from the left end. Make the horizontal line a timeline. In chronological order, mark the ages and years that correspond to the memories. This means your earliest memory will be closest to the left and the latest memory will be closest to the right. You'll need to look at both lists together in order to get all the ages and years in order on the graph. Try to spread the dates out on the timeline.

2. Mark the numbers one through ten both above and below the point of intersection on the left-hand vertical line. Evenly space the numbers. Mark a minus sign before each number that falls under the horizontal line.

3. Graph your memories. Place life's "downs" below the horizontal line and life's "ups" above it. Plot each memory in relation to age/date and ranking. I like to show the kids an example or two before they start.

4. After plotting, use one set of lines to connect the positive events and negative events.

5. Once the spacing is worked out on the plain paper, I hand out real graph paper so that students can create a really neat final draft. When all the memories are plotted on this version, the final step is to create an accompanying visual symbol for each event. Students can draw, cut out magazine pictures, or use clip art for their graphics. Jacque chose to use a combination of clip art and scanned photographs to illustrate her important life events.

When the kids get to the graphing, don't forget to have them do a preliminary rough draft graph on a plain piece of paper so that they can work out the spacing, years, format, etc. It might be

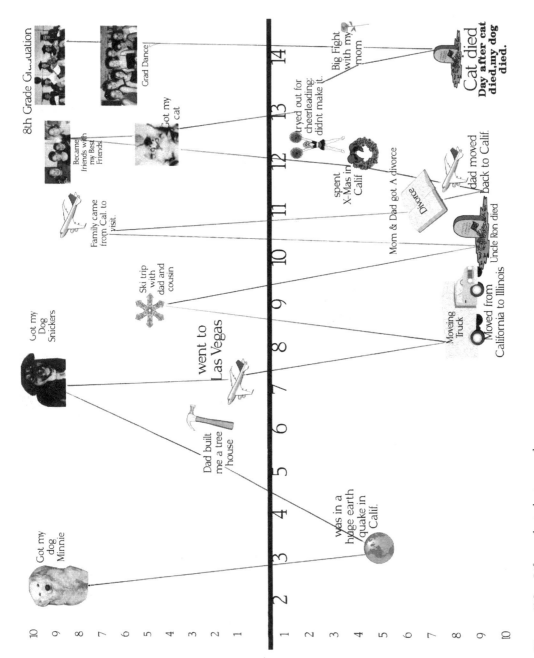

Figure 7.2 *Life graph student example*

cheaper where you live, but around the Chicago area, graph paper is expensive and having each kid burn through three sheets of it before they get the layout right can really run up the tab, particularly when it's coming out of your pocket.

The finished graphs can be shared just like the neighborhood maps. Both the graph and the maps also serve as great prewriting activities that can be re-examined later. Once we're done with them for now, tell the kids to save the maps and graphs in the Writing Archive section of the binder.

Using Family History to Extend Beyond the Classroom

Once the kids are in the groove of listening and asking questions, a great way to expand their skill usage is to take it home to their parents and relatives. One of the projects my students work on throughout the year is collecting and writing up interviews with family members. The final result is the creation of a family newspaper complete with photographs, captions, and articles. For the most part, teenagers and adult family members don't talk to each other much, and that's probably been the norm since the dawn of mankind. However, teenagers will talk to their relatives if they have an assignment to complete, and family members are usually thrilled that their teens have finally noticed they exist and might even be interesting. Before you start any outside interviews, it is a good idea to inform the parents. I explain the family history angle and assure them that the class is not doing this assignment just to be nosy (Zemelman 2000). Also, family members need to know that it is all right to decline to answer questions that make them uncomfortable. I'll never forget the mother I met during conference night who asked me why I insisted that the kids ask their parents about what kinds of trouble they got into when they were teenagers. I told the mother that the question was entirely her daughter's choice, not mine. The mother went on to describe how the girl badgered her with that question for days. Whoops, there's another skill I forgot to teach: how to interview in a respectful manner! After that incident, I started sending out a "warning letter" before any interviews begin. I discovered that parents are much more cooperative when they know in advance. Also, they know it's their child's poor planning not mine, which makes them complete an interview the night before it's due. The letter I now send out really sets the stage for the project.

When the class first gets started on interviewing, I give them the initial topic: find out how you got your name and what family events and activities surrounded your birth. Together we brainstorm generic follow-up questions.

1. How did you come up with my name?
2. Who was I named after?
3. What other names did you consider?
4. What name would I have had if I had been the opposite gender?
5. What does my name mean?
6. What is the story behind my middle name?
7. What time of day was I born?
8. How much did I weigh?
9. Who was at the hospital?
10. How long was Mom in labor?
11. What was the weather like that day?
12. What happened prior to Mom leaving for the hospital?

Dear Parents and Guardians,

I am writing to let you know that one of the components of the English 9 curriculum is the study of family history. Over the next several months, students will be asked to conduct interviews with a parent and a grandparent. A third interview will focus on researching a relative who has passed away, so students will be interviewing survivors who knew that person. Students will also be looking to you for information about their name and birthday events, genealogy, and family migration. Therefore, the input of you and other family members will be extremely important.

In class we will be developing interview questions and practicing interview skills. Let me assure you that no interview will be assigned with the expectation that it be due the following day. Your student will be expected to make an appointment with each relative he/she plans to interview. Of course, if there is information you are not comfortable sharing, either with your child or with our class, your privacy will be respected. In those cases, please encourage your child to come up with some alternative interview questions. After each interview, students will write an article for his/her family newspaper, a project that will be completed during fourth quarter. Please do not be surprised when you are asked for photographs; these will be scanned and then accompany the articles. My hope with this project is to provide the opportunity for conversation between generations. The author Christopher Paul Curtis sums this up admirably in the afterword from his Newberry award-winning book *Bud, Not Buddy* (1999), the story of a boy searching for his father during the depression.

> Much of what I discovered about the depression I learned through research in books, which is a shame—I didn't take advantage of the family history that surrounded me for many years. I'm afraid that when I was younger and my grandparents and parents would start to talk about their lives during the depression, my eyes would glaze over and I'd think, "Oh, no, not those boring tall tales again!" and I'd find the most convenient excuse I could to get away from them. Now I feel a real sorrow when I think of all the knowledge, wisdom, and stories that have been forever lost with the deaths of my grandparents.
>
> Be smarter than I was: Go talk to Grandma and Grandpa, Mom and Dad and other relatives and friends. Discover and remember what they have to say about what they learned growing up. By keeping their stories alive you make them, and yourself, immortal.

Thank you for your help. If you have any questions, please give me a call at school. Also, if you would like to look at some of last year's newspaper projects, I'll have them available during conference day.

Sincerely,

Nancy Steineke

Figure 7.3 *Family history interview parent letter*

Of course, after we come up with these questions, I ask for a volunteer to be "my parent" and model how to interview respectfully, demonstrating such skills as making an appointment, being ready for the interview, taking notes, asking follow-ups, asking if there's anything else the parent might think of, and thanking the parent for his or her time. This is fun for the class because the volunteer can make up answers about my past. (Before we start, I do quietly remind the volunteer that I don't want to be embarrassed.) Afterwards, I share the real information, which is usually in stark contrast to whatever the volunteer made up. Finally, students practice respectful interviewing in pairs. If time permits, have a few pairs model their interviews for the class. Give students a few days to complete their name and birth interviews.

On the day the interviews are due, students present their notes to their partners first. Putting the page face down, a partner talks about his interview information for one minute. When students can't read their notes verbatim, they tend to converse in a more animated and spontaneous manner. Afterwards, the listener asks two or three Follow-up Questions which either can be answered on the spot or provide some ideas for further interviewing. Then partners switch roles.

After this initial interview, students again brainstorm questions they would like to ask their parents or grandparents. Typically, kids want to find out about what relatives were like when they were in their teens. Here are some questions that usually pop up.

1. What was your neighborhood like when you grew up?
2. What historical events happened during your life?
3. What was school like when you were growing up?
4. How did you and Mom meet?
5. What did you do for fun as a kid?

If the kids have trouble coming up with interesting questions, an excellent source for ideas is a book by Bob Greene and D. G. Fulford called *To Our Children's Children: Preserving Family Histories for Generations to Come* (1993). The book has extensive question lists under categories such as holidays, school, and careers. It is a great resource. Once a variety of questions are listed, students need to pick about six questions that they find most interesting. Even though the kids have practiced and used follow-up questions quite a bit in class, I often find that even when students have great lead questions, they still fail to explore them thoroughly in the interview because they forget to ask those follow-ups. There are two ways to combat this. Students can roleplay the interviews and afterwards write down possible Follow-up Questions. A more advanced strategy is for each student to write down a Lead Question (the starter question) and then, imagining the conversation path, list all the potential Follow-up Questions. After completing this activity alone, students can work together with a partner to see if they might think of additional questions. I tell students that each Lead Question needs to have at least four Follow-up Questions that are open-ended, not yes/no questions.

Lead Question	**Follow-up Questions**
How did you and Mom meet?	Where did you meet?
	Who was there with you?
	When was your first real date?
	What did you do/where did you go?
	What were your first impressions of Mom?

Lurquin's Legend

Volume 1, Issue 1   May 8, 2001

A heroic effort to save a Lieutenant

I asked my Grandpa many questions about his life. He was born in 1922 in Greece and lived in Greece until he was about 40, and then he came to America to live. This is from my mom's side.

Back in Greece, he had no cars, no electricity or running water. It was a small town, with a small school and only had dirt roads. The place that he used to live in is a total change now. There is electricity, running water, cars, and yes, now they actually have toilet paper because back then they didn't. It was really nice to them, but to think about it, it is horrible to us. To walk around it was very, very safe. There was no crime at all. He felt really sad when he had to leave Greece for America. He had to leave his house, family, and his country.

Everything cost barely anything. It was very inexpensive for things that he did have. He barely had anything. He didn't have shoes, and he had to walk around barefoot. Everything there now is pretty much how it is here. Some of the things were expensive and some things aren't.

He didn't have any technology. The best things he had were candles. Seeing that

he barely had anything, the things he did

have, were really cheap. It is very much more high tech now then it used to be. Nothing came new to them until he came to America. He thought it was different, but it was great.

The clothes that they wore around his time were really different. Women wore long dresses and men wore plain old work clothes. Most colors were browns and blues. He didn't consider himself different from anybody.

(Continued on page 2)

A goody-good teenager

The parent that I interviewed was my mom. She was born in 1959 and she didn't live in America until she was about seven. This describes about herself and her childhood.

I asked my mom many questions about her childhood. Her neighborhood was totally different than it is now. She lived in Greece. There were no sidewalks, indoor

plumbing, or electricity. The houses were mostly cold in the winter and hot in the summer. Instead of wood or chain-linked fences, they had ones made of rock. At the time, they thought it was nice because they thought that it was what everyone else had and they weren't bothered by it, but now,

(Continued on page 4)

Figure 7.4 *Family newspaper student example of front page*

The final form these interviews take is only limited by your imagination. My students turn their interviews into a family newspaper using Microsoft Publisher. We write up the interviews and scan family photographs to accompany them.

I've also had students do speeches on the most interesting member in their family. Often some great stories are revealed, stories that might have been lost had these students never been forced to seek them out. One student, Ray, told a family story that had been passed down for several generations. During his long boat trip from Italy to the United States, Ray's great, great, great grandfather slipped and hit his head. The resulting blow left him with temporary amnesia. When Ray's ancestor landed at Ellis Island, he couldn't remember his last name, so the immigration official pulled out a New York phone book and randomly assigned him one. Even though Ray's grandfather eventually recalled his real last name, his family continued to go by the assigned name since that was the official one listed on his immigration documents.

The integrated curriculum (English, Biology, Geometry) sophomore team in my building has taken the Family History project a step further; their culminating experience is a Family History Fair. Students choose to explore one family member in depth while also delving into genealogy charts and genetics. On the day of the fair, each student has his charts and written up interview on display along with family photographs and artifacts. Family members are invited to come and visit with students and celebrate the stories they uncovered. Students stand by their displays and must orally explain their projects in as interesting a manner as possible to anyone who asks. After completing the newspaper or fair projects, students leave with a greater understanding of their own family and how they fit into its history. In addition, they are taking their questioning and listening skills beyond the classroom!

Trial and Error

The first time we tried the Family Newspaper project, the kids enjoyed it, but, in terms of final draft quality, I thought it was pretty much a disaster from start to finish. First of all, the interviews were stultifyingly shallow. Second, most of the kids failed to bring in any family photographs to scan. As a matter of fact, there were several who took great glee in searching the Internet photo galleries for "grandparents" and substituting images of these anonymous souls in place of their real relatives! Of course, I did my best to discourage such nonsense, but that only made "photo finding" more fun. At the end of the exercise, the final drafts of the newspapers were rife with errors: grammatical errors, typing errors, missing headlines, vast expanses of blankness, stories that continued to nowhere. The finished papers forced me to conclude that there were a lot more steps to the process than I had originally anticipated. I did a lot of things differently the second time.

First, I spread out the interview write-ups and spent more time up front on how to complete an in-depth interview. We completed the first interview in mid-October and finished the last interviews the following February. Before students embarked on each interview, they had to get their lead and follow-up questions stamped. This ensured getting the detailed information that the previous year's interviews lacked. Also, each time we went to the computer lab to type up another interview, I told the kids to bring in their photos so that we could start scanning them. By the time we put the final newspaper together, almost all of the students had at least a couple of genuine photos ready for placement. Finally, I consulted with my computer teacher friend, who was more than happy to give me a desktop publishing checklist he used, and I modified it for my project. When we went back to the lab to put the newspapers together, I pointed out the components on the checklist as I demonstrated the necessary desktop publishing steps. Later, as the kids worked on their own, I noticed many of them referring to the checklist, marking off the items as they were completed. This time they had a much clearer picture of what the newspaper needed to include. In the end, the newspapers still weren't perfect, but they were at least one hundred times better than the previous year's!

> **Moral:** *Whenever you try a new project, don't expect perfection the first time around. It usually takes at least one very rough trial before you can anticipate all of the steps needed in order to make the process run smoothly and the final product high quality.*

How Do I Assess This?

Almost any of the activities described earlier in the chapter can be stamped and saved in the binder for later counting. Students can keep a running log of their own interaction skills via individual Processing Sheets or pages in their Reflection Journal. Just like the Partner Grids from Chapter 2, I can eyeball and stamp the entries while they are working on something else. My goal is always to collect as little paper as possible. Besides, when I walk around and stamp, I am also engaged in monitoring the ongoing activity.

In the case of the Neighborhood Maps and Life Graphs, completion of each major step (listing memories, sketching rough drafts, etc.) gets stamped, and the final drafts get graded on the basis of having the necessary number of memories, neatness, graphics, and color. Before I grade these final drafts, I have the kids self-evaluate each of those categories on a scale of 1–5 by having them compare their products with high-quality samples I've saved from previous years. Also, don't forget that these projects get an audience assessment as well, because they'll be shared with all of their Appointment Clock partners. Every assignment connected with the maps and graphs is stored in the Writing section of the binder.

The family newspaper also involves quite a bit of stamping. Students must meet deadlines for writing their interview questions, bringing in their interview notes, and completing a computer-typed rough draft of each interview. Students can also get extra stamps on each rough draft when they show me the family photo that they'll scan to accompany the text. The final draft of each interview is graded separately according to a simple rubric. All pieces of newspaper text are graded separately from the final project. When the "big edition" is assembled, it is graded against a simple checklist. Notice that the paper is self-evaluated and peer-evaluated before it is teacher-evaluated. Ideally, before students turn the paper in for final evaluation, there should be some opportunity to go back to the computer and fix the omissions they have detected.

<table>
<tr><td colspan="2">Interview</td></tr>
</table>

Interview

Name _____

Relative's Name _____   Date _____   Hour _____

Subject clear to reader			5		4		3	2	1		no
In-depth versus superficial information	10	9	8	7	6	5	4	3	2	1	no
Error free	10	9	8	7	6	5	4	3	2	1	no

Figure 7.5   *Interview grade sheet*

Parting Words

Over the years I've found that asking Follow-up Questions is probably one of the most difficult collaborative skills to master. As a teacher, you're going to need patience and perseverance. Because so much personal focus is needed to ask Follow-up Questions that truly build on what others have said, students will often fight this skill because it takes a lot of hard work. Besides the careful listening, students also have to become more mentally nimble; Follow-up Questions require quick, spontaneous thinking.

As I mentioned earlier, students find very few models for this type of behavior in their own daily lives or even on television talk shows, a media genre that theoretically should model the art of discussion and interview. Talk show hosts routinely interrupt their subjects or even abruptly change the topic altogether. Shows that supposedly feature "lively debate" aren't much better. I remember once trying to watch the show *Politically Incorrect*. I thought the topic of politics paired with a discussion group composed of diverse members would be entertaining and interesting. Unfortunately, the *Politically Incorrect* discussion participants operated with only one goal in mind: out-talking and out-shouting everyone else. No one tried very hard to learn from each other's viewpoints, and I never heard anyone ask Follow-up Questions that might clarify another's

Family Newspaper Evaluation

Name _____

Date _____ Hour _____

Date		Date		Date		
Self		Peer		Teacher		
Yes	No	Yes	No	Yes	No	
						1. Is your name in the paper's title?
						2. Do you have a catchy title that uses alliteration?
						3. Do you have an accurate date and volume header?
						4. Did you separate the volume and date header with a horizontal line (to separate top headings from articles)?
						5. Have you filled in the "special points of interest"?
						6. Have you listed articles and page numbers under "inside this issue"?
						7. Do you have a consistent serif font style for all text?
						8. Did you use no larger than a 12-point font for the articles?
						9. Do you have a consistent font style for all headlines?
						10. Are your headlines directly above the article?
						11. Are the article headlines slightly larger than the article?
						12. Did you bold the headlines?
						13. Did you leave at least one blank line before and after each heading?
						14. Did you single space the body of each article?
						15. Does a scanned photograph accompany each interview?
						16. Does your newsletter use two or three columns for its articles?

Figure 7.6 *Newspaper checklist—front*

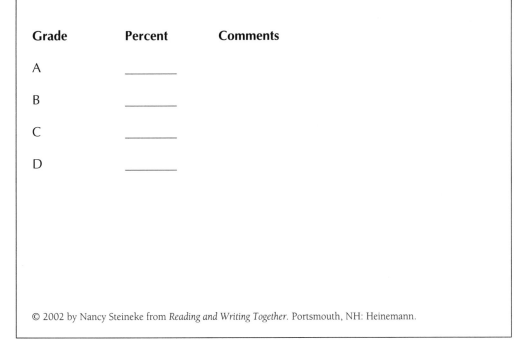

Peer Evaluator's Name _____

Date		Date		Date		
Self		Peer		Teacher		
Yes	No	Yes	No	Yes	No	
						17. Do you have articles about your name and birth?
						18. Do you have a parent article?
						19. Do you have a grandparent article?
						20. Do you have an "other relative" article?
						21. Do you have a poem?
						22. Is it clear where articles are continued?
						23. Does a graphic accompany each history story?
						24. Are headlines and titles free of typos or grammatical errors?
						25. Are articles free of typos or grammatical errors?

Grade   **Percent**   **Comments**

A   _____

B   _____

C   _____

D   _____

Figure 7.7   *Newspaper checklist—back*

idea. All I heard were a lot of fragmented, half-explained opinions. Though the show had the potential for interesting thought, the content frustrated me with its shallowness.

Getting back to the classroom, though, keep remembering that the skill of asking Follow-ups will be brand new and even foreign to most of your students. My experiences have shown me that it takes students one or even two full semesters before this skill becomes a natural part of their discussion technique. The more opportunities that you can provide for practice, reflection, and refinement, the sooner you'll see real ownership of this skill. Once students are good at using questions in a social context, Literature Circles provide the best academic context for growing as questioners.

Resources

Curtis, Christopher Paul. 1999. *Bud, Not Buddy.* New York: Delacorte Press.
    If you haven't read this book or his other one, *The Watsons Go to Birmingham—1963,* you are missing out on some wonderful stories.

Greene, Bob and D. G. Fulford. 1993. *To Our Children's Children: Preserving Family Histories for Generations to Come.* New York: Doubleday.
    This book gives a few tips for researching family stories, but it's mostly just made up of extensive lists of questions you might ask your ancestors.

Zemelman, Steven, Patricia Bearden, Yolanda Simmons, and Pete Leki. 2000. *History Comes Home: Family Stories Across the Curriculum.* York, ME: Stenhouse Publishers.
    Don't stop with a family newspaper. This book tells you how to research family history and integrate it with any subject area.

Question Books

There are lots of good books of questions that can be used for discussion or writing prompts. Here are a few:

McFarlane, Evelyn and James Saywell. 1995. *If . . . (Questions for the Game of Life).* New York: Villard Books.
    There are two more volumes in this series, copyrights 1996 and 1997.

Nicholaus, Bret and Paul Lowrie. 1992. *The Conversation Piece: Creative Questions to Tickle the Mind.* New York: Ballantine Books.

Schwartz, Linda. 1989. *Think on Your Feet.* Santa Barbara, CA: The Learning Works, Inc.

Schwartz, Pepper. 2000. *201 Questions to Ask Your Kids/201 Questions to Ask Your Parents.* New York: Avon Books.
    This book is actually two books in one. Face-up it focuses on questions parents can ask. Flip it upside down, and it focuses on questions kids can ask their parents.

Stock, Gregory. 1988. *The Kids Book of Questions.* New York: Workman Publishing.
    Many of these questions are of the "moral dilemma" variety, so it's best to think about the level of controversy you wish to create before randomly choosing a question.

Overhead Timer

The Kagan product catalogue refers to this as a Teach Timer. You can order it online at <www.kaganonline.com> or by calling Kagan Publishing at 1-800-933-2667.

CHAPTER 8

Literature Circles
Getting Them Started
and Keeping Them Going

Training Students for Literature Circles

Thanks to the regular use of SSR and Book Talks, students do gradually become much more skillful at reading and small group discussion. In addition, they'll be fairly competent at most of the skills that members of a Literature Circle need for success: support and friendliness, good listening, and asking Lead and Follow-up Questions. Finally, students will be in a better position to use and analyze reading strategies such as finding passages, making connections, and drawing inferences. That's why I like to save Literature Circles for later in the semester.

When training students for effective functioning in genuine Literature Circles where each group is reading a different book, I use a specific progression. Before committing groups to any novels, I've found it best to first work students through two or three short stories in order to get them focused on asking good questions. I define a good question as one that creates interesting discussion and new insight, but also gets members to look back in the text. The stories I like to use for this kind of introductory training are those that are only a few pages long. Students can read them in ten minutes or less, which gives more time for skill practice and question discussion. Also, doing the individual work in class eliminates the preparedness issues that may arise when the class moves to a novel. Some stories that lend themselves to this activity are "The Jacket" by Gary Soto, "Eleven" by Sandra Cisneros, and "The Bridge" by Todd Strasser.

Students start by reading the story and jotting down two or three questions that would be interesting to discuss with their partners. I have the students write each question on a separate sticky note and paste each question on the page of text right where they thought of it. Next, before the discussion, students get out a sheet of loose leaf, put their names on, and create the usual Lead and Follow-up Questions columns. Then they trade papers with their partners; this is a new twist. Partner A reads his question aloud and jots down the page number on the note before removing it from the text. Then he hands it to Partner B who pastes it in the Lead question column of Partner A's sheet. Before Partner B answers the question, both students make sure their stories are open to the same page. Only then can Partner B answer; afterwards, Partner A asks a Follow-up Question. However, before Partner B can answer this next question, he has to write it down next to the sticky note in the Follow-up Question column. What's interesting about this reversal, compared to the way questioning is done on the Partner Grid, is that it builds in some wait time. Students seldom give pause to think of what they will say; they hear a question and blurt out whatever enters their heads first, probably because this is the kind of rapid-fire responses that large group discussions often generate. Once three or four Follow-up Questions have been pursued, the roles are reversed. It's never a good idea to let one person ask all of his Lead Questions because it might leave the other student with nothing new to discuss. After the process, papers are traded back so that each person has a record of his questioning. The next step is for each student to mark the lead question that produced the most extended and interesting discussion. In large group, these questions are shared on the board or a transparency.

Once everyone's best question is out for examination, the class can draw some general conclusions on what kinds of questions work the best. Usually they'll come up with observations such as these:

1. They make you think.
2. There's more than one possible answer.
3. It makes you fill in details from your imagination.
4. It brings up a controversial idea.
5. It makes you notice something you didn't before.
6. It makes you see something in a different way.

I like to practice this partner strategy and question analysis a few times. Once the kids know the drill, I increase the group size to four and move on to the next phase, reading a whole class novel Literature Circle style. Though I am the first one to support choice, I also know that almost every English curriculum in the United States contains at least one or two required texts. In my own department, ALL freshmen are expected to read *Of Mice and Men* and ALL sophomores read *To Kill a Mockingbird*. So, why not "kill two birds with one stone"? Get that "must read" book out of the way and teach the kids how to work in small groups at the same time. Really, having everyone read the same book has some advantages.

First, students become aware of the careful reading needed for a Literature Circle discussion. I find that students who are used to large class discussion formats often need to rethink how they approach their homework reading. In the past, skimming, watching the movie, reading the *Cliff's Notes*, or just careful listening and notetaking during the teacher led discussion was enough for them to finish with a C or B on the unit test. However, while talented bluffing might be a useful skill to save face when singled out in a large group discussion, that sort of behavior in a small group just frustrates members and wastes everyone's time. A whole class book is a good opportunity for kids to learn the following concept: a successful small group discussion requires that everyone has read carefully and knows what he's talking about.

Second, a whole class novel is a good trial run for assessing individual accountability. *To Kill a Mockingbird* offers me excellent insight into who is consistently ready for discussion, who is inconsistent in preparation, and who is highly undependable. Once in awhile, I run across a group with only one or two members who are really ready for discussion. A whole class novel lets me easily shift these kids to other groups for that meeting while their unprepared members are *strongly* encouraged to use the class period to get ready for the next discussion. Also, those groups with temporary members get to learn how to greet and include guests in their discussion. I find that this individual accountability track record is highly useful later when putting together true Literature Circles where every group is reading a different book. If I know up front that a student is inconsistent in her preparation, I'll try to make sure that kid gets her first book choice since I want her motivated to read. Also, I'll make sure the group is a bit larger since that member might not be ready to participate in all the discussions.

1. Why do you think Kenny went into the water at Collier's Landing after he knew people had died there? Ch. 13
2. If you were in Kenny's place, would you go to Collier's Landing? Ch. 13
3. What do you think was going through Kenny's mind when he heard the bomb go off? Ch. 14
4. "A guy just came by and said somebody dropped a bomb on Joey's church." How would you react if that sentence had your loved one's name in it? Ch. 14
5. Why was Kenny the only one who went into the church after the bombing? Ch. 14
6. Why do you think someone would put a bomb in a church with little kids in it? Ch. 14
7. Why does Kenny become so traumatized (after the church bombing)? Ch. 15
8. Why do you think Kenny imagined the magic behind the couch? Ch. 15
9. Why weren't the parents helping Kenny get over his trauma? Ch. 15
10. How has Byron changed from before he left for Birmingham? Ch. 15

Figure 8.1 *Class examples of questions that created good discussion*

Third, on the days between small group discussions, the class can come together to compare and discuss how to improve their Literature Circle notes and their discussion skills. Because everyone is reading the same text, comparing the usefulness of specific questions or passages is easy. Here are some questions we gathered from the last three chapters of *The Watsons Go to Birmingham—1963* by Christopher Curtis.

When I notice that students still aren't pursuing Follow-up Questions enough in their "same book" Literature Circles, I use a skill drill similar to one the students have used earlier in a social rather than academic context. As students read the novel chapters assigned, each member has to come up with two or three Lead Questions. This time, the questions and the corresponding page numbers are written on note cards rather than sticky notes. In their groups of four, all of the questions are shuffled and placed in a deck.

1. #1 picks a card from the deck and reads it to #2.
2. #2 counts to five silently (building in wait time) and answers.
3. #3 asks a follow-up question.
4. #4 asks a follow-up question.
5. #1 gives #2 a specific compliment based on that member's answers.
6. #2 picks up the deck and a new round begins.

After this activity, once again gather the two most interesting questions from each group and display them on the board or overhead. Now it is time to analyze the questions in a bit more depth. You can use the different levels of Bloom's Taxonomy. Here's an example that uses questions based on the fairy tale "Cinderella."

Knowledge (fact recall): What were the mice turned into?

Comprehension (summarize/explain): Recap the main plot points in "Cinderella."

Application (relate to real life): When was a time you wanted to do something that your parents forbid you to do?

Analysis (compare/contrast): What kind of person is Cinderella? What does she have in common with Snow White?

Synthesis (create something new): How would Cinderella have gotten to the ball if her fairy godmother had never appeared?

Evaluation (give an opinion): What do you think about Cinderella's generous decision to allow her stepsisters to live in the castle with her?

A somewhat simpler way to examine questions is a framework used by Project CRISS called QARs: Question Answer Relationships (Santa 1996). Questions are first divided into two main categories: "In the Book QARs" and "In My Head QARs." "In the Book" questions are further categorized into "Right There" questions whose answers are short and can be found directly in the book, and "Think and Search" questions whose answers are still text dependent but require the reader to look up information in different parts of the text. "In My Head" questions are subdivided into "Author and You" questions that require the reader to make inferences, while "On My Own" questions focus on the reader's prior knowledge and experiences; these questions encourage discussion of personal connections. Here is a Cinderella question that fits into each category.

Right There: What material were Cinderella's slippers made out of?

Think and Search: What happened during each of the three evenings Cinderella attended the prince's ball?

Author and You: What do you think made Cinderella's stepsisters so mean and selfish?

On My Own: If you had to live in a family like Cinderella's, what would you do to survive it?

The nice thing about the QARs is that with only four, it's easy to code them. After a couple of Literature Circles, students can go back over their notes and highlight their questions with crayons or markers, using a different color to represent each type of question. This is a very visual way of getting kids to recognize whether or not they are in a question rut. Once question after question highlighted in the same color glares back from a page, students quickly start writing questions that reflect greater diversity.

If I'm feeling too lazy to drag the crayons out of the cabinet, I have each student write her best question on a slip of paper. After getting them typed up and run off, I hand a copy out to each student and make an overhead as well. Instead of colors, we code the questions with numbers: 1 = Right There, 2 = Think and Search, 3 = Author and You, 4 = On Your Own. First, I have the students do the labeling on their own. Then, using the overhead, I record the class' judgments. If there is disagreement, we go back to the question type definition and example and discuss it. Lots of times we conclude that a question could fall into a couple of categories depending upon how it is pursued by the group. This presents an excellent opportunity to re-emphasize the importance of Follow-up Questions since they can have such an effect on the depth of a question's answer. I like to examine questions early on and then again later in the Literature Circle cycle. Comparing the early and later transparencies shows the class how far they have come in their development of sophisticated discussion questions.

Getting Literature Circles Up and Running

While SSR offers students a wide range of choice and challenge depending on the students' individual inclinations, Literature Circles are definitely more teacher driven in the sense that the choice is finite. When creating a book list, you've first got to think about the goal. Is it to learn more about a certain period in history? Is it to provide the support needed to read some of the classics that your curriculum requires? Is it to show kids the fun of sharing ideas together as one reads a book? At one time or another, I have used Literature Circles for each of these purposes. Currently, my favorite Literature Circle books are text sets, groups of novels that focus on a specific theme. After we watch the film *Schindler's List*, students form Literature Circles around novels which all connect in some way to the film. However, all of the books are not directly about the Holocaust. Choices include *Hate Crime*, a novel about contemporary anti-Semitism; *The Giver*, a futuristic story about a "too perfect" society; and *After the War*, a novel about the challenges death camp survivors faced once released. After reading *To Kill a Mockingbird*, the subsequent Literature Circles revolve around books that hopefully will broaden my students' understanding of the ongoing discrimination African Americans face in the United States. While many of the books have southern settings, this text set also includes *There Are No Children Here* by Alex Kotlowitz, a nonfiction narrative that depicts in stark detail the difficulty any urban child faces growing up in the public housing projects of Chicago. My most recent text set was developed in response to the events of September 11, 2001. The turn of world events made me realize that we all needed to learn more about the Middle East and Arabian culture.

When choosing your books for a Literature Circle unit, the trick is to find books that need a discussion, ones that challenge yet are not so difficult that they will frustrate the reader. At the same time, I look for books of varying levels of difficulty so that the various reading levels present in a heterogeneous class can be addressed. Also, I try to look for books that students wouldn't necessarily pick up on their own.

Picking Books and Forming Groups

On the day scheduled for students to make their selections, I have a ballot already prepared that lists the books, asks for ranking (#1 is first choice, #2 is second choice, etc.), and provides designated blanks for the ever-necessary name, date, and hour. After passing out the ballots, I tell the students that I want them to make informed choices so they need to go through two steps before they rank their selections.

First, I do a quick Book Talk on each book so that students have some idea of the plot, its connection to the Holocaust (or whatever theme is being studied), and also any caveats or previous readers' opinions (i.e., "starts slow, but then it really moves").

Next, I group the kids in rows or circles so that the number in the row or circle matches the number of choices: eight books equals a circle with eight kids. Then we do a quick book pass; each student gets to look at each book for one minute and then the book gets passed. Before we do the pass, we have a quick discussion listing what one might look for in a book during a minute's worth of examination. Students conclude that one minute is enough time to look at the cover, skim the summary on the back, check how long it is, and maybe read a bit of the first page. During the book pass, I emphasize that this activity is solo; that means no talking! Once the book pass is completed, everyone ranks the selections. I always tell them to rank their top four choices out of the eight or nine titles available.

After collecting the ballots, I warn everyone that there are limited numbers of copies, so everyone will not automatically get his first choice; usually a student gets one of his top three choices.

Name _____

Date _____ Hour _____

Rank your choices in numerical order.
Make your first choice #1, second choice #2, etc.

_____ *Briar Rose*

_____ *Gentlehands*

_____ *The Giver*

_____ *Hate Crime*

_____ *If I Should Die Before I Wake*

_____ *Summer of My German Soldier*

_____ *The Wave*

_____ *The Cage*

Figure 8.2 *Literature Circle ballot*

I always try to give myself a cushion of at least two days between the voting and actually passing out of the books. That gives me a chance to catch anyone who was absent on voting day. It also gives me a little time to form the groups and organize the books. Once I've got the ballots, I sort them out by first choices. Any book that doesn't have at least three people choosing it gets dropped, and those students are reclassified by their second or third selection.

Next, I look at numbers. The best Literature Circle is a group of four. If one member is absent, a fine discussion can still be had with three. On the other hand, when someone is absent from a group of three, having a full-blown Literature Circle discussion with only two is difficult for most students. I'll never forget the senior Novel class I had several years ago. I was just beginning to experiment with Literature Circles and had no financial backing, which meant my offerings were limited to what I could scrounge from the English department book closet. Being inexperienced, I assigned a group of three seniors to *Around the World in Eighty Days*. All of them had good attendance records, so I assumed a group of three would not be a problem. Unfortunately, I never anticipated the week-long disappearance of the student council member when he was called upon to oversee the high school's spring festival activities, nor did I predict the absences generated from "college visits." For seniors, these days are akin to personal leave days: use 'em or lose 'em. This combination of factors resulted in that group of three having only one meeting out of a potential five where everyone was present. After that experience, I now try my best to avoid groups of three whenever possible. On the other hand, five is the ideal number when you have a student with a high absence rate or one who seldom comes to class prepared. Since these students will probably not be participating in every discussion, it's still mainly a group of four. However, a group of five is not ideal when everyone is present and prepared. Try as I might with reinforcing the discussion skills and processing after each discussion, a group of five always has one member who is a shadow, letting the other four do most of the talking.

Finally, I look at the faces in the current groupings and try to tweak the groups for optimal success based on personality, discussion skill level, and homework habits. If the high achiever's first choice puts him with the kids who seldom do their homework, I'll move him to his second choice. It would be nice to fantasize about him being just the role model these less-motivated kids need, but, being a pragmatist, my gut tells me that he'll probably be the only one prepared, quickly get frustrated, and then have his angry parents call me about the punishment these Literature Circles are inflicting upon their child. On the other hand, if I can put a less-motivated student with several stronger ones, that often can push that student in a positive way if the book was this kid's first choice.

Gender and personality balance are also considerations. If a group consists of one girl and three guys, I think about whether the guys will be skilled enough to include her, and I'll also think about whether the girl is going to be comfortable in that situation. I also always try to make sure the kids are working with some new people, since one of my goals is for all of the students to meet and work with everyone else before the end of the year. All of these are individual judgment calls, but if you've been working with a class for a while you can usually make them pretty quickly.

By now you're probably wondering if anyone ever gets the book she really wants to read. The answer is yes. I'd say that ninety percent end up getting their first choice and close to one hundred percent have gotten their first or second choice. With all my meddling, how can that be? Thanks to SSR, the kids have already read at least a half dozen novels on their own; they've become book connoisseurs, so to speak. They know what they like and don't like. Choosing books based on who else wants to read a particular title or which one has the fewest pages takes a back seat to choosing a book based on potential reading enjoyment. This fact hit home just recently. One of the choices from the Holocaust text set is *The Giver* by Lois Lowry. Since I put this list together several years ago, the middle schools that feed into the high school have also put this book on their reading lists; therefore, many of the ninth graders have already read it. If students were looking for the easiest way out, they'd opt for a book they'd already read, right? When I looked at the most recent ballots, hardly any students listed *The Giver* as a top choice, instead opting for books they hadn't read before. *I repeat: readers know what they want.*

The other reason why the groups seem to fall into place is that the selection is an absolutely silent, individual process. It is completely solo. I purposely do not give them the opportunity to negotiate with their friends because I want them to choose the book that interests them versus the book that "Susie" wants them to read. I know this makes me sound like a control freak, but groups of friends do not necessarily create the best Literature Circles. They have too many other agendas and common experiences to share, discuss, plan, or review. If these kids really want to read a book together, they can start a junior chapter of Oprah's book club! What's stopping them? Also, there are always one or two kids in class who don't have a lot of friends, whatever the reason. Still suffering the pain of being chosen next to last for high school P.E. teams, I never want to put my students in that position. In the end, I'm always aiming for heterogeneous groups made up of people with diverse experiences and opinions since these are the ingredients necessary for lively discussion.

Meeting the Group

After I have my groups nailed down, I type up a list for each class naming the members and book title for each group and print up a couple of copies. One copy goes in my grade book and the other copy goes to my student aide, who counts out the books and puts a rubber band around them. I always find that the better organized you are on the day you pass out the books, the happier you'll be. Also, do not pass the ballots back to the kids unless you want to hear a lot of whining about why they didn't get their first choice, why they don't want their first choice, or why they want to change their first choice. If you wait a few days between voting and passing out the books, most of the kids will not remember their exact rankings. This will make your life easier; go with it!

The day the books get passed out, I like to immediately follow with about 15 or 20 minutes of SSR time so that students can get a bit of a feel for how their books read before they meet with their group. There are certain tasks that need to be completed during the first meeting.

Membership Grid: Often, we teachers want students to move directly into the task when what the group really needs at first is some "get to know you" time. The Membership Grid works very much like the Partner Grid from Chapter 2 except that there is room for details on more members and students don't need to write anything about themselves. That way, the sheet still works for a group of five. The grid is an activity that should be the first item on the agenda of each Literature Circle meeting because it loosens everyone up and lubricates the wheels of discussion.

Ground Rules: By the time students begin working in Literature Circles, they've already worked with groups in several other capacities, definitely enough to have a pretty good idea on what behaviors create success versus failure. Therefore, at the first meeting I have each group develop a list of three to five ground rules that everyone agrees to follow. You might have students think about how they'll deal with a member who hasn't done the reading/notes, how to share equally in discussion, or how not to get on each other's nerves. Students often bring some pent-up frustration with them from their previous experiences in dysfunctional groups, so this is a way to clear the air and lay the cards on the table so that all members are clear on each other's expectations. Here's an example of the ground rules one group negotiated.

1. Take TURNS talking and doing discussion things.
2. Come prepared.
3. Be NICE to each other no matter how much pain you're in.

I like that third rule. I'm glad students also recognize that personal baggage needs to be put aside in order for academic activity to take place. Along with the first and last names of their members, I have each student list their group's rules on a sheet of loose leaf labeled Literature Circle Processing. This sheet comes out at each meeting for review, reflection, and goal setting.

Reading Calendar: One of the things I like best about Literature Circles is that it promotes student responsibility and decision making. At this first meeting, I give each group some calendars with the Literature Circle meeting dates circled and any other important dates (holidays, prom, etc.) marked. I tell students that the book needs to be finished by the last meeting date, but they need to decide what reading is due for the other dates. It's interesting to listen in on the conversations and the strategies. Often, inexperienced groups will start by figuring out how many pages are in the book and then dividing by the number of meetings. Sooner or later, though, someone else will suggest that finishing a certain number of chapters for each meeting might be a more logical approach, while someone else recognizes that it makes sense to assign more pages to the meetings that have more reading time between them. Each member of the group keeps a copy of the calendar but also turns in a copy to me. Double check to make sure the groups have recorded the actual page assignments rather than listed the chapters. Knowing the pages each group should

MEMBERSHIP GRID

1st

Megan

TOPICS	GROUP MEMBERS			
	Amy Ricchiuto	Matt Withrow	Christine Rems	Rich Hansen
5-4 Best Places to see a movie	- friends house - comfy - rent movies - watch a lot of them	- Sony home theater @ Best buy - monster surround sound	- friends house w/ DVD & big screen - cheaper - eat what you want	- Marcus - big screen - food = good - popcorn
5-7 Andrew fest Day 1	- no $ - don't know what's going on - 2nd hr. + 5th - walk around	not here	- wants to go to pie throw - no $ - walk around	- buy food - going 3rd hr. - wants to eat - obstacle course
5-8 Andrew fest Day 2	Absent	- was working - snow cones - lots of snow cones - raining	- walked around - thought it was boring - circus boy	- was fun - elephant ears - pizza - obstacle course = fun
5-14 3 day weekend	- went to aunts - spent night w/ cousin - saw charlies angels	- lincoln way - track meet - weather = bad - got cancelled - didn't have equipment	- got sick - Friday went to friends house - Sun = Grandparents over	- saw Driven - Marcus - German guy talked funny - Good Movie

Figure 8.3 *Megan's Membership Grid*

be discussing on a given date makes accountability monitoring much easier for you. Of course, some groups completely mismanage the reading schedule at first and then need to change it. That's okay; it's part of the learning process.

Large Group: While the students are still in their groups, I have one member from each group share their ground rules and also the strategy for how they decided on their reading schedule. Then I give the groups a few minutes to review their own rules and schedule since the sharing might have jogged some refinement of their own.

Processing: Before the group disbands, I want them to immediately begin to recognize and reinforce their positive accomplishments. So on the same sheet that has their ground rules listed, I have them discuss and list three specific things that helped the group get along, get the jobs done, and enjoy each other's company. If time permits, it's nice to quickly share these in large group as well because it publicly affirms behaviors that contribute to group success. Also, when the kids aren't specific in their observations (i.e., "We cooperated"), this gives me the chance to

MEMBERSHIP GRID

GROUP MEMBERS

TOPICS

TOPICS	GROUP MEMBERS			

Figure 8.4 *Blank Membership Grid*

prod them for an example that illustrates the skill. Last but not least, I tell the members to turn to their group and say, "Thanks for your help; I'm glad you were here today." Yeah, it sounds phony, but when I don't remind the kids to frequently thank each other, I notice a drop in positive interaction. Hmmm, imagine how differently we might feel at school if we were frequently and genuinely thanked for our hard work.

Getting Ready for the First Discussion

You'll notice that the Literature Circle instructions that I use are very similar to the preparation of the Book Talk Discussion Sheet. This was not due to laziness but design. I purposely wanted the preparation to be similar in order for the students to keep refining certain reading skills. Also, it is quicker and easier to explain new tasks that are already familiar in some ways. The one big difference in preparing for a Literature Circle discussion versus a Book Talk is that the kids have to come up with good discussion items that will get others involved and thinking. Though role sheets are often suggested for Literature Circles, by the time the kids are in high school, I want them to be focusing on all of the typical elements one would bring to a group discussion: questions, passages, connections, illustrations. When each student is preparing in this manner, there is usually plenty to discuss. Ideally, there is too much to discuss, which forces students to choose their most promising items when it is their turn to contribute. Depending on the class, I might or might not offer class time for preparation. When I taught senior Novel, I often gave them class time for reading and notetaking since most of the students held what amounted to full-time jobs. As much as I wished I could use the class time for something else, I knew that this group made no time for homework. On the other hand, my ninth graders are too young for jobs, so they are expected to prepare outside of class.

Along with the rubric, I always find it helpful to show students what high-quality notes look like by showing them work from previous students. Of course, the samples are from novels other than the ones they're reading. I also emphasize that high-quality notes cover ALL the pages, not just the first ten! When preparing the notes, I give students the choice of using sticky notes or writing directly on a sheet of paper. Besides the usual name, date, and hour, the paper must be headed with the title of the book and the page range due for that discussion. The paper is folded in half lengthwise to create two columns. The left-hand column is for questions, the right-hand column is for passages, and the reverse side is for connections. A separate blank sheet of paper is used for the illustration.

The First Discussion

Before the time for the first discussion arrives, you need to decide how you'll handle those who come unprepared. If you let the groups handle that issue in their ground rules, it's important for them to have a short meeting a day or two before that first discussion so that they can motivate each other to complete the reading and notes and also to review the consequences of being unprepared.

On discussion days I recommend planning some sort of ten-minute individual activity so that you have some time to take a quick look at the notes. You could always give them the time to read, but I've found a good ongoing assignment is writing a Character Journal based on what the students have read in their Literature Circle book so far.

A Character Journal encourages students to explore inferences related to character and examine multiple perspectives. They must write as that character would think. Though students can be assigned characters, they'll probably be more invested in the writing if they can choose the character. However, since this activity is designed to stretch the reader, you might add one requirement such as making the student choose a character of the opposite gender or choose a character that is most unlike the student's personality. Even with these guidelines, students sometimes turn their journals into summaries rather than ongoing explorations into character. If that happens, ask students to brainstorm what real people or fictional characters might put in a diary. You'll notice in the list below that "moment by moment account of what happened that day" is not included. While the students write their journal entries in their composition books, I take a walk around the room and briefly examine the notes.

After the notes are checked, it's time for the groups to move together. Between the Membership Grid, journal, and notes there should be enough there for at least a twenty-minute discussion. Keep in mind that English teachers can gab for hours about what they've read, but high school students aren't English teachers; it's always better to have them begging for more time rather than finishing early and then have extra time to start throwing wadded up candy wrappers at another group. For the first meeting, I use an agenda similar to this. My times are based on a 50–55-minute class period.

1. **Membership Grid** (5 minutes)
2. **Read Character Journals aloud and discuss** (5–10 minutes)
3. **Take turns guessing at, explaining, and asking questions about each other's illustrations** (5 minutes)
4. **Discuss questions, passages, connections** (10–20 minutes)
5. **Group Processing** (5 minutes). What were three things we did well today? What is one thing we can do differently so that our next discussion improves? Remind group members to thank each other before disbanding.
6. **Large Group Processing** (5 minutes)

---

1. Emotions/feelings
2. Memorable events
3. Fights
4. Gossip
5. Confessions
6. Personal problems and possible solutions
7. Depressing stuff
8. Death/loss
9. Friends, family
10. Secrets
11. Ideas/beliefs
12. Goals/future plans
13. Favorite things
14. Hopes and dreams
15. Missing scenes from the book
16. Relationships—what people did, what you wish they did

Figure 8.5   *Character Journal ideas*

Literature Circle Discussion Notes

Questions (spread out through assigned reading)

What would be interesting to discuss with others? Your questions need to reflect your thoughtfulness after reading and have the potential for extended discussion and follow-ups. Note the *page number* for each question. Below the original question *write three potential follow-ups* you might use.

Passages (spread out through assigned reading)

Pick passages that seem especially important, interesting, or puzzling. Record the *page numbers, passage locations,* and *three potential follow-up questions* that could direct thought and conversation about your passage. Be ready to read the passages aloud and explain why you chose them.

Connections

What does this story remind you of? Does it make you think of another story or novel you've read? An incident from your own life? Something in the news? A television program, movie, play? Jot down a *specific connection* and *notes that explain them.* Be ready to talk about them and tell your group the whole story.

Illustration

On a plain sheet of paper, sketch a picture related to your reading. This can be a drawing, cartoon, diagram—whatever. You can draw something that's specifically talked about in the reading, or something from your own experience or feelings, something the reading made you think about. Be ready to show your picture to your group and talk about it. On the back side, jot down the pages you were thinking about and some notes about the novel. **Make the drawings detailed and full page.**

Figure 8.6 *Literature Circle notes instructions*

Amy
9/21/00
1

5/5

Book 6

5/5

Questions

What posessed Helenus to say
that Diomedes was the best
of the Greeks & they didn't
even fear Achilles as much?
    p. 238 C1B

How come, in those times,
two rivals were so formal
and polite to their enemies,
even before dueling?
    p. 238 C2B + p. 239

In the Trojan War, Andromache
greatly supports Hector &
keeps him fighting. But in
this version, she's more
selfish & tells him not to
leave her famililess. Why is
this? p. 242 C1

Passages

p. 242 C2 paragraph 4:
  The similes in this passage
are awesome. The author
really reaches deep into this
scene & just spits it back
out at you in very loose, proud
vocab.

p. 240 C1 paragraph 3:
  I liked this passage because
the author expresses in
depth how Hecuba was
willing to offer her dresses to
Athena if she'd help the
Trojans. And I think it's cool
how its summed up by
simply saying, "But Athene
would not."

p. 238 C2 paragraph 3:
  I liked this passage
because it's really exaggerated.
Instead of just saying Hector
walked away, the author
really leaves a more developed
image in your mind.

Figure 8.7   *Student Literature Circle notes*

Literature Circle Notes Rubric

Questions	1	2
	• Neat • Original • Page number indicated • Meets quota • Open-ended • Spread out • Follow-ups if required	• Questions consistently reflect potential for prolonged, interesting, thoughtful discussion

Passages	1	2
	• Neat • Original • Page and location (T, M, B) indicated • Meets quota • Spread out/do not overlap questions • Notes on reason for choice • Follow-ups if required	• Notes explain choice and discussion potential in detail

Connections	1	2
	• Neat • Original • Meets quota • Connection to specific part of book • Notes	• Lots of specific details • Connection explained thoroughly

Figure 8.8 *Literature Circle rubric*

Vocabulary

1	2
• Neat • Original • Meets quota • Page number and location indicated • Correct definition for context	• Notes related to author's craft and context

Illustration

1	2
• Neat • Original • Fills the page • Some detail • Text location and caption on back	• Foreground and background details • Very detailed • Thought and effort apparent • Original—did not pick the most obvious image

Figure 8.8 *(Continued)*

Literature Circle Skill Accountability Rating

Assignment: _____ Date _____ Hour _____

Name _____   **1 – 2 – 3 – 4 – 5**

___ Support & Liking   ___ 12" voices
___ Focused on group members . . . On task   ___ Follow-up Questions
___ Actively using book and notes   ___ Encourages equal participa-
                                               tion and idea sharing

Name _____   **1 – 2 – 3 – 4 – 5**

___ Support & Liking   ___ 12" voices
___ Focused on group members . . . On task   ___ Follow-up Questions
___ Actively using book and notes   ___ Encourages equal participa-
                                               tion and idea sharing

Name _____   **1 – 2 – 3 – 4 – 5**

___ Support & Liking   ___ 12" voices
___ Focused on group members . . . On task   ___ Follow-up Questions
___ Actively using book and notes   ___ Encourages equal participa-
                                               tion and idea sharing

Name _____   **1 – 2 – 3 – 4 – 5**

___ Support & Liking   ___ 12" voices
___ Focused on group members . . . On task   ___ Follow-up Questions
___ Actively using book and notes   ___ Encourages equal participa-
                                               tion and idea sharing

Figure 8.9 *Literature Circle accountability ratings*

Literature Circle Skill Accountability Rating—*Advanced*

Chapters: _____ Date _____ Hour _____

Name _____   **1 – 2 – 3 – 4 – 5**

___ Support & Liking
___ On task . . . 12″ voices . . . using books/notes
___ Getting everyone's opinions
___ Extending/Disagreeing

___ Lead Questions/Passages/
Vocabulary/Illustration/
Connections
___ Follow-up Questions

Name _____   **1 – 2 – 3 – 4 – 5**

___ Support & Liking
___ On task . . . 12″ voices . . . using books/notes
___ Getting everyone's opinions
___ Extending/Disagreeing

___ Lead Questions/Passages/
Vocabulary/Illustration/
Connections
___ Follow-up Questions

Name _____   **1 – 2 – 3 – 4 – 5**

___ Support & Liking
___ On task . . . 12″ voices . . . using books/notes
___ Getting everyone's opinions
___ Extending/Disagreeing

___ Lead Questions/Passages/
Vocabulary/Illustration/
Connections
___ Follow-up Questions

Name _____   **1 – 2 – 3 – 4 – 5**

___ Support & Liking
___ On task . . . 12″ voices . . . using books/notes
___ Getting everyone's opinions
___ Extending/Disagreeing

___ Lead Questions/Passages/
Vocabulary/Illustration/
Connections
___ Follow-up Questions

Figure 8.9   *(Continued)*

Before the groups meet, I make it very clear to them the kind of behaviors I expect to see as I observe the groups. First, on a poster, overhead, or on the chalkboard, I make an "I'm Looking For . . ." list.

1. Desks touching.
2. Plenty of space between groups so that I can walk around and observe. Put the bags under the chairs.
3. Members focused only on each other.
4. Equal participation, taking turns.
5. Support and friendliness.
6. Books open, everyone on the same page.

Besides the general requirements of the list, I also give each group an Accountability Rating sheet. Each member signs his name in a blank. As I monitor the groups, I also try to do some specific observation, checking off skills being used, and jotting down exactly what students say or do that are specific examples of those skills. Though the number rating (1 is low and 5 is high) is always present on this form, I don't necessarily assign the number myself. Usually, I let each student rate himself along with a note explaining why. Direct observation for skill usage is an important guide for deciding on the following day's lesson. Also, your observations can be useful to the group during that end-of-discussion processing. Always leave some time for skill discussion, refinement, and review for the day following a Literature Circle.

The Day After that First Meeting

I usually schedule Literature Circle meetings for Tuesdays and Fridays and use some time during the in-between days to refine the discussion process so that, hopefully, each meeting will be better than the last one. I always make a point to set some time aside for large group processing, because usually time runs short at the end of Literature Circle meetings. After that first discussion, it's very helpful for the groups to share their processing in order to see what strengths and frustrations they have in common. Here are the lists one of my classes developed after their first discussion.

Things Done Well

1. Stayed on-task.
2. Used 12-inch voices.
3. Asked a lot of questions.
4. Encouraged each other.
5. Listened to each other's ideas.
6. Compromised on different answers.
7. Asked for sections to be reread.
8. Made good eye contact.
9. Didn't interrupt the speaker.
10. All our desks touched.

Things to Improve

1. Work faster.
2. Pay better attention to the speaker.

3. Ignore other groups.

4. Ask more questions.

5. Sit closer together.

6. Use 12-inch voices.

7. Have more fun.

8. Take turns reading aloud.

9. Share work evenly.

10. Include others.

These lists offer an interesting comparison: the same skill can be strong in one group yet weak in another.

After the whole class processing lists are compiled, groups need to gather for a quick meeting so that they can review their original improvement goal, possibly changing or modifying it so that they are working on the element most critical to improving their next discussion. Once the group goal is set, then they need to figure out three specific actions that all members can take to achieve the goal. Here are a few examples:

Goal: Include everyone equally

1. Let the person who talks the least go first.

2. Address each other by name.

3. Take turns in the discussion rather than letting one person ask everything from his notes.

Goal: Have more fun

1. Address each other by name.

2. Work on bringing more interesting passages and questions to discussion.

3. Give members compliments whenever they contribute positively.

Goal: Share work evenly (i.e., everyone comes prepared)

1. Call each other up and remind each other of what's due.

2. Tell the group exactly when you are going to do the assignment.

3. Celebrate with a treat if everyone is prepared.

Groups are more likely to own a problem and work together towards a solution if they are the ones who set the goal. Therefore, it is best that teacher intervention occur subtly. If a group asks for answers on how to solve a problem, turn it back to them first. If you return later and they are still stumped, ask them this question, "Would you like to hear how other groups have solved this problem?" Then give them some examples and leave so that the troubled group can develop its own plan. From this point on, goal review now becomes a regular part of each meeting agenda.

Literature Circle Meeting #2

For all meetings there are some constants, namely the "I'm Looking For . . ." list, the Literature Circle Accountability Rating form, the Membership Grid, and the Literature Circle notes. As groups progress, though, the meeting agenda begins to evolve.

1. **Membership Grid** (5 minutes). Don't be tempted to discard this activity once it seems that groups have bonded. This is a warm-up for the discussion to come. Talking about a silly, nonthreatening topic like what toppings you like on your pizza creates a friendly atmosphere that is much more conducive to the risk-taking necessary for sharing ideas in depth. During portfolio interviews, I am always surprised by the number of students that use an old Membership Grid as one of their artifacts. For them, the grid symbolizes the birth of some new friendships or at least the creation of some good working relationships. The grid gives students the excuse to talk to new people and get to know one another. I often notice that the grid notes get more detailed the longer students use the Membership Grid. I think this happens because as students get to know each other better, they become more interested in each other. Therefore, it's natural to ask more questions and get more details. This interest in the ideas of other members is what makes a Literature Circle discussion engaging.

2. **Read Character Journals aloud and discuss** (5–10 minutes). A variation of this might be for members to trade journals and respond in writing as if they were another character or possibly even the same character rereading the entry at a later date. Or, have the kids read the entry aloud without first disclosing the perspective and make the listeners guess which character it is by pointing out relevant clues.

3. **Review the goal and action plan from the last meeting** (5 minutes). Discuss how each person is going to meet that goal in today's discussion.

4. **Share Illustrations** (5–10 minutes). Take turns guessing at, explaining, and asking questions about each other's illustrations.

5. **Discuss questions, passages, connections** (10–20 minutes).

6. **Group Processing** (5 minutes). What were three specific things we did today that helped us meet our goal? What is one thing we can do differently so that our next discussion improves? What was an interesting idea that came up in our discussion that we could tell the rest of the class about? Remind group members to thank each other before disbanding.

7. **Large Group Processing** (5 minutes). If you have an extra five minutes, use it for a quick round-up of one positive accomplishment and one goal from each group.

The Following Day

Now students need to get back into their Literature Circles to discuss a couple of items. First, what solution worked best in helping the group meet its last goal? Everyone should put a star on his Processing Sheet by that item. Next, under the new improvement goal, which was agreed upon the day before during group processing, each person needs to come up with three specific things he can say or do to meet that goal. Last time the group came up with a group plan; this time each person comes up with his own plan. In the example below, one group decided they needed to ask more follow-up questions, so each person came up with three all-purpose follow-up questions she could use in the next discussion.

Goal: Ask more Follow-up Questions
1. Where did you find that?
2. How does that make you feel?
3. What did that make you think about?

This was one person's action plan. Ideally, each member would have different questions to truly extend the discussion.

Next, each group reviews how they will explain their interesting idea, also from yesterday's group processing, to the rest of the class so that everyone will understand their summary even though each group is reading a different book. I tell the students that this time there will be no volunteers; individuals will be chosen at random. A really good way to make the randomness fun is to get a transparency spinner. Have the kids number off, pick a group to start, and then spin; the number the pointer lands on is the one who stands up and addresses the audience. This is a great way to increase individual accountability. Aim for no more than a ten-minute large group discussion unless students seem really interested and involved. It's important to remember that all groups don't have to share in regards to each of the processing questions. Also, since this discussion is taking place while the kids are still in their groups, it's important that whoever "wins the spin" stands so that it's easier for the rest of the class to focus on the speaker. Equally important is for the audience to swivel around in their chairs or desks so that they are always trying to give the speaker eye contact. Do not let half the class sit with their backs to whoever is speaking; that is a recipe for nonlistening. Furthermore, as a teacher, if you let this behavior occur, the message being sent is that this large group discussion isn't very important anyway.

The rest of the time spent on those off-days depends on how the groups are doing. If some of the skills are sagging, I'll take some time to review a skill by looking back at an old T-Chart and getting the class to add more "Looks Like" details and "Sounds Like" phrases to the lists. Once in a great while those Membership Grids just don't do the job of creating blissful group harmony. I remember one class where half of the groups spent most of their meeting time angrily arguing over who was right. Those kids wanted to tear each other's throats out by the end of almost every Literature Circle meeting. Group processing time was spent finger pointing and blaming each other for the lousy discussion that just transpired. At first I thought those initial bad discussions were just isolated phenomena, but after a few more fiascos that approached fisticuffs, I woke up and realized a completely new skill needed to be discussed.

For some reason, this group of students all believed that there was only one correct interpretation of a text. To top it off, each student believed that his interpretation was the only correct one! First, I clued the kids in on the fact that different readers can have different responses, and in many instances, divergent views can both be valid. They needed to view conflicting perspectives as something that makes discussion interesting rather than something frustrating and negative. Plus, they needed to agree to disagree. Then I told them that rather than immediately falling into an argument mode, they needed to figure out how Follow-up Questions could help them investigate these differences of opinion productively. The groups put their heads together and brainstormed questions to ask when conflicting ideas arose. Once we had the master list, the class then divided them up into two categories: questions to ask when members disagree and questions to ask in order to better understand a member's idea. Though the students in that class never became buddies, their discussions began to progress beyond arguments and bad feelings. In the end, they were able create positive working relationships with each other.

Sophisticated Follow-up Questions: Disagreeing with an Idea

1. What makes you feel that you are right?
2. Why do you think that?
3. What parts of the text lead you to believe this?
4. What else could that passage/word mean that is different from what you said?

5. Where did you find this in the text? Give us some support for this idea.

6. I disagree. What about the instance in which . . .?

7. What examples are there that might also support this other viewpoint?

Understanding Another Person's Idea

1. What other parts of the story does this remind you of?

2. Where did you find that?

3. What information do you have to back this up?

4. What examples of this can you think of?

5. I don't understand; explain your idea in more detail.

6. How do you feel about this?

7. What did that part make you think about?

Sometimes groups reflect a higher level of skillfulness, which in turn requires less time for tune-ups. In that case, those off days can provide some time for whatever curricular agenda you wish to cover. I like to spend those days experimenting with the performance options I offer to students for planning their group Literature Circle projects. I'll cover those assessment options later in the chapter.

The Remaining Literature Circle Meetings

By the third meeting, the groups should have developed a certain rhythm and familiarity that often allows them to facilitate more in-depth discussion. Also, Literature Circle experience gives students direction in refining their notes so that better discussion is created. Starting with the third discussion, I encourage each group to develop its own discussion agenda. I've noticed that groups quickly fall into ruts, trudging through their questions on a death march towards their connections. Groups need to experiment with different ways to start. They might save the journals for last and start with each person's favorite passage, or each person might prioritize his discussion notes, picking only the best two items to bring up with the goal of using the text and follow-up questions to extend the discussion. At this point, after the day's agenda is set, I also encourage members to put their notes face down because what they bring up from memory will probably be more spontaneous. Of course they can return to their notes for a page reference. Here's a sample agenda for a later meeting:

1. **Membership Grid** (5 minutes). I keep on using the Grid because the routine is familiar and needs no explanation. However, if you have some other favorite icebreaking activities, use them. After all, variety is the spice of life!

2. **Negotiate the discussion agenda** (5 minutes). Now the group decides how they want to use their discussion materials. I encourage them to try a different agenda for each meeting. After an agenda is determined, all members write it down on their individual Processing Sheets.

3. **Review the goal and action plan from the last meeting** (5 minutes). Discuss how each person is going to meet that goal in today's discussion.

4. **Discussion** (15–25 minutes).

5. **Group Processing—Compliment Pass** (10 minutes). This activity works exactly like the Compliment Card processing described in Chapter 4. The only difference is that the

students pass their Processing Sheets around rather than an index card. Each member passes his Processing Sheet to the person to his right. That person compliments the owner of the paper on something specific that she said or did that helped the group that day. The writer signs his compliment. When everyone is finished writing, the papers are passed again. By the time the owner gets his paper back, he has a signed compliment from each member of the group. *Warning*: the compliment pass is a more advanced processing strategy, and the groups must really value each other in order to make it work. If you're worried that someone might break the trust with a nasty anti-compliment, continue with the simpler consensus style processing discussed here and in Chapter 4.

When a Literature Circle group concludes it's cycle, each student's Processing Sheet records the group's progression in regards to successful functioning and skills refinement. Figure 8.10 shows Dana's record of her meetings.

Literature Circles and Group Design

When troubleshooting Literature Circle dysfunction or, in "Emeril speak," just trying to "kick it up a notch," the place to start is with those five elements of group design. Groups that aren't working or are working at a minimal level, probably have weak or missing ingredients. If you were to look back at the Literature Circle agendas, you would find that they all had the following elements in common:

Positive Interdependence: The group needs each other to create a discussion. The better the discussion, the more students will have to write about in their journals or discussion reports, and the more knowledgeable they will be about the text when it comes to writing an essay or taking a test. Contributing to a good discussion is in everyone's best interest. Groups also have specific social skill goals. They must practice taking turns, reading from the text, and asking questions that require group members to elaborate and explain their ideas in greater depth.

Individual Accountability: Students need to complete the reading and have their notes ready on time for each meeting. While notes are checked, all students complete individual Character Journals. Each student keeps a Processing Sheet. Though groups set goals together, individuals also set skill goals and then work to achieve them. After a discussion, students write summaries or journals that highlight how well they listened to the ideas of others. When a Literature Circle concludes, students might complete a project together but each individual is also responsible for completing his own essay or test.

Social Skills: Students use checklists and processing to monitor and practice important skills such as asking Lead and Follow-up Questions, getting everyone's ideas, offering support and friendliness.

Group Processing: After each meeting, students reflect on the strengths and weaknesses of the group. If time allows, large group processing takes place so the class can compare problems and generate solutions. At the conclusion of a Literature Circle, each student writes an individual Processing Letter that focuses on accurately assessing that member's contributions to the group and setting new goals for improvement as a member of future groups.

Face-to-Face Interaction: Students focus on each other, sit far enough away from other groups so as not to be distracted, and engage each other in continual conversation via the Membership Grid, Illustration, Character Journal, and notes.

3/19/01   Members of Group #5

Dana
Rich
Lee
Val
Matt

Ground Rules

1. Keep an open mind to comments and questions.
2. Let everyone have a turn to talk.
3. Ask good follow-ups to further the discussion.
4. Do your homework.

3/20/01   Agenda

1. Grid
2. Passages
3. Questions
4. Connections

Skills We Want to Use Today

1. Getting everyone's opinion.
2. Asking follow-ups.
3. Taking turns.

3/23/01   Agenda

1. Grid
2. Illustration (save the last word for me)
3. Passages (save the last word for me)
4. Questions (mix 'em up—pick your best)
5. Connections

Three Specific Ways Today's Discussion Improved

1. We asked interesting lead questions.
2. Had fun and stayed on-task.
3. Asked a lot of follow-up questions.

Most used skill: Follow-ups
Least used skill: Reading passages aloud

3/27/01   Agenda

1. Grid
2. Goal setting (based on previous discussion weaknesses)
3. Questions

(continued)

Figure 8.10   *Completed Processing Sheet*

4. Illustrations
5. Best of connections and passages

Goal: Get around to all the different discussion starters (questions, passages, illustrations, connections)

3/30/01   Agenda

1. Grid
2. Choose a skill focus for the observer
3. Best of notes—make discussion lively, unpredictable

4/2/01   Becoming a Better Observer

1. Collect descriptive information
2. Watch for nonverbal messages (nods, smiles, etc.)
3. Don't try to record everything
4. Write down specific words/phrases that members say
5. Give each group member personal feedback

Today's goal: Work on using names

4/4/01   Agenda

1. Grid
2. Ways to make this discussion our best:
   - Everybody is encouraging and encouraged by others.
   - Everyone gets to give his opinion.
   - Don't interrupt somebody in the middle of a thought.
3. *Goal:* get more follow-ups
4. TKM Discussion

Observation Sheet Predictions   Before the observer shows the data, have the group make predictions for each of the following categories. After seeing the sheet, put stars by the predictions that were accurate and cross-out and correct those that weren't.

- Best Group Skill: Using Names *
- Weakest Group Skill: ~~Discussion Starters~~ Supporting answers with text
- Most Improved Group Skill: ~~Supporting answers with text~~ Asking follow-up questions
- Best Personal Skill: Asking follow-ups and using names *
- Weakest Personal Skill: Supporting answers with text *

Biggest Positive Skill Changes I Made in the Literature Circle

1. Talked a lot more—not so shy.
2. Staying on-task.
3. Keeping people involved by using names and asking specific questions.

Figure 8.10   *(Continued)*

Refining Literature Circle Skills

As the Literature Circles progress, I often notice that many groups have the same skill problems, so here are some strategies that are helpful. If the problem is contained to one group, gentle yet direct teacher intervention is the best course to take. Most of the time all you need to do is make an explicit statement such as, "I've noticed that only two people do most of the talking during a discussion. What could your group start doing differently so that everyone participates more equally? I'm looking forward to hearing your solutions. I'll be back in five minutes; be ready with them." When severe dysfunction occurs, it's best to interview each member separately and discreetly before deciding the best course of action. I once had a girl who ended up in a Literature Circle with another girl who had harassed her in junior high. No monitoring, T-Chart, or processing would have ever uncovered the root of the problem. In that case, allowing the girl to switch books and groups was the necessary solution. On the other hand, many times a majority of the groups will struggle with the same skill problem, so here are some skill tune-ups you can introduce during the off-days and then practice in the next discussion.

One person dominates the conversation.   Have students use "talking chips." Before the discussion begins, each member gets three or four chips. You can use poker chips, pennies, or squares of paper. Whenever a member answers a question or voices an opinion, he must surrender one of his chips. They can just be placed in the center of the table or each group can assign a banker. Once you're out of chips, you can only listen and ask Follow-up Questions until everyone else has used up his chips as well. Once all members are "out," the chips are redistributed and round two begins. After one or two discussions, the chips can be abandoned. By then, most groups develop a more even participation pattern.

Students are not using Follow-up Questions.   This might be a time when the teacher needs to assign the goal of increasing the number of Follow-up Questions asked during a discussion. Instead of a full Literature Circle meeting one day, students might break up into pairs in order to review Follow-ups using the drill activity mentioned earlier in the chapter.

It is also useful for a class to brainstorm different kinds of Follow-ups that can be used with different parts of the Literature Circle notes. Here is a list of questions that a class brainstormed for increasing the discussion about each person's illustration.

1. Why did you choose that character to draw?
2. What interested you about this part of the story?
3. Where was this in the story? What passage would you use for a caption?
4. What details would you have added if you had more time?
5. What feelings does this scene show?
6. What's another part of the story that would make a good illustration?
7. Which details in your drawing are most important to the story?
8. What were you thinking while drawing this picture?
9. How does your illustration show symbolism, irony, or a moral?
10. If you became a new character in the story, where would you be in the drawing? What would you be doing?

Before the next discussion, each member can pick the two or three questions he wants to use when discussing the illustrations of others. Be sure to challenge each group to think of some new questions that could be added to the master list.

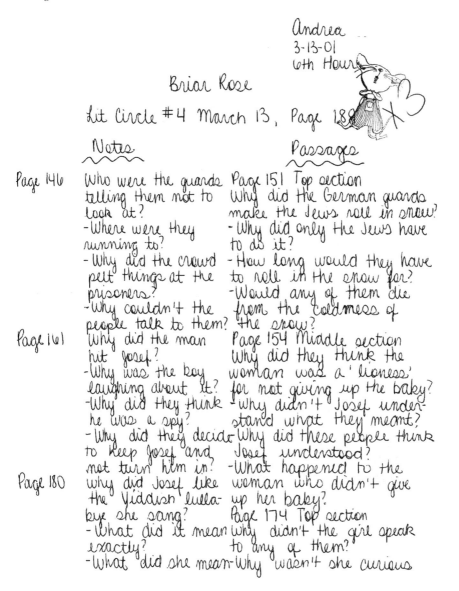

Andrea
3-13-01
6th Hour

Briar Rose

Lit Circle #4 March 13, Page 18

Notes	Passages

Page 146 — Who were the guards telling them not to look at?
- Where were they running to?
- Why did the crowd pelt things at the prisoners?
- Why couldn't the people talk to them?

Page 161 — Why did the man hit Josef?
- Why was the boy laughing about it?
- Why did they think he was a spy?
- Why did they decide to keep Josef and not turn him in?

Page 180 — Why did Josef like the Yiddish lulla-bye she sang?
- What did it mean exactly?
- What did she mean—

Page 151 Top section — Why did the German guards make the Jews roll in snow?
- Why did only the Jews have to do it?
- How long would they have to roll in the snow for?
- Would any of them die from the coldness of the snow?

Page 154 Middle section — Why did they think the woman was a 'lioness' for not giving up the baby?
- Why didn't Josef understand what they meant?
- Why did these people think Josef understood?
- What happened to the woman who didn't give up her baby?

Page 174 Top section — Why didn't the girl speak to any of them?
- Why wasn't she curious

Figure 8.11 *Student notes with Follow-ups*

Another way to get students to use more Follow-up Questions is to have them think while they are doing their notes of ones they might use with each of their lead questions and passages. Students can list the Follow-ups directly underneath the item or they can set up the paper in the two-column Lead and Follow-up format, using the left-side column for questions or passage notes and the right-side column for potential follow-up questions they could ask. This assignment forces students to imagine what kind of conversation their questions and passages might illicit. Hopefully, if they can't imagine any kind of conversation, they'll think of a new discussion item for their notes!

Students are coming up with weak connections.   Students seem to have a particularly rough time with this part of the notes. Many times students find making a connection to the text overwhelming because they think they have to connect with the entire text. A student might be reading a novel about the Holocaust and say, "I don't have anything to connect with. I've never been in a war, and I've never felt discrimination." What students fail to grasp at first is that connections can be much smaller. While most students have never experienced anything remotely like the Holocaust, most have lost a pet, a relative, been forced to be nice to relatives or family friends they detest, etc. Once students begin to understand this, their connections become much more personal, meaningful, and interesting.

Making good connections takes practice. Though personal connection is what makes reading come alive, many students don't automatically use this skill. A teacher modeling connections with her own reading is very instructive for the class. An important part of the modeling is describing the thought process behind the connection. Likewise, some students will be much more adept than others at making meaningful connections. Ask them to explain how they do it. What do they think about? The more students can share their thought processes with each other, the better they will all get at reading and making connections.

Students immediately explain their illustrations and passages rather than letting the others comment first.   A great way to solve this problem is using the strategy called "Save the Last Word for Me." Here are the steps:

1. One student shows her illustration or reads her passage aloud.
2. In turn, each student in the group explains why the passage was chosen or why the illustration was important to the story. Each student is challenged to add something new to the comments.
3. Once everyone else in the group has given his opinion, the student with the illustration or passage adds anything that wasn't already mentioned.
4. Before moving on to a new passage or illustration, the group asks some Follow-up Questions to get more information about the artist's thinking or the meaning behind the chosen passage.

Some groups finish earlier than others.   If everyone is finishing early, then consider shortening up the time or reviewing Follow-up Questions. If a group is finished a couple of minutes early, that's really okay as long as they can continue talking together as a group rather than breaking off into cliques or starting to distract other groups. If a group is consistently finished well before the others, it's a signal that the teacher probably needs to intervene directly. It might be because their discussion notes aren't very useful, they aren't using Follow-up Questions, or they just aren't interested in each other. In any event, once the real problem is uncovered, turn it back to the group to solve and then monitor them more closely in subsequent meetings.

If you notice it's a different group finishing early here or there, a universal back-up plan is helpful. On a day when Literature Circles are not meeting, have the class brainstorm questions or activities to pursue when they finish early. Have the kids copy the list and put it with their Literature Circle Processing Sheets. When that extra time arises, there should be lots more to talk about if they look back to the list. Here's part of a list my Novel class developed.

1. What's your favorite part from the story so far?
2. Based on what we've read so far, how do you think it's going to end?

3. Who is your favorite character? Why?

4. Everyone rereads a page and finds a new passage or vocabulary word to share/discuss.

5. What do you think the author thought about or experienced in order to write this story?

6. How do you feel about the story now compared to when we first started reading it?

7. Look through the text for literary devices: simile, metaphor, irony, symbolism, alliteration. After everyone finds one, discuss them.

8. What advice would you give each of the characters?

9. If this story were made into a movie or television show, how would the story need to be changed?

10. If this story were made into a movie, how would you cast it?

Some students read ahead of the rest of the group.   You'll probably be able to pick these kids out at the same time you hand the books to them, since because of SSR, you already know what kind of readers they are. Pull the speed readers aside for a chat. If you can, get them to agree not to read ahead. Have them mark the place they need to stop for each upcoming discussion with a sticky note or, better yet, put a rubber band around the "off-limits" pages as long as they can be trusted not to shoot someone's eye out with it! If they won't promise to quit reading, then at least make them promise not to ruin it for the slower readers. Kids hate it when a group member tells them how the book ends before they're even half-way through. Just a few weeks ago, I pulled a few kids from various groups to model a small group discussion. One student, who apparently had read *To Kill a Mockingbird* before, gleefully revealed story details to her group that wouldn't appear until six chapters later. After the demonstration, I asked the class to list discussion Do's and Don'ts. At the top of the "Don't" list was "Don't talk about parts of the book that the other members haven't read yet." Whenever the message can come from the class rather than from you, it is much stronger. From now on, I am going to purposely try to choose a "repeat reader" for demonstration, just so that the students can come to the conclusion that "spilling the beans" is never helpful to the group. A "repeat reader" is a valuable asset since a second or third reading will always reveal details never noticed on the first trip through a book. In the case of fast readers, remind them to skim through the assigned reading the night before a Literature Circle meeting so that they can remember what took place in that part of the story. Otherwise, these members will unwittingly reference story events in their answers that the other members haven't run across yet. Another option is to offer the fast reader a chance to read any of the other Literature Circle books as well, since his extended reading might offer the group the opportunity to discuss a different kind of connection.

Some students come unprepared.   Since more and more employers are making use of work teams out there in the business world, it's getting easier to find business books on the topic of teamwork. Christopher Avery makes an interesting point in his book *Teamwork Is an Individual Skill: Getting Your Work Done When Sharing Responsibility* (2001). He says that a work team can only be as strong as its weakest, least-motivated member. If I notice that preparation is an issue, I talk to the kids about workplace skills. On the days notes and reading are due, they write down the date and pages due in their composition books. Underneath that heading they write Asset or Liability. Then I tell them that a member will be an asset to her group if she's finished the reading, remembered and thought about the reading, and completed the notes with high quality. Someone is likely to be a liability if they've done less than what was due that day. Next, I have each student list as many specific contributions they think they can make to the discussion that day, keeping in mind that learning more about the book and gaining greater insight is a goal of a Lit Circle discussion. Finally, I have the kids go back to the words Asset or Liability, and I ask them, "Are you going to help your group learn more about the book or are you going to slow them down? You decide whether you will be an asset or liability to your group." I think it's really important that students acknowledge how lack of individual accountability hurts an entire group, not just themselves. The students who decide they are assets join their groups. The students who are insufficiently prepared need to take personal responsibility and decline to join the group of their own volition rather than making me call the shots. After all, they can more accurately estimate their possible contributions than I can. I instruct those who choose not to join the group to first figure out what's holding them back from being prepared, and then make a homework plan so that the subsequent preparation gets done.

While the Literature Circles are meeting, I also try to get to the solo workers to discuss their plans and encourage them to get back on track. The other thing I like about this approach is that sometimes, even though students haven't done all the work, they can still participate effectively as long as they finished the reading. Lisa wasn't much for completing her Literature Circle notes and often didn't finish the reading, but for her last meeting she chose to participate. Now, if it were up to me, I would have barred her because she had no notes. However, she did have a beautiful illustration from the last chapter of *To Kill a Mockingbird*. It was readily apparent that she had read, remembered, and paid attention to detail as she drew. Her picture created lots of discussion, and because she wanted to be with her group, she was highly involved, responding to the ideas of others and asking her own spontaneous questions.

Students know how to use the skills but need to use them more in discussion.   When students are starting to engage in Literature Circles or Books Talks, I always use a Skills Checklist as I observe and monitor the groups. Signing names on the sheet next to a specific role or a set of skills reminds students of the skills needed for a successful discussion and it seems to help them stick more closely to the academic task. However, as students become more experienced, I try to turn the observation and assessment over to them.

One of the best ways to help students focus on specific skills in order to increase their usage is through the use of an Observation Sheet. When this device is used, one student's main job is to observe the interaction of the remaining members, recording who is using what skills as well as jotting down any notes on specific things members say that are good examples of the skills being observed (Johnson 1998, 6:11). Though teachers are often concerned that an observer is shortchanged because he can't actively participate in the discussion, this is far from the truth, because the observer is engaged in a different kind of learning. Whoever observes leaves the experience with a heightened awareness of which skills are important and how those skills influence discussion. The next time that student is an active participant, he'll more than likely use the discussion skills he previously observed with greater fluency. Using observers and Observation Sheets is particularly useful when there are four or five people in a group since these sizes are conducive to those shadow members who the others forget to encourage. Also, taking one person out of the discussion completely shifts the discussion dynamics in interesting ways.

Since using an observer effectively is a more complicated strategy, steps must be taken so that students understand what to do. The best way to begin is by using a fishbowl demonstration where one group engages in a Literature Circle discussion while the rest of the class observes them. If every group has a different book, recruit one confident group to repeat its last Literature Circle discussion for the entire class. If you are using Literature Circle style discussions for a whole class book, choose students from different groups to repeat a discussion or use the demonstration in the place of a Literature Circle meeting. While the demonstration group is dragging

Figure 8.12   *Lisa's illustration of Boo Radley*

their desks into position, pass the Observation Sheets to the rest of the class. On the overhead, show them where to put the names of those being observed and how to record the skills being observed by using tic marks and notes. Then sit down with the observers and let the demonstration group proceed with about ten minutes of discussion. At the end of that time, thank the group and let them return to their original seats.

Now, the rest of the students tally the results from their individual observations. Students add the numbers across each row to determine how many times the group used each skill, and students add the numbers going down each column to determine how many times each person in the group participated while using the observed skills. Then we compare the results between students. When numbers widely differ, such as one student recording twelve Follow-up Questions while another student has thirty-three, we discuss what could have accounted for the difference in perception. It might turn out that one student counted all questions, while the other one didn't count Lead Questions or yes/no Follow-ups. What I try to emphasize is that, as an

OBSERVATION SHEET

DATE __5-14-01__   PERIOD __1__   OBSERVER __Brittany__

SKILLS	GROUP MEMBERS					TOTAL
	Kathryn	Joanna	Andy	Dana	Christine	
Follow-ups	||	||||	|||	|||	|||	16
Have Fun	||||| |	|||||||	|||||	||||| |	||||	28
New Discussion Starter	|||	||	||	||||	|||||	16
Keep Everyone Involved	||||	|||	||	||	|||	14
Using Names	|||| |||| ||||||||	||||| ||||| |||| ||||	||||| ||| ||	||||| ||||| ||||	||||| ||||	71
TOTAL	34	36	22	29	29	

OBSERVATION NOTES:

"What do you think, Kathryn"
"Christine should explain it"
"Joanna move back"
"Andy we haven't heard from you"
"Christine, what do you think?"
"I can't hear"
"Everyone listen"

"Christine, why don't you go"

"Any concluding thoughts"

Figure 8.13   *Observation Sheet data*

observer, you have to be clear on how you are defining a skill and then be consistent in your recordkeeping. We also talk about whether observing was easy or difficult. Often, some students will notice that for a while they forgot to observe because they became focused on the content of the conversation. Another will comment on how hard it is to keep up; while you're trying to decide where to record a comment, the discussion keeps moving forward. It's important for students to know that they'll never catch everything, but they need to be as accurate as possible with what they do record. We end the analysis by looking at the numbers, trying to detect discussion patterns and skill strengths and weaknesses.

OBSERVATION SHEET

DATE _____ PERIOD _____ OBSERVER _____

SKILLS	GROUP MEMBERS				TOTAL
TOTAL					

OBSERVATION NOTES:

Figure 8.14 *Blank Observation Sheet*

Once I start using Observation Sheets, I try to use them in at least four or five consecutive Literature Circle meetings so that everyone gets a chance to be observed several times and be an observer at least once. Always choose the skills you really want to emphasize as the ones being observed. It's best not to try to observe for more than four or five skills at a time. When groups are using Observation Sheets, I collect them and make a photocopy for each member. Being able to set them out side-by-side is a useful tool when students begin to analyze their own skill growth. Also, as students get more adept in the use of Observation Sheets, I let each group decide which skills will be observed. Here is a list of observable skills that one class brainstormed.

Observable Skills

- Using quiet voices
- Directing the group's work
- Describing personal feelings/reactions to the reading
- Paraphrasing
- Using the text to support an idea
- Being friendly and supportive
- Recognizing good ideas
- Energizing the group
- Disagreeing with ideas respectfully
- Asking follow-up questions
- Using names
- Taking turns to start discussion with one's notes
- Answering questions

Trial and Error

Probably one of my most personally humiliating moments of epiphany came at the hands of Edye Holobec Johnson, a fact that I never revealed to her until now. I was enrolled in a week-long summer course entitled *Advanced Cooperative Learning*. I had that beginner course under my belt, I had been diligently using cooperative learning for a whole year, and, boy, did I know everything! To top it off, I was the best cooperative group member anyone could ask for; just ask me! Of course, it did not take long for my own hubris to take me down a few notches.

Mid-week we were practicing using groups with observers. Because I was such a *useful* group member, I let someone else volunteer to be the observer. Our group task was to rank items necessary for survival in the dead of winter after a plane crash. We had five active participants and one observer. Though I can't remember all of the skills observed, the two that stick out now were "Encouraging the Contributions of Others" and "Giving Information." As I recall, another woman and I did most of the talking. We had lots of opinions and did not hesitate to share them. As a matter of fact, we had so much to share we never even bothered to ask the rest of the group members if they knew anything about winter camping or cold weather survival. Our domination reduced the rest of the members to shadows. One woman who we totally ignored kept murmuring, "I've done this exercise before; the steel wool is important; it needs to be ranked near the top." Did we listen? Of course not, we were too busy talking!

When we scored the rankings, our group froze to death because we had discarded the one item that would have helped us start a fire: the steel wool. Then it was time to look at the Observation Sheet. I think I had "Giving Information" checked off about eight hundred times and "Encouraging the Contributions of Others" two times. How pathetic. I was mortified! If I had only listened to that woman who SAID she had done this ranking before, we would have lived! From that time on, I've tried my best to hear others before trying to be heard.

Moral: Teach your students that listening and asking follow-up questions might be more important than voicing every thought and opinion that comes to mind. The Observation Sheet is just the tool to drive this point home!

How Do I Assess This?

When I assess students during Literature Circles, I think of assessment in terms of four categories: preparation, participation, idea expansion (thinking deeply in a new way), and summation.

Preparation

Each time students meet in their Literature Circle, their notes are turned in and evaluated by me. Remember the stamp system I described earlier? Literature Circle notes plus the illustration are worth up to three stamps. When I scan the notes, I look for legibility, good discussion questions, page references, full coverage of the assigned reading, and opinion details related to the passages, and connection. I make sure that students have some good samples and a rubric to work from (see Figures 8.6 and 8.8). If there's time at the end of a meeting, I like to have the students do a self-evaluation and explain how their notes contributed to the day's discussion. After all, that's the whole point of doing the notes! Few students can successfully argue their notes' usefulness when they must defend why their questions were all fact-oriented and their passage selections were all from the first three pages. With the illustration, I'm looking to see if they followed the directions. Does it fill the page? Are there lots of details? True artistry is not the issue; it's whether the illustration reflects time, effort, and thinking. If lots of extra effort is apparent, I'll award an extra point if I'm feeling generous. Stamped notes get stored in the Reading section of the binder.

Before you panic and think, "Oh my goodness, I don't want to have to read all of these," keep in mind that I used the word "scan" not "read." Once you know what you're looking for, it's easy to move through a class set in about fifteen minutes. But, let's say you don't even want to do that. Figure out how you can collect them at random. When the kids say, "Are you going to grade these?" just reply, "I haven't decided yet." Collect the notes some days but not all days. I follow-up more closely on the kids that tend to be unprepared. However, before you get too lackadaisical about all this, I strongly recommend that you regularly inspect the notes from at least the first two meetings so that you can get the kids on the right track of creating truly useful discussion notes.

Participation

I've already mentioned two "gradable" ways to assess participation: direct observation via Observation Sheets and ongoing post-discussion group processing. After any discussion using Observation Sheets, I collect them from the observers and make photocopies for each group member. These are stored in the Leadership section of the binder so that they can be easily accessed for goal setting or examination of group skill progression. I collect the individual Processing Sheets every few discussions and stamp each entry. Current Processing Sheets get stored in Miscellaneous for easy retrieval. Once a Literature Circle cycle is completed, these sheets go into Leadership. Another assessment, though a more informal one, is the sharing during the large group processing which takes place at the end of a Literature Circle meeting or the following day.

Sometimes, particularly when working with older students, I use another form of participation self-assessment by having students write more detailed reflections in their composition books, reflections which describe the course of the interactions among the group members. The composition books work particularly well for this because they keep the entry dates in order. In the end, when students look back at the entries in order to draw some final conclusions about their group's interactions, these entries become chapters that chronicle their Literature Circle experience. When requiring a post-discussion journal, I use some specific prompts. The thing

5/6   Group Discussion Reflection

Present: Rhonda & Melissa

I felt comfortable with Rhonda and Melissa. They helped me understand things that were confusing me. We shared good ideas about the possible plot of the book. We also discussed our opinions on the book, whether we liked it or not. I need to work on letting other people answer questions. When a question is asked, I always am the first to answer.

5/10   Group Discussion Reflection

Present: Rhonda & Melissa

I felt even more comfortable. This discussion was based on opinions. We talked about what we thought was going to happen, what we wanted to happen, and what we thought of what had happened already. Today I did not answer as fast. I wanted to see if anyone else had something to say. If they did, I let them talk. If they didn't, I talked. We had a great discussion.

5/10   Group Discussion Reflection

Present: Rhonda & Melissa

Today was the best discussion yet. We discussed so many confusing ideas. We all helped each other understand better. I let everyone answer, but also answered some questions myself. We discussed what the author went through to write this story. Our group never argues; we get along great.

5/12   Group Discussion Reflection

Present: Rhonda, Melissa, & Jennie

This discussion was not so good. One member told the rest of us that we were stupid and she didn't like us. I thought this was ignorant and rude and said so, but ever since this incident everything has been fine. We discussed the book's humor. We also talked about next week's assignments. I didn't talk as much, maybe because of the remark made by that one person. Whatever the reason, it was a good time to allow the others to give their opinions. Next time my goal is to not get involved in an argument.

5/17   Group Discussion Reflection

Present: Rhonda, Melissa, Jennie, Nicole

This discussion was a lot better from last time. The one person I mentioned didn't say anything rude. I think maybe she realized I wouldn't listen to it because last time I told her she was ignorant. But anyway, we all discussed opinions about the conclusion of the book. Some of us thought McMurphy would remain in the hospital and some of us thought he would escape. We also discussed the essay questions a bit. It was a good discussion.

Figure 8.15   *Julie's Literature Circle reflection journal for* One Flew Over the Cuckoo's Nest

that needs to be emphasized most as students record their experiences is to describe them in as much detail as possible. What was said? Which skills were being used? How did you know it? Giving specific examples is what makes these journals useful in the end because upon rereading students can really remember specific discussions.

Group Discussion Reflection

When writing, consider/reflect on:

Strengths

Weaknesses

Emerging patterns

Successful skills/techniques/plans

Breakthroughs

Personal improvements

How problems were solved

Interesting ideas

It never hurts to use student samples to show what a good journal looks like. A way to improve this kind of reflection is to get the crayons out after a few entries (remember the question coding activity from earlier in this chapter?) and have the kids highlight the anecdotal evidence and specific details that illustrate their descriptions of each group meeting. This exercise sends an immediate message to the students who write in vague, general terms because they won't be doing much coloring. How to recall and cite anecdotal evidence is another minilesson to address during a Literature Circle off-day. Students can offer a few of their general interaction descriptions and the entire class can brainstorm what kind of descriptions or stories would illustrate them. I also recommend that if you choose to use this journal approach, tell students to examine problems objectively and not slam other students; avoid using names. That's another reason to show some good examples before embarking on this assignment.

The nice thing about the journals is that they lead directly to a concluding activity I often use called a Processing Letter, previously mentioned in Chapter 4. The letter is addressed to me and is written after the conclusion of a Literature Circle cycle. Its focus is a series of questions that, hopefully, get kids to look back at the participation artifacts they've stored in the Leadership section of the binder. In order to write a good letter, students need to re-examine their group Processing Sheets and large group processing notes. Journal reflections and Observation Sheets, if used, provide further evidence from which some conclusions can be drawn.

Idea Expansion

A problem that sometimes arises in Literature Circles is that a few students will think they know everything and there is no point listening to the opinions of others because all opinions are inferior to their own. The flip side of this is the student who doesn't pay much attention to anything anyone says, whether it's his opinion or someone else's. In both cases, some individual accountability is needed to increase the value of listening to those diverse opinions. Unfortunately, the only way I've figured out how to get kids to document their idea gathering is through writing about it. The good news is that these pieces of writing don't need to be very long nor do they need to be done after every discussion. Before a meeting begins, I always remind students to remem-

Literature Circle Processing Letter

DIRECTIONS: Write a letter to me, Mrs. Steineke, thoughtfully answering the following questions. Use complete sentences and a separate paragraph for each question. Fragments, one-word answers, or cryptic responses will receive no credit. Your letter should be at least a page long and needs to answer each question thoroughly, using specific events/anecdotes for evidence.

1. How would you rate your most recent group? What were your group's strengths and weaknesses? Out of all the groups this semester, which one worked together the best? How do you explain it? What skills did this group have that the others were missing? Tell me about some specific successes; explain using specific anecdotes. What problems arose? How did you deal with them? If the solutions did not work, what would you do differently the next time?

2. Examine your group Processing Sheet and Observation Sheets carefully. How have you changed and grown as a contributing group member? What are your best skills? What is your weakest skill? What do you need to start doing differently so that you continue to improve and grow as an effective group member?

3. Later in the semester, we will once again be moving into Literature Circles. From working in the last group, how would you try from the very start to make this group enjoyable and academically productive? If it were up to you, what should be the ground rules that everyone functions under? What skills would you want to emphasize?

4. What's new in your life? What's happening in your other classes? What have you been up to since the last Processing Letter?

Figure 8.16 *Processing Letter instructions*

ber the prompts and their need for listening to others carefully just in case they may be writing about it. Here are some prompts I often use:

1. What did people talk about when they looked at your illustration? What was something you hadn't thought about before during this conversation? Which illustration did you find the most interesting? Why?

2. Which of your passages created the best discussion? What did people talk about? When other people read their passages and discussed them, what was something you hadn't thought about or noticed before?

3. Describe an interesting idea that originated from a recent Literature Circle discussion. Describe the discussion progression in detail.

Once again, I'm looking for specific details concerning what took place in a discussion. The better the student listens and pays attention to his group members, the better he will be able to write about the ideas discussed. Sometimes, I have students write a short discussion summary at the conclusion of a meeting. If time permits, students can write them during the last few minutes of the period; otherwise, they are done as homework. When a student remembers the specific academic contributions of others, it shows she's been a good listener.

9/28/01   Discussion Report

Today was a very good discussion, for everyone was very well prepared to answer each other's questions. We talked about the arrival of Aunt Alexandra. We wondered if Atticus had really told her to come or if she kind of invited herself. We don't think Atticus wanted her to come and tell him he is raising his kids poorly and to get rid of Cal. We talked about how Cal kind of has two personalities, one with the Finches and one with the Black people. We wondered how Dill really got to Maycomb after running away because Dill lies a lot, so it is hard to believe what he has to say. We also talked about how Scout isn't afraid to say or do anything in front of others. All together, it was the best discussion so far.

Allison

Figure 8.17   *Allison's discussion report on* To Kill a Mockingbird

Another kind of writing, the Discussion Journal, helps students record how their ideas and opinions change in the course of reading and discussion. In the example on the next page, Jill recorded her thoughts as she and her group worked their way through the often perplexing novel *One Flew Over the Cuckoo's Nest* by Ken Kesey. Though the wording reflects the roughness of a first draft, the evolution of ideas through the entries creates a map of the reader's changing opinions in regards to the book, as well as an illustration of how important a discussion group becomes when the reading is challenging.

A slightly different route to text insight and reflection is the Literature Circle Pen Pal Letter. This is an idea I've used when I've had two or more classes reading the same books. Each student writes to a member of the corresponding Literature Circle in the other class. I tell students to write about what they think of the book so far, anything interesting that their group has thought about, and what questions they have thought about as they've read. On the day the letters are due, students bring in three copies: one to keep, one for me, and one for their pen pal. The following day I distribute the letters and the students write back. This can be done in class or at home that night. A couple of days later, the students get their return letters. Kids always enjoy this assignment and it's a way to get more conversation going about a book outside of class, since students often seek out their pen pals for further discussion. The examples on the following pages are somewhat of an anomaly. A trio of senior girls in my 7th hour Novels class chose to read *The Rainmaker* by John Grisham, but they had no matching group in the other class. Since I had wanted to read that book anyway, I became the unofficial fourth member of their Literature Circle. Whenever the other groups looked like they were functioning well without my monitoring, I would join the Grisham group. Of course, I had my sticky notes ready! When it came time for the Pen Pal Letters, that group corresponded with me.

The thing I like best about Pen Pal Letters is that they're fun. Even though students have to do a significant amount of thinking about the text in order to come up with interesting points and questions, there is only positive feelings apparent when students get a letter in response to their own. After a round of Pen Pal Letters, the most frequently asked question is "When are we going to write back?"

5/7/93   Pre-Discussion

The story is starting out pretty slow, so it is not that exciting. I don't think the main person, McMurphy, is really crazy. He just wants to get into the mental home and change it. He seems like the type of person that wants to take charge all the time. Maybe the book will get better once the characters start getting some action. Otherwise, this whole book will pretty much suck because it does already. The only good thing about this book is the fact that the author wrote a lot of it under hallucination, so it's interesting to see what kind of things he can come up with. Hopefully, something better than what I've read so far will happen. Otherwise, this book is probably going to be a waste of time.

5/11/93   Post-Discussion

After reading the first couple chapters, I started to enjoy the book a little more. The characters seemed to pick up with interest and the action seemed to pick up the pace After the discussion with my partners, I gained some useful insight on what McMurphy is actually doing and how the Big Nurse thinks and reacts. I also gained some information on how Chief thinks. I really didn't understand how the Chief thinks concerning the white fog and how the black boys mistreated him while shaving and washing him. After discussing my partners' responses, I realized the points of the book I was missing out on.

5/13/93   Post-Discussion

After the second discussion I was able to understand the story a little bit better. McMurphy now has pretty much established his place in the institute, and the battle has begun between McMurphy and the Big Nurse. McMurphy had begun to influence the other patients into doing what he wanted. I recognize the actions the Big Nurse is taking. She does not appreciate how someone is belittling her authority and making things run out of sync. That is how some teachers seem to run classes. People don't appreciate it when others run things the way they don't like it. That's why I feel the war between McMurphy and Big Nurse began.

5/17/93   Post-Discussion

After each discussion I realize that I learn more and more about this book. I really do enjoy this book because it's interesting to read about the brave and wild things that McMurphy does. I admire the way he stands up to the Big Nurse. I think that's what the world needs most: people that will stand up for what they believe is right. I like people that aren't afraid to take a stand and voice their opinions. Our discussions made me realize that that is what the book is really trying to say. People need to stay awake and take charge of their lives. Otherwise, people will continue to run things their way for you and take advantage of you for their own personal benefits of gain and power.

5/19/93   Post-Discussion

It has now become very clear to me after our group discussions that no matter what happens, authority can pretty much overrule everything and everyone. The Big Nurse had such power of

(continued)

Figure 8.18   *Jill's Discussion Journal*

the institution that she literally ran the patients' lives. I feel one very important fact was learned after reading this book and discussing it: people should not allow others to run their lives for their satisfaction. Everyone should have a say in what happens in his life. People, even mentally unstable ones, need to be respected and not treated like robots that are trained and manipulated by any other authority figure.

5/25/93   Post-Discussion

I'm really happy we read this book. I found it highly entertaining and intellectually stimulating. The characters, especially McMurphy, had such a unique outlook on life, even if it was in a crazy, irrational way. However, I do believe that in most cases, authority will rule the majority of the time. Somehow the people with the most power will usually come out on top, even if it's for the worse. A lot of unfairness occurs to people who have the best intentions for others. They are trying to help make a difference and make the world a better, more respectable place to be. That is what McMurphy tried to do.

Figure 8.18   *(Continued)*

Nancy Steineke
12/15/96
7th Hour
The Rainmaker

Dear Readers,

Right now my cat, Cleopatra, is doing her best to sabotage my typing by nudging my hands with her nose and stepping on the keyboard, but I'll do my best to try to pull my thoughts together.

First of all, I was somewhat surprised by how entertaining this novel is so far. The last Grisham novel I read was *The Chamber,* and that novel took itself *very* seriously. By the time I was finished, I had learned a lot about the arguments against the death penalty, but I can't say that I was very entertained. The only novel by Grisham that I haven't read so far is the one that is still out only in hardcover. One of the things that's different about this book is that it is written in present tense and first person. I'm not sure, but I think this is a departure from the previous novels. If it isn't, then this is the first narrating character that I've found engaging.

Speaking of Rudy, I still can't figure out how he made it all the way through law school considering how much he seems to loathe his colleagues, fellow students, classes, lawyerly practices (looking for business in the hospital cafeteria), etc. Although he said he did it just to spite his father, his father has been dead for years. Maybe Rudy likes being a lawyer better than he's letting on at the moment, or he's just tremendously stubborn. How did you feel about him starting to befriend that abused wife, Kelly, he met at the hospital? As I read that part, I couldn't decide whether she was pathetic or manipulative or both. However, I do think Rudy is nuts to continue that relationship in any way, shape, or form. Kelly's husband is *very* dangerous, and I

(continued)

Figure 8.19   *Literature Circle Pen Pal Letter*

don't doubt for a moment that he would not hesitate to kill Rudy and Kelly if he thought there was something going on between them.

What do you think about Miss Birdie? She's another one who has more to her than she's letting on. On page 116 she off-handedly mentions that she's done twenty wills already and knows all about them. What is that all about? Also, all of that money her second husband left her when he died. I've got the feeling that this money was gotten illegally. Otherwise, why would Birdie keep it a secret and even refuse to spend it? She definitely could hire a full-time gardener and not have Rudy hauling those bags of bark chips around. Is she afraid of spending the money for some reason, or is she just too cheap?

Finally, why do you think the Lake firm got torched? (Jill, don't spill the beans; try to remember what you were thinking the first time you read it.) Though I don't think Rudy was involved directly, does it have something to do with that insurance case he handed over to them?

Looking forward to hearing from you,

Mrs. S.

Figure 8.19   *Literature Circle Pen Pal Letter (Continued)*

12/16/01

Dear Mrs. Steineke,

I think this novel is very entertaining as well. I think it's entertaining because the characters are written down to earth and you kind of feel like you know them. I have read other Grisham novels such as *The Firm, The Client*, and *The Pelican Brief*. I enjoyed all of those books, but they were all much more serious, like you stated about *The Chamber*.

I also don't understand how Rudy could stay in law if he hated it. I just can't believe he'd devote himself to such a difficult, time-consuming career just because of his father. I do not think Rudy should get involved with Kelly because she has a lot of emotional problems which I do not think Rudy can handle. Also, she has that psycho husband who could hurt Rudy.

Miss Birdie is a very strange character. She seems to be very with it for her age and very smart. However, if she is so smart, why doesn't she let Rudy in on some information about her money if he is going to draw up her new will? I also thought that the money was somehow illegal. I don't think Miss Birdie would have done anything illegal. Maybe her husband did something, but I don't think she knows about it. I never thought Miss Birdie was hiding anything serious about the money. I just think she is a cheap old lady who knows how to get the good end out of the deal.

I thought the Lake Firm got torched to cover up some type of scandal, maybe about the insurance case. I never thought that Rudy torched the firm because he just seems too good to do that.

Jill

Figure 8.20   *Literature Circle Pen Pal Response*

Ideas for Replacing the Unit Test

Summative assessment takes place after all groups have finished their books. I like this assessment to be a combination of individual and group activities. Some ideas follow.

Final Letters

Just as the ongoing group processing can serve as notes towards a final Processing Letter, the shorter pieces of discussion content writing mentioned in the Idea Expansion section can contribute to a final content-oriented letter, which takes the place of the traditional final. Letters make nice reading for the teacher because they can take on a more personal tone and voice, something often absent in the more traditional essay forms. However, like those traditional forms, students can still focus on all of the conventions that they normally need to use such as paragraphing, topic sentences, supporting details, correct grammar and punctuation, correct format. You'll notice that I am very firm in my directions about length. As you have probably found, many students have mastered the art of going on for pages without saying much. After years of wading through this muck in the search of a cogent thought, I finally concluded that having to write with brevity and conciseness creates a much more challenging assignment since students have to make every word count.

The letter example in Figure 8.22 was written by a freshman student after her Literature Circle had finished discussing two books that connected with the class novel *To Kill a Mockingbird*.

These photos show a student group acting out their tableau scenes from To Kill a Mockingbird. *In scene #3, Calpurnia calls Atticus to warn him of the mad dog. In scene #6, Atticus, Calpurnia, Heck Tate, Jem, and Scout look on after Atticus has shot the dog. The accompanying scripts for these tableau scenes can be found on page 187.*

Literature Circle Letter

Counts as a Test!

Directions: Write a letter to me, Mrs. Steineke, that is interesting and also convinces me that you spent some time thinking about your book and your discussions. Your letter will have three paragraphs, each focusing on one of the following questions. Your letter should be one-page long, no longer, 1″ margins all around, 12-point Times New Roman, letter format. Don't forget to sign your name!

1. Describe an interesting idea that originated from one of your Literature Circle discussions. What was the initial topic/question? What ideas were presented? How did it relate to the text? How did you think differently after you listened to the ideas of others?

2. Explain a specific connection between your Lit Circle book and another book that we have read as a class or one that you have read on your own this year. Be sure to show depth of thought in your explanation. Use lit circle text references.

3. Explain a point that explores a feeling of yours related to the book. Below are some topic ideas; however, these are just suggestions.

   • How did this book make you feel after you finished reading it? What did it make you think about that you hadn't thought about before?

   • What connections can you make between this book and your own life?

   • To what degree were you involved with the characters and their actions?

   • I think the relationship between ___ and ___ is interesting because . . .

   • I like / dislike (name of character) because . . .

   • Why or why not would you recommend this book to other readers?

This paper will be counted as a 100 point test. We will not be spending class time on this; it must be done for homework. Since final draft quality is expected, I strongly suggest that you use the following writing process: outline or other form of detailed notes, rough draft, final draft.

Point Break Down:

Question #1	25 points
Question #2	25 Points
Question #3	25 points
Conventions	25 points
Total	**100 points**

Figure 8.21   *Literature Circle Letter directions*

May 21, 2001

Dear Mrs. Steineke,

Our Literature Circle read two books, *Montana 1948* by Larry Watson and *Spite Fences* by Trudy Krisher, but one of our most interesting discussions occurred while reading *Spite Fences*. It started off when Lee asked, "How do you think Maggie was feeling when Virgil was trying to rape her?" This question made our group explode with answers. The thought of fear came into play. She felt fear of her mother because of the laundry that was strewn over the dirty ground. Virgil caused most of her fear. Val brought up, "She might have been thinking of escape. She was thinking of how she could get out of the situation without hurting herself more. She was thinking of hurting him also." This coincided with Gina's idea . . . revenge! "Maggie was probably having thoughts of murder, how she could hurt Virgil without any consequences." When Gina brought that up, I was taken aback. I never thought of Maggie thinking of revenge as Virgil was molesting her. It put a different perspective on her character and her innocence. This discussion made me think about the different views that characters in books can have.

The second thing I would like to bring up is another part of our discussion. This specific part showed a connection between *Montana 1948* and *To Kill a Mockingbird*. Jill felt the father in each book showed characteristics that were very similar. "Atticus and Wesley were both reserved. They felt it was their duty to have their children on the correct path and were always willing to teach a lesson." Lee seemed to disagree with Jill when she first brought up that connection. Lee said, "I think the complete opposite!" However, once Jill described her point of view more thoroughly, everyone understood the comparison and agreed with her. I also brought up two particular scenes in which the fathers were alike. In *Montana 1948*, Wesley has to take charge of the situation when he finds out that his brother has been molesting Indian girls. Wesley arrests Frank, his own brother, and tries his hardest to do the right thing. In *To Kill a Mockingbird*, Atticus tries to do the right thing by defending Tom Robinson even though he knows that it will expose his family to ridicule and possible danger. In both cases, the characters needed a lot of courage to make those decisions. Everyone agreed that this connection was one of great importance.

The third point I'd like to make is a feeling I acquired while reading *Spite Fences*. One thing that bothered me in particular was the character of Maggie Pugh. She was the main character in the book. She caused me distress because I felt she was so unlike me. While reading, I wanted to reach into the book and give her some common sense! I hated that she didn't do anything about her mother beating her. She told her best friend, Pert, but that did little in the long run. Her mother needed a slap in the face from Maggie herself. Maggie should have left the house in the beginning of the book, not in the last section. The whole situation with Virgil made me feel sadness towards Maggie, but I wish she would have reacted more quickly and run away. The best thing would have been to talk to the police after the first incident! I wanted to give her some confidence and make her gain respect from others. I think her character really enhances the book; my strong feelings were actually the reason I kept reading.

Rachel

Figure 8.22   *Literature Circle Letter–student example*

Literature Circle Letter Rubric

Discussion	3	4	5
	• Topic introduced in first sentence • Stays on *one* topic • Some description of "who said what" • Concluding sentence	• Describes evolution of conversation in detail • Shows members ideas/viewpoints	• Cites strong text details to connect with discussion points • States how personal interpretation changed as a result of hearing other ideas

Text-to-Text Connection	3	4	5
	• Topic sentence introduces comparison • Clear comparison between 3 novel incidents and 3 details from connection text • Concluding sentence	• Reflects repeated reading of connection text in the thought and details discussed • Comparisons explained in greater depth	• Shows in-depth thought/feelings/personal opinion when comparing details from novel and connection text

Figure 8.23 *Literature Circle Letter rubric*

Personal Opinion	3	4	5
	• Topic introduced in first sentence • New topic versus rehash of something discussed earlier • Opinion points are clearly stated • Some specific details from novels • Concluding sentence	• Traces topic through entire story	• Personal interpretation clearly and thoroughly explained • Opinion backed up by strong, specific text details

Conventions	3	4	5
	• All words spelled correctly • No homophone errors • Complete sentences • Complete paragraphs • Writing is clear, easy to follow • Book title underlined/italics	• Correct comma usage • No run-ons, comma splices, or fragments	• Error free

© 2002 by Nancy Steineke from *Reading and Writing Together*. Portsmouth, NH: Heinemann.

Figure 8.23 (*Continued*)

The Traditional Five-Paragraph Essay

Coming up with something worthwhile that fills an extra long final exam period is always a challenge when students have spent most of the semester in Literature Circles. One super-duper long Scantron test just won't do the trick. That's when I thought of this idea for my second-semester seniors who had already been showing serious signs of senioritis since the beginning of fourth quarter. Besides finishing up discussion of the novel, the other Literature Circle assignment for the last meeting was to come up with three good essay-style questions on their book that could be turned into a five-paragraph essay. The questions had to reflect the entire book rather than one portion. I told the groups that they could create and discuss the questions together, but the group didn't have to reach a consensus. Each member was free to choose the three questions he would be most interested in writing about. At the end of the period, students wrote their questions in their composition books and also on index cards. As I collected the cards, I told them that on the day of the final exam, I'd return the cards with one of the three questions circled. That question would be the topic of their essay. Therefore, they would be best prepared if they thought about and took notes on all three questions. Here are some examples of the group-generated questions.

One Flew Over the Cuckoo's Nest
- Why did the patients need McMurphy in order to realize they didn't need to be hospitalized?
- Do you think McMurphy has helped or hurt the other patients' chances of becoming well again?
- In the end, who do you think really won the battle: Big Nurse or McMurphy?

The Chocolate War
- Compare Archie to one of the rabbits from *Watership Down*.
- Compare your experiences as a freshman and a senior with those of the characters in *The Chocolate War*
- Why are the Vigils tolerated by Brother Leon and Brother Eugene? Explain.

Around the World in Eighty Days
- How would the story be different if Passepartout hadn't gone on the trip?
- What were the advantages and disadvantages of rescuing Aouda and taking her with them?
- How would the story have changed if it took place in the 1990s?

The Catcher in the Rye
- How would Holden fit in at a public school like Andrew?
- What significance did the "ducks in the park" have in relation to Holden and his life?
- What does Holden think of himself? Does he think he's wonderful or terrible?

On the day of the exam, I passed back the cards with the question I wanted them to answer. Though I was stuck with a bunch of essays to grade right at the end of the semester, there were a few advantages. First, since final exams are never returned, grading them goes quickly because there is no need for written comments. Second, each student wrote on a different question, so I never got bored reading them.

After the exams were turned in, we still had a few minutes left, so I had the kids do a little processing on the back sides of the index cards. Here was the prompt: *If another class did this same type of final exam, what advice would you give them?* Here were some of the responses.

- Go over the book the night before and get quotes and pages that describe each question so that you are prepared.
- Think of questions that you would want to write about. Pick something from the book that you liked. Don't write a question down until you've thought about how you would answer it.
- You should tailor the questions to your knowledge of the book. Don't necessarily choose the same questions everybody else chooses.
- Don't just write down two good questions because you may be stuck with the third one.
- Don't rely on your partners for ideas and information because they won't be able to hand the information to you during the test.
- Read the book. If you don't, you won't be able to think of any good questions and you won't be able to bluff your way through the answers.

Literature Circle Portfolio

A portfolio is a collection of artifacts, usually some "best" pieces but also artifacts that demonstrate "work in progress." I think a portfolio would be particularly useful if a class were to engage in more than one Literature Circle. That way, each student would have a starting point, the chance to develop improvement goals between the first and second Literature Circle, and then the chance to compare artifacts in order to show that growth. The final "test" grade on the second portfolio would be based on how well a student met or surpassed his goals. What categories would I use for a Literature Circle Portfolio? Students would have to show accomplishment and growth in the four assessment areas: *preparation*, *participation*, *idea expansion*, and *summation*. The portfolio contains no more than eight pieces, possibly four from the first Literature Circle and four comparison pieces from the second. Each artifact pair would have an explanation of the growth demonstrated or the reason why the student failed to move past her roadblock. If this assessment intrigues you, Chapter 10 discusses the portfolio process in much greater detail.

Book Talks

Here's a structure that's already established in the classroom and needs little further explanation or class time. Besides giving students the opportunity to engage in some interesting discussion around a common book, another purpose of Literature Circles is to get the class interested in reading more of the books on the list. Book Talks are an excellent way to get the word out. Also, since each student will be preparing her Book Talk Sheet individually, it's another way to see how much of the book each student has taken with her.

Projects

If you've read Harvey Daniels' book *Literature Circles* (2002), you've definitely thought about concluding your Literature Circles with projects. On the plus side, projects can be a lot of fun and also give students a wider choice in how to show what they know. On the minus side, high-quality projects require the class time for each group to develop its own grading rubric based on specific criteria and benchmarks (Burke 1993). Unless students take the time to clearly define what an "A" project looks like, project presentations will range from highly entertaining to highly excruciating. For this reason, I tend to limit the performance choices to formats we've already studied as a class. My favorite projects revolve around oral interpretation and drama.

Found Poetry Project

This really works if students have been keeping character diaries. After a brief introduction of the book, the group highlights different parts of the novel by having each student read a journal entry. The presentation concludes with a free verse poem created from the most powerful lines in their journals. An alternative to using journal lines is for students to choose a particularly powerful passage from the text and rearrange the lines to create a "found" poem (Bleekers 1996). In either case, students perform the poem in Readers Theater style. This means that all members share in the reading and certain lines are read in unison by the group in order to create emphasis. This example of a "found poem" originated from pages 130–131 of *Whale Talk* by Chris Crutcher.

Whale Talk
I never knew what it is to be human
I'm just finding my way
Mad at myself, my parents, my relatives, my teachers
They never warned me that this kind of pain
Even exists in the world
Their true thoughts and feelings secret
I walk outside and scream
My anguish travels maybe two blocks

Whale songs travel for thousands of miles
A cry unleashed
Every whale in the ocean
Will run into that song
Whales don't edit
The joy of lovemaking
The crippling heartache of a lost child
All heard and understood
No secrets
Whale talk is the truth
If you're a whale
You know exactly what it is to be you

Figure 8.24 *Found poem from* Whale Talk

Readers Theatre

Watership Down, Chapter 2: "The Chief Rabbit"

(adapted from pages 19–21)

Introduction: After Fiver's horrific vision, the brothers try to warn the rest of the warren about the impending disaster. Bigwig, a close friend of Hazel's and a respected Owsla member, uses his connections to arrange a meeting for them with the Chief Rabbit. Unfortunately, Hazel's audience with the Chief Rabbit does not bring the results he had hoped for. Rather than taking Fiver's prediction seriously, the Chief Rabbit treats the brothers as though they were suffering from over-active imaginations.

Parts: Chief Rabbit (Chief)
Hazel
Fiver
Narrator (Narr)

Chief: Ah, Walnut. It is Walnut, isn't it?

Hazel: Hazel

Chief: Hazel, of course. How very nice of you to come and see me. I knew your mother well. And your friend—

Hazel: My brother

Chief: Your brother . . .

Narr: Said the Threarah with the faintest suggestion of "Don't correct me anymore, will you?" in his voice.

Chief: Do make yourselves comfortable. Have some lettuce.

Narr: The Chief Rabbit's lettuce was stolen by the Owsla from a garden half a mile away across the fields. Outskirters seldom or never saw lettuce.

Chief: Now, how are things with you? Do tell me how I can help you.

Hazel: Well, sir . . .

Narr: Said Hazel rather hesitantly.

Hazel: It's because of my brother—Fiver here. He can often tell when there's anything bad about, and I've found him right again and again. He knew the flood was coming last autumn and sometimes he can tell where a wire has been set. And now he can sense a bad danger coming upon the warren.

Chief: A bad danger. Yes, I see. How very upsetting.

(continued)

Figure 8.25   Watership Down *Readers Theater example*

Narr: Said the Chief Rabbit looking anything but upset.

Chief: Now, what sort of danger I wonder?

Narr: He looked at Fiver.

Fiver: I don't know. B-but it's bad. It's so bad that—it's very bad.

Narr: He concluded miserably.

Chief: Well, now, and what ought we to do about it, I wonder?

Fiver: Go away. Go away. All of us. Now. Thearah sir, we must all go away.

Chief: That's a rather tall order, isn't it? What do you think yourself?

Hazel: Well, sir, my brother doesn't really think about these feelings he gets. He just has the feelings, if you see what I mean. I'm sure you're the right person to decide what we ought to do.

Chief: Let's just think about this a moment, shall we? It's May, isn't it? Everyone's busy and most of the rabbits are enjoying themselves. No elil for miles, or so they tell me. No illness, good weather. And you want me to tell the warren that your brother here has got a hunch and we must all go traipsing across country to goodness knows where and risk the consequences, eh? What do you think they'll say?

Fiver: They'd take it from you.

Chief: Well, perhaps they would, perhaps they would. But I should have to consider it very carefully indeed.

Fiver: But there's no time, Thearah, sir. I can feel the danger like a wire round my neck—like a wire—Hazel, help!

Narr: He squealed and rolled over in the sand, kicking frantically, as a rabbit does in a snare. Hazel held him down with both forepaws and he grew quieter.

Hazel: I'm awfully sorry, Chief Rabbit. He gets like this sometimes. He'll be a all right in a minute.

Chief: What a shame! What a shame! Poor fellow, perhaps he ought to go home and rest. Yes, you'd better take him along now. Well, it's really been extremely good of you to come and see me, Walnut. I appreciate it very much indeed. And I shall think over all you've said most carefully, you can be quite sure of that. . . . Bigwig, just wait a moment, will you?

Narr: As Hazel and Fiver made their way dejectedly down the run outside the Threarah's burrow, they could just hear, from inside, the Chief Rabbit's voice assuming a rather sharper note. Bigwig, as he had predicted, was getting his head bitten off.

Figure 8.25   Watership Down *Readers Theater example (Continued)*

Introduction: Our tableau is from Chapter 10 when Tim Johnson, the mad dog, wanders into the neighborhood. In these scenes you are about to see, Scout and Jem will learn something astonishing about their father. We chose courage as the motif that best reflects this part of the book because Atticus showed courage when he took the gun from Mr. Heck Tate.

Scene #1
One Saturday Jem and Scout decided to go exploring with their air rifles to see if they could find a rabbit or squirrel.
"Watcha looking at?"
"Mr. Tim Johnson, down yonder," Jem replied.
"What's he doing?"
"I don't know Scout; we better go home and tell Cal."

Scene #2
When they arrived at the house, Jem described the dog's unusual behavior to Cal.
"Are you telling me a story, Jem Finch?"
"No Cal, I swear I'm not!"

Scene #3
When Calpurnia saw the dog, she stared and then grabbed the children by the shoulders and ran them home.
She shouted into the telephone, "Mr. Finch! This is Cal. There's a mad dog down the street, and he's headed this way!" She hung up and called Miss Eula May, the town operator. Cal told her, "Can you call Miss Rachel and Miss Stephanie, and tell them a mad dog's a comin'."

Scene #4
Mr. Heck Tate was the sheriff of Maycomb County. He carried a heavy rifle as he and Atticus stepped out of the car.
"Stay inside, son," said Atticus. "Where is he, Cal?"
Calpurnia pointed down the street at Tim Johnson.

Scene #5
"Take the rifle, Mr. Finch," Mr. Tate told Atticus.
"You know I can't shoot that well. I'll hit the Radley's house!"
Atticus slowly took the gun and walked to the middle of the street. He bent down, adjusted his glasses, and aimed the gun. After what seemed like forever, Atticus brought the gun to his shoulder and the rifle cracked.

Scene #6
Tim Johnson leaped, flopped over and crumpled on the sidewalk. He didn't know what hit him.
"You were a little to the right, Mr. Finch," Heck Tate called.
"Always was," answered Atticus. "If I had my 'druthers I'd take a shotgun."
Jem was paralyzed.

Figure 8.26 *Tableau script example taken from* To Kill a Mockingbird

Readers Theater Rubric

Scripting

	1	2	3
	• A few "alls" • Everyone has a part • Predictable script divisions—parts are all in big clumps or show repetitious order	• More "alls" • Everyone has a part • Parts are more split up—not predictable/repetitious	• "Alls" are at the parts that need unity or emphasis • Parts for 2 or 3 in unison or echo • Line divisions play with words and emphasis, catch poem mood of text

Interpretation

	1	2	3
	• Some eye contact • Easily heard (outdoor voices) • Clear diction • Good posture	• Good eye contact with audience • Most lines convey emotion • Enthusiastic • Correct pacing • Facial expressions show emotion	• Emotion comes through on all lines • Vocal control: variation in volume and pitch • Advanced pacing: speed up, slow down, pause—for emphasis

Figure 8.27 *Readers Theater rubric*

Collective Performance	1	2	3
	• Well practiced, few stumbles • Group stands so that members can see/cue each other • No upstaging • Everyone knows where to stand	• Good eye contact with each other • "Alls" are in unison • Individual parts read with emotion and confidence	• "Alls" are precise • Lines feed off each other—smooth transitions • Choral parts ring with feeling • Script is close to memorized
Originality	1	2	3
	• Stationary	• Some movement and gestures • High energy	• Movement and gestures regularly incorporated • Play with levels/line arrangement • Props • Something "new"

Figure 8.27 Readers Theater rubric (Continued)

Theater Tableau Rubric—Actor

Facial Expressions	3	4	5
	• Face can be seen clearly	• Some emotion, fits context	• Clearly identifiable, exaggerated expression, accurate characterization

Pose	3	4	5
	• Remains frozen entire time	• Identifiable gestures, fits context	• Exaggerated gestures, accurate characterization

Theater Tableau Rubric—Narrator

Reading Pace	3	4	5
	• Slow enough to hear all words easily	• Uses pauses appropriately	• Varies pace to intensify emotion and emphasis

Interpretation	3	4	5
	• Reads loudly and clearly • No stumbles	• Moments of identifiable, appropriate emotion	• Pitch and volume vary for emphasis and intensity • Feeling/emotion constant

Figure 8.28 *Tableau rubric*

Theater Tableau Rubric—Group

Blocking	3	4	5
	• All actors fully visible • Tight compositions • Well practiced	• Body heights staggered • Spacing shows relationships between characters	• Each frame is substantially different

Scene Selection	3	4	5
	• Makes sense to those who have not read the book • Holds the audience's interest	• Scene is important to the story	• Scene reflects high drama, conflict, action

Script	3	4	5
	• "Key information" introduction given before tableau is performed • 5–6 Frames presented • Script is typed/written out	• Scene progression/flow makes sense • Uneven editing (some good "captions," some too long)	• Well edited • Captions fit scene perfectly with tableau frame

Props/Costumes	3	4	5
	• Slight suggestion of character/scene • Contributes positively	• Definite planning and thought reflected	• Creativity and obvious outside effort reflected

© 2002 by Nancy Steineke from *Reading and Writing Together*. Portsmouth, NH: Heinemann.

Figure 8.28 *Tableau rubric (Continued)*

Readers Theater Project

Another oral interpretation project I like is Readers Theater. The group starts by taking a high-interest excerpt from their novel and dividing it into parts. An ideal excerpt has a mixture of dialogue and narration. For example, let's say an excerpt contained two characters speaking to one another plus narration. If the Literature Circle group contained five members, two members would take the speaking parts while the remaining three would divide up the narration (Latrobe 1993). Along with creating the Readers Theater piece, students would also need to write an introduction. (See Figure 8.25 pp. 181–182.)

Tableau Project

A good drama project is for students to take an important passage and turn it into a series of four or five tableau scenes. While one student reads the text, the others create the scene by freezing in position (Wilhelm 1998, 54). This project requires students to be ruthless in their scripting since the narration is reduced to a series of captions. Also, students must think seriously about the accuracy of their blocking and characterization; this requires them to reread the text carefully. As in the readers theater project, the tableau also requires an introduction to the scene. It's fun to videotape these, because upon playback, the getting into position movement is eliminated and the audience just gets to see the tableau with the narration. However, I must repeat, for the kids to be successful at any of these three performance activities, they already have to know how to write found poetry, create a readers theater script, or block tableau scenes.

Parting Words

Always remember that Literature Circles will probably work poorly before they work well. When it comes down to it, a highly functioning Literature Circle is a complex endeavor. It requires thoughtful preparation and skillful discussion. Unless most of your students have already participated in well-structured Literature Circles, it's going to take some time to lead them to true enlightenment. Sometimes it takes a complete Literature Circle cycle before the kids finally understand what makes them work. I recently completed my Holocaust Literature Circle unit with my freshmen. When I asked them to suggest something that would make the next Literature Circles more successful, most wrote something about how they never realized how much the quality of their notes affected the quality of discussion. Well, duh! But as you well know, the only truth to an adolescent is something found through self-realization. Celebrate the positives publicly and greet the disasters as opportunities to problem solve. Observe carefully and keep revisiting the skills that seem weak or lacking. Never forget to have students monitor and process their group's functioning as well as their growth as individual members. Gary wrote this letter after participating in several different Literature Circles over the course of his freshman year.

Dear Mrs. Steineke,

The skill that I have most improved on is support and friendliness. In the first semester, I did not get used to that very well, so I concentrated on that skill the most

(continued)

Figure 8.29 *Gary's Literature Circle Processing Letter*

second semester. It helped because I got that checked off more on my sheet than I did before. I have been able to relate to other people's ideas better too. By doing that, I mean I can see their point of view and look at both sides. What I need to concentrate on the most next year will be follow-up questions. I did not do well on that either semester because I probably wasn't prepared enough and couldn't think of topics that related to the conversation.

I will be best remembered for my questions that related to the person more than the book. For example, "What would you do in Lennie's place at that time" or "Do you think that was wrong of Curley to go after Lennie?" Those questions give you more of an understanding of the person you are talking to, their thinking processes, and even how they react in real life. A lot of people's opinions reflect how they are in life. If somebody says, "That was mean of Curley to go after Lennie," they are probably a nice person and forgive others for their mistakes. If they say, "Curley should have finished off Lennie," they are probably a little too aggressive and would probably be good at being a manager for a company.

I have learned *many* things working with my group members. Each person is better at some skills and weak in others and some people have fewer weak skills than others. To learn successfully with your group members, you must use everyone's strengths. You must also give in and listen to their reasoning as if it were your own so that you don't take their differing opinions as an insult to your ideas. There is probably just about no one that would have the exact same opinion as someone else for every question, so differences are part of being in a group. Therefore, you just have to say, "That is a good point; that might be why he did that" or something like that. The variation in people's thinking and questions is what makes your group better not worse. If you have a different idea, you should state it so there will be a *discussion,* and not everyone just agreeing to someone's answers. In my opinion, that is what makes a group succeed: when everyone is not afraid to say what's on his mind and not be worried about another person putting them down or arguing with them.

Sincerely,

Gary

Figure 8.29 *(Continued)*

Resources

Bleeker, Gerrit and Barbara Bleeker. 1996. "Responding to Young Adult Fiction Through Writing Poetry: Trying to Understand a Mole." *The ALAN Review* (Spring): 38–40.

This is a fantastic article that offers several different ideas for connecting the writing of poetry with reading novels. The even better news is that you can actually find this article on line! <http://scholar.lib.vt.edu/ejournals/ALAN/alan-review.html>.

Burke, Kay. 1993. *The Mindful School: How to Assess Thoughtful Outcomes*. Palatine, IL: IRI/Skylight Publishing, Inc.

When I started diving into alternative assessment, this book was my bible. All of the chapters are short and practical with lots of examples: rubrics, checklists, reflection sheets, you name it.

Daniels, Harvey. 2002. *Literature Circles: Voice and Choice in the Book Clubs and Reading Groups*. York, ME: Stenhouse Publishers.

Daniels is to Literature Circles what Atwell is to reading/writing workshop (do they still have that analogy section on the SAT test?). I found this book an invaluable resource on the topic. Your library is incomplete without it.

Dixon, Neill, Anne Davies, and Colleen Politano. 1996. *Learning with Readers Theatre*. Winnipeg, Canada: Peguis Publishers.

If you want to dive into the dramatic depths of readers theatre, this book offers specific tips on oral interpretation, scripting, and blocking. It is very thorough.

Latrobe, Kathy. 1993. "Readers Theatre as a Way of Learning." *The ALAN Review* (Winter): 46–50.

Bad news. This article is going to be hard to find since the online version of ALAN doesn't go back this far. You'll have to search the bound periodicals of a university library for this one. However, once you find it, you'll be rewarded by great ideas on how to turn any novel into a Readers Theatre script.

Santa, Carol M., Lynn T. Havens, and Evelyn M. Maycumber. 1996. *Project CRISS: Creating Independence Through Student-owned Strategies*. Dubuque, IA: Kendall/Hunt Publishing Company.

This handbook is available only to those who go through the CRISS training. However, if you are looking to expand your repertoire of reading strategies for adolescents, particularly those that cut across all curricular areas, you are looking in the right spot. Here's the web address: <www.projectcriss.org/>.

Wilhelm, Jeffrey D. 1998. "Not for Wimps! Using Drama to Enrich the Reading of YA Literature." *The ALAN Review* (Spring): 52–55.

This article explains the steps for creating tableau scenes as well as several other drama-inspired reading strategies. The good news is that you can find this article online. <http://scholar.lib.vt.edu/ejournals/ALAN/alan-review.html>.

Workshops/Courses

The Walloon Institute 847-441-6638 or <www.walloon.com>.

This institute, run by Harvey Daniels of Literature Circle fame, is language arts/integrated curriculum heaven. A week at the institute offers keynote speakers, a variety of break-out sessions, and daily afternoon strands devoted to your particular grade level and learning interest. This past summer offered over twenty different workshops per day. Topics included reading and writing workshop, Literature Circles, poetry writing, dramatic performance, portfolio creation, and interdisciplinary teaming.

Supplies

Transparency Spinner: available at <www.kaganonline.com> or by calling Kagan Publishing at 1-800-933-2667.

CHAPTER 9

I Only Want to Read It Once
Writing and Conferencing Strategies That Do the Work for You

One of the big benefits of having kids practice discussion skills on a regular basis is that those skills seamlessly translate to Peer Conferencing. The main thing I want kids to do during a conference is to ask the writer lots of questions: questions that ask for more detail, questions about why something was included, questions about how they used their research. You name it! When teaching kids how to peer conference, I really emphasize questions because I HATE it when someone tells me how to revise something unless I've begged that person for her advice. I'll never forget the time I was signed up to attend a week-long summer workshop sponsored by the Illinois Writing Project. On the first day, we wrote personal narratives. I wrote about the recent loss of my best friend, who had just moved away, and the parallel closing of the coffee shop (pre-Starbucks!) where we always hung out. My piece was rather melancholy and depressing, but I thought it expressed my emotions and feelings about that point in my life.

Later in the day, we traded pieces with a partner. Mine was a rather officious looking English teacher. She never asked me a single question, just told me how to change my piece. Her final suggestion was to change the ending: keep the coffee shop open and find a new best friend. When I told her that this new ending didn't reflect my personal experience or my feelings, she explicitly stated that I needed a happier ending. Boy, it's a good thing that I can't remember that woman's name or face because I'm still pretty peeved! However, the good news is that the workshop location was an hour and a half drive from my home, and that incident gave me a good reason not to return since I didn't want to waste one more second of my precious summer vacation in the presence of that woman. I spent the rest of that week sitting on my deck reading a good book. Ironically, years later, I ran into the workshop instructor who said, "I remember you in that workshop, but then you just disappeared." Sharing one's writing in a conferencing group takes at least as much trust as sharing ideas in a Literature Circle. Therefore, many of the same skills and icebreaking techniques students practiced in their book discussion groups are just as important when it comes to their new roles as peer conferencers.

Trial and Error

I'll never forget how excruciating conference days once were in my Basic Writing class. I had yet to learn how to have a quick conference or how to teach the kids to peer conference. While ninety-nine percent of the class restlessly fidgeted as they tried their best to keep quiet and busy when all they really wanted to do was to talk to the kid in the next row, I would meet with one student at a time and laboriously go though a paper line by line. I touched the paper. I held the red pen. I jotted down the notes. I was happiest when a student actually wrote the final draft according to my conference specifications. Though I did ask students questions, there is only one I distinctly remember: "This sentence is awkward. How can you change it so that it would make more sense?" Of course, had I been able to step back and look at what I was doing, I should have asked myself, "Why are the kids still writing so many awkward sentences after all these conferences?" Instead, I blamed. "Why didn't those middle school teachers ever bother to teach those kids anything about writing?" or "Why don't these kids pay attention to anything I tell them?" At the time, I never noticed that these conferences were always about editing, never about content or ideas. In the end, I gave up on the conference days because I had too much trouble keeping the kids quiet for an entire period and whether or not I conferenced with them had little influence on a paper's quality.

> *Moral: Conferencing needs to occur at every stage of the writing process. If the students are dependent on you for those conferences, the situation quickly becomes unmanageable and unrewarding. Instead, kids need to learn how to talk about their writing with each other.*

Getting Peer Conferencing Groups Up and Running

The more students are used to working together and sharing ideas in a successful manner, the better they will function in Peer Conferencing groups. Therefore, whenever possible, I always try to have a writing project follow the conclusion of a Literature Circle. Conferencing groups work best with three members rather than the four or five necessary for Literature Circles. When conferencing, groups of four take too much time to share and pairs just don't seem to create enough input. Therefore, I use the writing project as a means to reshuffle the groups. After a class' Literature Circles have concluded, I have an excellent idea of how each student functions in a group and I use this knowledge to form successful new groups. Based on what students say in their Processing Letters (along with what I've observed during my monitoring) I try to form triads with students who have complementary skills. The nice thing about the Peer Conferencing groups following the Literature Circles is that all students will enter the new groups with more refined social skills than they had earlier in the year. Also, every student now understands what helps a group function in a positive manner.

Building Trust

Before students get down to the nitty-gritty of a serious writing project, the groups need to get to know each other and feel comfortable together in the preceding weeks. This trust building is probably even more important in a conferencing group, because in a Literature Circle, the members always have the book to fall back on; after all, someone can always read another passage. However, in a conference group the members have to be truly interested in each other's writing in order to listen and give useful feedback. If you don't care about someone personally, you're not going to care much about their paper either, so the conferencing will end up being quick and superficial and the attitude will be "Okay, thank goodness that's over with!"

Using the Membership Grid to Explore Writing Topics

Before students get into their Peer Conferencing groups for the first time, I have each person turn to the next blank page in his composition book and head it "What I Know About/What I'm Interested In." I give the class a few minutes to think about their own life experiences and jot down whatever comes to mind. Afterwards, we go around the room to get all the different ideas so that a master list is created. Here are some of the topics my Basic Writing class came up with.

1. Vacations
2. Driving
3. High school classes
4. Skiing
5. Winning money
6. Dances
7. Jobs
8. Camping
9. Fishing
10. Hobbies
11. Rehab
12. Music/Concerts
13. Hunting
14. Surgery
15. Good teachers
16. Moving

After this list is complete, I have them star the topics that most fit them because of their own personal experiences. Next, students move into their new groups and compare lists. Their goal is to come up with one topic that everyone is interested in talking about. If none of the topics "ring a bell," then the group has to think of some new topics that all members have in common. Finally, I pass out fresh Membership Grids. Each group writes down the topic they agreed on and interviews each other using the same rules that were in place for the Literature Circles. Students keep going back to this list for subsequent Membership Grid topics. Groups can either look for other topics they have in common, or each member can choose the topic that they want the other members to use in their interview. Returning to the topic list repeatedly also has an ulterior motive. The list is a fertile topic source when it is time to pick something to write about. Even better, the groups have already engaged in some prewriting activity without even knowing it! They have already talked about and elaborated on some of the topics they may choose to write about later

Also, as soon as Literature Circles have concluded, I take the kids back to the library for some new SSR books. Unless Literature Circles are in progress, SSR is always a part of daily classroom life. Therefore, Peer Conferencing groups always have the option to interview each other on whatever books they are reading that week.

Dialogue Journals

In the beginning stages of Peer Conferencing, Dialogue Journals can be another way to develop group trust and cohesiveness. At the start of the hour, I give the class a writing prompt such as "If you could turn invisible whenever you wanted to, how would you use your talent?" or "How would your life be different if you had an identical twin?" Students write on the topic in their composition books; their goal is to at least fill one page. Afterwards, this activity segues quietly and seamlessly into SSR because the second instruction is to put the comp book aside and read. After SSR, students meet with the group, comp books in hand. At the signal, members pass their books to the partner on the right, read the entry and write back. However, before the written dialogue exchange begins, I give some specific instructions.

1. Greet your partner by name as if you were writing a letter.
2. Use specific details in your response that show you remembered and thought about what your partner had to say.
3. Make your handwriting clear and legible so that your partner can read it.
4. Sign your first and last name clearly.

The first couple of times we do this, I have the partners trade, read, write back, and return the composition books so that each member can read the response. Afterwards, it's fun to let the group talk about the topic together and then maybe gather a couple of ideas from the class in a quick group share. Later, when students are familiar with the procedure of reading and responding, I use the assignment in true Dialogue Journal fashion, having partners trade their journals back and forth two or three times so that a real conversation in writing is created. Besides teacher-directed prompts, this Dialogue Journal activity is another opportunity for students to choose their own topics by looking back on the "What I Know About/What I'm Interested In" page in their composition books. Also, there is no reason why students in a Peer Conferencing group cannot double as a literature discussion group. Here is a Dialogue Journal written after a group read the Kafka short story "Metamorphosis." While significant thought is apparent, Dialogue Journals often create a sense of playfulness.

Picture books also offer another rich source for Dialogue Journal prompts. When introducing literary elements such as metaphor or irony, reading a picture book that illustrates that

---

11/30/95 "Metamorphosis"

I think Gregor's insect symbolized the problems he had in his real life such as how he couldn't talk to his family. When he was an insect, they still didn't understand him. Also, he still lives at home and supports his family because he feels guilty about them being in debt, but his family just ignored him whether he was a human or an insect. I don't think that his family's debt should have been his problem. I think Gregor should have been able to get any job he wanted and get a home of his own. He shouldn't have to support his family. That should have been his father's job. I wonder how old the sister is. She seems like she is old enough to get married and move out.

Kathy

Dear Kathy,

I agree with you. Gregor should have lived a life of his own, not the life his parents wanted him to lead. Maybe he felt that he had to take care of his parents because they took care of him as a child. I think the sister was just a year or two younger than Gregor. She also is living at home. What a nut! I would have moved out a long time ago. Where does this story take place?

Amy

Amy,

I have no idea where this story takes place. It doesn't really matter. Oh wait, I just thought of something. It takes place in his head!

Kathy

Kathy,

It matters for the test, doesn't it? Geek—just kidding.

Amy

Figure 9.1   *Dialogue Journal entry based on a short story*

"The Sweetest Fig"

    I thought this story was cute. I liked how the dog ate the last magic fig and then dreamed that he would switch places with his owner. It reminds me of how I was when I was little. I always saved my favorite pieces of candy for last, but then my big sister would steal it. At least she didn't turn me into a dog.

Christina

Christina,

    Yeah, that kind of reminds me of family too. This story <u>was</u> cute. Did you ever see that one movie where the man turns into a dog? It is so funny. It's kind of old, so I don't know if you would have seen it.

Jan

Jan,

    Yeah, I did see a movie like that, but I don't know if we're talking about the same one. The beginning of the story was sort of like all the typical fairy tales, but the end was ironic and that's what I liked.

Christina

Christina,

    Yeah, I like stories that get ironic at the end—it makes it so much more exciting. I hate boring stories. I could never finish a boring story.

Jan

Figure 9.2   Sweetest Fig *Dialogue Journal*

element is a good way to start. Telling the students to listen carefully because they will be writing about it afterwards also keeps the heads off the desks as well! For some reason, I always have a couple of students who automatically equate story time with nappy time. Here is a Dialogue Journal written after listening to *The Sweetest Fig* by Chris Van Allsburg. This picture book is a great introduction to irony. In their dialogue, students discuss irony but they also connect to a film experience they have in common.

Creating Found Poetry

This idea was discussed in the last chapter on Literature Circles, but it's also a great icebreaking strategy for building peer conference teamwork. Students can look back over the journal entries in their composition books and decide together which prompt they want to use. Then, each student rereads his entry and response, highlighting the most interesting or powerful words and phrases. The group puts together a free verse poem by recombining the lines so that they fit. When the groups ask if they can add some new lines, the answer is "Of course!" See, the groups already want to tackle revision before you've even broached the subject.

    Many times I use a variation of the found poetry strategy as a follow-up to another assignment. A frequent convention attendee, I often have to come up with multiple-day lesson plans that will fit any sub, keep the kids busy, and hopefully keep them learning and engaged. Yes, this is when the kids finally get to watch a movie! But, after each day's viewing, every student

The Autobiography of Miss Jane Pittman

This film was adapted from the book of the same title by Ernest Gaines. Elderly Miss Jane Pittman is celebrating her 110th birthday. Jane Pittman is a woman with many stories to tell. Born into slavery, she lives through the Civil War, Reconstruction, life on a Southern plantation, and the Civil Rights movement of the 1960s. Life as an African American woman has not been easy for her. Acts of racism and prejudice result in the deaths of her friends and closest family members. A writer by the name of Quentin discovers Miss Pittman and begins to interview her about her extraordinary life. Pittman's story is told in a series of flashbacks, beginning with her memories of being a slave during the Civil War and continuing on until her past meets the present, the early 1960s. For those of you who have read *To Kill a Mockingbird*, think about how the struggles of Jane Pittman mirror the struggles of the African American population in Maycomb, the book's setting.

Pivotal Events in the Life of Miss Pittman

1. Life as a slave
2. New found freedom
3. Escape from the plantation
4. Attacks by the Ku Klux Klan
5. Life in east Texas/the white horse/Joe Pittman's death
6. Ned's return, his fight for civil rights, and his death
7. Raising Jimmy
8. Jimmy's return, his fight for civil rights, and his death
9. Jane Pittman's decision to participate in a civil rights demonstration

Character Journal

Days 1, 2, 3 & 4: After watching the film each day, write a diary entry as if you were Jane Pittman looking back at one of the pivotal events listed above. Write about a different event each day. Do not summarize what happened in the film. Write about how Miss Pittman is reacting to the events she's experienced and her interactions with other characters. Use your imagination, but don't forget that all entries must be consistent with Jane Pittman's character and the storyline! Outlandish, bizarre entries that are not consistent with the character will receive no credit; 200 words (filling a full composition book page, normal sized handwriting) will get you full credit. Take a look at the Character Journal example below.

Character Diary Example (Quentin, the writer who interviews Jane Pittman)

Dear Diary,

   I have been interviewing the most incredible woman: Miss Jane Pittman. When I first came to Louisiana to cover the Civil Rights movement, a friend of mine

Figure 9.3 *Character Journal assignment instructions*

told me about this elderly woman who still lived on one of the local plantations. I took a chance and drove out there. She was reluctant to talk to me at first, but when she found that I was truly interested in her life, she opened up. I cannot believe what a hard life she's lived. Within weeks of attaining her freedom from slavery, racists murdered her family and friends. Rather than giving up, Jane and Ned, the only survivors, journeyed northward in the hopes of finding a better life. They had no money or anything; they were only teenagers. I'm almost forty and I still struggle with setbacks that seem inconsequential compared to what Jane has had to endure. I am so lucky to have such an easy life. Jane has seen her closest friends and family murdered for their beliefs in equality. After all that, I'm not sure that I would be able to keep living, determined to see a better future for the next generation. I can't imagine being killed just for saying that African Americans deserve the same treatment as whites. I don't know if I could be as brave as Miss Jane. Her family members lost their lives sticking up for their beliefs, yet she didn't try to stop them or encourage them to "play it safe." Despite all the tragedy, Miss Jane remains upbeat and determined. There is much I can learn from her.

Quentin

(Not counting greeting or closing, the above paragraph contains 266 words)

Figure 9.3   *(Continued)*

has to write a page-long Character Journal entry in his composition book. Figure 9.3 shows some typical instructions.

This assignment is great incentive for watching the film versus taking a nap, and also encourages the students to think about the characters well after the day's viewing is completed. The problem I run into is that when I return from the conference, I'm always trying to finish up whatever I had previously left half-done. The Character Journals get checked in, but then get pushed to the side in order to make way for more pressing concerns. However, even months later, the Character Journals offer a good opportunity for writing found poetry. Plus, resurrecting a long-forgotten assignment reinforces the concept that every assignment becomes important sooner or later! Here are three poems, all based on the same film.

One Hundred Years

Over one hundred years old
Walked down to the water fountain
Straight to the fountain
Head held high
Not once did my head drop
Took a drink
My head held high
More proud than ever
I felt as if no one could stop me
By Renee

Miss Jane

Not thinkin' of still bein' alive
Blowin' out all of these candles
Ku Klux Klan
Friends shot dead
Saw wars, saw slavery, saw hardest of times
But I loved my life
By Joe

A Slave

A Yankee soldier told me my name was a slave's name
Said to pick another
I did and felt free
Even though I never knew what free was
I found out later when the boss said we were free to go
We left and stayed in a barn
Sleeping, I was awoken by gun shots
Me and Ned were the only ones left
Now I was free
No where to go
By Mike

For this kind of assignment, I first have each student write an individual poem based on his journals. Next, students meet with their groups and read their poems aloud. The poems always end up being quite different, even though they are all based on the same film. Groups can compare and contrast the styles and content of their poems in an informal discussion, good practice for talking about their writing during Peer Conferencing. Then I challenge the groups to take their poetry writing a step further by creating a brand new collaboratively written poem. Each group has the option to go back to their journals for lines, combine lines from their individual poems, or write a new poem entirely from scratch. Once the poems are written, groups script them Readers Theater style, practice a few times, and then perform for the class.

When I'm confident that the conference groups have sufficiently bonded, I'm ready to move them to a specific writing project and start teaching them how to work as a conference team.

Peer Conferencing Procedure

Due to class rosters that often run beyond thirty students and periods of under 50 minutes, I find that Peer Conferencing is a much more efficient use of time than trying to conference with each student individually. However, though most conferencing takes place in the arena of student groups, that doesn't mean I'm not part of the conferencing process. It's just that I am conferencing more informally. Nothing stops me from asking a question or making a suggestion as I listen to students read their pieces to their partners.

Basic Peer Conferencing Agenda.   Even though various writing projects may differ in content and genre, the basic conferencing procedures always remain the same.

1. The group focuses on one paper at a time.
2. The writer starts by reading his paper aloud to the group while the members listen carefully.

3. After reading the draft, the writer takes a deep breath and reads his paper to the group a second time. This time, the members should think about what details they wish the author had included. They should also think about what parts really work well.

4. After the second reading, the listeners should each tell the writer what their favorite parts were, narrowing it down to a phrase or sentence.

5. Last, each listener should ask the writer at least two open-ended questions. The writer does not answer but writes them down on his Conference Sheet.

6. Before moving to the next paper, the writer thanks his listeners for their help.

I learned the "reading it aloud twice" trick from Toby Fulwiler, and when you stop to think about it, it really makes a lot of sense. When you hand a rough draft, particularly handwritten, to someone, the reader is immediately distracted or confused by the handwriting. Plus, the mis-spelled words and grammatical errors are further distractions. Reading aloud is good practice in listening and forces the members to devote their full attention to the content. The first time listeners hear a piece, they are getting the gist of it while the second time allows them to think about the parts that are missing and the parts that are working really well. Fulwiler also suggested not answering the questions for two reasons. One, discussing the answers takes up precious class time. Two, ideally, the listeners will get to find out those answers when they hear a subsequent draft. I always tell the groups that they can go back and discuss the answers if they have some time left after all pieces have been heard. Before adjourning, students spend a few minutes pro-cessing their group's functioning. The processing is located on the back side of the Conference Sheet. Of course, if time permits, it's interesting to share the processing or invite some volunteers to read a portion of their piece aloud.

I have all groups conference on the same day at the same time because I found that talking and silent writing just didn't go together. When I let groups choose when to conference, off-task conversations would sprout up within moments among the solitary writers. As soon as I put one fire out, another would spring up. My kids just couldn't ignore the talking going on in the "con-ference corners"; they wanted to get in on the act themselves! I also found that some students used Peer Conferencing as an excuse not to write; a few groups tried to take up permanent resi-dence in those "conference corners"! Because I wanted to spend my time on conferencing as well, I just couldn't seem to successfully oversee the Peer Conferencing as well as the solitary writing, so I finally concluded that all conferencing would take place on the same day at the same time. I also started giving the groups a strict time limit, five to ten minutes a paper depending on length. One of the group members must take on the role of time keeper so that every student in the triad gets some attention before the time is up.

Though most are more than willing to continue using the "Sharing Conference" model that the Conference Sheet delineates, I also try to expand their conference repertoire by showing them how a writer can use a "Problem-Solving Conference." Learning how to get good at different types of conferencing takes a lot of repeated modeling and practice.

Types of Conferences and Their Procedures

Sharing Conference

Purpose: Getting general feedback from listeners in order to find out which parts of a piece are working and which parts need more detail

	Peer Conference Record		
02/98			
NAME _____		HOUR _____	

DATE	QUESTIONS	QUESTIONS	FAVORITE PARTS
TITLE OF WRITING			
TYPE OF DRAFT			

SIGNATURES OF PEER CONFERENCERS _____

DATE	QUESTIONS	QUESTIONS	FAVORITE PARTS
TITLE OF WRITING			
TYPE OF DRAFT			

SIGNATURES OF PEER CONFERENCERS _____

© 2002 by Nancy Steineke from *Reading and Writing Together* Portsmouth, NH: Heinemann

Figure 9.4 *Blank Conference sheet*

Skills You Need to Use in Order to Have a Good Conference

- Eye contact/focus on writer
- 12-inch voices
- Reading so that others understand

- Asking open-ended questions
- Writing down questions and favorite parts on sheet
- Support and liking

Conference Steps

1. Writer reads the story aloud while other listen carefully.

2. Listeners ask writer specific open-ended questions—at least 4 per listener.

3. Writer writes down questions on conf. sheet, rewording when necessary. Writer **does not** answer the questions.

4. Writer writes down each listener's favorite part on conf. sheet.

Processing

Date:

What were three specific things your group did today to get along well and get the job done?

How could you improve your conferencing the next time you meet?

Date:

What was/went better in this writing conference compared to the last one?

List one way each person got some specific help from the group on his writing.

Figure 9.5 *Conference Sheet processing—back side*

Procedure

1. Writer reads her draft aloud.
2. Listeners comment on what worked, what was interesting, which parts really grabbed their attention.
3. Listeners ask questions about the parts that they would like to know more about.

Problem-Solving Conference

Purpose: Focuses on a specific part of the paper that the writer is having trouble with. Listeners ask questions, make suggestions, or give ideas that will help the writer solve his problem

Procedure

1. Writer reads the draft aloud.
2. Listeners first comment on what worked, what was interesting, which parts grabbed their attention.
3. Writer explains where he is stuck and what help he needs.
4. Writer reads that part of the draft again.
5. Listeners give suggestions and ask helpful questions.

I give students a handout defining the steps for the two types of conferences, but they really need to see them roleplayed before they have a clear procedural vision in mind. I model the first roleplay with my own writing and have a couple students or the entire class be my partner. As I listen to the feedback, I take notes on the overhead using a transparency copy of the Conference Sheet; showing how the author listens and take notes is an important part of the modeling. I find that revisiting the role play from time to time to model effective conference behaviors keeps students sharper and more focused in their own groups. It's particularly important to return to discussion of the Problem-Solving Conference so that students can begin to recognize the various writing issues their group might take up. Here is a list one class eventually generated.

Problems for a Problem-Solving Conference

1. Brainstorm more interesting words.
2. Listen for awkward sounding sentences and help writer rephrase them.
3. Improve/expand dialogue.
4. Find the good parts and get rid of the parts that don't fit.
5. Improve/expand descriptive parts.
6. Add specific examples or support to a point.
7. Make introduction more interesting.
8. Give readers something to think about in conclusion.
9. Make sure the point of the topic sentence is explained thoroughly.

Once students start to personalize their conferencing needs, it's much harder to develop a generic Conference Sheet like the one I referenced earlier. Instead, I have them keep a Peer Conference Log which lists date, draft information, partner's name, type of conference, at least two specific suggestions/ideas/questions the writer can use, and some quick skills processing. As kids get better at conferencing, conference time can be extended because the groups will know how to examine writing in greater depth.

Peer Conferencing Skills

When writing projects and Peer Conferencing follow Literature Circles, students have already practiced many of the skills that they will need. Here is a list of the basic skills that students need in order to have a successful peer conference.

1. Eye contact
2. Using quiet voices
3. Ignoring other groups
4. Looking interested in the writer
5. Friendliness and Support
6. Following task directions
7. Asking open-ended questions
8. Giving specific feedback
9. Recognizing missing details
10. Recognizing unimportant details

The first five items on this list are group maintenance skills, while the last five are academic task skills. Remember that both types of skills are equally important to the success of a group. While the first five skills lend themselves to traditional T-Charts, the last five skills lend themselves more to lists of what to say. The best way to improve performance in academic skills is to have a large group share after the day's peer conferences have concluded. Name an important skill such as "Asking open-ended questions," and have the writers individually look at the feedback notes they took from their partners' suggestions, highlighting the questions that will be most helpful to them when they revise. Then gather the examples on a transparency. Right before the next peer conference begins, put the transparency back up and have each student write down a personal goal that will help him give better and more useful feedback to his peers. Just as students must continually examine and refine the usefulness of their notes for a Literature Circle meeting, students must work to refine their skill at giving useful feedback in a conference group. As always, as you monitor their conference group, think about what you want to see kids doing and saying during their conferences. If it's not there, it's time to teach that skill explicitly!

Peer Conferencing and the Elements of Group Design

Peer Conferencing and group writing projects will always work best when all elements of successful collaborative design are present. Here's an examination of how a conference group fits the model.

1. **Positive Interdependence**: The group needs each other for feedback (academic task interdependence); together partners must practice specific skills (social skill interdependence); groups work on helping each other improve their papers in subsequent revisions—they are always focusing on what is working well and recognizing it (celebration interdependence); the groups sit together and are as far away from other groups as the room size allows (environmental interdependence).

2. **Individual Accountability:** Students must have the assigned piece of writing ready for the conference. During the conference, students must take notes on the feedback they receive from their peers. Afterwards each student uses the feedback to make significant changes to the draft. Ultimately each student produces a final draft.

3. **Group Processing:** After each meeting, students examine how they functioned as a group. From time to time, whole class processing is used to celebrate consistently seen strengths and discuss and refine skills that seem to be weak.

4. **Social Skills:** During Peer Conferencing, students are specifically instructed to use skills such as attentive listening, giving specific feedback, and showing support and friendliness.

5. **Face-to-Face Interaction:** Students sit knee to knee and eye to eye with the purpose of ignoring other groups and talking about each member's paper in turn.

When Peer Conferencing isn't working, the first course of action is to go back to the elements of group design. Think about the noneffective behaviors the groups are exhibiting and then match it to the element that most needs to be reinforced. Though increasing and strengthening the modes of positive interdependence is always a good place to start, consider all of the elements. Groups fail for all sorts of reasons. Sometimes the solution is simple. If the groups are talking to each other, they need to sit closer together and sit further apart from other groups. Sometimes the solution is complex. If kids aren't giving useful feedback, refinement will require some skill lessons and more modeling on how to record and examine feedback from a peer conference. I would also look for ways to make each student more individually accountable so that she gives the best feedback possible. Dysfunctional groups require careful examination, clinical diagnosis, and then rejuvenating therapy!

Large Group Share

If you've ever read any books on writer's workshop, they always talk about the wonders of "Author's Chair." Everyone pulls his chair up in a circle and waits with bated breath for a peer to jump into the center stage chair and read some simply fantastic piece that leaves everyone else in emotional nirvana. After that, the next child jumps up and asks for help on his metaphors. I swear, I've read about this class in several books. Each time I leave the text wondering why I don't get kids that dote on each other's words like the ones all these other teachers have. Therefore, I've never been much for "Author's Chair," because all I can do is imagine the pitfalls. I worry about the kids who don't read aloud very well. I worry about the underlying competition involved. Have you ever gone to any kind of English workshop where the participants have to write something? Ninety-nine times out of a hundred, after some individual writing, the presenter always asks, "Is there anybody who would like to share what they wrote?" That's when the best writer in the room jumps up and shouts, "I would!" Following her exclamation is the reading of a piece no one can top. What kind of effect would that experience have on a group of students? Consequently, I don't offer the opportunity for any large group sharing of writing until I'm certain that all class members can be supportive and no one will leave feeling uncomfortable. As students get used to reading their work to each other and giving useful supportive feedback, the class's ability to perform as a unified and empathetic audience emerges and writers are more willing to read before the group. Even then, some kids like to volunteer and some kids don't, so I don't make a big deal out of who's reading aloud and who's not. I know that everyone's writing is being heard and discussed during peer conference time. For me, large group share is an interesting and occasional change of pace and a good opportunity to practice Quiet Patient Listening.

Using Partners for Grammar and Editing

Constance Weaver was absolutely correct when she wrote her book *Teaching Grammar in Context* (1996). Isolated grammar exercises do not guarantee improved editing and proofreading skills. Students need to learn how to recognize and correct the errors in their own writing. I know some proponents of the technique referred to as Daily Oral Language (DOL). For those who are uninitiated, basically it's just a daily minilesson on grammar with about four or five sentences the kids correct, check with a partner, and then put up on the overhead. I've noticed that the kids seem to have no problem finding and accurately correcting the errors in these sentences, but when it comes to their own papers, they miss the same errors. This happens even when the example sentences are taken from the class's own papers!

Many years of frustration have led me to the following conclusion: kids know more about grammar and punctuation than we think; they just don't want to take the time to pay attention to detail. What the kids hate about editing is what everyone hates about editing: it's nitpicky and laborious. The difference is that as adults we've "gotten over it" and realize that we need to carefully proofread anything meant for widespread publication. In addition, if it's really important, we'll have others proofread our work as well. Hey, here's a newsflash. The kids have already picked out whom they want to proofread their papers: you! They keep hoping that their superficial proofreading and repetitious errors will result in you marking up their papers and then letting them correct them for a higher grade! What a deal! Now, of course I'm not saying to quit teaching grammar and punctuation altogether. By all means, if certain errors crop up in a majority of papers, cover it in a minilesson. Then think about how to get the kids to start really using it in their own writing.

Step 1: Learning to Pay Attention to Detail

Have you ever heard of the Kagan structure called Same/Different (Kagan 1997)? To start, students work across the table from each other in pairs. Each partner is given a picture, but the picture cannot be shown to the other member. The pictures are similar at a glance, but if you start to study the details, you begin to notice subtle differences. In pairs, each student studies his picture and takes turns asking questions about his partner's picture in order to make a list of the differences between the two. However, at no time can the students put the pictures side to side and just compare them. This activity focuses on attending to detail while also remembering what one's partner has said. You don't even have to spend any time trying to create these pictures. The Kagan catalogue has several different volumes you can order and reproduce.

Step 2: Finding Differences in Text

Once the kids get the hang of Same/Different, the next step is to use the same activity with paragraphs. Students work in pairs again. Both have the same paragraph, but just like the pictures, there are two versions with different errors in each. Partners take turns reading aloud, one sentence at a time, while both students put their index fingers on each word as it is read. Afterwards, the partner who read the sentence begins to point out possible differences, asking questions like, "Which "there" do you have? Mine is spelled *t-h-e-i-r*. Which one would be the right one?" As students detect differences, they negotiate the correction and mark it on both papers before moving on to the next sentence. Then the other partner reads aloud. Like the original exercise, at no time can the papers be laid side by side and just quickly compared. All corrections must take place via reading aloud, asking the right questions, and negotiating correct answers.

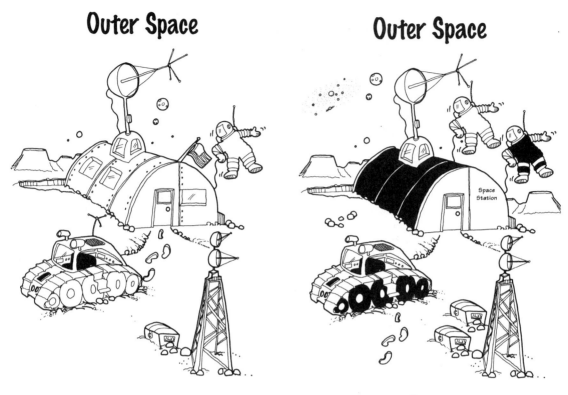

Figure 9.6   *Same/Different—Picture 1*   **Figure 9.7**   *Same/Different—Picture 2*

Source: From Cooperative Learning Structures for Teambuilding. © 1997 Kagan Cooperative Learning.

Step 3: Partner Proofreading

One of the important parts of proofreading that students refuse to accept is that you'll always find more errors if you read aloud and put your finger on each word than if you read silently. This is because reading aloud slows you down while the finger pointing helps you look at each word individually. Actually, good proofreading is pretty much the opposite of good silent reading. As a skilled reader reads silently, she aims for speed and grouping ideas together as opposed to seeing the words as individual entities. Unfortunately, using silent reading for proofreading results in missing many errors because the brain will automatically ignore repeated words (for example, two *thes* in a row), fill in missing words, and not recognize missing or incorrect punctuation because the brain is reading for meaning.

When students are ready to edit their final drafts, have them print out two copies, double spaced. If they are long papers, have them print out the first two pages. Then have students work with their partners to proofread one paper at a time. Sitting across from each other, the writer's partner reads one sentence aloud at a time and then both students discuss any corrections that are necessary. Before the next sentence is read, the writer makes the corrections on his copy of the paper. Sitting across from each other prevents partners from just putting the papers side by side and reading silently. While this activity is going on, you can walk around and read over shoulders, offering assistance when asked or when you recognize it is needed. Prior to partner proofreading, it's a good idea to have the class brainstorm a list of specific errors that they frequently make so they can be on the look-out for those.

Now, I know this procedure is going to take some time. However, start to think about how much time has already been wasted (yours and theirs!) with years of grammar lessons that haven't worked. As Jim Trelease points out in his *Read Aloud Handbook,* "We make time for what we value most." If poorly proofread papers are a pet peeve of yours too, making the time to really work on editing skills might be worth it.

Using Peer Conference Groups for Narrative and Fiction Writing

While the first part of this chapter gave you some tips for making Peer Conferencing groups more productive, the following section provides some process models for writing personal narratives, short stories, and research papers.

Personal Narrative

As you've probably already discovered, the personal narrative can produce some pretty good, entertaining pieces of writing. Unfortunately, in the state of Illinois, our junior year competency tests only include expository and persuasive writing, so personal narrative and fiction writing have become somewhat of a luxury these days. However, narratives have always been a surefire winner and a great introduction to Peer Conferencing and revision, so I'm hoping your hands aren't as bound by the state as mine are. Here are the steps.

Step 1: Talking about ideas.   One of the habits I want kids to get into is to talk about writing possibilities before committing to paper. For the personal narrative, some of the best idea-generating strategies are the Neighborhood Map and the Life Graph, which were described earlier in Chapter 7. When students trade and talk about their maps or graphs with many different partners, the process gives audience feedback since it shows which stories seem interesting to others. Also, each time a different partner is attracted to the same story, the writer performs impromptu revision; it's natural for anyone to try to tell his story a little better each time.

When the personal narrative project is beginning, I have students retrieve the maps from the writing archive section of the binder and meet in their groups. Each person picks his two best stories to tell. Partners have three minutes apiece to tell one of their stories; any remaining time is used to ask detail questions. At the end of three minutes, the group focuses on the next member. The cycle can be repeated if you have time for a second round of stories. Next, in order to avert those long, dreary, endless descriptions of the family vacation, I insert a quick minilesson on the different kinds of conflict. Before they commit one word to paper, I want my writers to understand that a story without conflict will not make an interesting read! All I do is ask the groups to make a list of the conflicts in their composition books. After three minutes (have you noticed that three minutes is the perfect time for just about anything, eggs included) the groups volunteer the different conflicts: man vs. man, man vs. himself, man vs. technology, man vs. society, man vs. nature, man vs. the supernatural, etc. After this, members return to their group discussions. First, the writer explains his story's conflicts; then his peers give suggestions for making the story more interesting to other readers. As the meeting adjourns, members thank their partners for their help and return to their seats.

Before the next step, I like to have a quick large group share. Even though everyone has an idea, it's still a good idea to go around the room and have each student announce his topic to the class. This gives you one last opportunity to possibly head off a bad choice, but it also gives the class one last chance to think of something better. Oftentimes, hearing the other ideas can jog the memory, leading to a better story.

Step 2: Using guided imagery for the first draft.   Once everyone is firm on a topic, I have each student get out a couple of sheets of paper and a pen. Everything else goes back into the backpacks. Then I tell the kids to put the paper and pen on the floor so that there is nothing on their desks. I introduce guided imagery by explaining how guided imagery is often used in sports. In diving, the person on the high dive is often coached to move through an imaginary dive before executing it. Most coaches will tell you about imagination exercises they use to help athletes mentally prepare for the physical challenge of competition. Thanks to the deep respect our society has for athletic achievement, students never question guided imagery after I've connected it with sports. Next, I tell everyone to sit up straight and close his eyes or cover them with a hand. The posture thing is important; if you let the kids put their heads down, a few of them will fall asleep. If a class is comfortable with and trusting of one another, closing their eyes will not be an issue. Therefore, I don't recommend using guided imagery until a positive climate is consistent. In any case, I always emphasize that this memory exercise won't work if anyone is distracted by someone else or if a person is distracted from his own memories by keeping his eyes open. I also emphasize and repeatedly use the phrase "in your mind's eye" and remind the kids that no physical movement will ever take place; this is all taking place in their imaginations. Otherwise, I can guarantee that one goof will jump out of his seat and exclaim something like, "Well, you said to turn around!" If you really emphasize the mind's eye concept, usually everyone stays seated. After everyone is situated correctly, I move through the script that I adapted from *A Community of Writers: Teaching Writing in Junior and Senior High School* (Zemelman and Daniels 1988).

Guided Imagery Steps

1. Keeping your eyes closed, take a couple of silent deep breaths and listen to background noise in the room. Do you hear the heating ducts rattling? That person screaming in the hallway? The cement truck dumping a load of concrete underneath our window? (As I write this, our school is undergoing a giant new construction project.) Good. Acknowledge those sounds and then ignore them. Start to move back in time to your story.

2. Find yourself in the story. In your mind's eye, look down at the floor. What kind of shoes were you wearing? Imagine that you were looking in a mirror. What were you wearing that day? How did you look different then than you do now? How were you feeling that day? What were you doing? What were you thinking?

3. Now, in your mind's eye, look directly ahead. Where are you? What do you see? What details can you notice? Are you inside or outside? What time of day is it? What kind of light is there? Natural? Electric? Campfire? Listen to the background noises. What is loudest? What can you faintly hear in the distance? Are there any odors? What is the weather like? How does the temperature feel against your skin?

4. In your mind's eye, slowly look to your right and left. What new details can you notice? Now, in your mind's eye, turn around and look behind you. What else can you see?

5. Now, in your mind's eye, face forward again. Who else is in this scene with you? What are they wearing? What kind of conversation is taking place? What emotions and feelings are the other people experiencing? How are these people reacting to one another? How do you fit into that conversation and scene?

6. Imagine that this entire incident was on a videotape. In your imagination you can play the tape. You can pause, stop, rewind or zoom in whenever it is necessary. In your mind, play this tape and watch it carefully. Try to notice and remember as many

details as possible. When you have reached the end of the incident, rewind the tape and watch it a couple more times. See what else you can notice that you missed the first time. (I give students about two minutes of silent visualization time for this.)

7. As you finish playing the tape in your mind's eye, return to the present. Do not talk; focus on holding those memories. Silently pick up your pen and paper and begin to write. Try to get everything from your imagination down on paper. Do not worry about spelling and grammar. Write as fast as possible so that you do not lose any of the memories.

Students will finish this last step at different times, so it's important to remind everyone in the class to offer others the quiet writing time they enjoyed as they finished their first drafts. After they finish, they need to silently pick up their SSR books and use the time to get in a few pages as they practice Silent Patient Waiting. Now is a good time to put on one of those soothing classical music CDs.

Step #4: Personal narrative revision.   Teachers often complain that students never substantially revise their papers. Maybe a sentence is added here or a word is changed there, but the paper itself stays pretty much the same. I think this kind of writing is the result of two problems. First, most writers, no matter how unskilled, don't appreciate or readily act upon unsolicited suggestions. Studies show that all of those comments English teachers traditionally make on student papers are essentially worthless because, for most students, it doesn't result in noticeable improvement in their writing. Second, for most people, revision is pretty much a mystery. Everyone knows it involves making a piece of writing different from how it began and hopefully better, but where do you begin? Luckily, some people in the field have begun to figure this out.

To start with, I try to emphasize to students that if you take the word *revision* and separate it into two parts, you have "*re*" and "*vision*." What does the prefix "*re*" mean here? To repeat or do something again. What does *vision* mean? Seeing. Therefore, *revision* means to see something in a new light, to look at it differently. When I have students work on revisions, they do not rewrite the entire paper. Instead, they pick one part of the paper to rewrite in a completely different way. As a rule of thumb, I tell students that each revision should be about one page (front side only) of average size handwriting. Here are the different types of revisions I use for the personal narrative. I adapted most of these ideas from Barry Lane, so be sure to check out his book *After THE END*. He has lots of great examples and tons of revision ideas.

Whenever we work on different kinds of revisions, I first model it with a piece of my own writing. Showing them my writing demonstrates my trust in them and my own willingness to take a risk, the same attributes I want them to show with each other. When I read aloud my example drafts, I follow the same format as they did in the initial peer conference. Students have to listen to it twice, ask questions, and indicate which parts seem to work while I take down the notes on a conference sheet transparency. After students write each revision draft, usually as a homework assignment, they return to their groups for a sharing conference to ask questions and point out best parts.

Personal Narrative Revisions

1. **Dialogue Draft:** The quickest minilesson I've found on writing dialogue is to have the kids go back to their SSR books and look for a page of dialogue. As they study the page, it's easy for them to see the nuances of punctuation and the way a new paragraph starts whenever the speaker changes. Afterwards, I have students find a part in their stories in which the characters talk to each other. If no part exists, I have them find a part

"What happened?" my dad exclaimed. "Why did the boat slow down?"

"Maybe you hit something," my mom suggested.

"No, I didn't hit anything," my dad snapped. "I'm going to check the engines. Could you put the boat in neutral?"

"Sure," my mom said nervously.

"What's wrong?" I said. "Will we be able to make it?"

"We'll be fine, honey," my mom reassured me.

"Well," my dad started, "it looks like we'll be driving there on one engine. The left engine won't start."

"How are we going to do that?" my mom asked.

"We have no choice. Our best bet is to try to make it to Saugatuck, but we may have to find a closer place to stop. We can only go about ten miles per hour," my dad told us.

"What can I do to help?" my mom asked.

"Just make sure the kids are okay."

"Mom, I feel sick," whined my sister Katie.

"Get some fresh air and look at the beach."

"How much longer is it going to take?" I asked.

"I don't know; we have to go slow. We'll get there soon enough," soothed my mom.

Figure 9.8   *Student example of a dialogue draft*

where characters *could* talk to each other. If no other characters exist, I tell them to imagine the character having a conversation with his conscience or inner voice. Then I tell students to pick up the story from that point and continue to tell it strictly through dialogue. No narration can be used, only dialogue tags.

For her dialogue draft Christina, a freshman, wrote about her family's ill-fated boat trip from New Buffalo to Saugatuck, Michigan. An hour away from their destination, the boat broke down, stranding them in the middle of Lake Michigan during a storm. In her final draft, Christina did not use all of the dialogue in this draft. She picked out the most emotional pieces that best captured the moment, but she also added dialogue to other parts of the story as well.

2. **Snapshot Draft:** This time students pick a part of the story that needs more description. After a quick review of the five senses, I once again send students back to their SSR books to find a descriptive passage. Students share with their partners, discussing what senses were used. This is also a good time to have students look for similes and metaphors since they are often used to enhance description. After a short large group share, I tell students to think of the scene they've chosen from their narrative as if it were a snapshot. With only words, how can they create the picture that's in their imagination so that a reader will see it too? I also remind them of the original guided imagery exercise; lots of times refocusing on the picture seen in the mind's eye is very helpful (Lane 1993, 35).

In his snapshot, freshman student Vince describes the disastrous conclusion to a birthday party. What starts as roughhousing quickly escalates into a brawl.

I was grabbing at my hat, and in the struggle we were knocked to the ground. To the others it seemed that I had jumped on and was pummeling Jim, but nothing could be further from the truth. I had just gotten my hat back, when I felt a sharp jab in my back. I bellowed and turned around to see Wes jamming his long nails into my spine. Everyone else was running at me, too. Wes only got there first because he was so light and wiry. I braced myself for the rest of them, knowing that no matter how I dodged them I would get hurt. Adrenaline flowed through my veins as my heart pounded in my ears. A punch came from the left! I jumped and countered with a punch to the stomach. Pete let out a ragged gasp and fell to the ground. Most everything else was a blur, but I remember the end of the fight. When Wes punched me in the jaw, I ran after him but Mark got in the way so I just let my fist fly. After my hand connected with his eye, he stopped fighting, but then Wes tackled me from behind and my head bashed against the concrete. Pain exploded from the back of my head. I shuddered and closed my eyes.

Figure 9.9 *Snapshot draft*

As the end credits for *Halloween* rolled on the television screen, I numbly sat there thinking, "Is Mike Myers out there lurking in the darkness?" I heard a rustle outside. Oh my God! He is out there! To try to take my thoughts off the movie, I started picturing myself safe at home. But neighbors had not come home yet, so I wondered what time it was and how much longer it would take before they came back. I looked at my watch. Ten-thirty! "What's taking them so long?" I asked myself. Unfortunately, this started me thinking about all of the accidents or other mishaps that could possibly detain them. I nervously wrung my hands as I thought of car accidents and kidnappings and all sorts of other strange fates. Why haven't they called? What if they never come back? What should I do? Should I call my parents? Where are my neighbors? These questions ran over and over in my mind, and each time they resulted in different answers. They haven't called because they're dead! They will never come back! The questions in my mind continued as I nervously waited.

Figure 9.10 *Thoughtshot draft*

3. **Thoughtshot Draft:** I explain thoughtshots by drawing a rudimentary comic strip character with two balloons: one with a traditional pointy tail and one that looks like a cloud with some bubbles trailing to the character's head. When I ask them what is the difference, all of the students can tell me that the tailed balloon shows what the character is saying, while the cloud and bubble balloon indicates what the character is thinking. Then I tell them that this draft, a thoughtshot, explains what was going through one of the character's minds at a specific point in the story. As you might have predicted, students go back to their SSR books and look for a thoughtshot (internal narration) to share with their partners and the class. Students then pick a point in their

own stories and write a new part that explains what the character is thinking about (Lane 1993, 46). Leann, another freshman, wrote the preceding thoughtshot about her scary babysitting adventure.

4. **Beginnings Drafts:** This is the last revision students do before putting all the different parts together into a final paper. Students start solo by reviewing all of the previous conference questions that they have recorded and then highlighting the three most interesting or helpful questions. Next, they get out three sheets of loose leaf and write one question at the top of each. Now, they study the question and answer it by starting to tell the story from that point. Each beginning should be about three-quarters of a page. The conferencing for this draft is a little bit different than the others. Instead of recording questions, the writer reads each beginning once while the others listen. After all three beginnings have been heard, the listeners tell the author which beginning got them hooked. Of course, the author can choose whatever beginning he likes the best. He's not obligated to take his group's advice.

After each draft, students return to their groups and follow the standard conferencing process. The amazing thing I find in this process is that the kids, for the most part, don't view it as drudgery because it's fun to hear what the others have come up with. The writing has now become intertwined with the social element and that's what makes this kind of revision fun. Also, since each draft is significantly different, the "Why do I have to do this again?" mindset doesn't rear its ugly head.

Step #5: Putting the pieces together.   It's ironic that after students do all this work on a paper they'll still go back to the first original draft, make a few corrections, and turn it in as the final. Just as students need to be taught specific strategies for revising different types of papers, students need to learn how to put all the pieces together. This starts solo with the students getting all their drafts out, reading them over, and thinking about which parts of each draft should be used. They need to be encouraged to number sections, make notes to themselves, and use a highlighter. After this individual planning time, the groups come back together to hear the pieced together draft. One at a time, each student reads his writing from start to finish while the others listen and think about how the pieces fit. Listeners need to point out the parts they don't understand and the parts that are really working well. In addition, this is the time for members to give each other suggestions for making those puzzle pieces fit better.

Using a Model for Writing Short Stories

Though I believe writing absolutely original fiction takes some skill, determination, and imagination, almost any student can write a pretty good story when starting from a model. These stories can be written individually but have great potential for group writing. When students work to write a story in a group, the group not only conferences but also *creates*.

By now I must sound like a broken record, but I cannot emphasize strongly enough that to make this group writing process work, you've really got to pay attention to skills. In this case, I've found that the most important skill for collaborative writing is honoring members' ideas. Often, one member will steamroll the others or even unintentionally shut someone else down by ignoring an idea; hurt feelings early on often result in that member withdrawing and participating in the most minimal sort of way. Before groups even start the brainstorming and writing process, it's best to discuss how important keeping an "open mind" is and then developing a T-Chart for this skill.

Honoring the Ideas of All Members

Looks Like	Sounds Like
Leaning forward	"Let's get everybody's ideas before we decide"
Smiling	"Where would you put that part?"
Eye contact	"These are all good ideas. How can we combine them?"
Focused on the group	"I like your idea; tell us in more detail how it fits in with the rest of the story."
Looking interested in members	"What kind of personality does this character have?"

I have the group work as a unit to create the first written draft. Left to their own devices, a group will typically elect one person to be the scribe. Instead, I recommend that all students write down the first draft the group comes up with. That way if the scribe is absent, the process can continue because everyone has a copy of the group's work. Also, when everyone has to write, everyone stays involved in the process. Often a scribe can become a dictator, taking over the project, doing all the writing, ignoring the ideas of others, and then in the end bitterly complaining about her lazy members making her do all the work.

The nice thing about fiction is that you can employ the same revision techniques used for a personal narrative. In a group writing project, these revision techniques also serve as individual accountability checkpoints. After the first draft is done, I have the groups work through the different revisions. For example, each member has to write a full page of dialogue for the story. However, before the dialogue drafts are written, the group decides together where the story needs dialogue and assigns each member to a different story part. That way there are no duplicates, the group has more new material to work with, and it is more likely that the final piece of writing will reflect the contributions of all members versus just one. This process of individual revisions continues for the thoughtshots and snapshots.

When the groups are ready to produce the final draft, I prefer to take the kids to the computer lab rather than having the final draft typed up by one member. The best typist can man the keyboard, but the other two have the handwritten copies and dictate to the typist. All three members should keep an eye on the screen, correcting errors and suggesting impromptu revisions as they see the final story taking shape. Once the story is typed up double-spaced, the group prints three copies. Another Peer Conferencing day is scheduled, this time for editing. While one member reads aloud, the other two follow along with their fingers on each word. Any member can say "stop" whenever they detect a potential error. All members discuss the correction and mark it on their individual drafts. The task of reading aloud is rotated after each page. At this point, depending on class time and computer lab availability, the groups can return together to correct their stories or complete this final part of the process on their own. Here is a time when you can let the most dominant member take charge of the finishing touches.

Grading a Group Project

Even though the final product is a group effort, there are many layers of individual accountability built in. Each member has to write his own copy of the first draft; write specific dialogue, thoughtshot, and snapshot drafts; keep a process journal; tangibly participate in proofreading/editing by marking corrections on his copy of the paper; and write a Process Letter. If you decided to give points out for all of these activities rather than stamps, the total value of the parts would probably equal or surpass whatever points the final draft was worth. However, that still doesn't

Pesonal Narrative Rubric

Engaging Story

3	4	5
• Beginning, middle, end • Easy to follow • Focused on one incident/event	• Clear conflict • Succinct wording, avoids details that don't add to story • Strong, specific nouns and verbs	• Opening grabs reader's attention • Crisp, effective ending—leaves reader thinking • Story has an overall feeling (humor, fear, sadness) • Story is tight

Dialogue

3	4	5
• Punctuated correctly • Speakers are clear to reader	• Used in more than one place • Reveals characters' personalities	• Snappy, lively, adds to story

Thoughtshots

3	4	5
• At least one is used	• Used in more than one place • Expanded—interesting "inside" details	• Gets reader to understand/sympathize with character • Shows how feelings change through story

(continued)

Figure 9.11   *Personal narrative rubric*

Snapshots	3	4	5
	• At lease one is used • Some good details words related to the five senses	• Snapshots used in more than one place	• Vivid imagery (metaphors and similes) • Paints memorable scenes

Conventions	3	4	5
	• Words spelled correctly • Complete, clear sentences • No homophone errors	• No run-ons, comma splices, or fragments • Correct comma usage	• Error free

© 2002 by Nancy Steineke from *Reading and Writing Together*. Portsmouth, NH: Heinemann.

Figure 9.11 (*Continued*)

get past the group grade that will ultimately fall upon any paper written together, so here are a few tips. First, always start the project with a rubric and some previous student examples. Ideally, if you have the time, let the students study some good models and have them come up with the rubric. Second, let the group self-evaluate their final draft against the rubric before turning it in to you. As the groups work through the grading, I have them use different colored pens or highlighters to delineate where they've met certain requirements and to write explanations in the margins. I find that when the group has to match their final draft to the rubric that carefully, their assessment and my assessment of the paper are seldom dissimilar.

When the self-evaluation of a project doesn't line up with my assessment, I find the documentation in the Process Journals and Letters very useful. As the groups work through the various stages of their piece, they maintain a daily record of what was done during the meeting. This record is kept in the same manner as the Literature Circle Processing Sheets discussed in Chapter 8. The anecdotal records from the Process Journal are then used to write an individual Process Letter.

Process Journal Questions
1. What do you plan to get done during today's meeting?
2. What did you get done during today's meeting?
3. What specific behaviors and actions contributed to your group's success?
4. How will you work together differently during the next meeting so that you get more done, make your story more interesting, or get along with each other better?
5. What does each person need to do on his own before you meet again? What goals do you need to set for your next meeting?

As students meet in their groups, I walk around, inspecting and stamping their Process Journal entries to make sure the reflection is ongoing. If you don't make this part of the routine, the kids will write the journal notes at the last minute just like they write their outlines after the term paper is finished. By the time a Process Journal is completed, it should have a stamp for every meeting.

When the project is due, these journals are turned in with a cover letter. No member of a group will receive a grade on the final project unless his journal and letter are attached. The Process Journal letter highlights that person's specific contributions to the project plus anything else I, as the teacher, should know. Yes, this does give the kids an opportunity to rat on their partners, though few do. The most memorable set of letters I ever read was from one self-selected group. Each member claimed to have done all the work, and there were four members in the group. I guess this meant that the work must have been evenly divided and everyone worked hard. Who knows! Hey, they picked each other. At least no one was blaming me for their poor partner choices.

Do not prepare to tear your hair out over all these letters and journals you're going to have to read and grade; take a breath and relax. Before the groups turn their projects in, have them present them to the entire class or at least another group as you monitor the class. Or have them defend their self-evaluation to another group as "the prosecution" keeps asking them to cite specific evidence on how each rubric criteria was met. By the time you collect the projects and associated detritus, you'll be pretty familiar with them. Give them a quick eyeballing to see if there are any big discrepancies between the self-evaluations and what you would assign. If there is, it's time for some negotiation. If the differences are minor, go with their grades and make your life simpler. Also, be sure to skim the letters for any ugly incidents that you need to be aware of as you grade so that a surprise parent phone call doesn't catch you off guard. Finally, if it looks like angry

---

Process Letter

General Instructions: Write a letter to me, Mrs. Steineke, describing your role in the completion of this project. Before writing, review the day-to-day accomplishments and notes detailed in your Process Journal. Be sure to answer all of the questions posed and give specific details to back up your points/opinions.

1. What specific contributions did you make to your group? Think about ideas, specific project parts, other skills (typing, art, etc.), and attendance.

2. What specific cooperative skills did you consciously use so that your group worked well together and produced the best project possible?

3. What problems did your group run into during the process? When and where did your group get stuck? How did your group solve the problem? Were you happy with the solutions?

4. If you had to do a similar project in the future, what would you do differently to make the project process go more smoothly and successfully? What do you know now that you didn't know before?

Figure 9.12   *Process Letter instructions*

parents are ready to start World War III, wave the white flag and grade that student only on her individual work. Honestly though, if you set the groups up, train them to work together, keep those five group design elements in mind, and start with a rubric, I doubt you'll ever run into that last problem. But, forewarned is forearmed.

Good Story Models

The following are some of my favorite models for group story writing.

1. "The Secret Life of Walter Mitty" by James Thurber
   Students follow Thurber's model of moving the story back and forth between the worlds of daydream and reality. The challenge is for students to create new "Mitty" adventures that fit into contemporary society. Nowadays, Mitty often daydreams he is James Bond, Arnold Schwarzenegger, or the Crocodile Hunter.
      Another spin-off from Mitty is to change the daydreams to flashbacks. Rather than a commonplace item sending the character into a fantasy, the prop sends the character into a recollection of an important earlier memory. Students enjoy choosing settings that stir important memories for them: graduation, weddings, funerals, prom.

2. "Night Club" by Katharine Brush (see appendix)
   This story takes place in the dressing room (women's washroom) of a 1920s night club during the height of prohibition. Each mini-story begins as some characters enter and ends when they leave. The character maintaining continuity is the ladies room attendant. Students pick a location and a narrating character and then create three mini-stories. In the past, the narrating characters have included a piece of gum stuck under a high school classroom desk and a housefly buzzing around the family reunion picnic of presidential hopeful Gary Hart (remember the Donna Rice scandal?).

Story Title: _____   Names _____

Date: _____   _____

Watership Down New Rabbit Mythology Rubric

Not There Yet (1–2)	On the Way (3–4)	El-ahrairah Would Be Proud (5)
• Less than 3 pages • Rehash of original novel incident	• 3–5 pages • Details of original story intact	• 5 or more pages • Basic story intact while drama, action, intrigue, humor, heroism or magic have been expanded upon
• Summarizes story—little dialogue	• Story told by specific character • Characters in myth use dialogue when speaking	• Equal mix of narration and dialogue • Word choices and descriptions reflect creative use of rabbit dialect/traditions

1. What part or parts of this story do you like the best?

2. What difficulties did you run into while completing this assignment?

3. If you had more time, what would you change or revise? Which part of the story are you least satisfied with?

Figure 9.13 *Rubric and self-evaluation for Watership Down mythology project*

3. *Watership Down* by Richard Adams

Of course, I definitely don't have students writing novel length pieces, but when we study mythology we often read this book. Within *Watership Down* there are a series of rabbit tales surrounding the mythical rabbit called El-ahrairah, who is the ultimate trickster rabbit. After reading the novel, I allow students to work alone or in groups to write a new tale that the rabbits might tell.

Fairy Tales

Teachers probably invented rewriting fairy tales as a writing assignment the moment after the Brothers Grimm told their first story. However, you can't knock this assignment because it has high "fun potential" and it offers another way to practice the revision drafts described earlier. When I first tried this assignment, what surprised me the most was the number of students who were rather unfamiliar with many fairy tales. Unless it's been depicted in a recently released Disney movie, many kids probably aren't going to have the extensive background knowledge you might have expected. Therefore, before we try writing new stories, I make sure they are familiar with the original ones. The best way to do this is to have students work with a partner. Each pair has a different story, and their job is to read the story, learn it, and be able to tell it to the rest of the class. A professional storyteller whose workshop I recently attended also recommends that students first rewrite the story in their own words.

After the performances, choose one of the stories to rework; it doesn't have to be the story they performed. There are many published examples of fairy tale retellings. I've included a list of these in the resources section of this chapter. After listening to a few read alouds, students brainstorm a list of possible changes. Here are some ideas that usually come up.

1. Have a different character tell the story—change the point of view.
2. Change some plot elements.
3. Combine parts of two different stories.
4. Put the story in modern times or change the setting.
5. Add new characters.
6. Make the good guys the bad guys.
7. Write a sequel.
8. Tell the story backwards—start at the end—use character flashbacks.
9. Give the story a different ending.
10. Make the story ironic.
11. Change characters (occupation, gender, species).

Extending the Audience: Class Books

A great way to conclude a group writing project unit is with a class book. It makes a wonderful class souvenir because each person has something in the book. I've done books of "Walter Mitty" spin-off stories, fractured fairy tales, *Watership Down* myths, and personal narratives. Or, if the class has done lots of different kinds of writing, each student can submit his one favorite piece for a multi-genre class magazine. Be sure to also specify a page limit and require that all submissions are single spaced. Two single-spaced pages for an entry works best because thirty entries boil down to fifteen pages, and each entry starts on the right-hand page, just like the chapters in a real book. If you use the standard-style binding machine found in the main offices of most schools, you'll find that long books become unwieldy when trying to punch the holes, so running the stories back to back is an absolute must. Also, the bigger the plastic binding comb necessary, the more expensive. Enlist the aide of your budding artists to design a cover and add illustrations to the stories. In the past, I got everyone's disks and combined them for a single document so that the pages would be numbered consecutively, but that takes way too much time, so I recommend numbering the pages by hand unless you can get a student to do the disk work for you. Even if the page numbers are added by hand, it doesn't take much time to type up an official and accurate looking table of contents for the beginning.

One of the things that always worried me about the class books was that the pieces of writing were not perfect; I feared that some adult would pick up the book, notice a misspelled word, and immediately report my students' illiteracy to a newspaper columnist such as the late Mike Royko, an author who thoroughly enjoyed humiliating an unsuspecting victim. Luckily, Randy Bomer came to my rescue by suggesting the use of a prominently displayed disclaimer (1995). Here's the letter I always put at the beginning of any class book.

> Dear Readers:
> We hope you take pleasure from reading our pieces. You might notice some mistakes, but please don't think it's because we don't care about making our work as perfect as possible. We proudly admit to being learners still in some areas of writing, so please read with a forgiving eye. If any of the mistakes get in the way of your reading, we apologize and hope they won't detract from what we have created. It's more important for us to get our stories out to you than to wait until the day when they would be absolutely free of mistakes. Enjoy!

The Research Paper

Personal narrative and structured fiction assignments are nice ways to get the kids in the groove of writing significantly different revisions and also using Peer Conferencing time well. Being in the habit of writing and conferencing makes the segue to nonfiction that much easier. Though at times I do have students experiment with different nonfiction genres, most of the time high school nonfiction writing falls into the "research paper" category. Therefore, the ideas presented here don't focus on creating unique revisions but instead focus on developing a topic, synthesizing research, and putting it all together in a final draft that is interesting and informative. Of course, since this is a book about collaboration, an important part of the research and writing process is the Peer Conferencing.

If you've ever read any of Tom Romano's books (his specialty is the multi-genre paper), he often describes the Dialogue Journals/Learning Logs his students keep (Romano 1995, 113). They read and write about the topics they are researching, and he writes back to them, posing questions, giving input, offering redirection when necessary. It's absolutely wonderful! If I had a single section of one class with no more than twelve students, I think I could do this and truly enjoy it, but the reality is that most of us in the upper grades are working with class sizes of thirty or more, and teaching two or three sections of the same class. There's just no way one teacher can offer that kind of support to ninety or more students. I once tried this approach with one class of thirty. Besides the fact that lugging those journals to and from school was a burden, I found it very difficult to keep up this kind of continual and meaningful correspondence; it really took a lot of time from my evenings and weekends. By the end of the semester I was exhausted and resolved that I wouldn't continue my role as educational martyr no matter how much heavenly penance I was earning! That was when I decided that I had to teach my students how to talk with each other about their research. It's my belief that when students can have regular and meaningful conversations, this interaction can serve the same purpose as those Dialogue Journals. Also, it's not like the teacher has left the room. Providing the time for small group conversations about research still lets you listen in and provide direction when necessary.

Choosing a Topic

This past year, our fall semester started unseasonably late due to a series of construction delays. Our school year finally began on September 10, 2001. Before the second day of school had even gotten underway, the first plane had hit the World Trade Center. The horrific catastrophes of that day unnerved and stunned us all and trivialized the typical start of the school year activities. Just the previous day I had passed out copies of *To Kill a Mockingbird*. In previous years I had waited to read the book until the students had mastered some group skills, but the city of Chicago had started a reading initiative called "One Book One Chicago" and *To Kill a Mockingbird* was the program's inaugural title. Throughout September and October, programs, newspaper articles, and discussion groups would be encouraging the populace to read and discuss Harper Lee's classic. What seemed like a good idea on September 10 seemed like an unimportant idea on September 11. Instead, my classes spent the rest of that first week writing, talking, watching television news reports, talking, and writing some more. It was a difficult week. The terrorists had really caught the United States off guard.

The two biggest questions that arose those first days were "Why would someone do this to us?" and "How will the United States respond?" Three pieces of writing that came out of discussions follow. Students read their pieces to the class on Friday, September 14. Our writing and discussion revealed that the events of September 11 created a multitude of questions. We realized that our collective knowledge of terrorism, foreign policy, emergency defense, and military retaliations was minimal.

We began our research by collecting articles and reading newspapers. Students read their articles for homework and met with their groups to summarize the information, talk about what others had heard or read on various topics, and begin to make a list of possible research topics related to September 11. After a couple of days, each group made a poster of the ten most important topics their group had come up with. The members of each group presented their posters and explained the reasoning behind their topics; then all of the posters were displayed around the room for a gallery walk. Students had to get up, move around, study the lists, and think about

---

9/13/01

Reaction to 9/11/01 Terrorist Attacks

When I heard about all this, it really angered me. I felt a sense of hatred towards the people who did this to us. Then I relaxed, but when the world around me didn't, I noticed something. I noticed America turning into a ball of hate fueled by the media. The patriotic people of this country won't be happy until every Middle Eastern country is in ruins. Despite the innocent deaths we suffered, killing more innocent people will not bring back our dead. It will not fix our economic suffering. It will not rebuild the Pentagon or the World Trade Center. Innocent people should not be held accountable for the actions of terrorists. We must find those responsible and then seek peace once again.

Tony

Figure 9.14   *Tony's response to the terrorist attacks*

9/13/01

Reaction to 9/11/01 Terrorist Attacks

My reaction is mostly worry about the retaliation we will have. After the bombing of the U.S. Embassy in, I think, Kenya, we sent cruise missiles to try to devastate Osama Bin Laden's followers and try to kill him. This then gave the message to Muslim and Bin Laden followers that they must be a big threat to America. In a way this gave Bin Laden more followers, which meant more power. Don't get me wrong. Something has to be done, but we cannot just bomb them. We have to think the retaliation thoroughly. I hate to say this, but America is known in other countries for making rash decisions without all of the facts. I heard "war" being said by politicians and students, which makes me wonder if war is really the answer. War is how Bin Laden got his power. We made him and now we have to deal with him. I see on the television the carnage and rescue efforts. They say this is one of the worst moments in America's history. I have to say it might be one of its finest. Everywhere people are volunteering blood and saying prayers for the lost. Look, I know something is going to happen, and I really hope President Bush makes the right decisions. I don't know what those decisions should be.

Andy

Figure 9.15 *Andy's response to the terrorist attacks*

what topic they would like to pursue in their own research. Just as students are more likely to read when they can choose the books, students are more likely to invest themselves in research-related writing when the topic interests them. Here is a partial list of the topics the groups came up with.

Possible Research Topics Connected to September 11, 2001
- Afghan Refugees
- Military Attacks on Afghanistan
- Osama bin Laden
- Rescue Dogs
- Airline Security
- Biological Terrorism
- Terrorist Organization Funding
- Patriotism
- New York City/World Trade Center Victims
- 9/11/01 Effect on Film and Television
- National Security versus Invasion of Privacy
- Collin Powell
- Rudolph Giuliani
- The Taliban
- Navy Seals

9/13/01

Reaction to 9/11/01 Terrorist Attacks

On Monday there were people fighting against praying in schools. On Tuesday you would have had a hard time finding a school that wasn't. On Monday there were people trying to separate each other by race, sex, and color. On Tuesday they were holding hands. On Monday we thought that we were secure. On Tuesday we learned better. On Monday we were talking about heroes being athletes. On Tuesday we relearned what hero meant. On Monday people went to work at the World Trade Center as usual. On Tuesday they died. On Monday people argued with their kids about picking up their rooms. On Tuesday the same people could not get home fast enough to hug their kids. On Monday people picked up McDonalds for dinner. On Tuesday they stayed home. On Monday people were upset that their dry cleaning was not ready on time. On Tuesday they were lining up to give blood for the dying. On Monday politicians argued about budget surpluses. On Tuesday, grief stricken, they sang "God Bless America." On Monday we worried about the traffic and getting to work late. On Tuesday we worried about a plane crashing into our house or place of business. On Monday some children had solid families. On Tuesday they were orphans. On Monday the president was going to Florida to read to children. On Tuesday he returned to Washington to protect our children. On Monday we emailed jokes. On Tuesday we did not.

    These are just some of the things that have changed since September 11. It is sadly ironic how it takes horrific events to place things in perspective, but it has. The lessons learned this week, the people we have taken for granted, the things that have been ignored or overlooked, hopefully will never be forgotten again.

Terra

Figure 9.16   *Terra's response to the terrorist attacks*

- Army Rangers
- Islam

Creating a Focus for Research

Once everyone picks a topic, each student starts a modified KWL chart in his composition book since examining one's background knowledge can help to narrow a topic and focus the research. I only have students use the first two columns: what do you *know* about the topic and what do you *wonder* about the topic. In the *Know* column, I tell students to list everything they know or think they know about the topic. In the *Wonder* column, they list all of the questions they have about the topic. It's important for students to realize that their own personal curiosity is what will drive the research. If you have no questions about your topic, now is the time to pick a new one! Once students have completed their charts solo, it's time to rejoin their groups to share information and help each other come up with more details and questions. This sharing will be more productive if you set a quota: each group needs to come up with five more questions for each member's topic. When all of the students have a good selection of research questions, everyone turns to the next blank page in the composition book and heads it "Research Strategies." Then the groups proceed to discuss and take notes on the following questions.

Questions to Discuss Before Beginning Research

1. What kind of resources will I use to find out my answers?
2. How will I search for the information? This relates particularly to using the Internet, everyone's favorite research tool! Groups can help each other brainstorm different key word search combinations. Students might even know of specific sites or organizations that another member might find useful. Also, students might know someone to interview.
3. How am I going to limit my topic?
4. What format will my piece take? How might I write about what I find out?

The nice thing about having the kids talk about this in their groups is that you can monitor easily, make some suggestions, answer some questions, and move on. Most of the time, I don't think students get enough practice helping each other solve their writing/research dilemmas. Every student is an expert at something school related, and the only way the other students will ever know about that expertise is if they talk to each other about academic issues. It turned out that some of the best Internet sites related to the topics of September 11 were suggested by other class members.

Researching the Topic

Nowadays, I much prefer that kids use the Internet and databases for their research rather than books and periodicals, mainly because getting pages copied is so much simpler. All you have to do is hit print rather than standing in line for the photocopy machine only to realize that you don't have the correct change or you lined the document up wrong against the glass so that half of it is cut off. Also, the Internet provides students with graphics that can be easily placed in a file and then pasted into a document. Here are the big mistakes I see when kids start doing research via the Internet.

1. Failure to narrow the search—nothing like getting a million hits!
2. Taking the first hit they see rather than skimming through the first five or so pages of potential sites.
3. Copying anything and everything.
4. Pasting text into a word processing file and then forgetting to copy the web address.
5. Never stopping to examine the reliability of the source.

There are some ways to combat these problems. First, I only accept printed research that clearly includes the web address. Second, I require students to read their first two or three articles in class. First, I model a piece of text, showing how I read, stop, have a conversation with myself, refer back to my own KW chart and mark notes on information that relates to my questions. Then, with pen, highlighter, and KW chart in hand, students mark important passages and write notes as they read. While they're working, I monitor their solo work, making sure that they are taking the time to write specific notes rather than just underline. Every other day or so, students return to their groups to summarize their articles, explain interesting details, and talk about how the information relates back to their questions. The main job of the others is to listen and ask for more details.

Before the groups meet, it's important for the students to see a model discussion so that they have a clear idea of what skilled and detailed sharing looks like. Without this modeling, I find that group members summarize their articles in the briefest manner possible and little effort is given to truly aiding each writer. Therefore, after each meeting, be sure to include some group processing. One of the questions that frequently needs to be addressed: *In what specific ways did we help each other to continue and refine our research*?

Part of my goal with these frequent group meetings during the research and writing process is to get the kids to start thinking out loud. Having to explain yourself to others forces you to organize and refine your ideas much more than if you only have to read and write on your own. The discussion of the research also gives students a chance to question each other in regards to the reliability of the information. Students need to constantly ask each other, "How do you know if this information is accurate?" Finally, talking about how they've conducted their research gives other group members new ideas on how they might proceed.

Organizing the Details

After students have read and taken notes on about three articles, they return to the KW charts in their composition books to review their original questions and add new ones. Next, students pick out the four most interesting questions related to the topic and put stars by them. Then each question becomes the heading for a different blank page in the composition book. Before proceeding, the kids need to review their four questions to make sure that they are all different enough; sometimes one question is actually the sub topic of another. In that case, the similar question needs to be written on the same page as its companion and a new question needs to be chosen to replace it. Finally, the students go back to their question lists and search for other questions that relate to the four main ones they've chosen. Any questions in a similar vein are listed on the same page as the main question.

After the questions are finalized, each student individually brainstorms what pieces of information would answer the question thoroughly. What do they still need to find out? What kinds of examples would be useful? What kinds of details and statistics are needed to back up the answer? Groups then meet to further brainstorm the types of information needed for each of the questions, trying to go beyond what each individual initially listed. Then the members adjourn and individually comb back through their pieces of research, jotting down specific information under the appropriate question. I tell students that they should have at least a full comp book page of details for each question. Less than that means further research is necessary or that the question is too narrow to create much of an answer. In that case, a new question needs to be created, probably by combining two or three smaller ones from the KW chart.

Direct notetaking is one way to organize information, but many students respond to a more graphic representation. Although, I never had much luck with traditional mapping, my students love using the computer program *Inspiration*. This program allows you to easily manipulate graphic symbols and lines in order to create organizational maps. The nice thing about mapping with the computer is that if you don't like the way you've arranged the information or what you've written, it's easily revised. When it's finally done, a nice neat hard copy is printed. In comparison, when I tried to get kids to map on a piece of paper, they either just stared at its blankness after they put their topic in the center circle or quickly became frustrated with cross-outs, erasures, and various other mistakes and changes. Visually, the end product just wasn't very attractive. In contrast, the kids move quickly because *Inspiration* is very intuitive, and, unlike the paper version of mapping, it even seems to encourage the kids to add more supporting detail because of its visual nature. A near empty computer screen just seems to goad the kids into writing more. Here's a tip, though. Have the kids put each of their research questions in a separate file. If the questions print out separately, there will more room on each page for specific details. Maybe it's the way my students' brains are programmed from playing all those video games! All I know is that for most kids, inspiration really works. Interestingly enough, the only group this program flopped with was my honors class. They hated creating the maps and begged me to let them write outlines with Roman numerals! Go figure. Writers need to experiment with different organizational strategies and pick the ones that work best for them.

Of course, as you might have guessed by now, whether they've taken notes by hand or created an *Inspiration* map, the students are soon back with their Peer Conferencing groups. They need to explain their notes or maps to the others, focusing on how these points and details will answer their questions. Partners need to listen for support, details, weaknesses, or vague points. A good way to do this is for each listener to take on a specific audience role. For example, if the topic was Airport Security, one member might listen to the details pretending to be an anxious passenger while another member might pretend to be an airline pilot. Each member then listens to the details and thinks, "If I were going to get on a plane, what else would I want to know in order to feel secure?" Having students pick specific audience roles also makes individual accountability easier. After listening, each member makes a list of further details the author needs to include so that the question is thoroughly answered. By using different roles, the writer gets a broader response than if his listeners were only thinking in the roles of high school students.

Once this step is completed, students finish their research and write the answers to each of their questions in their composition books. My standard rule of thumb is that if you can't write at least a one-page answer (normal sized handwriting) then you don't have enough to write about yet. After the entries are finished, students return to their conferencing groups and read their questions and answers aloud while their peers listen for specific details and examples along with the writer's insight and opinions related to the information.

Putting the Research Paper Together

Have you noticed that I teach expository writing in a nonlinear fashion? I'm not sure if it's just the way my brain is wired, but I always find it much easier to come up with an introduction after I have a good idea of what the rest of the paper looks like. Also, when I have students focus on writing parts of the paper, it makes it easier for them to see that revision can also focus on one part rather than the whole paper.

When the research has reached the point of being ready to put into a final form, I like to use the I-Search format (Macrorie 1988). While traditional research papers are typically written in a voiceless third person drone, I-Search papers are written in first person and the paper focuses on explaining what the information means to the writer. After students write each part of the I-Search paper in their composition books, they return to the groups for some feedback. While the writer reads, the listeners keep the rubric in mind (see pages 230–231), watching for missing elements and also paying attention to general flow and wording. Now is the time for members to listen carefully and think, "Does this make sense the way it was written? Can I follow the thoughts easily?"

Introduction.   When students start the paper, their introduction explains and answers the following questions:

- How did I get interested in this topic?
- What other topics did I consider?
- What did I already know about the topic?
- How does this topic relate to the overall theme?

Megan's introduction describes her interest in the rumors that swirled about our nation after the September 11 attacks.

On September 11, 2001 America was attacked, but humanity across the world was affected by the cold blooded killers whose leader is too cowardly to come forth and take responsibility for the thousands of innocent lives he took. Rumors are an important part of the terrorist attacks. As soon as the first plane hit, people picked up telephones or got online and began to talk and channel information. As the messages were passed along, stories got twisted and people began to just make things up. I first became interested in this topic because I began to hear a lot of information about the attacks and I wanted to know if it was true. Also, the topic of rumors is something I can relate to due to the fact that I am in high school and rumors are, unfortunately, a primary source of information for students. I found that many of the rumors about September 11 were passed along through the Internet. In the days after the attacks, I received about five emails a day; their subjects included stories about U.S. retaliation, stories about bin Laden, stories about the attacks, and some stories that seemed completely made up. I wanted to know if all this information was true, so I did some research. It turns out that four out of five of the emails I received were false. Before deciding on a topic, I thought about looking into Islam, bin Laden, or holy war, but I thought since everyone is exposed to rumors this topic would be interesting and informative.

Figure 9.17   *Megan's I-Search paper introduction example*

The search.   This part of the paper explains exactly how the topic was researched and where the information came from. A good description of the search should read like a treasure hunt. Describing problems, missteps, and dead ends are as much a part of research as finding the buried treasure: a really good article. Students are encouraged to consider and write about all of their leads. Mentioning the specific help one's group or one's grandmother provided is just as important as listing websites. Figure 9.18 tells the story of Megan's search as she looked for reliable information about the September 11 related rumors.

The fruits of my search.   This is the body of the paper where the questions and their answers appear. However, once again, though students need to answer their questions clearly with detail and specific examples, they are still writing in first person. As the writer talks about the information, it's important that she also relates the research to her own feelings and opinions. What was surprising? Interesting? What information connects to personal experience or other topics? How does this information make the writer feel?

Conclusion.   Consistent with the rest of the I-Search paper, the conclusion is written in first person. Though the writer is expected to revisit the main points mentioned in the introduction, the main purpose of the conclusion is to talk about how the research and learning process changed the writer's viewpoint or gave her insight. Also, any new knowledge almost always creates further curiosity. If the research continued, what direction would it take? What new questions need to be answered? What sources of information are still untapped?

Megan's conclusion appears in Figure 9.20, p. 229.

My search to get as much information as possible was harder than I thought. I found absolutely no information in the newspapers, and obviously books were of no help because the topic was a current event. I began to wonder if I should switch to a topic that would be easier to find articles on, but then I decided to stick with my original topic and see how much information I could get.

I began on the Internet, looking at a website that a classmate suggested: <www.snopes.com>. This site had lots of information about the rumors of the September 11th tragedies, and I gathered most of my articles from this site. There were a variety of true and false rumors, so I chose two true stories and two false stories from this site. I then remembered that we needed different sources of information, so I started to look for another site that might provide different rumors than the ones snopes.com offered. I went to <www.askjeeves.com>. Askjeeves is a site where you can type in a question and it will then give you suggested sites and links. The only useful link I got from Askjeeves was <www.about.com>. This site supplied a few useful rumors and I used them one day when some articles were due, but I used none of them when deciding on my final I-Search questions. I'm glad I chose my topic because it was interesting to learn about and easy to find good information on snopes.com.

Figure 9.18 *Megan's I-Search paper: the Search example*

Should Americans avoid local malls on Halloween?

An email has been forwarded through millions of computers warning American citizens not to go to any shopping malls on Halloween. This was the most common rumor I found. I even received this email, so that's why I decided to investigate it. Here is the rumor.

A girl claimed to have gotten a letter from her Afghan boyfriend who said he loved her and would never see her again. He also told her not to get on any planes on September 11, 2001 or go to any shopping malls on Halloween. The email continued saying that the girl gave the letter to the F.B.I.

When I received this email, I went to snopes.com and researched what I could. The link gave me a lot of information about this story, and it was in fact proven false. These were the details I found out. The email began circulating on October 5, 2001. Also, the F.B.I.'s National Press Office stated that they got many calls about this email. When they checked it out, they found that no letter from a girl with an Afghan boyfriend ever existed. Now I know that when I receive these forwarded emails, I need to read into them to see if the facts add up. For instance, why would that boyfriend take the chance of ruining his entire terrorist mission just to warn his girlfriend? Also, wouldn't he have known if she were planning a trip? Many people are falling for these email hoaxes.

Figure 9.19 *Megan's I-Search question example*

As a result of my search, I would say that rumors are a troublesome problem for our nation. I feel that making up rumors in connection with the attacks on America is morally wrong. Our country is going through some rough times. Thousands of innocent citizens have lost their lives, yet some people have the nerve to stir up trouble and worry people unnecessarily. There is enough going on in this world without having people create more problems. As I come to the end of this paper, I feel I am much more informed on rumors. I received many emails in connection with September 11, most of which turned out to be false. This should be a time for our nation to pull together, not scare and misinform each other.

Figure 9.20   *Megan's I-Search paper conclusion*

I-Search bibliography.   When I was in high school, I remember struggling over bibliography cards, trying my best to get the commas, periods, and indentations all in the right order. Well, guess what? The computer age has eliminated the hassle. Search the web and you will find sites that organize and alphabetize source information automatically. All you need to do is plug it in. <www.Easybib.com> is my favorite one. This site offers you a multitude of source options ranging from online news sources, specific websites, email, speeches, and, surprise, books. Call me lazy, but I've never seen a better and more complete bunch of bibliographies than when I told the kids to start using Easybib. The kids really owned it too because they were recommending it to their friends in other classes who were writing research papers. One girl even reported that she noticed another girl struggling at a nearby media center computer, desperately trying to put a bibliography together from scratch. Carolyn took pity on the girl, gave her a quick Easybib lesson, and then proceeded to educate the media specialists on the merits of the website.

We also refer to a rubric to evaluate the research papers once they are completed.

Increasing Positive Interdependence and Individual Accountability

When peer conferences take place, it's important to monitor the conversations carefully to see if true writing-related work is getting done. When groups get off-task, the first thing to determine is whether they're lazy or whether they don't have a clear enough picture of what they need to do. Very often I find that when students move from conferencing fiction and personal narrative writing to conferencing research and nonfiction, their level of functioning diminishes. Though groups have some mastery of listening, asking Follow-up Questions, offering friendly support, and using quiet voices, conferencing nonfiction is challenging because the nature of the discussion and use of these skills changes subtly. Students might need some minilessons on how to orally summarize an article to others or how to point out specific and important details. Students also need to learn and practice how to detect research weaknesses while listening and then asking helpful follow-up questions. These skills are subtle and complex. You'll need to model them for the class and then have students participate in some model discussions as the rest of the class observes and takes notes. Don't forget to have the conference groups process their progress. Each student needs to keep a Peer Conference Process Log that records suggestions and contributions. Once again, the elements of this log are very similar to the Literature Circle Processing Sheet students keep,

I-Search Rubric

Introduction

	3	4	5
	• Correct format • Personal interest in topic explained • No longer than one page double spaced • Easy to follow	• Path of topic choice/ thought process explained in detail	• Details from KW chart used

Search

	3	4	5
	• Correct format • Basic search path described • Some relevant details • No longer than one page double spaced • Easy to follow	• Thought process in search explained • More relevant details	• Search explained thoroughly • Dead ends and rethinking explained

The Fruits of My Search: Questions Answers

	3	4	5
	• Correct format • Question clearly displayed • Answer reveals specific research details • Answers the question • Easy to follow • In writer's own words— not copied from sources • No longer than 1 page double spaced for each answer	• Answer reveals serious research • Many relevant details and examples • Interesting	• Writer includes some personal reaction/response

Figure 9.21   *I-Search rubric*

	3	4	5
Conclusion	• Connects to ideas presented in introduction • Easy to follow • No longer than 1 page double spaced	• Still unanswered questions/new questions discussed • Path to further research explained	• Personal reaction/change in thinking as a result of research
Bibliography/Works Cited	• 5 sources cited • Correct format (hanging indent) • Correct order of source information • Basic information for all sources • 100% focus on topic	• Full information on all sources	• More than 5 sources with full information
Conventions	• Correct format • Consistent paragraphing • Complete sentences that make sense • Correct spelling • Correct homophone usage • Double spaced, 12 pt. Times New Roman	• Correct use of punctuation • No run-ons, comma splices, or fragments	• Error free

Figure 9.21 (Continued)

as described in Chapter 8. You might make up a hand-out or just have the kids keep the log on loose leaf paper or in their composition books. Either way, certain information would have to be recorded for each meeting.

Research Process Log Information

1. Date, members present, nature of meeting (discuss research, share beginning ideas, etc.)
2. What *specific* questions or ideas did others give me about my research/writing? List at least three.
3. What *specific* questions or ideas did I give others about their research/writing? List at least three
4. What was the most helpful thing our group did today to get along and enjoy our time together?
5. What was the most helpful thing our group did today to improve the quality of each individual's writing project?
6. What specific writing or research do I need to do before our next Peer Conferencing meeting?

If time permits, have the groups share their ideas with the rest of the class. I always tell students that I want them to learn how to find help from their peers since they'll be around longer than I will be.

Groups fall off-task when one or more members comes unprepared. Therefore, it's up to you to make that option as unattractive as possible. First, students have to bring the research, writing, etc. to the group on the day it's due. Those assignments are their admission tickets to their Peer Conferencing groups. Be sure to date stamp whatever is due that day! Getting to conference with the group should be worth some points, but it should also be seen as socially rewarding. However, without the necessary materials, members can't contribute fully. Unprepared students need a little mini-conference with the teacher followed by silent solo time to catch up and get back on track for the next meeting.

I-Search Success

When you combine the I-Search format along with the research process steps I've outlined previously, getting kids to write research papers is a breeze. Having to talk and write at frequent intervals throughout the process tricks the kids into getting the project done. This past semester, out of ninety kids, I only had one student fail to turn in a paper. Also, writing in first person definitely cuts down on the cut and paste Internet plagiarism or out and out term paper stealing that is so common these days. Since most source articles are written in third person, the information has to be rephrased in order to fit into the first-person narration of an I-Search paper. Also, most online term papers are written in a traditional "boring" objective third-person narration, so downloading one of those doesn't do much to meet the criteria of the more personal I-Search paper. Plus, when it comes time to grade the papers, the first-person narration lets the individual voices shine through and makes the reading far more interesting.

Expanding the Audience: Reading the I-Search Aloud

A final twist that I added to the research papers was an oral interpretation component. About a week before the finished paper was due, the first completely typed up draft was due. That day, the students met with their editing partners and practiced reading their papers aloud to each other. I made them stand and told the readers to keep a pen in hand because whenever you hear your words aloud you always want to correct errors and make changes. As I monitored, I was happy to see a lot of impromptu editing taking place. Partners were instructed to watch and listen and use the following coaching phrases as often as necessary.

"Eye Contact—look up from your paper!"

"Posture—feet shoulder width apart, hands out of pockets, back straight!"

"Slow down!"

"More energy—ham it up!"

Two days later, two copies of the new and improved paper were due. This time the partners worked together to proofread the papers, using the procedure I outlined earlier in this chapter. The following week, each student turned in a final draft to me, but also retained a second copy to read aloud to the class. When called upon to read, the student wrote her name and paper topic on the board, which the audience copied into their composition books. While the author read the introduction, search, two of the four questions, and the conclusion, the audience listened carefully and then wrote down three specific facts they learned about the topic of the paper. Later, these notes were checked during a binder, planner, and composition book check.

I decided to have the students read the papers aloud for several reasons. First, after all that work, I thought the papers deserved an audience of more than just me. Second, having to read the paper to the class increased individual accountability; students were much more concerned that the paper made sense and sounded right! Third, I always enjoy hearing an author read his own work; a good reader makes his words take on greater life than they have just sitting on the page. Plus, the oral interpretation saved me grading time. Having already heard most of the papers, I could read and grade them much more quickly than if I were meeting each one cold. Also, because I wanted to grade the papers when they were fresh in my mind, I didn't procrastinate. After a paper was presented, I made a point of having it graded within twenty-four hours.

Expanding Nonfiction Writing

Once students have a handle on conducting focused research and putting the information into their own words in an organized fashion, it's fun to experiment with other nonfiction genres. I like the kids to start by examining the nonfiction that they read regularly. Most upper-grade students do read magazines, so I have them start to keep folders of articles they think are interesting and well written. Collecting articles also serves as a good group icebreaker—it's a good way to learn about interests and hobbies outside of school.

When a group has collected some articles between them, they can begin to look at the craft within the writing. First, each member presents his favorite article to the group, summarizing it but also explaining why it is interesting and well written. Here are some of the things I want them to start thinking about.

Examining Nonfiction Craft

1. What kind of research did the author have to do to write this piece?
2. What makes the article interesting?
3. How does the author grab your attention in the beginning?
4. How does the author connect the information so that it makes sense to the reader?
5. How does the author conclude the piece?

Performance Evaluation

I-Search Paper Presentation   Name _____

Title _____   Date _____ Hour _____

- **First impression:** confidence stance   no   1   2   3   4   5   Times 1 =
  ready to perform

- **Practiced:** no stumbles   no   1   2   3   4   5   Times 2 =

- **Voice:** audible, clear enunciation,   no   1   2   3   4   5   Times 2 =
  even pace, holds audience's
  attention

- **Interpretation:** practiced,   no   1   2   3   4   5   Times 2 =
  makes paper sound interesting,
  not monotone

- **Eye contact:** regularly looks at   no   1   2   3   4   5   Times 1 =
  audience, face is not buried in
  paper

- **Posture:** continued confidence   no   1   2   3   4   5   Times 1 =
  stance

Total _____

Maximum Points: 45

Figure 9.22   *I-Search performance grade sheet*

6. Which passages really stand out?

7. What format did the author choose?

8. Who is the audience this article is aimed at?

9. What does the author want the reader to do or think about after reading the piece?

After some discussion of the articles, the group adjourns for another solo activity with their article files. This time I instruct them to read just the first couple of paragraphs of each of their articles and jot down how the writer catches the audience's attention. After reviewing all articles, students return to their groups, each ready to read the three best examples they found. From the small groups, the class reconvenes to make a master list of opening devices and volunteers are asked to read their examples so everyone gets to hear those devices in use.

The RAFT is the most useful device I've found in moving the kids towards different genres. RAFT is an acronym that stands for Role, Audience, Format, Topic (Buehl 2001, 87). Keeping their research in mind, students make specific decisions. They pick a perspective from which to write (*role*), decide who the writing will be aimed at (*audience*), and decide how the information will be presented (*format*). Figure 9.23 is an example that I wrote for a class. My role is that of a Jonestown Massacre survivor, my audience is a newspaper reader, and my format is that of a first-person account.

Once students have seen the example and understand the RAFT components, it's time for them to get their article collections out and choose one to use as a model. It's also a good idea to gather format ideas in a large group before students make their writing decisions. Here is a list one class came up with.

Different Writing Formats

Reviews

- Books
- CDs
- Movies
- TV shows

News Stories

Feature Articles

Editorials and Opinions

Parodies

Eulogies

Interviews

This part of the decision process ends with a peer conference where each person presents his RAFT idea. The members need to ask questions about the RAFT components so that the writer thinks them through.

RAFT Peer Conferencing Questions

1. Why did you pick that audience?

2. How does your format fit your research topic?

3. How does your format fit your audience?

4. How will the reader know what role you are taking?

I Survived a Death Cult

When I first joined the people's temple, our leader, our messiah Jim Jones promised that we would create heaven on earth. Most of the church's followers, including myself, were African Americans. Life had always been hard in the United States. The "Land of Opportunity" never seemed to offer us much, so we felt little apprehension or regret when Jim Jones announced we were moving our congregation from San Francisco to a small South American country called Guyana. There we would build our society from scratch, everyone connected by common beliefs and goals. We were going to create the perfect world for ourselves.

At first the work was hard and tiring yet challenging. Gradually though, the atmosphere of harmony slowly changed to one of persecution and paranoia, fueled largely by our leader, Jim Jones. He told us that people in the United States wanted to destroy us, that Satan would take our souls if we did not put our complete faith in our messiah. We were captives of Jonestown: he held our passports, money, and controlled any communication we had with the outside world.

By the spring of 1978, followers lived in constant fear of Jim Jones. Small rule infractions led to torture and death threats. He began preaching that there could be no utopia on earth. All 915 of us began practicing an elaborate suicide ritual. When the speaker announced it, we would line up for a cup of Kool-Aid that might be laced with cyanide.

I found hope once again on November 17 when congressman Leo Ryan arrived in Jonestown with several reporters and concerned relatives. A friend of mine secretly slipped a note to one of the reporters; that gave me the courage to defy Jim Jones and ask Congressman Ryan for help in escaping Jonestown. By the following day, fifteen people left with Ryan for the airstrip. Though no one voiced it, we knew that Jim Jones would not let his followers leave this easily.

As it turned out, two of our "defectors" were actually Jim Jones's hit men, who opened fire on us both in the plane and on the tarmac. Wounded, I watched helplessly as Congressman Ryan and three reporters were shot dead. I only escaped by pretending to be dead. Recovering from my wounds in the hospital, I learned that over 900 people took their lives that day by drinking poisoned Kool-Aid. Jim Jones was found with a bullet hole in his head. I will never forget that day as long as I live.

www.rickross.com/reference/jonestown/jonestown8.html
www.netcentral.co.uk/steveb/cults/jones.html

Figure 9.23   *RAFT Example*

5. Which information from your research will you be using? How will you make the information appealing to your audience?

6. How will you make the research your own and avoid plagiarizing?

Since a RAFT paper is generally much shorter than a research paper, conference groups would probably meet once after members wrote their first drafts and once after their revision. As mentioned much earlier, students work only with a partner when the paper has reached the editing/proofreading stage.

Examples of RAFT Assignments

Role	Audience	Format	Topic
Newspaper Reporter	Readers in the 1870s	Obituary	Qualities of General Custer
Lawyer	U.S Supreme Court	Appeal Speech	Dred Scott Decision
Abraham Lincoln	Dear Abbey	Advice Column	Problems with his Generals
Mike Royko	Public	News Column	Capital Punishment
Frontier Woman	Self	Diary	Hardships in West
Constituent	U.S. Senator	Letter	Gun Control
Newswriter	Public	News Release	Ozone Layer has been formed
Chemist	Chemical Company	Instructions	Combinations to Avoid
Wheat Thin	Other Wheat Thins	Travel Guide	Journey through the Digestive System
Plant	Sun	Thank You Note	Sun's role in Plant's Growth
Scientist	Charles Darwin	Letter	Refute a Point in Evolution Theory
Square Root	Whole Number	Love Letter	Explain Relationship
Repeating Decimal	Set of Rational Numbers	Petition	Prove You Belong to this Set
Cook	Other Cooks	Recipe	Alcoholism
Julia Child	TV Audience	Script	Wonders of Eggs
Advertiser	TV Audience	Public Service Announcement	Importance of Fruit
Lungs	Cigarettes	Complaint	Effects of Smoking
Huck Finn	Jim	Letter	What I learned During the Trip
Joseph Stalin	George Orwell	Letter	Reactions to *Animal Farm*
Comma	9th Grade Students	Complaint	How is Misused
Trout	Self	Diary	Effects of Acid Rain on Lake

Figure 9.24 *RAFT example chart*

RAFT Grade Sheet   Name_____

Role _____   Date_____Hour____

Format _____

- Topic clear to reader   5   4   3   2   1   no

- Role is clear and fits format   5   4   3   2   1   no

- 3 sources listed: 2 Internet addresses   5   4   3   2   1   no
  and one print source

- Original and interesting piece   10 9 8 7 6 5 4 3 2 1 no
  created from historical research

- Error free   10 9 8 7 6 5 4 3 2 1 no

Figure 9.25   *RAFT Grade sheet*

Newspapers and Brochures

Another way students can create more original research writing is to put it in the format of a multi-genre paper (Romano 1995). I'll typically have kids use their research to write a poem, a straight news story, and an interview. The best way I've found to get an audience for this project is to put the writing into a desktop publishing format. *Microsoft Publisher* has loads of templates for just about any occasion. Plus, if you have a scanner, students can include personal photographs. And if you don't have a scanner, it's very easy to get pictures from the Internet to accompany each article. Whereas the traditional double-spaced paper comes off as boring, students enjoy reading each other's brochures and newspapers. And, if you have extra time in the computer lab, send your kids to <http://puzzlemaker.school.discovery.com/CrissCrossSetupForm.html> where the kids can create and print out their own crossword puzzles based on the information in their publications. This is a fun way to get classmates to read each other's writing more closely.

How Do I Assess This?

During the writing process I use a lot of stamps. Entries in Process Logs get date stamped, each revision gets stamped, articles with notes get stamped. If it's part of the process, it's going to get a stamp! Ongoing pieces that are stamped are stored in the front of the writing section.

Throughout the writing process, I also try to get students to frequently refer to the rubric, which ideally not only lists the components that will be graded but also defines variations in quality. As you'll notice, some of my rubrics are much more clearly defined than others; it's something that I'm continually working on. Also, don't forget to involve students in the rubric process. The more they study models that demonstrate quality, the better they'll be able to define quality and then execute it in their own pieces. Only final drafts are graded against the rubric. These scores count in my grade book as tests.

Parting Words

In some respects, I think that training and managing Peer Conferencing groups is more challenging than running Literature Circles. While a Literature Circle always has a book at its foundation, in a conferencing group everything has to come from the members: the writing, the revision ideas, the questions. If students are not taught how to respond to writing and create meaningful conversation for the writer, the groups may appear to be on-task, but their true usefulness will be minimal. However, taking the time to teach the skills is well worth it. An individual teacher is only around for a fraction of a student's life as a writer, so knowing how to talk about writing with one's peers and get help when needed is a skill that will come in handy often. When thinking and talking as a writer becomes a practiced behavior, kids own writing in a way they didn't before.

A colleague of mine told me about a student who was in my Basic Writing class the previous semester. Springtime is high-stakes testing time in Illinois, so my colleague decided to give her class a short review of writing structures before the kids took the big test. After my friend went over the steps of writing a personal narrative (before Illinois eliminated that writing genre) my former student pulled the teacher aside and took her to task. "You didn't need to go over personal narratives. I know all about what a good story needs. I already *know* how to write dialogue, thoughtshots, and snapshots!"

Resources

Lane, Barry. 1993. *After THE END: Teaching and Learning Creative Revision.* Portsmouth, NH: Heinemann.

Barry Lane has tons of great ideas for revising fiction and narratives. It's one of my very favorite professional books. I wish he would write a companion book that focuses on revision strategies for nonfiction genres.

Macrorie, Ken. *The I-Search Paper.* 1988. Portsmouth, NH: Heinemann.

Though sometimes this book gives you a little more information than you might have wanted, it is the best source out there if you are looking for a more thorough discussion of how to write an I-Search paper.

Romano, Tom. 1995. *Writing with Passion: Life Stories, Multiple Genres.* Portsmouth, NH: Heinemann.

Romano is *the* expert when it comes to the multi-genre format. His book shows many, many different examples.

Fairy Tales Retold

Garner, James Finn. 1994. *Politically Correct Bedtime Stories: Modern Tales for Our Life & Times.* New York: Macmillan Publishing Company.

Hilarious read-alouds for older students who understand the meaning of the phrase "politically correct."

Granowsky, Alvin. 1993. *That Awful Cinderella.* Austin, TX: Steck-Vaughn Company.

From the Point of View Stories series, this book tells the original story on one side. Flip it over and the story is retold from an evil stepsister's perspective.

_____. 1993. *The Unfairest of Them All.* Austin, TX: Steck-Vaughn Company.

From the Point of View Stories series, this book tells the original story of Snow White on one side. Flip it over and the story is retold from Snow White's stepmother's perspective.

_____. 1993. *Grow Up, Peter Pan!* Austin, TX: Steck-Vaughn Company.

From the Point of View Stories series, this book tells the original story on one side. Flip it over and the story is retold from Captain Hook's perspective.

Jacobs, A. J. 1997. *Fractured Fairy Tales.* New York: Bantam Books.

Yes, all of those great stories from *The Rocky and Bullwinkle Show* have finally made it to the printed page.

Minters, Frances. 1996. *Sleepless Beauty.* New York: Viking.

A contemporary retelling in which Beauty is awakened by a rock star.

Scieszka, Jon. 1989. *The True Story of the 3 Little Pigs!* New York: Viking.

Told from the wolf's perspective, he complains that the tabloids have exaggerated and exploited his story.

_____. 1991. *The Frog Prince Continued.* New York: Viking.

In this version, the prince does not live happily ever after and longs to return to the pond.

Trivizas, Eugene. 1993. *The Three Little Wolves and the Big Bad Pig.* New York: Macmillan Publishing Company.

As three mild-mannered wolves try to maintain their homes and play a game of croquet, the mean pig of the neighborhood bullies them endlessly.

CHAPTER 10

Portfolios
A Tool for Refining
Collaborative Literacy Skills

I remember when my curiosity was first piqued in regards to portfolios. "Portfolio" was the total buzzword of the moment. Everyone seemed to be doing them, but no one seemed very good at explaining them. I attended several different workshops and left feeling no better informed on the topic. It wasn't until I attended an alternative assessment conference led by Kay Burke that I realized a portfolio could be a collection of work that was already graded; portfolios didn't have to contain brand new, never before seen artifacts. Those previous portfolio examples discussed at the workshops had been restricted to writing samples, mainly new pieces and new revisions. I just couldn't imagine how to grade 100 of those at the end of a semester. Kay Burke and later Janell Cleland and Carol Porter in their book *The Portfolio as a Learning Strategy* (1995) were the first ones who showed me how to build a portfolio around previously graded work. Rather than re-grading the artifacts, these pieces now serve as tools to demonstrate what stands out to students about their learning.

My main portfolio goal is to get the students to reflect on their past accomplishments and their future learning goals. Therefore, I give students as much choice as possible when it comes to selecting artifacts for inclusion. However, I also insist that they demonstrate skill competence in each binder category: *Reading, Writing, Speaking and Listening,* and *Leadership*. What follows are the steps I take within a semester so that presentation portfolios are ready by final exam week.

Maintaining the Binders

The binder is a complete collection of student work. In fact, it is a working portfolio. The better a student does to categorize and maintain the organization of his binder, the better off he will be when it comes time to create a presentation portfolio. Students are already encouraged to keep proper order because of the binder checks I do every four weeks or so. It is also very helpful to take some class time to work on organization. The best way is to have the students work with partners and just go through their binders together page by page. When they come to a discrepancy, they can decide where the paper really belongs, ask someone else nearby, or, as a last resort, ask the teacher! When they are kept organized, the binders come in handy when you want kids to compare their progress (or lack thereof) on a series of assignments. For example, before students do the next Book Talk Discussion Sheet, I have them get out all of their old sheets in order to see what areas need more effort. When working on corrections for the final draft of a paper, I have students get out all of their old corrected drafts and make a list of their frequent errors. Now when editing this latest draft, they know what to look for. At least once every quarter, I have students put all of their old reading sheets in order to examine how their reading speeds have changed. An organized binder makes these comparisons a snap. That's why I always require students to have their binders with them on a daily basis. Believe me, they'll want to leave them in their lockers. However, if you make them an integral part of class routine, the kids will stop nagging you about them after awhile!

The binder also helps the kids to review what they've learned and accomplished. Towards the middle of second and fourth quarters, I have the kids list the four binder categories and leaf through their papers, listing the skills they've mastered. For example, under *Reading* students might list their improved reading speed, the different fiction genres they've explored, the new words they've learned through reading, or how they now go about the task of picking good passages. This certainly helps the kids realize how far they've come.

Becoming Familiar with the Portfolio Content Categories

Students begin working on their semester portfolios about four weeks before the semester ends. I start by giving them some basic instructions and showing them what a finished portfolio looks like. I complete my own portfolio as an example and also show them old student examples. Though most kids want to keep their portfolios, flattery will almost always get you some really good souvenir portfolios. Also, I always end up with extras from the kids who never bother to come pick them up on the last day of school. It's good to have a variety of quality samples to show, since students always want to know what an A would look like compared to a C.

Once students have a handle on the idea that a portfolio is a collection of work that demonstrates accomplishment, the discussion needs to turn towards what could actually go into it. The only artifact I require either semester is the reading list; the rest of the contents is the choice of the students. A problem I run into, particularly when students are working on their first portfolios, is that they often don't choose the most illustrative pieces of work to include. I finally solved this problem by taking class time to actually go through the binders together and make a master list of artifacts that could be used to prove accomplishment in *Reading, Writing, Speaking and Listening*, and *Leadership*. Quickly, students begin to see that many artifacts overlap. For example, an Observation or Processing Sheet from a Literature Circle discussion could be used as proof of accomplishment in either *Speaking and Listening* or *Leadership*. I try to get students to start thinking about *which* artifact would be the best choice to show accomplishment. At this point I also emphasize that a portfolio should show variety in the artifact choices. Therefore, no type of artifact can be repeated. In other words, if a student uses a Book Talk Discussion Sheet as a *Reading* artifact, she cannot use another Book Talk Sheet for *Writing*.

After completing the lists for the four categories, I turn to the "Choice" artifact. This is an opportunity for the students to place one additional piece in their portfolios. Students might choose something they are proud of but couldn't use because they had already filled their artifact allotment in all of the other categories, or a student might have an artifact that demonstrates learning but just doesn't seem to fit into any of the other categories. I always make "Choice" an optional category. If a student is going to add an additional artifact, I want it to definitely mean something to her. As you've probably noticed, I want these portfolios to be as thin and as light as possible. I don't want to lug boxes of these things around. Besides, limiting the number of artifacts forces the students to make careful choices.

Semester 1 Portfolio for Sophomore English

What is a portfolio for this class?

Your portfolio represents your participation, performance, and growth in this class. This portfolio may contain some of your best work but may also contain work that needs improvement but represents a realization or breakthrough in learning. It is your written reflection on the pieces that is most important.

Portfolio Contents:

You may use only <u>one</u> artifact for each category, and you can have no artifact duplicates (i.e., two journals, two Book Talk Discussion Sheets, etc.). Each artifact must have an explanation sheet attached to it. *Part of creating a presentation portfolio is to carefully pick the artifact that best represents accomplishment or growth in each category.*

Content Categories:

1. **Reading:** Complete reading list (required) plus an additional artifact of your choice
2. **Writing**
3. **Speaking and Listening**
4. **Leadership**
5. **Choice Artifact** (optional)

What do I need to do prior to the due date?

1. Neatly and carefully complete the artifact explanation sheets.
2. Address a reflective letter to the portfolio reader that explains how the pieces in your portfolio reflect your accomplishments of this past semester.

What do I need to do prior to my interview appointment?

Display and explain the contents of your portfolio to an adult family member. This is meant to be practice for your portfolio interview with me. Afterwards, that person should write a response that becomes part of your portfolio.

How will my portfolio be graded?

Your portfolio will count as your final exam grade, which is 20% of your overall semester grade. Be sure to carefully study the grading scale and the rubric.

What will I be doing during the final exam period for this class?

We will be watching the film version of *To Kill a Mockingbird.*

Figure 10.1 *Portfolio instructions*

Artifact List for Semester 1

This list is not finite; you might run across an artifact not on the list. As long as an artifact represents your work from first semester and it reflects the proof of the accomplishments you are seeking, don't be afraid to use it.

Reading

- Reading List
- Reading Log Sheets
- Book Talk Discussion Sheet
- Literature Circle Notes
- Literature Circle Letter

- Reading Surveys
- Illustrations
- Books I Want to Read List
- *Mockingbird* Quizzes

Writing

- I-Search Paper
- *To Kill a Mockingbird* Letter
- Various Composition Book Entries
- *Mockingbird* Discussion Summaries
- September 11 Entries
- What I Know/Questions for I-Search

- Notes on Research for I-Search Topic
- Editing/proofreading Copy of I-Search Paper
- *Autobiography of Miss Jane Pittman* Journals
- Book Talk Discussion Sheet

Speaking and Listening

- Membership Grid
- Composition Book Reflections
- I-Search Paper Presentation
- Leadership/*Mockingbird*/ Book Talk Processing
- *Mockingbird* Notes
- Composition Book I-Search Audience Entries

- *Mockingbird* Question Improvement Analysis
- Various Composition Book Entries
- Book Talk Discussion Sheet
- *Mockingbird* Illustration

Leadership

- Membership Grid
- Composition Book Reflections
- Leadership/*Mockingbird*/ Book Talk Processing
- *Mockingbird* Quizzes

- *Mockingbird* Discussion Summaries
- 12/21/01 grade sheet
- I-Search Paper Listening Notes
- Class Rules
- Appointment Clock

Figure 10.2 *Artifact lists*

Choosing the Artifacts

Before students begin choosing their artifacts, I give each one a file folder; this is the artifact receptacle. As I said earlier, I want to be able to easily carry these things. Also, if I'm storing them in the room, I want them to take up as little space as possible. As students choose their artifacts, I tell them to label them with sticky notes, noting the category and why they chose it. These are quick reflections in preparation for more elaborate ones. I give the kids class time to get started on this process in case they have any questions. Without fail, someone always asks if they can use more artifacts than the designated limit for a category. The only exception I make is if they want to show contrast such as two reading sheets in order to show a speed increase, one from early in the semester and one from later. Since recognizing improvement is an integral part of portfolio creation, I never discourage this kind of doubling up.

Writing the Reflections

Rather than relying solely on sticky notes and highlighting, I like students to take a further step in formalizing their reflections with the use of Explanation Sheets that are attached to each artifact. Each sheet is duplicated on a different color of paper. The color coding makes it easy for grading since you can immediately notice any missing categories, and it also helps the students to make sure the right reflection is attached to the right artifact. It's a good idea to run off double the amount of these, since most students need two: one for a rough draft and one for the final portfolio version. Yeah, they could write the rough drafts on loose leaf, but somehow writing directly on the colored sheets helps emphasize the portfolio organization scheme.

Though the question on each Explanation Sheet might be worded a bit differently, the bottom line, basic question is "How does this artifact demonstrate accomplishment, new learning, or refinement of a skill?" Before writing, it is helpful for students to work with a partner and talk about their chosen artifacts. Students generally seem to have great trouble citing specific proof of accomplishment, so the more you can have a listener point to the artifact and say, "Where is the proof that you're better at _____?" the more specific the reflections will be. Of course, showing good examples from previous students is also helpful, but I still notice a big difference when the kids spend more time actually talking about their artifacts and proving their accomplishments before they write. I tell the kids to start with the artifact they feel they can defend the best. After each partner has defended a couple of artifacts, it's time for the class to get back together and talk about how different statements of accomplishment could be supported by specific details within an artifact. I let them use the examples they've just been discussing with their partners. This is also a good way to detect which categories are giving them the most "proof/support" troubles. If many students have ideas on how to show reading improvement but no one has offered any ideas for *leadership,* that's the category to discuss. After this work in class, students are ready to finish up the Explanation Sheets at home. At this point, I encourage them to type their final reflections and glue or tape them onto the sheet. Since this is a presentation portfolio, neatness counts. Also, typing allows them to get more information on one side of the sheet. The examples that follow were taken from the first semester portfolios of some of my freshman students.

The Cover Letter

Once the students have their reflections finished and attached to the artifacts, the cover letter is easy to write. The cover letter is meant to be a substitute for anyone who would not have the

Name _____
Date _____ Hour _____

Reading

How do these artifacts demonstrate an accomplishment, a new skill, or a refinement in regards to your reading ability, habits, or attitude?

Name _____
Date _____ Hour _____

Writing

How does this artifact reflect organization, supporting detail, clear thought, creativity, and mastery of conventions (punctuation, spelling, sentence clarity)?

Name _____
Date _____ Hour _____

Speaking and Listening

How does this artifact demonstrate an accomplishment, new skill, or refinement in your public speaking, small group discussion, or attentive listening?

Name _____
Date _____ Hour _____

Leadership

How does this artifact demonstrate your positive contribution towards the academic and emotional environment of this class? How do you contribute to the well-being and success of others?

Name _____
Date _____ Hour _____

Choice

How does this artifact represent your learning? Why do you feel pride in it?

Figure 10.3 *Portfolio artifact explanation sheets* (Each category would head a different sheet.)

Name <u>Jacque</u>

Date <u>12/00</u> Hour <u>4th</u>

Reading

How do these artifacts demonstrate an accomplishment, a new skill, or a refinement in regards to your reading ability, habits, or attitude?

Artifacts: <u>Reading List, Book Talk Discussion Sheet</u>

Before the beginning of the year, I only read maybe one book over the last twelve months. Since I started high school, I have read a total of 1800 pages over first semester. That is a total of nine books. I have made a huge accomplishment. I recorded every book I read on the reading list. I also did Book Talks on some of the books I read.

For my Book Talk sheet, I typed it out so that it could be more easily read. When I wrote out the plot points, I made sure to include the main characters' names and some important conflicts. When I chose my passage, I picked one that grabbed my attention and would get someone to read the book. A part of *The Lost Mind* made me think of something that happened to me. I remember one time I was accused of doing something that I didn't do. When I was questioned, my answer was always, "I don't know." Saying that made me look guilty. I used this for my connection because the same thing happened to one of the characters. I also took the time to draw and color my picture and made sure it related to the book. I drew a picture of the young teenager who was murdered by the lake.

Name <u>Andrea</u>

Date <u>12/00</u> Hour <u>6th</u>

Writing

How does this artifact reflect organization, supporting detail, clear thought, creativity, and mastery of conventions (punctuation, spelling, sentence clarity)?

Artifact: <u>Found Poem created from a personal narrative</u>

In this poem, I wrote about the time when I got a black eye; I felt it was very descriptive and emotional. I describe the setting very well and I also go into detail. I used different sound words to make the poem more interesting. Words such as "boom" and "ahh" give the readers a better vision in their heads. When I read this poem to myself, I can picture that day all over again. I feel as if I were there in the poem making this happen all over again. I also picked this poem because having a black eye was something I still remember very well. I could tell anyone exactly how it happened.

(continued)

Figure 10.4 *Portfolio artifact explanation sheet student examples*

Name __Zack_____

Date __12/00_____ Hour __6th____

Speaking and Listening

How does this artifact demonstrate an accomplishment, new skill, or refinement in your public speaking, small group discussion, or attentive listening?

Artifact: Family Newspaper Interview Notes

Of the three kids in my family, everyone has interviewed my dad when they had to do a family interview assignment for school. I don't know why. I guess they thought that my dad's childhood was more interesting than my mom's. I thought, for once, I'd interview my mom instead. I had to think of some good questions to ask her. I asked my mom questions about her childhood and listened to her answers and then wrote them down. I accomplished having a nice conversation with my mom and learning a little about her childhood. One of the questions I asked my mom was "How did your childhood differ from mine?" I wanted to know where she grew up, where she went to school, what sports she played, and what she did for fun. I learned a lot of things about my mom that were pretty interesting.

Name __Jacque_____

Date __12/00_____ Hour __4th____

Leadership

How does this artifact demonstrate your positive contribution towards the academic and emotional environment of this class? How do you contribute to the well-being and success of others?

Artifact: Person Search (Classbuilding Activity)

This artifact shows that I went around the room to find each person that could fill out a square of my sheet. When doing this, I contributed positively by signing other peoples' sheets, and I didn't go off and talk to my friends about something else. I did what I was supposed to do without going off task. By doing this, I contributed to the academic and emotional environment of the class. I learned something about each person, and I got to know a lot more people by getting up and talking to them.

Figure 10.4 *Portfolio artifact explanation sheet student examples (Continued)*

Name <u>Jacque</u>

Date <u>12/00</u>   Hour <u>4th</u>

Choice

How does this artifact represent your learning? Why do you feel pride in it?

Artifact: <u>Neighborhood Map</u>

For my choice artifact I chose my Neighborhood Map. This artifact represents my learning by showing how I had to look back and remember all of my important memories. This project really made me think. I wanted to make sure this project looked presentable. To do this I used a wide variety of colors, and I took my time when writing in all of the memories so people could read them. I feel pride in this project because I put a lot of work into it. My favorite memory was "When I Graduated from Prairie View." I drew in details to show how that memory was special to me.

Figure 10.4   *(Continued)*

12/7/00

Dear Reader,

Welcome to the beautiful Hotel Del Coronado. This elegant hotel has been around for centuries. Many famous people have come to visit this hotel. U.S. presidents, Babe Ruth, Jack Dempsey, and Marilyn Monroe are just a few of the celebrity guests. A Marilyn Monroe movie called *Some Like It Hot* was filmed at the Coronado. This film was a big success and caused the hotel to become the most popular hotel on the western side of the United States. Today I will be taking you on a little tour of the Hotel Del Coronado.

When you first pull up to the hotel, you will see red carpeted stairs which will take you into the luxurious lobby. In order to enter the hotel, you must provide something to prove that you can be a leader. I have taken the liberty of providing a grade sheet. The sheet shows how good my grades have been this quarter. It also provides the hotel reassurance of how well I can keep track of my own belongings and assignments. This will help them know that I will not lose anything valuable and then blame the hotel for my loss.

Once you have entered the lobby, you may notice the closed doors off to your right. A speech is just beginning in the Crown/Coronet Room. The speech is based on a grid of life's ups and downs. The speech is to provide the speaker with practice for giving big speeches when the time comes. The speech shows how well

(continued)

Figure 10.5   *Megan's portfolio cover letter*

the speaker has communicated her ideas and feelings about her life. The speaker has provided the grid as a visual aid for the listeners.

Over the years, writers have been drawn to The Del. This hotel can transport a person's imagination to a time long ago. With its large red turrets and beautiful Victorian woodwork, many believe this alluring architecture inspired the literary efforts of L. Frank Baum, who wrote several books for his Oz series while staying at the hotel. It is said that the hotel was his inspiration for the design of the Emerald City. The hotel offers a writing class in which you can learn how to write many kinds of literature. I jumped at the chance to take that class. I learned how to take a story of what happened to me and turn it into a beautiful poem. Of course, the poem is not a rhyming poem, but, nevertheless, it is still a poem. I am proud of that poem. I learned how to take important facts from my story, and, word by word, set them on paper.

Sitting by the pool with a full view of the Pacific Ocean, a person can relax and enjoy reading some of her favorite books. A personal favorite of mine is *Chicken Soup for the Pet Lover's Soul.* The Coronado offers many books in its gift shop; you can choose from fantasy to mysteries. One of the mysteries I really enjoyed was *Out of the Dark* by Betty Ren Wright. I do believe that the hotel inspired me to read my current book: *The Legend of Kate Morgan.* This is the story of a ghostly woman who haunts the Hotel Del Coronado. I can't wait to finish the book and find out why she haunts the hotel.

I hope you can come to the Hotel Del Coronado to find a room for a night or two and, more importantly, to experience all that I have learned in my first semester. With the great atmosphere I found success in my writing. With the mystique of the hotel, I couldn't help but be creative. When you look at the architecture and strength of this hotel, you can't help but want to improve your sentence structure. The Hotel Del Coronado has been a pearl in the making since 1888. With the hotel as my inspiration, I too know that with time I can only improve.

Sincerely,

Megan

Figure 10.5   *Megan's portfolio cover letter (Continued)*

opportunity to directly question the portfolio owner. The letter's goal is to introduce each artifact with enough detail so that the reader wants to examine the pieces further. The letter also requires students to review and refine their thinking in regards to their accomplishments.

Another stipulation I give students is that they need to frame their letters within the context of an extended metaphor. This is what makes the letters fun to read since these metaphors quite often reflect the individual students' interests. Once I give students the idea list along with a good example, they seem to have no problem coming up with new metaphors; as a matter of fact, most of the letters seem to reflect some fun in the voice that comes through. This past semes-

Portfolio Reflection Letter

Directions: Write a thoughtful letter to the portfolio reader that highlights this semester's personal accomplishments, learnings, and areas of improvement. Use some imagination: take the portfolio reader on a trip, tour, etc. This letter needs to be of final draft quality and no longer than two single-spaced pages, 12 point Times New Roman. Remember that this letter, the portfolio, and your interview are worth 20% of your overall semester grade. Your letter needs to start with an introduction paragraph and end with a concluding paragraph. Each of the portfolio categories should be discussed in a paragraph or two.

Introduction

- Welcome the reader and invite him/her to browse your portfolio's contents.

Reading

1. How do these artifacts demonstrate an accomplishment, a new skill, or a refinement in regards to your reading ability, habits, or attitude? What proof do you have?
2. How have you challenged yourself as a reader this past semester?
3. Which book has been the most memorable for you? Why?

Writing

1. How does this artifact demonstrate your ability to explain your thoughts in detail or take on the perspective of another person? What proof do you have?

Speaking and Listening

1. How does this artifact demonstrate an accomplishment, new skill, or refinement in your public speaking, small group discussion, or attentive listening? What proof do you have?

Leadership

1. How does this artifact demonstrate your positive contribution towards the academic and emotional environment of this class?
2. How has your participation changed in your Book Talks, partner work, or other group work? Why would someone want to work with you?

Choice Artifact (optional)

1. How does this artifact represent your learning? Why do you feel pride in it?
2. How did you decide on this piece? What others were you considering?

Conclusion

1. Explain what you hope to improve on and accomplish in second semester.
2. Thank the reader for taking the time to examine your portfolio.

Figure 10.6 *Portfolio cover letter instructions*

ter I discovered that the show *Crocodile Hunter* was pretty popular with the freshman males. Here's the introduction of one letter:

> Good Day Mate,
>
>   My name is Tom and today I'm going to be taking you on a trip through the Australian artifact outback. Now I have to warn you there are some pretty ferocious species of artifacts in the outback, so please keep your hands and arms in the vehicle at all times.

I'm always amazed with the creativity and uniqueness some students bring to this assignment. Megan's family vacation to California left a lasting impression. Her portfolio letter from first semester takes the reader on a tour of the Hotel Del Coronado while also pointing out some of her accomplishments in Freshman English (see pages 249–250).

My class came up with the following list of metaphor ideas.

Portfolio Letter Metaphor Ideas

New galaxy	Time machine
Tapestry	Multiple course dinner
Painting	Sea of Knowledge/Diving
Self-portrait	Website
Field trip	Disney World
Safari	House under construction/Construction site
Amusement park	Museum
Space shuttle ride	Art gallery
Recipe	Book: my life as a freshman student
Train ride	Cruise ship
Hike	Archeological dig site
Mountain climbing	Time capsule

Trial and Error

Before I figured out the entire portfolio process (and believe me these steps took years to figure out), I saw a lot of really pitiful portfolios. I'll never forget the one kid that turned in a portfolio crammed with anything he could grab out of his binder. There were no explanation sheets or a cover letter, just random artifacts. Though he failed the portfolio, luckily he had done enough to pass the semester. Since most of the other kids turned in okay portfolios compared to this aberration, I blamed the kid for his own ineptitude. After all, I gave them some time in class; he could have asked questions; he could have taken some responsibility for himself! Now that I look back, I realize that his portfolio symbolized his total confusion in regards to the process. Whoops!

Recently, as I introduced the portfolio concept to my first-semester freshman class, a kid blurted out, "What's the point of all this?" I could feel my blood pressure rising and my hands itching to strangle the kid, but I held my cool and tried to explain that it gives students the chance to verify their progress while also preparing them for the world of professional work, where a portfolio is often required for a job interview. Being attuned to my body language, the kid backed down, but I knew he wasn't really buying my explanation.

It wasn't until months later that I got a real-life example of why a portfolio can come in handy. As the kids started working on their second-semester portfolios, I told my student teacher that I wanted her to prepare one as well. Though Danielle pretty much stuck to the same categories as the kids, her artifacts emphasized how she addressed *Reading, Writing, Speaking and Listening*, and *Leadership* in her teaching. Within a day of finishing her portfolio, I heard that another high school in our district was conducting interviews for several new English positions. I called the division chair immediately. She asked if Danielle had filed her requisite application paperwork with the district. Since the answer was no (she hadn't even finished her student teaching yet), the division chair hesitated to put her on the schedule until I told her that Danielle had a professional portfolio prepared. That was what got her in the door for the interview. Of course, I went back to my classes, including the one with the nay sayer, and told them the story.

> *Moral: Just because portfolios are a very useful learning tool and later a valuable job-seeking tool, it doesn't mean that the kids are going to automatically understand and buy into the idea. Taking the time for each step is critical to success.*

The Interview Process

Once the portfolios are finished, I have students go through an interview process at least twice: once with their classmates and once with their parents. Beforehand, I give students a list of basic questions that could be asked about the various artifact categories in the portfolio. I feel that actually presenting the portfolio and being questioned by others is very important; knowing how to prepare for an interview will come in handy later on during employment searches.

Portfolio Interview Instructions

General: Imagine that you are interviewing for a job and your goal is to convince the employer that you've got the skills it takes to succeed. With little prodding, you can give ample evidence and proof of these skills. You, the person being interviewed, should be doing most of the talking. Since the interview is only eight minutes long, you should show ample evidence that you have thought about and prepared for the following questions. Wasted time will not impress the interviewer.

Reading

1. How do these artifacts demonstrate accomplishment, new skill, or a refinement in regards to your reading ability, habits, or attitude? What proof do you have? Point out some specific details.
2. How have you challenged yourself as a reader this past semester?
3. Which book has been the most memorable for you? Why?
4. What do you think you need to do at this point to become a better reader?

(continued)

Figure 10.7 *Interview questions*

Writing

1. How does this artifact demonstrate your ability to explain your thoughts in detail or take on the perspective of another person? What proof do you have? Read some specific parts aloud to illustrate your accomplishments.

2. If you had a choice, what kinds of writing would you like to do second semester?

3. What do you think you need to do at this point to become a better writer?

Speaking and Listening

1. How does this artifact demonstrate an accomplishment, new skill, or refinement in your public speaking, small group discussion, or attentive listening? What proof do you have?

2. What is the speaking or listening skill you most need to improve? How do you know? What will you do to improve?

Leadership

1. How does this artifact demonstrate your positive contribution towards the academic and emotional environment of this class? Cite some specific artifact details for proof.

2. How has your participation changed in your Book Talks, partner work and other group work? Why would someone want to work with you? What consistent contributions can a group depend upon you for?

3. Which class rule gives you the most difficult time? What have you been doing to make sure you follow it?

Choice Artifact (optional)

1. How does this artifact represent your learning? Why do you feel pride in it?

2. How did you decide on this piece? What others were you considering?

Figure 10.7   *Interview questions (Continued)*

On the day before the portfolios are due, I model the interview rehearsal by letting two students interview me about my portfolio. I start by presenting an artifact, purposely leaving out some important detail. It is the interviewer's role to listen carefully and then demand further proof if I've been vague in giving specific examples to back my claim of accomplishment. The following day when the finished portfolios are due, students count off to make groups of three. Each student needs his portfolio, a pen, and three sheets of loose leaf paper. During an eight-minute time limit, one member presents his artifacts while the rest of the group grills him for more specific proof in any weak areas they detect. When the time is up, each student writes a short five-minute reflection, and all three papers become part of the presenter's portfolio. To get credit for the reflections, members must write for the full five minutes and remember to sign their first and last names to each reflection. Now the second person presents and the process is repeated.

Interviewer
1. What was interesting about the presentation?
2. Which proof/evidence of achievement was most convincing/impressive?
3. What was the most effective part of the presentation? How could you use your partner's good ideas for your own presentation?
4. Which parts of the presentation were weak? What should your partner practice/improve?

Presenter
1. What was it like to present your accomplishments? How did you feel?
2. What were the strengths and weaknesses of your presentation?
3. How will you improve your portfolio presentation for your final interview?

Figure 10.8 *Portfolio group Interview written response questions*

5/10/01

Dear Self,

I was very strong with my interview because I completely answered all of the questions. I also had a lot of detail in my examples and remembered to use my post-its. I think I should have had more examples, though. I also kept the conversation going. I didn't hesitate at all. I just need to make my portfolio presentation longer. I did a good job explaining how I accomplished things.

Sincerely,

Tim

Dear Tim,

Your strengths were explaining your artifacts without reading off the sheets. With the post-its you explained certain things; that was good. The interview went really smooth and you knew what you were going to say. Some things that you may want to work on are making your presentation a bit longer and explaining your accomplishments in a little more detail. That's the only thing that you may want to work on. Nice job!

Sincerely,

Dave

Figure 10.9 *Partner interview reflection examples*

After the class interviews, each student must take his portfolio home and present it to one or both of his parents. Ideally, the student also shows his parents the interview questions so that some interaction takes place. Afterwards, I ask the parents to write a positive note to their child, which also becomes a part of the portfolio. I emphasize that this note is to the child, not the teacher. Our society seems to offer few chances for family writing; my hope is that in ten or twenty years some of these notes might become precious souvenirs. I like including the parent interview because teenagers seldom show their parents anything that they do at school. Looking at a portfolio is a good way for parents to get some insight into the curriculum. It is also an excellent opportunity for parents to see what kind of quality work students are turning in. I also find it useful to give parents explicit instructions for responding.

Turning in the Portfolio

By now you're probably wondering how I manage to grade all of these portfolios in the limited and restrictive schedule most high schools call final exam week. Before you dismiss this as too time consuming compared to the traditional machine-graded multiple-choice test, here are a few things to think about. First, remember that all of the artifacts are already graded; you've seen this work before. Second, the kids have been working on these portfolios for a couple of weeks off and on in class, so you probably already have some idea of what you'll find in them along with the quality of reflection. Third, you had the chance to listen in when the students were presenting their portfolios to their peers. To tell you the truth, when I collect these portfolios, I don't feel too

---

Dear Partner in Learning,

After your student has explained the significance of the artifacts contained in his/her portfolio, please take a few minutes to write a note to your child, which will then become a part of the portfolio. If you are suffering from writer's block, here are a few topics you might find useful for responding.

1. What surprised or impressed you the most about your student's accomplishments?
2. How has your student improved his/her skill in working with others and participating in a successful literature discussion?
3. How has your student changed and grown as a reader?
4. If you were demonstrating pride in your student in a conversation with another person, what would you tell that person about your student's accomplishments in English?

As you write this note, remember that its goal is to celebrate your student's success and accomplishments. Thank you for your time and interest in this project!

Sincerely,

Nancy Steineke

Figure 10.10   *Parent response instructions*

1/10/95

Dear Casey,

    After reading your portfolio, I was quite surprised to see how you compared situations in your life to situations in some of the books that you read. It was most educational since I had never heard you say anything close to being comparable to what you wrote.

    I am sorry that you do not enjoy reading every book you can get your hands on, but I recall you mentioning your approval of reading the *Dragon's Den* because you could pick how the story ended. Whatever gets you to read is okay with me!

    One thing I can agree with you on is your dislike for *Of Mice and Men*. I recall reading that book in high school and I did not care for it. Of course, I might pick it up some day soon and read it again to see if I still have the same opinion since twenty-five years have gone by since I was a freshman.

Love,

Mom

Figure 10.11   *Parent response example*

bad about skimming through them quickly because my main goals are to get the kids to reflect on where they are with their own learning and then practice presenting their accomplishments to others. Considering how much the process has been discussed and how many people have already looked at these portfolios, I don't feel guilty at all. I can whip through a class of thirty in about ninety minutes. Yeah, it's not like the sixty seconds that the machine can crank those tests out (provided the scoring machine is working; ours always likes to break when grades are due), but I feel the learning that results from turning in the portfolio is worth the additional effort.

    Now, if you can swing it, here's a way to reduce that end-of-semester grading crunch. I always make sure that the portfolios are finished a week before final exams begin. During that last normal week of the semester, I conduct portfolio interviews. Students sign up for ten-minute appointment slots before school, during homeroom, or during final exam week after the testing ends for the day. Luckily, in my district, 1st hour does not begin until 9:00 a.m., so if I start the interviews at 7:30 a.m., I can get quite a few done by the end of the week. Students must be on time (I'm focusing on those job interview skills again) and I only reschedule an interview appointment if an absence is due to an extreme emergency, proof required! I give each student exactly eight minutes for the presentation, and I use a stopwatch. If the student has taken all of the other interviews seriously (and most do), these interviews are a lot of fun because it is one of the few times I get to have an extended conversation with each student. It's also interesting to find out what assignments students value because they are reflected in their portfolio choices. I'm always comforted when I see a great variety of assignments in the portfolios because it tells me that different activities are connecting with different kids. On the other hand, if I start to notice that a few assignments are conspicuously absent from the portfolios, I have the opportunity to ask students why that assignment didn't click.

How Do I Assess This?

Like other class projects, the portfolio has check-in points. Students can list the due dates right inside the portfolio folder. I usually have four due dates:

1. The day artifacts must be selected for all categories.
2. The day all explanation sheets are finished and attached to each artifact.
3. The day the cover letter is due.
4. The day the completed portfolio is due.

For each due date, I stamp the inside of the folder. The third due date occurs a couple of days before the practice interviews. This gives students a last chance to talk about their portfolios with their partner while they work together on proofreading the cover letters. As always, they're required to bring in two copies.

Also, from the very start of the portfolio process, students work with a rubric that clearly defines quality expectations. A 3 is equal to a C, a 4 is a B, a 5 is an A. When students finish their interviews with me, I have them self-evaluate their portfolio using the rubric, checking off the criteria that were met. Most often, students are very accurate. If I differ from the student's opinion, it's seldom by more than one number. In any case, if conflicts arise upon their return, students always have the option of appealing. So far no one ever has.

Parting Words: Where's the Collaboration?

Though on the surface the portfolio activity seems rather solitary compared with Peer Conferencing groups and Literature Circles, it isn't. First, this individual work sets a stage for individual reflection and improvement that enhances the functioning of future collaborative groups formed in that class. Second, when students are working on their portfolios in class, a great deal of informal collaboration occurs. Students ask each other for artifact ideas and advice on how to present accomplishment and read parts of their cover letters to each other for feedback. In fact, portfolio time gives the kids the chance to use their collaborative skills the way they would in an actual workplace environment, a place where cooperation depends upon the initiative of the co-workers rather than elaborately structured strategies provided by the boss. Also, direct collaborative structure is provided when students practice their interviews together. Portfolios also bridge the collaboration between students and adults. Parents become part of the process, and the final step is a conversation with the teacher and student.

Portfolio interviews are always full of surprises. Even when students haven't been doing much work, they still usually come in for the interview and talk very candidly about themselves. In one of these conversations, I found out that Missy was very happy with a C– grade in English because most of her spare time was spent at the dance studio. Someday she hoped to dance professionally. Though we talked about her artifacts, the best part of the conversation was when we compared notes on the recent dance film *Center Stage*. Another girl, one who was well behaved but dropped hints that she had the potential for an aggressive volcanic explosion, presented me with her Leadership artifact, a copy of the class rules that we had negotiated. During her interview she explained, "It's a lot harder to break the rules when I was the one who made them up." At that point, I knew why she had kept herself in check: we were on the same team. Hey, collaboration can't get any better than that!

Writer_____   Title Semester 1 Portfolio

Grade Level 10   Subject English   Type of Assignment FINAL EXAM – 20%

Partners_____   Date January 7, 2002

FACTOR (Traits)	Score	Wt.	Total Pts.
• CONFERENCE			
Well Prepared, Carries Interview	5 4 3 2 1	X3	15
Convincing & Specific Proof in ALL CATEGORIES	5 4 3 2 1	X3	15
• PORTFOLIO CONTENTS			
Organization & Neatness	5		5
Cover Letter Content	5 4 3 2 1	X4	20
Cover Letter Conventions	5 4 3 2 1	X2	10
Artifacts & Colored Sheets	5 4 3 2 1	X5	25
Self & Peer Response	5		5
Parent/Guardian Response	5		5

Scoring Key

5—Excellent   4—Good   3—Average   2—Weak   1—Poor

Point Totals Converted to Grades:

100 to 90 = A
89 to 80 = B
79 to 70 = C
69 to 65 = D
64 to 0 = F

Organization
1. Cover Letter
2. Reader response
3. Reading
4. Writing
5. Speaking and listening
6. Leadership
7. Choice artifact
8. Self & peer response

Figure 10.12 *Portfolio score sheet*

Portfolio Rubric

Interview	3	4	5
	• Carries interview—needs little prompting • Displays correct artifact while explaining • Cites specific accomplishments in each category • All categories covered in 8 minutes • Does not read from half-sheets	• Citing of accomplishments sometimes supported by specific artifact evidence	• Well prepared, practiced • Each accomplishment is always supported by specific artifact evidence which is clearly displayed

Portfolio Cover Design	3	4	5
	• Colorful • Neat • School appropriate • Inviting to portfolio reader	• Design reflects portfolio categories	• Original • Illustrates specific accomplishments • Thought and effort apparent

Artifacts and Half-Sheets	3	4	5
	• All required artifacts are present • Correct half-sheet stapled to each artifact in correct fashion • Correct order • Half-sheets neatly printed or typed clear • Explanation of importance of each artifact	• Significant specific details accompany most half-sheets	• All half-sheets refer to specific artifact details • All half-sheets connect specific details with a well-defined accomplishment • Artifact details highlighted and/or explained with sticky note

Figure 10.13   *Portfolio rubric*

Cover Letter Content 3 4 5

- Extended metaphor used
- Each artifact category is discussed in a separate paragraph
- Specific accomplishments are cited along with some support details

- Specific proof of accomplishment is present in all artifact paragraphs

- Support details cited can easily be found in artifacts—marked with highlighter and sticky note
- Energetic voice
- Creative and consistent use of metaphor

Cover Letter Conventions 3 4 5

- Correct format: date, greeting, closing, signature
- Clear paragraphing
- No typos
- Words spelled correctly
- All sentences make sense

- Commas used correctly
- No run-ons or fragments

- Error free

© 2002 by Nancy Steineke from *Reading and Writing Together*. Portsmouth, NH: Heinemann.

Figure 10.13 *(Continued)*

Resources

Porter, Carol and Janell Cleland. 1995. *The Portfolio as a Learning Strategy*. Portsmouth, NH: Heinemann.
    This was the book that made me realize that the best portfolios are created when students get to choose which pieces to put in them. Also, a portfolio is not strictly for writing; it can reflect many aspects of class work.

CHAPTER 11

Collaborative Literacy
in Action
Strategies to Remember
and Practice

Remember the very first chapter? The one about how good teachers are made not born? It's time for you to think about that idea in more personal terms. By now, if you've read this whole book, you're probably feeling a mixture of excitement, hope, information overload, and depression. I'm only guessing, but that's always the way I feel when I finish any professional book. However, the compulsion to compare our worst classroom moments with an author's best serves no useful purpose. I mean, teaching is frustrating enough. Why submit to this personally administered abuse as well? The thing to remember when reading any teacher book is that the author's story is like one of those *Reader's Digest* condensed books. Quite a few chapters have been cut; only the best parts remain. As I combed through my old files in the search of suitable student examples, I realized that this book is the culmination of fifteen years worth of struggles and successes. Had I documented all of the time I wasted on things that didn't work, I probably could have produced a book at least three times this size. But who would buy that? I like to think of this book as my own presentation portfolio. Though I'm showing you my best stuff, the last thing I want you to conclude is that I'm "Miss Perfect Superteacher." My life as a teacher is pretty much like yours: I have great days, good days, bad days, and disastrous days. Ironically, it's those bad days that we need to appreciate more, because once we're done licking our wounds, those are the days that really spur us on to revise our teaching and learn new strategies. Since this book is all about strategies, I thought it might be helpful to gather up the main ones for a final curtain call.

Explain Your Strategy Choices

As I've mentioned many times already, students run across a wide variety of teaching styles and methodology in the course of their middle school and high school careers. If your colleagues are traditional, the more likely the strategies in this book will be questioned. After all, almost anything that diverges from the norm is often suspect. Don't be intimidated, be up front. Explain why icebreaking is important for classroom success. Teach the five elements of cooperative learning so that students can analyze the structure of a group task. Demonstrate the real-world applications of interviews and portfolios. Make the invisible visible. Be the unmasked magician and explain your teaching decisions to your students. Open house is an excellent time for educating parents. I always tell them why I choose to use Sustained Silent Reading, Literature Circles, peer writing groups, and cooperative learning. I also emphasize that I do not rely on group grades because this is usually the key reason why parents oppose collaborative activities. I recommend you do the same.

Revisit Icebreaking Activities Often

You don't need to keep using the icebreaking activities listed in this book. By all means, look for new ideas; there are a lot of community-building books out there. The important thing to remember is that you need to engage in whole class icebreaking and collaborative team icebreaking activities at least twice a week. You don't need to spend loads of time; lots of activities take only five minutes. The important thing is that these activities continue throughout the entire year. If you offer a variety of activities and keep them fun, the kids won't complain. If you try an activity that totally gets out of hand, don't give up. Reassess the class' maturity and social skill level and then pick a different activity that more closely matches where they are. Immature and socially inept students need these activities more than any other students so that they can grow and learn to respect the needs and feelings of others.

Think in Terms of Foundation Activities

Whenever I plan for a class, I always think in terms of how I want the kids to act as well as what I want to cover, because I know that behavior can make or break any content coverage. The successful use of any strategy in this book depends upon kids who can work quietly by themselves as well as listen respectfully in a group, so that's what I always address at the beginning of the school year. Once we're past that hurdle, I think in terms of building upon past experience. Rather than always throwing new activities at students, I try to focus on repetition and refinement. Sustained Silent Reading segues into Literature Circle reading, student Book Talks segue into Literature Circle discussions, Literature Circle discussions segue into peer writing conferences. Follow-up questions should be used in as many different venues as possible because this is a difficult skill and students need many opportunities for practice before mastery occurs. If you like to do projects, give the kids at least two different shots at them with some time in between to reflect on what worked, analyze what didn't, and revise or develop rubrics. Whatever you do, think about how projects or assignments can be recycled so that they offer new challenges but also offer opportunities to build upon previous experiences. Give students the time and practice they need to get better at a task rather than always moving in a new direction.

Negotiate with Students

The more students can be a part of classroom decisions the more they will own classroom activities. The class rules are a start, but aim for regular class meetings where problems and successes can be discussed. Work to get students to volunteer to be moderators at these meetings after you have modeled the format. The more students are up front and center, the better students will see themselves as part of the decision-making process. Negotiation also plays an important role in the development of rubrics. Teach students how rubrics work and then have them come up with the important categories and criteria for an assignment. Whenever possible, have students conduct a self-evaluation against the rubric before you grade anything. Self-evaluation deflates the emotional power of your grade because students usually have a pretty good idea of an assignment's quality level before it ever gets turned in.

Provide Choices

It's human nature to enjoy choice because it lets us take control of the situation. That's why more students will read and enjoy books during SSR or Literature Circles than when the class is doing one book together. This semester I had a girl who typified this. During SSR she read two or three books a week. Sometimes she would read a book a day. Yet she absolutely refused to read *To Kill a Mockingbird*. After she saw her grade plummet, I think she was a little sorry that she had chosen to be that stubborn. Though her official explanation was that the book was too boring to hold her interest, I think, at least on a subconscious level, the real problem was that she didn't like someone else telling her what to read. Of course, learning how to deal with situations that offer no choice is part of life too, so I'm not recommending that you abandon all curriculum requirements. Instead, I'm suggesting that whenever choices can be made available to students, be sure to offer them.

Model and Demonstrate: A Picture Is Worth a Thousand Words

Take a risk and start with yourself. Share your own writing. Believe me, the kids won't think it's that good; you won't intimidate them! Before sending them out to conference in groups, have them practice on you and be sure to run them through all of the steps. Take part in a roleplay to show a new skill or highlight a common problem that needs to be solved. Regularly talk about the books you're reading. Point out good passages, new words, your own personal connections. Teach kids how to participate in and observe roleplay discussions. Do it regularly enough so that most students have had a chance to model at least one discussion. Buy a cabinet and start saving student samples. Though a project seems perfectly clear to you since you've been using it for years, that same project is often a fuzzy picture to someone new to it. Examining samples is a great way to challenge students to improve upon last year's product. Show, don't tell!

Use the Binders Every Day

If you don't like my categories, then think of your own; no one's stopping you. Those binders are a foundation cornerstone. Because points are recorded only two or three times a quarter, students keep everything rather than getting a graded paper back and immediately tossing it in the garbage. As a result, students have a great variety of artifacts from which to choose when it comes time to develop portfolios. The binders encourage unorganized students to develop a new skill. The need for organization is reinforced by the binder check and stamp counting. Remember to give the kids some class time now and then to compare binders with a partner and get everything up to date. Finally, the binder decreases your time entering and figuring grades. Rather than having dozens of little homework/classwork grades, you'll only have two or three numbers to add together and divide. However, remember that for the binders to work, the kids have to bring them to class every day. That means that you need to refer to the binder contents frequently throughout the period.

Teach Social Skills Explicitly

Do not bemoan the fact that your students have no manners or cannot listen respectfully to one another. Teach them how and give them opportunities to practice. Do not let romantics criticize you for reducing discussion into its mechanics. Tell those squares to get real: everything is mechanical before it becomes fluent. Neurosurgeons begin as medical students who learn how to manipulate scalpels and other instruments of incision by practicing on cadavers! A golf swing can be broken down into dozens of different parts; adjusting one component affects everything else. I'm willing to bet Tiger Woods has spent some quality time analyzing and refining his swing. Children don't automatically speak their native language; someone has to teach them. Social skills are no different. You've got to meet the kids where they are and move them forward. Keep in mind that the more unskilled students are at collaboration, the more challenging it will be to get them to change because the new skills are so different to them. Persist longer than they can resist. You are improving their chances for future happiness by teaching them how to get along and work with other people.

Build Reflection into Daily Classroom Life

Get kids to think about their interactions with others and remember what worked and how they can change or refine what didn't. This kind of thinking gives groups power because recognizing accomplishment and solving problems becomes an integral part of the process. Likewise, provide opportunities for students to regularly reflect upon their own individual accomplishments, learning, and roadblocks. Teach students to set goals and then develop steps and measures to help them achieve those goals. Model your own reflection whenever possible. A common pitfall in all this reflective thinking is that teachers often forget to show how reflection governs their own decisions. Many times students don't value reflection because it's not modeled by the adults that surround them.

Observe the Elements of Cooperative Learning

Cooperative learning is complex; there's no way to get around it. Creating well-designed lessons takes practice and thought. Make a poster of the five elements and display it prominently in your classroom and paste a smaller version of it to your desk. Every time kids work together, look at it and see if you can identify all of the components. When groups aren't working well together, see what components are weak or missing. Also, I can't urge you strongly enough to take some professional development classes in cooperative learning. Though I've been using collaborative groups for years, I still try to make regular pilgrimages to the University of Minnesota. The Johnsons always have something new to teach me or something old that I've forgotten and need to be reminded of.

Teach Students the Art of Asking Questions

The ability to ask questions is the most important academic skill one can teach and reinforce. When students ask questions about a text, another student's writing, or someone's opinion in a discussion, it requires thinking on a deeper level than when students are asked to answer the questions of the teacher or the textbook author. Asking questions is what drives new thinking and continues a discussion. The more opportunity you can provide for students to create and discuss their own questions, the better they will get at thinking in depth.

Find the Time for Sustained Silent Reading

If you haven't done this before, giving up ten or fifteen minutes of class time on a daily basis will be difficult, but do it. I repeat: DO IT! The more kids read and start to like what they read, the more interested they are going to be in Literature Circles, authors' craft, and their own writing. Plus, the more practice they get at reading, the better they will become at reading. Also, be sure to read yourself; model how important that reading time is for you. Take this opportunity to become familiar with books that you can in turn recommend to your students.

Make Sticky Notes a Way of Life

Find ways to encourage the kids to use sticky notes with their reading on a daily basis. Make sticky notes so much a part of the regular routine that they automatically have them ready to go along with some loose leaf paper and a pen. Some students take immediately to sticky notes while others will not and need more reinforcement. All can benefit from the habit of reading with sticky notes in hand. Model it yourself. Center conversation around text ideas marked with sticky notes.

Think of Assessment as an Ongoing Process

Look for lots of ways to evaluate and grade. Try to make the steps in the process worth as much as the final product. When you take this route, the final product is already somewhat familiar and, therefore, takes you less time to grade. Use rubrics that define specific criteria.

Use Peer Conferencing Groups Regularly

Though teacher–student conferencing has its place, in the long run teaching students how to talk with each other about their own writing is far more valuable. Though you'll be out of their lives at the end of a year or a semester, there is an excellent chance that current classmates will work together again in future classes. If students are encouraged and taught how to help each other while they're with you, they are far more likely to turn to their peers for help in the future. Also, frequent discussions during all stages of writing greatly reduces the likelihood of students downloading Internet term papers because it's hard to have an ongoing discussion on something that's plagiarized. Also, your regular monitoring should pick up any red flags long before a final draft appears.

Monitor Collaborative Groups Carefully

When the groups start working well, teachers are often tempted to drop out of the circuit and get some grading done. Don't be tempted. Now is the time to observe for skill usage and think about how student interaction might be further refined. Just because students own the process, it doesn't mean your expertise is no longer needed. There's nothing more flattering than when a group explains what they've come up with and then asks for your opinion. Also, there is nothing wrong with throwing in your own controversial question now and then. In the case of writing groups, monitoring is a good way to keep tabs on the progress of everyone's papers without having to collect and read them all.

Give Yourself Permission to Fail

Nothing starts to work right until it has flopped a few times. Try to get that "teachers need to be perfect" image out of your head. That old adage "Practice Makes Perfect" is right and wrong all at the same time. While it assumes that nothing is perfect from the start, it also mistakenly assumes that perfection can eventually be achieved. Imagine if that were true; a life of perfection would get boring pretty fast. Though I can't remember who said it, I've always loved the quote that goes something like, "Perfection bears no children." Think of all the science fiction stories that have used the "perfection is boring" premise. When it comes down to it, *imperfection* provides the opportunity to learn something new; imperfection makes life interesting. We always encourage our students to take risks and learn from their mistakes, so it's about time we jump on the bandwagon as well. When you try something new and the plan goes awry, celebrate the risk. Buy yourself a new outfit. Treat yourself to a massage. Open up a bottle of champagne and make a toast. Take some of those deep-calming belly breaths my yoga teacher is always yapping about and repeat my two favorite mantras:

> "Rome wasn't built in a day."
> "The journey of a thousand miles begins with one step."

Finally, glue your photo onto "The License to Make Mistakes," fill in your name, and fold over the corner of the page in this book so that you can find your license immediately in case of an emergency. Whenever a classroom disaster strikes, review the terms of that license! As you read, visualize your pulse rate returning to normal and then remind yourself of this important fact: even though people are often more manageable and easily controlled when they are kept apart, imagination, new ideas, and creative thinking take off when people work together. Teaching students how to collaborate can be difficult and time consuming, but creating a community that learns together and cares about each other is well worth the effort.

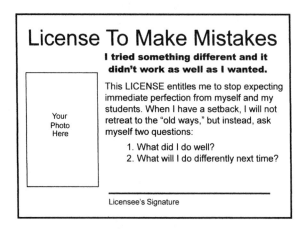

Figure 11.1   *License to make mistakes*

Appendices

EXAMPLES OF T-CHARTS

Quiet voices

Looks Like	*Sounds Like*
Eye contact	Whispering
Desks close together	"Lower your voices please"
Leaning in	"Let's try not to disturb any other groups"
Focus on the speaker	"Good job. I can hear you, but the other group cannot"
Ignoring other groups	"I'll talk to you after class"
Finger to lips	"Remember your 12-inch voice"

Encouraging Participation

Looks Like	*Sounds Like*
Eye contact	Using names
Desks close together	"What do you think?"
Leaning in	"Let's hear from (name)"
Focus on the speaker	"Give us an idea (name)"
Looking interested	"Let (name) go first this time"

Giving Help

Looks Like	*Sounds Like*
Eye contact	"Show me what you've done so far"
Desks close together	"Where do you get stuck?"
Leaning in	"How is this problem like this other one?"
Focus on the speaker	"Explain the steps you've taken"
Looking interested	"Now that I've explained, show me how you'd do the next one"
Smiling	"Ask me a specific question"

Checking for Understanding

Looks Like	*Sounds Like*
Eye contact	"How would you answer that question?"
Desks close together	"Sum up what we've just said"
Leaning in	"What are the three most important points?"
Focus on the speaker	"What will you say if the teacher quizzes you?"
Looking interested	"Good, now give me some examples to support your answer"
Taking notes	"Explain how to do that problem"

SOCIAL SKILL LESSON WORKSHEET

Social Skills Lesson Plan

Cooperative Skill: _____

Definition: _____

_____

What would you like your students to be like when this skill is mastered? _____

_____

Step 1:   How are you going to communicate a need for this skill? (teacher observation, news articles, class discussion, journal reflection, posters, read aloud, etc.)

_____

_____

_____

_____

Step 2:   How will you explain and model the skill? (class creation of T-Chart, partner T-Charts, roleplay skill usage, roleplay lack of skill, video, read aloud, journal assignment, posters, etc.)

_____

_____

_____

_____

Step 3:   How will you ensure that students actively practice this skill in their cooperative groups? (bonus points or other rewards for use, teacher reinforcement, individual grades, student observers, skill-related roles, etc.)

_____

_____

_____

_____

Step 4:   After a cooperative activity, how will group processing be used so that students reflect upon and improve their skill usage?

_____

_____

_____

_____

How will whole class processing be done?

___   Public announcement by groups of strengths and goals

___   T-Chart update

___   Journal writing, sharing, reading aloud

___   Large group discussion of teacher observations

___   Call attention to specific examples of excellent skill usage

___   Tally chart that graphs whole class use of skill

Step 5:   How will you ensure that students persevere in practicing this skill?

___ Teaching students how to become observers

___ Student planned role plays that demonstrate good skill usage

___ Assigning students to use the skill outside of the classroom

___ Intermittently spending some class time reviewing and refining the use of this skill

___ Outside enemy interdependence: competing between classes for best skill usage

___ Having another teacher or guest come in to observe the skill and give feedback

Other ideas: _____

_____

_____

_____

_____

_____

_____

_____

_____

_____

_____

_____

_____

_____

TO KILL A MOCKINGBIRD TEXT SET

Literature Circle Text Set for *To Kill A Mockingbird*

Burns, Olive Ann. 1984. *Cold Sassy Tree*. New York: Ticknor & Fields.
> Affectionate portrayal of a southern town circa 1906. Entertaining and humorous with little concern for the racism lurking just off stage. Interesting contrast to *Mockingbird*.

Conroy, Pat. 1972. *The Water Is Wide*. New York: Bantam Books.
> Personal account of the year Conroy worked as one of the few school teachers for the rural, impoverished, and isolated African American children in Yamacraw, an island located off the coast of South Carolina.

Gaines, Ernest. 1982. *The Autobiography of Miss Jane Pittman*. New York: Bantam Books.
> Fictional story of an African American woman whose life spans slavery to the Civil Rights movement of the 1960s.

Hazelgrove, William. 1995. *Tobacco Sticks*. New York: Bantam Books.
> Set in 1945 post-war Richmond, Virginia, young Lee Hartwell learns about prejudice and deceit when his father defends an African American domestic worker falsely accused of stealing from her employer.

Kotlowitz, Alex. 1992. *There Are No Children Here*. New York: Anchor
> True story of brothers Lafeyette and Pharoah as they try to navigate their childhood within the gang infested and violent atmosphere of a Chicago housing project.

Krisher, Trudy. 1994. *Spite Fences*. New York: Laurel-Leaf Books.
> Thirteen-year-old Maggie comes of age during the summer of 1960 when she secretly witnesses a violent hate crime committed against an African American member of her community.

Meyer, Carolyn. 1993. *White Lilacs*. San Diego, CA: Harcourt Brace Jovanovich.
> Fictional story based on historical fact. In the 1920s a thriving African American community in Texas was driven from their homes in order to make way for a new city park. The story is told from the perspective of Rose Lee, a teenager whose family loses their home.

_____. 1997. *Jubilee Journey*. New York: Harcourt Brace Jovanovich.
> Sequel to *White Lilacs*. Rose Lee is now a grandmother who is determined to accept the future with hope while also helping younger family members remember their roots.

Watson, Larry. 1995. *Montana 1948*. New York: Pocket Books.
> Twelve-year-old David Haydin comes of age quickly when he discovers that his respected uncle, the community doctor, has been sexually abusing the Native American women under his care. David's father, the town sheriff, struggles with the choice of covering the incident up or arresting his own brother for rape.

THE HOLOCAUST TEXT SET

Literature Circle Text Set for The Holocaust

Greene, Bette. 1973. *The Summer of My German Soldier*. New York: Puffin.
   During World War II, the army base in Patty Bergen's Arkansas town becomes a temporary prisoner of war camp for German soldiers. Patty, a Jewish girl, faces the wrath of her church, parents, community, and law when she hides a German escapee.

Karas, Phyllis. 1995. *Hate Crime*. New York: Avon Flare.
   When anti-Semitic graffiti covers his synagogue, Zack becomes personally involved in trying to discover the perpetrator of this hate crime. This book does an excellent job showing the disturbing power of a hate crime on the members of a community.

Kerr, M. E. 1978. *Gentlehands*. New York: HarperTrophy.
   Buddy is enamored with a grandfather he never met before now. Once he discovers that his grandfather is a fugitive Nazi war criminal, his feelings begin to change.

Levitin, Sonia. 1999. *The Cure*. San Diego, CA: Harcourt Brace.
   In the year of 2407, diversity is considered criminal because of the conflict it brings. When Gemm16884 tries to be different, he undergoes treatment for his condition. Via hallucination he becomes a German Jewish youth living in the year of 1348. When the plague appears, violent anti-Semitism erupts as the Jews are blamed for the Black Death.

Lowry, Lois. 1994. *The Giver*. New York: Laurel Leaf.
   When Jonas is chosen to become The Receiver of Memories, he comes to realize the price his community has paid for their utopian way of life. There's a reason why no one in his village is handicapped, unusual, or different.

Matas, Carol. 1997. *After the War*. New York: Pocket Books.
   Once Ruth is released from a concentration camp, she quickly finds it is difficult to restart a life without family, money, or respect. Though the war is over, the prejudice against Jews remains.

Nolan, Han. 1996. *If I Should Die Before I Wake*. New York: Harcourt Brace and Company.
   Anti-Semitic Hilary begins her story in a coma after a motorcycle accident. While unconscious she becomes Chana, a Jewish girl trying to survive the perils of the Polish Lodz Ghetto and later Auschwitz. The story's conclusion hints of the supernatural.

Sender, Ruth Minsky. 1986. *The Cage*. New York: Bantam.
   From the German invasion of Poland in 1939 to the liberation of her concentration camp in 1945, Minsky tells her story of survival and hope.

Strasser, Todd. 1991. *The Wave*. New York: Laurel Leaf.
   A high school history teacher conducts a group pressure experiment with his classes that mimics the way Nazi's pressured the German citizenry to join their movement. Based on a true incident.

Yolen, Jane. 1992. *Briar Rose*. New York: Tor Books.
   After her grandmother's death, Becca discovers a box of possessions that lead her to Poland in an attempt to uncover her grandmother's past. What she discovers is startling.

LEARNING ABOUT THE MIDDLE EAST TEXT SET

Literature Circles: Understanding the Middle East

Grades 6–10 Recommendations

One More River by Lynne Reid Banks
Paperback—256 pages. Reprint edition (May 1993) Avon; ISBN: 0380715635
YA: Shows both sides of the Palestinian-Israeli conflict during Israel's Six Day War.

Broken Bridge by Lynne Reid Banks
Mass Market Paperback—272 pages (April 1996) Flare; ISBN: 0380723840
YA: Sequel to *One More River* takes place in Israel some twenty-five years later and follows the lives of the characters introduced in the first book.

Samir and Yonatan by Danielle Carmi
Hardcover—183 pages (March 2000) Arthur A. Levine; ISBN: 0439135044
YA: Samir, a young Palestinian boy, dreads going to an Israeli hospital for an operation. There he befriends an Israeli boy named Yonatan. As their bodies heal, the boys begin to heal the differences between them.

Breadwinner by Deborah Ellis
Paperback—170 pages (November 2001) Groundwood Books; ISBN: 0888994168
YA: Contemporary novel based on refugee stories about the oppressive rule of Afghanistan by the Taliban. Eleven-year-old Parvana must masquerade as a boy to gain access to the outside world and support her destitute family.

Kiss the Dust by Elizabeth Laird
Paperback—288 pages (April 1994) Puffin; ISBN: 0140368558
YA: Story of a Kurdish family who flees to Iran in an effort to escape persecution and certain death. Gives the reader a glimpse into the dire circumstances that Afghan refugees currently face.

Habibi by Naomi Shihab Nye
Paperback—271 pages (June 1999) Aladdin Paperbacks; ISBN: 0689825234
YA: Even-handed portrayal of the present day Arab-Israeli conflict when Jewish Liyana befriends an Arabian boy and finds out what it is like for Palestinians living in Israel.

The Space Between Our Footsteps: Poems and Paintings from the Middle East by Naomi Shihab Nye (Editor)
School & Library Binding—144 pages (April 1998) Simon & Schuster (Juv); ISBN: 0689812337

YA: Anthology of poetry and paintings featuring more than 100 poets from 19 different Middle Eastern countries who share their innermost feelings about place, family, war, and peace.

A Hand Full of Stars by Rafik Schami, Rika Lesser (Translator)
Paperback—195 pages. Reprint edition (August 1992) Puffin; ISBN: 0140360735
YA: In his journal, a teenage boy living in Damascus, Syria tells of his frustration with the violence and corruption destroying his country.

Shabanu: Daughter of the Wind by Suzanne Fisher Staples
Mass Market Paperback—240 pages. Reprint edition (September 1991) Random House Children's Pub; ISBN: 0679810307
YA: Gives a vivid glimpse into the nomadic lifestyle, which is part of Pakistani culture.

Grades 11–Adult Recommendations

Children of the Roojme: A Family's Journey from Lebanon by Elmaz Abinader
Paperback—304 pages. Reprint edition (December 1997) Univ of Wisconsin Pr; ISBN: 0299157342
ADULT–Nonfiction: Spanning four generations, the true story of a family who emigrates from Lebanon to western Pennsylvania. Depicts the hardships of World War I, the disintegrating Ottoman empire, abandonment of centuries-old villages, and the New World conflict between cultural tradition and assimilation.

Islam Today: A Short Introduction to the Muslim World by Akbar S. Ahmed
Paperback—272 pages. Revised edition (March 1999) I B Tauris & Co Ltd; ISBN: 1860642578
ADULT–Nonfiction: Focuses on the culture and society of Islam and how Islam shows its practical side. Shows non-Muslims how they can be more tolerant of Islam and even celebrate Muslim culture.

A Woman of Nazareth by Jabbour Hala Deeb, Hala Deeb Jabbour, Cheryl Rubenb
Paperback—276 pages (April 2000) iUniverse.com; ISBN: 0595089291
ADULT: Novel portrays the Arab-Israeli conflict from a Palestinian woman's perspective.

An Unexpected Light: Travels in Afghanistan by Jason Elliot
Paperback—496 pages. 1st Picado edition (October 2001) Picador USA; ISBN: 0312288468
ADULT–Nonfiction: Account of Elliot's two visits to Afghanistan, first in 1979 and then nearly ten years later. Transcends the typical travelogue and gives a deep and personal insight into one of the world's most inaccessible regions.

Silent No More : Confronting America's False Images of Islam by Paul Findley
Paperback—336 pages (July 2001) Amana Pubns; ISBN: 1590080017
ADULT–Nonfiction: Easy to read book that debunks stereotypes and helps readers gain a better understanding of modern day Islam.

Children of Israel, Children of Palestine: Our Own True Stories by Laurel Holliday
Paperback—384 pages (March 1999) Washington Square Pr; ISBN: 0671008048
ADULT–Nonfiction: What is it like to grow up in the war zone of the Middle East? This disturbing collection of true life stories begins with memories about childhood before the 1948 war and ends with accounts of young Palestinians and Israelis growing up now.

Taliban: Militant Islam, Oil and Fundamentalism in Central Asia by Ahmed Rashid
Paperback—288 pages (March 2001) Yale Univ Pr; ISBN: 0300089023
ADULT–Nonfiction: Rashid, a Pakistani journalist, takes the reader inside Afghanistan and the Taliban.

Woman at Point Zero by Nawal El Saadawi, Nawal El-Saadawi, Sherif Hetata
Paperback—112 pages, Second edition (September 1997)
ADULT: Fictional tale of a woman's search for freedom from the restrictions of her Egyptian/Arabic society.

Ali and Nino: A Love Story by Kurban Said
Paperback—282 pages (October 2000) Anchor Books; ISBN: 0385720408
ADULT: A novel set in Central Asia during World War I. Ali is Muslim while Nino is Christian. Requires sophisticated readers. Good AP pick for a unit on world literature/world culture.

TEEN PLEASING PAPERBACKS

Title	Author	Paperback Edition
Skellig	Almond, David	2001
Speak	Anderson, Laurie Halse	2001
Go Ask Alice	Anonymous	1998
The Thief of Always	Barker, Clive	1997
Life in the Fat Lane	Bennett, Cherie	1999
Searching For David's Heart	Bennett, Cherie	1998
Violet & Claire	Block, Francesca Lia	1999
Tangerine	Bloor, Edward	2001
Forever	Blume, Judy	1996
Black Hawk Down	Bowden, Mark	2000
Smack	Burgess, Melvin	1999
In a Dark Wood	Cadnum, Michael	1999
Chicken Soup for the Teen Soul (series)	Canfield, Jack & Mark Hansen	1998
Ender's Game	Card, Orson Scott	1994
Speaker for the Dead	Card, Orson Scott	1994
The Perks of Being a Wallflower	Chbosky, Stephen	1999
Imitate the Tiger	Cheripko, Jan	1998
Net Force (series)	Clancy, Tom	1999
Driver's Ed	Cooney, Caroline B.	1996
Face on the Milk Carton	Cooney, Caroline B.	1991
The Terrorist	Cooney, Caroline B.	1999
What Child Is This?: A Christmas Story	Cooney, Caroline B.	1999
Tenderness	Cormier, Robert	1998
We All Fall Down	Cormier, Robert	1993
Timeline	Crichton, Michael	2000
Chinese Handcuffs	Crutcher, Chris	1996
Running Loose	Crutcher, Chris	1986
Say Goodnight, Gracie	Deaver, Julie Reece	1989
Dreamland	Dessen, Sarah	2002
On the Devil's Court	Deuker, Carl	1991
Painting the Black	Deuker, Carl	1999

Title	Author	Paperback Edition
Forged by Fire	Draper, Sharon	1998
Romiette and Julio	Draper, Sharon	2001
Tears of a Tiger	Draper, Sharon	1996
Don't Look Behind You	Duncan, Lois	1990
Gallow's Hill	Duncan, Lois	1998
I Know What You Did Last Summer	Duncan, Lois	1999
Locked in Time	Duncan, Lois	1991
The Twisted Window	Duncan, Lois	1991
Trapped!	Duncan, Lois	1999
The Rebounder	Dygard, Thomas J.	1996
Ultimate Sports	Gallo, Donald R.	1997
The Fat Man	Gee, Maurice	1999
Mary Wolf	Grant, Cynthia D.	1997
The White Horse	Grant, Cynthia D.	2000
The Client	Grisham, John	1995
The Firm	Grisham, John	1992
A Time to Kill	Grisham, John	1992
Among the Hidden	Haddix, Margaret Peterson	2000
Don't You Dare Read This Mrs. Dunphrey	Haddix, Margaret Peterson	1997
Leaving Fishers	Haddix, Margaret Peterson	1999
Look for Me by Moonlight	Hahn, Mary Downing	1997
Practical Magic	Hoffman, Alice	1997
I Have Lived a Thousand Years	Jackson, Livia Bitton	1999
Breaking Boxes	Jenkins, A. M.	2000
Gentlehands	Kerr, M. E.	1990
Night Kites	Kerr, M. E.	1989
Christine	King, Stephen	1997
Misery	King, Stephen	1998
The Green Mile	King, Stephen	1997
The Shining	King, Stephen	1997
Thinner	King, Stephen	1994
Danger Zone	Klass, David	1998
Blood and Chocolate	Klause, Annette Curtis	1999
The Silver Kiss	Klause, Annette Curtis	1992
The Voice of the Night	Koontz, Dean R.	1996
Watchers	Koontz, Dean R.	1996
Into Thin Air	Krakauer, Jon	1998
Beyond the Burning Time	Lasky, Kathryn	1996
The Wreckers	Lawrence, Iain	1999

Title	Author	Paperback Edition
I Want to Keep My Baby!	Lee, Joanna	1988
Where the Heart Is	Letts, Billie	1998
Iceman	Lynch, Chris	1995
Mick:Blue Eyed Son, #1	Lynch, Chris	1996
Shadow Boxer	Lynch, Chris	1995
Parrot in the Oven	Martinez, Victor	1998
The Last Mission	Mazer, Harry	1981
Twelve Shots	Mazer, Harry	1998
Cut	McCormick, Patricia	2002
Now I Lay Me Down to Sleep	McDaniel, Lurlene	1995
Till Death Do Us Part	McDaniel, Lurlene	1997
Swallowing Stones	McDonald, Joyce	1999
The Me Nobody Knew	McLinden, Shannon	1998
Petey	Mikaelsen, Ben	2000
Babylon Boyz	Mowry, Jess	1999
Way Past Cool	Mowry, Jess	1993
Fallen Angels	Myers, Walter Dean	1989
Hoops	Myers, Walter Dean	1983
Monster	Myers, Walter Dean	2001
Scorpions	Myers, Walter Dean	1990
Slam!	Myers, Walter Dean	1998
The Other Side of Dark	Nixon, Joan	1987
The Beet Fields	Paulsen, Gary	2002
Dogsong	Paulsen, Gary	1999
Harris and Me	Paulsen, Gary	1995
My Life in Dog Years	Paulsen, Gary	1999
Nightjohn	Paulsen, Gary	1995
Sarny: A Life Remembered	Paulsen, Gary	1999
Soldier's Heart	Paulsen, Gary	2000
The Car	Paulsen, Gary	1995
The Voyage of the Frog	Paulsen, Gary	1990
Woodsong	Paulsen, Gary	1991
Are You in the House Alone?	Peck, Richard	2000
A Child Called 'It'	Pelzer, Dave	1995
The Lost Boy	Pelzer, Dave	1997
Clockwork: Or All Wound Up	Pullman, Philip	1998
The Amber Spyglass	Pullman, Philip	2001
The Golden Compass	Pullman, Philip	1999
The Subtle Knife	Pullman, Philip	1999

Title	Author	Paperback Edition
Close to a Killer	Qualey, Marsha	2000
Missing the Piano	Rapp, Adam	2002
The Buffalo Tree	Rapp, Adam	2002
Angus, Thongs, and Full-Frontal Snogging	Rennison, Louise	1999
Demon In My View	Rhodes, Amelia Atwater	2000
In the Forests of the Night	Rhodes, Amelia Atwater	2000
Shattered Mirror	Rhodes, Amelia Atwater	2002
Choosing Up Sides	Ritter, John H.	2000
Holes	Sachar, Louis	2000
Darkness	Saul, John	1992
Second Child	Saul, John	1997
Sleepwalk	Saul, John	1997
When the Wind Blows	Saul, John	1990
Mindbenders: Stories to Warp Your Brain	Shusterman, Neal	2000
The Dark Side of Nowhere	Shusterman, Neal	1999
Thief of Souls	Shusterman, Neal	2000
Singularity	Sleator, William	1995
The Duplicate	Sleator, William	1999
Annie's Baby	Sparks, Beatrice	1998
Go Ask Alice	Sparks, Beatrice	1998
It Happened to Nancy	Sparks, Beatrice	1994
Treacherous Love	Sparks, Beatrice	2000
Stargirl	Spinelli, Jerry	2002
Wringer	Spinelli, Jerry	1998
Crosses	Stoehr, Shelley	1998
How I Created My Perfect Prom Date	Strasser, Todd	1998
Free Fall	Sweeney, Joyce	1997
Katie.Com	Tarbox, Katherine	2000
Doing Time	Thomas, Rob	1999
Slave Day	Thomas, Rob	1998
Plague Year	Tolan, Stephanie S.	1991
Stuck in Neutral	Trueman, Terry	2001
Companions of the Night	Velde, Vivian Vande	1996
Izzy, Willy-Nilly	Voigt, Cynthia	1995
Shots on Goal	Wallace, Rich	1998
Wrestling Sturbridge	Wallace, Rich	1997
Making Up Megaboy	Walter, Virginia	1999
Farm Team: A Billy Baggs Novel	Weaver, Will	1999
Hard Ball	Weaver, Will	1999

Title	Author	Paperback Edition
Striking Out	Weaver, Will	1999
Locked Inside	Werlin, Nancy	2000
The Killer's Cousin	Werlin, Nancy	2000
Whistle Me Home	Wersba, Barbara	1997
Deathwatch	White, Robb	1973
Hard Love	Wittlinger, Ellen	2001
From the Notebooks of Melanin Sun	Woodson, Jacqueline	1997
I Hadn't Meant to Tell You This	Woodson, Jacqueline	1995
Lena	Woodson, Jacqueline	2000
The House You Pass on the Way	Woodson, Jacqueline	1999
Never Die Easy	Yaeger, Don and Walter Payton	2000
Armageddon Summer	Yolen, Jane and Bruce Coville	1999
My Darling, My Hamburger	Zindel, Paul	1984

SHORT STORY: NIGHT CLUB

Promptly at a quarter of ten P.M. Mrs. Brady descended the steps of the Elevated.[1] She purchased from the newsdealer in the cubbyhole beneath them a next month's magazine and a tomorrow morning's paper, and with these tucked under one plump arm, she walked. She walked two blocks north on Sixth Avenue, turned, and went west. But not far west. Westward half a block only, to the place where the gay green awning marked *Club Français* paints a stripe of shade across the glimmering sidewalk. Under this awning Mrs. Brady halted briefly, to remark to the six-foot doorman that it looked like rain and to await his performance of his professional duty. When the small green door yawned open she sighed deeply and plodded in.

The foyer was a blackness, an airless velvet blackness like the inside of a jeweler's box. Four drum-shaped lamps of golden silk suspended from the ceiling gave it light (a very little) and formed the jewels: gold signets, or cuff links for a giant. At the far end of the foyer there were black stairs, faintly dusty, rippling upward toward an amber radiance. Mrs. Brady approached and ponderously mounted the stairs, clinging with one fist to the mangy velvet rope that railed their edge.

From the top, Miss Lena Levin observed the ascent. Miss Levin was the checkroom girl. She had dark-at-the-roots blonde hair and slender hips upon which, in moments of leisure, she wore her hands, like buckles of ivory loosely attached. This was a moment of leisure. Miss Levin waited behind her counter. Row upon row of hooks, empty as yet, and seeming to beckon—wee, curved fingers of iron—waited behind her.

"Late," said Miss Levin, "again."

"Go wan!" said Mrs. Brady. "It's only ten to ten. *Whew!* Them *stairs!*"

She leaned heavily sideways against Miss Levin's counter, and applying one palm to the region of her heart, appeared at once to listen and to count. "Feel!" she cried then in a pleased voice.

Miss Levin obediently felt.

"Them stairs," continued Mrs. Brady darkly, "with my bad heart, will be the death of me. Whew! Well, dearie! What's the news?"

"You got a paper," Miss Levin languidly reminded her.

"Yeah!" agreed Mrs. Brady with sudden vehemence. "I got a paper!" She slapped it upon the counter. "An' a lot of time I'll get to *read* my paper, won't I now? On a Saturday night!" She moaned. "Other nights is bad enough, dear knows—but *Saturday* nights! How I dread 'em! Every Saturday night I say to my daughter, I say, 'Geraldine, I can't,' I say, 'I can't go through it again, an' that's all there is to it,' I say. 'I'll quit,' I say. An' I *will*, too!" added Mrs. Brady firmly, if indefinitely.

---

1. *Elevated*: an informal name for a railway that runs on an elevated structure; sometimes called the El.

Miss Levin, in defense of Saturday nights, mumbled some vague something about tips.

"Tips!" Mrs. Brady hissed it. She almost spat it. Plainly money was nothing, nothing at all, to this lady. "I just wish," said Mrs. Brady, and glared at Miss Levin, "I just wish *you* had to spend one Saturday night, just one, in that dressing room! Bein' pushed an' stepped on and near knocked down by that gang of hussies, an' them orderin' an' bossin' you 'round, an' usin' your things an' then sayin' they're sorry, they got no change, they'll be back. Yah! They *never* come back!"

"There's Mr. Costello," whispered Miss Levin through lips that, like a ventriloquist's, scarcely stirred.

"An' as I was sayin'," Mrs. Brady said at once brightly, "I got to leave you. Ten to ten, time I was on the job."

She smirked at Miss Levin, nodded, and right-about-faced. There, indeed, Mr. Costello was. Mr. Billy Costello, manager, proprietor, monarch of all he surveyed. From the doorway of the big room, where the little tables herded in a ring around the waxen floor, he surveyed Mrs. Brady, and in such a way that Mrs. Brady, momentarily forgetting her bad heart, walked fast, scurried faster, almost ran.

The door of her domain was set politely in an alcove, beyond silken curtains looped up at the sides. Mrs. Brady reached it breathless, shouldered it open, and groped for the electric switch. Lights sprang up, a bright white blaze, intolerable for an instant to the eyes, like sun on snow. Blinking, Mrs. Brady shut the door.

The room was a spotless, white-tiled place, half beauty shop, half dressing room. Along one wall stood washstands, sturdy triplets in a row, with pale green liquid soap in glass balloons afloat above them. Against the opposite wall there was a couch. A third wall backed an elongated glass-topped dressing table; and over the dressing table and over the washstands long rectangular sheets of mirror reflected lights, doors, glossy tiles, lights multiplied. . . .

Mrs. Brady moved across this glitter like a thick dark cloud in a hurry. At the dressing table she came to a halt, and upon it she laid her newspaper, her magazine, and her purse—a black purse worn gray with much clutching. She divested herself of a rusty black coat and a hat of the mushroom persuasion, and hung both up in a corner cupboard which she opened by means of one of a quite preposterous bunch of keys. From a nook in the cupboard she took down a lace-edged handkerchief with long streamers. She untied the streamers and tied them again around her chunky black alpaca waist. The handkerchief became an apron's baby cousin.

Mrs. Brady relocked the cupboard door, fumbled her key ring over, and unlocked a capacious drawer of the dressing table. She spread a fresh towel on the plate glass top, in the geometrical center, and upon the towel she arranged with care a procession of things fished from the drawer. Things for the hair. Things for the complexion. Things for the eyes, the lashes, the brows, the lips, and the fingernails. Things in boxes, and things in jars, and things in tubes and tins. Also an ash tray, matches, pins, a tiny sewing kit, a pair of scissors. Last of all, a hand-printed sign, a nudging sort of sign:

Notice!
These articles, placed here for your convenience,
are the property of the <u>maid.</u>

And directly beneath the sign, propping it up against the looking glass, a china saucer, in which Mrs. Brady now slyly laid decoy money: two quarters and two dimes, in four-leaf clover formation.

Another drawer of the dressing table yielded a bottle of Bromo Seltzer, a bottle of aromatic spirits of ammonia, a tin of sodium bicarbonate, and a teaspoon. These were lined rip on the shelf above the couch.

Mrs. Brady was now ready for anything. And (from the grim, thin pucker of her mouth) expecting it.

Music came to her ears. Rather, the beat of music, muffled rhythmic, remote. *Umpa-um, umpa-um-mm*—Mr. "Fiddle" Baer and his band, hard at work on the first fox trot of the night. It was teasing, foot-tapping music, but the large solemn feet of Mrs. Brady were still. She sat on the couch and opened her newspaper, and for some moments she read uninterruptedly, with special attention to the murders, the divorces, the breaches of promise, the funnies.

Then the door swung inward, admitting a blast of Mr. "Fiddle" Baer's best, a whiff of perfume, and a girl.

Mrs. Brady put her paper away.

The girl was petite and darkly beautiful, wrapped in fur and mounted on tall jeweled heels. She entered humming the ragtime song the orchestra was playing, and while she stood near the dressing table stripping off her gloves, she continued to hum it softly to herself:

> "Oh, I know my baby loves me,
> I can tell my baby loves me."

Here the dark little girl got the left glove off, and Mrs. Brady glimpsed a platinum wedding ring.

> " 'Cause there ain't no maybe
> In my baby's
> Eyes."

The right glove came off. The dark little girl sat down in one of the chairs that faced the dressing table. She doffed her wrap, casting it carelessly over the chair-back. It had a cloth-of-gold lining, and "Paris" was embroidered in curlicues on the label. Mrs. Brady hovered solicitously near.

The dark little girl, still humming, looked over the articles "placed here for your convenience," and picked up the scissors. Having cut off a very small hangnail with the air of one performing a perilous major operation, she seized and used the manicure buffer, and after that the eyebrow pencil. Mrs. Brady's mind, hopefully calculating the tip, jumped and jumped again like a taximeter.

> "Oh, I know my baby loves me—"

The dark little girl applied powder and lipstick belonging to herself. She examined the result searchingly in the mirror and sat back, satisfied. She cast some silver *Klink! Klink!* into Mrs. Brady's saucer, and half rose. Then, remembering something, she settled down again.

The ensuing thirty seconds were spent by her in pulling off her platinum wedding ring, tying it in a corner of a lace handkerchief, and tucking the handkerchief down the bodice of her tight white velvet gown.

"There" she said.

She swooped up her wrap and trotted toward the door, jeweled heels merrily twinkling.

> " 'Cause there ain't no maybe—"

The door fell shut.

Almost instantly it opened again, and another girl came in. A blonde, this. She was pretty in a round-eyed, babyish way, but Mrs. Brady, regarding her, mentally grabbed the spirits of ammonia bottle. For she looked terribly ill. The round eyes were dull, the pretty, silly little face was drawn. The thin hands, picking at the fastenings of a spacious bag, trembled and twitched.

Mrs. Brady cleared her throat. "Can I do something for you, Miss?"

Evidently the blonde girl had believed herself alone in the dressing room. She started violently, and glanced up, panic in her eyes. Panic, and something else. Something very like murderous hate—but for an instant only, so that Mrs. Brady, whose perceptions were never quick, missed it altogether.

"A glass of water?" suggested Mrs. Brady.

"No," said the girl, "no." She had one hand in the beaded bag now. Mrs. Brady could see it moving, causing the bag to squirm like a live thing, and the fringe to shiver. "Yes!" she cried abruptly. "A glass of water—please—you get it for me."

She dropped onto the couch. Mrs. Brady scurried to the water cooler in the corner, pressed the spigot with a determined thumb. Water trickled out thinly. Mrs. Brady pressed harder, and scowled, and thought, "Something's wrong with this thing. I mustn't forget, next time I see Mr. Costello—"

When again she faced her patient, the patient was sitting erect. She was thrusting her clenched hand back into the beaded bag again.

She took only a sip of the water, but it seemed to help her quite miraculously. Almost at once color came to her cheeks, life to her eyes. She grew young again—as young as she was. She smiled up at Mrs. Brady.

"Well!" she exclaimed. "What do you know about that!" She shook her honey-colored head. "I can't imagine what came over me."

"Are you better now?" inquired Mrs. Brady.

"Yes, oh, yes. I'm better now. You see," said the blonde girl confidentially, "we were at the theater, my boy friend and I, and it was hot and stuffy—I guess that must have been the trouble." She paused, and the ghost of her recent distress crossed her face. "God! I thought that last act *never* would end!" she said.

While she attended to her hair and complexion she chattered gayly to Mrs. Brady, chattered on with scarcely a stop for breath, and laughed much. She said, among other things, that she and her "boy friend" had not known one another very long, but that she was "gaga" about him. "He is about me, too," she confessed. "He thinks I'm grand."

She fell silent then, and in the looking glass her eyes were shadowed, haunted. But Mrs. Brady, from where she stood, could not see the looking glass, and half a minute later the blonde girl laughed and began again. When she went out she seemed to dance out on little winged feet, and Mrs. Brady sighing, thought it must be nice to be young . . . and happy like that.

The next arrivals were two. A tall, extremely smart young woman in black chiffon entered first, and held the door open for her companion; the instant the door was shut she said, as though it had been on the tip of her tongue for hours, "Amy, what under the sun *happened?*"

Amy, who was brown-eyed, brown-bobbed-haired, and patently annoyed with something, crossed to the dressing table and flopped into a chair before she made a reply.

"Nothing," she said wearily then.

"That's nonsense!" snorted the other. "Tell me. Was it something she said? She's a tactless ass, of course. Always was."

"No, not anything she said. It was—" Amy bit her lip. "All right! I'll tell you. Before we left your apartment I just happened to notice that Tom had disappeared. So I went to look for him— I wanted to ask him if he'd remembered to tell the maid where we were going—Skippy's subject to croup, you know, and we always leave word. Well, so I went into the kitchen, thinking Tom might be there mixing cocktails—and there he was—and there *she* was!"

The full red mouth of the other young woman pursed itself slightly. Her arched brows lifted. "Well?"

Her matter-of-factness appeared to infuriate Amy. "He was *kissing* her!" she flung out.

"Well?" said the other again. She chuckled softly and patted Amy's shoulder, as if it were the shoulder of a child. "You're surely not going to let *that* spoil your whole evening? Amy *dear!* Kissing may once have been serious and significant—but it isn't nowadays. Nowadays it's like shaking hands. It means nothing."

But Amy was not consoled. "I hate her!" she cried desperately. "Red-headed *thing!* Calling me 'darling' and 'honey,' and s-sending me handkerchiefs for C-Christmas—and then sneaking off behind closed doors and k-kissing my h-h-husband. . . ."

At this point Amy quite broke down, but she recovered herself sufficiently to add with venom, "I'd like to slap her!"

"Oh, oh, oh," smiled the tall young woman, "I wouldn't do that!"

Amy wiped her eyes with what might well have been one of the Christmas handkerchiefs, and confronted her friend. "Well, what *would* you do, Claire? If you were I?"

"I'd forget it," said Claire, "and have a good time. I'd kiss somebody myself. You've no idea how much better you'd feel!"

"I don't do—" Amy began indignantly; but as the door behind her opened and a third young woman—red-headed, earringed, exquisite—lilted in, she changed her tone. "Oh, hello!" she called sweetly, beaming at the newcomer via the mirror. "We were wondering what had become of you!"

The red-headed girl, smiling easily back, dropped her cigarette on the floor and crushed it out with a silver-shod toe. "Tom and I were talking to 'Fiddle' Baer," she explained. "He's going to play 'Clap Yo' Hands' next, because it's my favorite. Lend me a comb, will you somebody?"

"There's a comb there," said Claire, indicating Mrs. Brady's business comb.

"But imagine using it!" murmured the red-headed girl. "Amy darling, haven't you one?"

Amy produced a tiny comb from her rhinestone purse. "Don't forget to bring it when you come," she said, and stood up. "I'm going on out; I want to tell Tom something."

She went.

The red-headed young woman and the tall black-chiffon one were alone, except for Mrs. Brady. The red-headed one beaded her incredible lashes. The tall one, the one called Claire, sat watching her. Presently she said, "Sylvia, look here." And Sylvia looked. Anybody, addressed in that tone, would have.

"There is one thing," Claire went on quietly, holding the other's eyes, "that I want understood. And that is, '*Hands off!*' Do you hear me?"

"I don't know what you mean."

"You *do* know what I mean!"

The red-headed girl shrugged her shoulders. "Amy told you she saw us, I suppose."

"Precisely. And," went on Claire, gathering up her possessions and rising, "as I said before, you're to keep away." Her eyes blazed sudden white-hot rage. "Because, as you very well know, he belongs to *me,*" she said, and departed, slamming the door.

Between eleven o'clock and one Mrs. Brady was very busy indeed. Never for more than a moment during those two hours was the dressing room empty. Often it was jammed, full to overflowing with curled cropped heads, with ivory arms and shoulders, with silk and lace and chiffon, with legs. The door flapped in and back, in and back. The mirrors caught and held—and lost—a hundred different faces. Powder veiled the dressing table with a thin white dust; cigarette stubs, scarlet at the tips, choked the ash-receiver. Dimes and quarters clattered into Mrs. Brady's saucer—and were transferred to Mrs. Brady's purse. The original seventy cents remained. That much, and no more, would Mrs. Brady gamble on the integrity of womankind.

She earned her money. She threaded needles and took stitches. She powdered the backs of necks. She supplied towels for soapy, drippy hands. She removed a speck from a teary blue eye and pounded the heel on a slipper. She curled the straggling ends of a black bob and a gray bob, pinned a velvet flower on a lithe round waist, mixed three doses of bicarbonate of soda, took charge of a shed pink satin girdle, collected, on hands and knees, several dozen fake pearls that had wept from a broken string.

She served chorus girls and school girls, gay young matrons and gayer young mistresses, a lady who had divorced four husbands, and a lady who had poisoned one, the secret (more or less) sweetheart of a Most Distinguished Name, and the Brains of a bootleg gang. . . . She saw things. She saw a yellow check, with the ink hardly dry. She saw four tiny bruises, such as fingers might make, on an arm. She saw a girl strike another girl, not playfully. She saw a bundle of letters some man wished he had not written, safe and deep in a brocaded handbag.

About midnight the door flew open and at once was pushed shut, and a gray-eyed, lovely child stood backed against it, her palms flattened on the panels at the sides, the draperies of her white chiffon gown settling lightly to rest around her.

There were already five damsels of varying ages in the dressing room. The latest arrival marked their presence with a flick of her eyes, and standing just where she was, she called peremptorily, "Maid!"

Mrs. Brady, standing just where she was, said, "Yes, Miss?"

"Please come here," said the girl.

Mrs. Brady, as slowly as she dared, did so.

The girl lowered her voice to a tense half-whisper. "Listen! Is there any other way I can get out of here except through this door I came in?"

Mrs. Brady stared at her stupidly.

"Any window?" persisted the girl. "Or anything?"

Here they were interrupted by the exodus of two of the damsels-of-varying-ages. Mrs. Brady opened the door for them—and in so doing caught a glimpse of a man who waited in the hall outside, a debonair, old-young man with a girl's furry wrap hung over his arm, and his hat in his hand.

The door clicked. The gray-eyed girl moved out from the wall, against which she had flattened herself—for all the world like one eluding pursuit in a cinema.

" What about that window?" she demanded, pointing.

"That's all the farther it opens," said Mrs. Brady.

"Oh! And it's the only one—isn't it?"

"It is."

"Damn," said the girl. "Then there's *no* way out?"

"No way but the door," said Mrs. Brady testily.

The girl looked at the door. She seemed to look *through* the door, and to despise and to fear what she saw. Then she looked at Mrs. Brady. "Well," she said, "then I s'pose the only thing to do is to stay in here."

She stayed. Minutes ticked by. Jazz crooned distantly, stopped, struck up again. Other girls came and went. Still the gray-eyed girl sat on the couch, with her back to the wall and her shapely legs crossed, smoking cigarettes, one from the stub of another.

After a long while she said, "Maid!"

"Yes, Miss?"

"Peek out that door, will you, and see if there's anyone standing there."

Mrs. Brady pecked, and reported that there was. There was a gentleman with a little bit of a black mustache standing there. The same gentleman, in fact, who was standing there "just after you came in."

"Oh, Lord," sighed the gray-eyed girl. "Well . . . I can't stay here all *night*, that's one sure thing."

She slid off the couch, and went listlessly to the dressing table. There she occupied herself for a minute or two. Suddenly, without a word, she darted out.

Thirty seconds later Mrs. Brady was elated to find two crumpled one-dollar bills lying in her saucer. Her joy, however, died a premature death. For she made an almost simultaneous second discovery. A saddening one. Above all, a puzzling one.

"Now what for," marveled Mrs. Brady, "did she want to walk off with them *scissors?*"

This at twelve-twenty-five.

At twelve-thirty a quartet of excited young things burst in, babbling madly. All of them had their evening wraps with them; all talked at once. One of them, a Dresden-china girl[2] with a heart-shaped face, was the center of attention. Around her the rest fluttered like monstrous butterflies; to her they addressed their shrill exclamatory cries. "Babe," they called her.

Mrs. Brady heard snatches: "Not in this state unless. . . ." "Well, you can in Maryland, Jimmy says." "Oh, there must be someplace nearer than. . . ." "Isn't this *marvelous?*" "When did it happen, Babe? When did you decide?"

"Just now," the girl with the heart-shaped face sang softly, "when we were dancing."

The babble resumed. "But listen, Babe, what'll your mother and father . . .?" "Oh, never mind, let's hurry." "Shall we be warm enough with just these thin wraps, do you think? Babe, will you be warm enough? Sure?"

Powder flew and little pocket combs marched through bright marcels.[3] Flushed cheeks were painted pinker still.

"My pearls," said Babe, "are *old*. And my dress and my slippers are *new*. Now let's see—what can I *borrow?*"

A lace handkerchief, a diamond bar-pin, a pair of earrings were proffered. She chose the bar-pin, and its owner unpinned it proudly, gladly.

"I've got blue garters!" exclaimed another girl.

"Give me one, then," directed Babe. "I'll trade with you. . . . There! That fixes that."

More babbling, "Hurry! Hurry . . ." "Listen, are you *sure* we'll be warm enough? Because we can stop at my house, there's nobody home." "Give me that puff, Babe, I'll powder your back." "And just to think, a week ago you'd never even met each other!" "Oh, hurry *up*, let's get *started!*" "I'm ready." "So'm I!" "Ready, Babe? You look adorable." "Come on, everybody."

They were gone again, and the dressing room seemed twice as still and vacant as before.

A minute of grace, during which Mrs. Brady wiped the spilled powder away with a damp gray rag. Then the door jumped open again. Two evening gowns appeared and made for the dressing table in a bee line. Slim, tubular gowns they were, one silver, one palest yellow. Yellow hair went with the silver gown, brown hair with the yellow. The silver-gowned, yellow-haired girl wore orchids on her shoulders, three of them, and a flashing bracelet on each fragile wrist. The other girl looked less prosperous; still, you would rather have looked at her.

Both ignored Mrs. Brady's cosmetic display as utterly as they ignored Mrs. Brady, producing full field equipment of their own.

"Well," said the girl with the orchids, rouging energetically, "how do you like him?"

"Oh-h—all right."

---

2. *Dresden-china girl*: a girl having a delicate prettiness. Dresden china is a fine, glasslike porcelain made in Dresden, Germany.

3. *marcels*: deep, soft waves made in the hair with a heated curling iron; named after Marcel Grateau, a nineteenth-century French hairdresser.

"Meaning, 'Not any,' hmm? I suspected as much!" The girl with the orchids turned in her chair and scanned her companion's profile with disapproval. "See here, Marilee," she drawled, "are you going to be a damn fool *all* your life?"

"He's fat," said Marilee dreamily. "Fat, and—greasy, sort of. I mean, greasy in his mind. Don't you know what I mean?"

"I know *one* thing," declared the girl with the orchids. "I know Who He Is! And if I were you, that's all I'd need to know. *Under the circumstances.*"

The last three words, stressed meaningly, affected the girl called Marilee curiously. She grew grave. Her lips and lashes drooped. For some seconds she sat frowning a little, breaking a black-sheathed lipstick in two and fitting it together again.

"She's worse," she said finally, low.

"Worse?"

Marilee nodded.

"Well," said the girl with the orchids, "there you are. It's the climate. She'll never be anything *but* worse, if she doesn't get away. Out West, or somewhere."

"I know," murmured Marilee.

The other girl opened a tin of eye shadow. "Of course," she said dryly, "suit yourself. She's not *my* sister."

Marilee said nothing. Quiet she sat, breaking the lipstick, mending it, breaking it.

"Oh, well," she breathed finally, wearily, and straightened up. She propped her elbows on the plate glass dressing table top and leaned toward the mirror, and with the lipstick she began to make her coral pink mouth very red and gay and reckless and alluring.

Nightly at one o'clock Vane and Moreno dance for the *Club Français*. They dance a tango, they dance a waltz; then, by way of encore, they do a Black Bottom, and a trick of their own called the Wheel. They dance for twenty, thirty minutes. And while they dance you do not leave your table—for this is what you came to see. Vane and Moreno. The new New York thrill. The sole justification for the five-dollar convert[4] extorted by Billy Costello.

From one until half past, then, was Mrs. Brady's recess. She had been looking forward to it all evening long. When it began—when the opening chords of the tango music sounded stirringly from the room outside—Mrs. Brady brightened. With a right good will she sped the parting guests.

Alone, she unlocked her cupboard and took out her magazine—the magazine she had bought three hours before. Heaving a great breath of relief and satisfaction, she plumped herself on the couch and fingered the pages. Immediately she was absorbed, her eyes drinking up printed lines, her lips moving soundlessly.

The magazine was Mrs. Brady's favorite. Its stories were true stories, taken from life (so the Editor said); and to Mrs. Brady they were live, vivid threads in the dull, drab pattern of her night.

---

4. *couvert* (cōō'var'): *French*, cover charge; a fixed charge added to the bill at night clubs, etc., for entertainment or service.

REFERENCES

Adams, Richard. 1972. *Watership Down*. New York: Avon Books.

Allburg, Chris Van. 1993. *The Sweetest Fig*. Boston: Houghton Mifflin Company.

Almond, David. 1999. *Skellig*. New York: Delacorte Press.

Anonymous. 1971. *Go Ask Alice*. New York: Avon Books.

Atwell, Nancie. 1998. *In the Middle: New Understandings About Writing, Reading, and Learning*. Portsmouth, NH: Heinemann.

Autobiography of Miss Jane Pittman, The. 1974. Directed by John Korty. 110 min. Tomorrow Entertainment Videocassette.

Avery, Christopher M. with Meri Aaron Walker and Erin O'Toole Murphy. 2001. *Teamwork Is an Individual Skill: Getting Your Work Done When Sharing Responsibility*. San Francisco, CA: Berrett-Koehler Publishers.

Burke, Kay. 1993. *The Mindful School: How to Assess Thoughtful Outcomes*. Palatine, IL: IRI/Skylight Publishing, Inc.

Bleeker, Gerrit and Barbara Bleeker. 1996. "Responding to Young Adult Fiction through Writing Poetry: Trying to Understand a Mole." *The ALAN Review* (Spring): 38–40.

Bomer, Randy. 1995. *Time for Meaning: Crafting Literate Lives in Middle and High School*. Portsmouth, NH: Heinemann.

Buehl, Doug. 2001. *Classroom Strategies for Interactive Learning*. Newark, DE: International Reading Association.

Chbosky, Stephen. 1999. *The Perks of Being a Wallflower*. New York: Pocket Books.

Cisneros, Sandra. 1991. "Eleven." *The House on Mango Street*. New York: Vintage Books.

Clark, Mary Higgins. 1998. *All Around Town*. New York: Simon & Schuster.

Condor, Bob. 1997. "Doctors urged to use big dose of patience: Study ties lawsuits to curtness." *The Chicago Tribune*, February 19.

Cromier, Robert. 1974. *The Chocolate War*. New York: Laurel Leaf Books.

———. 1985. *Beyond the Chocolate War*. New York: Laurel Leaf Books.

Crutcher, Chris. 2001. *Whale Talk*. New York: Greenwillow.

Curtis, Christopher Paul. 1999. *Bud, Not Buddy*. New York: Delacorte Press.

Daniels, Harvey. 1994. *Literature Circles: Voice and Choice in the Student-Centered Classroom*. York, ME: Stenhouse Publishers.

———. 2002. *Literature Circles: Voice and Choice in Book Clubs and Reading Groups*. York, ME: Stenhouse Publishers.

Danziger, Paula. 1989. *This Place Has No Atmosphere*. New York: Dell Publishing.

Gallo, Donald R. 2001. "How Classics Create an Aliterate Society." *English Journal* 90(3): 33–39.

Greene, Bob and D. G. Fulford. 1993. *To Our Children's Children: Preserving Family Histories for Generations to Come*. New York: Doubleday.

Harvey, Stephanie. 1998. *Non-fiction Matters: Reading, Writing, and Research in Grades 3–8*. York, ME: Stenhouse Publishers.

Harvey, Stephanie and Anne Goudvis. 2000. *Strategies That Work: Teaching Comprehension to Enhance Understanding*. York, ME: Stenhouse Publishers.

Hayes, Billy with William Hoffer. 1977. *Midnight Express*. New York: Dutton.

Heimberg, Justin and David Gomberg. 1997. *Would You Rather . . . ? Over 200 Absolutely Absurd Dilemmas to Ponder*. New York: Penguin Putnam.

_____. 1999. *Would You Rather . . . ? Over 300 Absolutely Absurd Dilemmas to Ponder*. New York: Penguin Putnam.

Hinton, S. E. 1967. *The Outsiders*. New York: Viking Press.

Homes, A. M. 1990. *Jack*. New York: Vintage Books.

Johnson, David W., Roger T. Johnson, and Edythe Johnson Holubec. 1998, 1991. *Cooperation in the Classroom*. Edina, MN: Interaction Book Company.

_____. 1994. *The Nuts & Bolts of Cooperative Learning*. Edina, MN: Interaction Book Company.

Johnson, David W. and Roger T. Johnson. 1997. *Learning to Lead Teams: Developing Leadership Skills*. Edina, MN: Interaction Book Company.

Kagan, Miguel, Laurie Robertson, and Spencer Kagan. 1995. *Cooperative Learning Structures for Classbuilding*. San Clemente, CA: Kagan Cooperative Learning.

———. 1997. *Cooperative Learning Structures for Teambuilding*. San Clemente, CA: Kagan Cooperative Learning.

Kagan, Spencer. 1995. "Group Grades Miss the Mark." *Educational Leadership* (May): 68–71.

Karas, Phyllis. 1995. *Hate Crime*. New York: Avon Flare.

Kesey, Ken. 1962. *One Flew Over the Cuckoo's Nest*. New York: Viking Press, Inc.

Klass, David. 1990. *Wrestling with Honor*. New York: Scholastic, Inc.

Klause, Annette Curtis. 1997. *Blood and Chocolate*. New York: Bantam Books.

Kohn, Alfie. 1986. *No Contest: The Case Against Competition*. New York: Houghton Mifflin Company.

_____. 1993. *Punished by Rewards*. New York: Houghton Mifflin Company.

_____. 1996. *Beyond Discipline: From Compliance to Community*. Alexandria, VA: ASCD.

Kotlowitz, Alex. 1992. *There Are No Children Here*. New York: Anchor.

Krisher, Trudy. 1994. *Spite Fences*. New York: Laurel-Leaf Books.

LaMeres, Clare. 1990. *The Winners Circle: Yes, I Can! Self-Esteem Lessons for the Secondary Classroom*. Newport Beach, CA: LaMeres Lifestyles Unlimited.

Lane, Barry. 1993. *After THE END: Teaching and Learning Creative Revision*. Portsmouth, NH: Heinemann.

Lasky, Katherine. 1999. *Star Split*. New York: Hyperion Press.

Latrobe, Kathy. 1993. "Readers Theatre as a Way of Learning." *The ALAN Review* (Winter): 46-50.

Lee, Harper. 1960. *To Kill a Mockingbird*. New York: Warner Books.

Lowry, Lois. 1994. *The Giver*. New York: Laurel Leaf.

Macrorie, Ken. 1988. *The I-Search Paper*. Portsmouth, NH: Heinemann.

Matas, Carol. 1997. *After the War*. New York: Pocket Books.

McDaniel, Lurlene. 1993. *Please Don't Die*. New York: Bantam Books.

Porter, Carol and Janell Cleland. 1995. *The Portfolio as a Learning Strategy*. Portsmouth, NH: Heinemann.

Rief, Linda. 1992. *Seeking Diversity: Language Arts with Adolescents*. Portsmouth, NH: Heinemann.

Romano, Tom. 1995. *Writing with Passion: Life Stories, Multiple Genres*. Portsmouth, NH: Heinemann.

"Rude, disrespectful doctors more likely to be sued, studies suggest." 1994. *The Chicago Tribune* November 25.

Salinger, J. D. 1951. *The Catcher in the Rye*. New York: Bantam.

Santa, Carol M., Lynn T. Havens, and Evelyn M. Maycumber. 1996. *Project CRISS: Creating Independence Through Student-owned Strategies*. Dubuque, IA: Kendall/Hunt Publishing Company.

Schindler's List. 1993. Produced and directed by Steven Spielberg. 197 min. Universal Pictures. Videocassette.

Schmuck, Richard A. and Patricia A. Schmuck. 2000. *Group Processes in the Classroom*. New York: McGraw-Hill Higher Education.

Soto, Gary. 1986. "The Jacket." In *Coming of Age in America: A Multicultural Anthology*, ed. Mary Frosch. 1994. New York: The New Press.

Steinbeck, John. 1937. *Of Mice and Men*. New York: Penguin Books.

Strasser, Todd. 1991. *Beyond the Reef*. New York: Laurel Leaf Books.

———. 1987. "The Bridge." In *Visions: Nineteen Short Stories by Outstanding Writers for Young Adults*, ed. Donald R. Gallo. New York: Dell Publishing.

Trelease, Jim. 1989. *The New Read Aloud Handbook*. New York: Penguin Books.

U.S. Labor Department. 1990. *The Secretary's Commission on Achieving the Necessary Skills (SCANS)*.

Venables, Hubert. 1980. *The Frankenstein Diaries*. New York: Viking Press.

Verne, Jules. 1872. *Around the World in Eighty Days*. New York: Sterling Publishing Co.

Watson, Larry. 1995. *Montana 1948*. New York: Pocket Books.

Ways We Want Our Class to Be: Class Meetings That Build Commitment to Kindness and Learning. 1996. Oakland, CA: Developmental Studies Center.

Weaver, Constance. 1996. *Teaching Grammar in Context*. Portsmouth, NH: Heinemann.

Werlin, Nancy. 1998. *The Killer's Cousin*. New York: Delacorte Books for Young Readers.

Wilhelm, Jeffrey D. 1998. "Not for Wimps! Using Drama to Enrich the Reading of YA Literature." *The ALAN Review* (Spring): 52-55.

Zemelman, Steven and Harvey Daniels. 1988. *A Community of Writers: Teaching Writing in Junior and Senior High School*. Portsmouth, NH: Heinemann.

Zemelman, Steven, Patricia Bearden, Yolanda Simmons, and Pete Leki. 2000. *History Comes Home: Family Stories Across the Curriculum*. York, ME: Stenhouse Publishers.